Investment Management Certificate

STUDY TEXT

Unit 1 – The Investment Environment

Syllabus version 8 (2nd edition)

In this January 2011 edition

- A **user-friendly format** for easy navigation
- **Exam tips** to put you on the right track
- A **Test your knowledge** quiz at the end of each chapter
- A full **index**

Published January 2011

ISBN 9780 7517 9421 2

British Library Cataloguing-in-Publication Data
A catalogue record for this book
is available from the British Library

Published by

BPP Learning Media Ltd
BPP House, Aldine Place
London W12 8AA

www.bpp.com/learningmedia

Printed in the United Kingdom

Your learning materials, published by BPP Learning Media Ltd, are printed on paper sourced from sustainable, managed forests.

£65.00

A note about copyright

Dear Customer

What does the little © mean and why does it matter? Your market-leading BPP books, course materials and e-learning materials do not write and update themselves. People write them: on their own behalf or as employees of an organisation that invests in this activity. Copyright law protects their livelihoods. It does so by creating rights over the use of the content.

Breach of copyright is a form of theft – as well being a criminal offence in some jurisdictions, it is potentially a serious beach of professional ethics.

With current technology, things might seem a bit hazy but, basically, without the express permission of BPP Learning Media:

- Photocopying our materials is a breach of copyright
- Scanning, ripcasting or conversion of our digital materials into different file formats, uploading them to facebook or emailing them to your friends is a breach of copyright

You can, of course, sell your books, in the form in which you have bought them – once you have finished with them. (Is this fair to your fellow students? We update for a reason.)

And what about outside the UK? BPP Learning Media strives to make our materials available at prices students can afford by local printing arrangements, pricing policies and partnerships which are clearly listed on our website. A tiny minority ignore this and indulge in criminal activity by illegally photocopying our material or supporting organisations that do. If they act illegally and unethically in one area, can you really trust them?

CONTENTS

The Study Text reference in the right-hand column below indicates the chapter and section in which each learning outcome is covered. For example learning outcome 2.1.4 is covered in Chapter 2 section 1.

Syllabus Item	BPP Ref Chapter–Section
Topic 1: The UK Financial Services Industry – a European and Global Context Demonstrate an understanding of the UK financial services industry, in its European and global context	1 – 3
Section 1.1: The Financial Services Industry and the Role of Government	
1.1.1 Explain the functions of the financial services industry	1 – 1
1.1.2 Evaluate the role and impact of the main financial institutions	1 – 2
1.1.3 Explain the role of government including economic and industrial policy, regulation, taxation and social welfare	1 – 4
Section 1.2: The Impact of EU Directives on the Investment Industry	
1.2.1 Explain the legal status of EU Directives within the UK	1– 4
1.2.2 Explain the purpose and scope of the Markets in Financial Instruments Directive (MiFID) with respect to: – passporting – roles of the home and host state – core and non-core investment services – financial instruments covered by the legislation;	1 – 5
1.2.3 Explain the purpose and scope of the UCITS Directives	1 – 6
Topic 2: Financial Markets Demonstrate an understanding of UK and International financial markets	
Section 2.1: UK Equity and Fixed Interest Markets	
2.1.1 Identify the main dealing systems and facilities offered in the UK equities market	2 – 1
2.1.2 Identify the nature of the stocks that would be traded on each of the above systems and facilities	2 – 1
2.1.3 Explain the structure and operation of the primary and secondary UK markets for gilts and corporate bonds	2 – 1.3
2.1.4 Explain the motivations for and implications of dual listing of a company	2 – 1
Section 2.2: Types of Markets	
2.2.1 Compare and contrast exchange trading and over-the-counter (otc) markets	2 – 1
2.2.2 Distinguish between the following alternative trading venues: – Multilateral Trading Facilities – Systematic Internalisers – Dark Pools	2 – 1.6

Syllabus Item	BPP Ref Chapter–Section
2.2.3 Distinguish between a quote-driven and order-driven market	2 – 1
2.2.4 Explain the roles of the various participants in the UK equity market	2 – 1
Section 2.3: Settlement Procedures in UK	
2.3.1 Explain the clearing and settlement procedures for UK exchange traded securities	2 – 2
Section 2.4: Regulation of UK Investment Exchanges	
2.4.1 Explain the role of an investment exchange	2 – 3
2.4.2 Explain the need for investment exchanges to be authorised	2 – 3
2.4.3 Explain the relevance of investment exchanges being recognised by the FSA	2 – 3
2.4.4 Identify the recognised investment exchanges and clearing houses in the UK	2 – 3
2.4.5 Identify and distinguish the roles of – the London Stock Exchange (LSE) – NYSE Liffe – LCH.Clearnet	1 – 3
Section 2.5: The UK Listing Authority and Prospectus Requirements	
2.5.1 Explain the role of the FSA as the UK listing authority	2 – 4
2.5.2 Identify the source of the listing rules as FSMA 2000 and relevant EU directives	2 – 4.2
2.5.3 Explain the main conditions for listing on the Official List, AIM and PLUS markets	2 – 4.2
2.5.4 Explain the purpose of the requirement for prospectus or listing particulars	2 – 4.2
2.5.5 Identify the main exemptions from listing particulars	2 – 4.5
Section 2.6: Information Disclosure and Corporate Governance Requirements for UK Equity Markets	
2.6.1 Explain the disclosures required under the FSA's disclosure and transparency rules relating to: – directors' interests – major shareholdings	2 – 5
2.6.2 Explain the purpose of corporate governance regulation	2 – 5.4
2.6.3 Explain, in outline, the scope and content of corporate governance regulation in the UK (the Combined Code)	2 – 5.4
2.6.4 Explain the LSE requirements for listed companies to disclose corporate governance compliance	2 – 5.4
2.6.5 Explain the continuing obligations of LSE listed companies regarding information disclosure and dissemination	2 – 5.4
2.6.6 Explain, in outline, the UK company law requirements regarding the calling of general meetings	2 – 5.7

Syllabus Item		BPP Ref Chapter–Section
2.6.7	Distinguish between extraordinary and annual general meetings	2 – 5.7
2.6.8	Distinguish between the types of resolution that can be considered at company general meetings	2 – 5.7
2.6.9	Distinguish between the voting methods used at company meetings	2 – 5.7
2.6.10	Explain the role and powers of a proxy	2 – 5.7
Section 2.7: Regulation of Derivatives Markets		
2.7.1	Identify the main features of the regulation of derivatives	2 – 6
2.7.2	Identify the main features of clearing and settlement on derivatives exchanges and for over-the counter derivatives trading	2 – 6.7
2.7.3	Explain the arrangements for market transparency and transaction reporting in the main derivative markets	2 – 6.6
2.7.4	Explain the impact of MiFID and International Accounting Standards on the regulation of derivative markets	2 – 6
Section 2.8: International Markets		
2.8.1	Explain the mechanics of dealing in equities and fixed interest securities in each of the following specific countries: – US – Japan – France – Germany	2 – 7
2.8.2	Identify the participants in each of the above markets	2 – 7
2.8.3	Explain the structure and operation of the primary and secondary markets for Eurobonds	2 – 7.8
2.8.4	Explain the general principles of dealing in other markets including emerging markets and settlement issues in those markets	2 – 7
Section 2.9: International Settlement and Clearing		
2.9.1	Explain the settlement and clearing procedures overseas including the role of international central securities depositories, an appreciation of different settlement cycles and issues in managing global assets	2 – 8
Topic 3: Legal Concepts Demonstrate an understanding of legal concepts relevant to financial advice		
3.1.1	Explain legal persons and power of attorney	3 – 1
3.1.2	Explain basic law of contract and agency	3 – 2
3.1.3	Explain the types of ownership of property	3 – 3
3.1.4	Explain insolvency and bankruptcy	3 – 4
3.1.5	Explain wills and intestacy	3 – 5
3.1.6	Identify the main types of trusts and their uses	3 – 6

Syllabus Item	BPP Ref Chapter–Section
5.1.4 Explain the FSA's risk based approach to supervision and the enforcement and disciplinary powers of the FSA relating to: – information gathering (EG 3) – variation and cancellation of Part IV permission (EG 8) – prohibition of individuals (EG 9) – restitution and redress (EG 11) – statutory notices (DEPP 1 & 2)	5 – 4 and 5– 5
Topic 6: The Regulatory Framework Demonstrate an ability to apply the principles and rules as set out in the regulatory framework	
Section 6.1: Approved Persons, Controlled Functions, Training and Competence	
6.1.1 Define an approved person	6 – 1
6.1.2 Define a controlled function	6 – 1.2
6.1.3 Identify the types of controlled functions defined within the FSA handbook (SUP 10)	6 – 1.2
6.1.4 Identify the main assessment criteria in the FSA's Fit and Proper Test for approved persons (FIT)	6 – 1
6.1.5 Explain the application procedure for approved persons (SUP 10)	6 – 1
6.1.6 Explain the procedure for an approved person moving within a group (SUP 10)	6 – 1
6.1.7 Explain the requirements relating to training and competence	6 – 2
Section 6.2: Record Keeping and Reporting Information	
6.2.1 Apply the rules relating to record keeping	6 – 3.1
6.2.2 Apply the rules relating to occasional reporting to clients (COBS 16.2)	6 – 3.2
6.2.3 Apply the rules relating to periodic reporting to clients (COBS 16.3)	6 – 3.3
Section 6.3: Market Conduct and Financial Crime	
6.3.1 Explain the various sources of money laundering and counter terrorism regulation and legislation – FSA rules – Money Laundering Regulations – Proceeds of Crime Act 2002	6 – 4
6.3.2 Explain the role of the Joint Money Laundering Steering Group (JMLSG)	6 – 4.8
6.3.3 Explain the main features of the guidance provided by the JMLSG	6 – 4.7
6.3.4 Explain the three stages involved in the money laundering process	6 – 4.2
6.3.5 Explain the four offence categories under UK money laundering legislation	6 – 4.6
6.3.6 Explain the meaning of 'inside information' covered by CJA 1993	6 – 5.1
6.3.7 Explain the offence of insider dealing covered by the CJA	6 – 5.3
6.3.8 Identify the penalties for being found guilty of insider dealing	6 – 5.4

Syllabus Item		BPP Ref Chapter–Section
6.3.9	Explain the FSA's powers to prosecute insider dealing	6 – 5.6
6.3.10	Understand the nature of behaviours defined as market abuse (MAR 1.3,4,5,6,7,8 & 9)	6 – 6
6.3.11	Explain the enforcement powers of the FSA relating to market abuse (MAR 1.1.4,5 & 6)	6 – 6.9
Section 6.4: Complaints Handling, the Financial Ombudsman Service and the Financial Services Compensation Scheme		
6.4.1	Explain the FSA rules relating to handling of complaints (DISP 1.3)	6 – 7
6.4.2	Explain the role of the Financial Ombudsman Service (DISP Introduction and DISP 2)	6 – 8.1
6.4.3	Distinguish compulsory from voluntary jurisdiction (DISP Introduction)	6 – 8.2
6.4.4	Explain the procedure and time limits for the resolution of complaints (DISP 1.4, 1.5 and 1.6)	6 – 7.5
6.4.5	Apply the rules relating to record keeping and reporting (DISP 1.9, 1.10)	6 – 7.10
6.4.6	Apply the rules relating to determination by the Ombudsman (DISP 3)	6 – 8.5
6.4.7	Explain the purpose of the Financial Services Compensation Scheme (FSCS) (COMP 1.1.7)	6 – 9.1
6.4.8	Identify the circumstances under which the FSCS will pay compensation (COMP 1.3.3, 3.2.1 (1)&(2), 4.2.1 & 2 (1) to (6))	6 – 9.2
6.4.9	Identify the limits on the compensation payable by the FSCS (COMP 10.2.1,2 &3)	6 – 9.3
Topic 7: The Regulatory Advice Framework Demonstrate the ability to apply the regulatory advice framework in practice for the consumer		
Section 7.1: Accepting Customers for Business		
7.1.1	Explain the purpose of client classification	7 – 1
7.1.2	Distinguish between a retail client, a professional client and an eligible counterparty (COBS 3.4, 3.5, 3.6)	7 – 1.6
7.1.3	Apply the rules relating to treating a client as an elective professional client (COBS 3.5.3)	7 – 1.6
7.1.4	Apply the rules relating to treating a client as an elective eligible client (COBS 3.6.4)	7 – 1.6
7.1.5	Apply the rules relating to providing clients with a higher level of protection (COBS 3.7)	7 – 1.6
7.1.6	Apply the rules relating to client agreements (COBS 8.1)	7 – 1.9
Section 7.2: Financial Promotions and Other Communications with Customers		
7.2.1	Explain the purpose and scope of the financial promotions rules and the exceptions to them (COBS 4.1)	7 – 2
7.2.2	Explain the fair, clear and not misleading rule (COBS 4.2)	7 – 2.4

LEARNING MEDIA

Syllabus Item		BPP Ref Chapter–Section
7.5.3	Explain the rules relating to the protection of clients' assets and having adequate organisation arrangements (CASS 6.2)	7 – 6.2
7.5.4	Explain the rules relating to depositing assets with third parties (CASS 6.3)	7 – 6.2
7.5.5	Explain the purpose of the rules relating to the use of clients' assets (CASS 6.4)	7 – 6.2
7.5.6	Explain the rules relating to records, accounts and reconciliations of clients' assets (CASS 6.5)	7 – 6.4
7.5.7	Explain the application and general purpose of the client money rules (CASS 7.2)	7 – 6.3
7.5.8	Explain the rules relating to the segregation of client money (CASS 7.4)	7 – 6.3
7.5.9	Explain the rules relating to records, accounts and reconciliations of client money (CASS 7.6)	7 – 6.7
Section 7.6: Dealing and Managing		
7.6.1	Explain the rules relating to best execution (COBS 11.2)	7 – 7.2
7.6.2	Explain the rules relating to client order handling (COBS 11.3)	7 – 7.4
7.6.3	Explain the rules relating to the use of dealing commission (COBS 11.6)	7 – 7.5
7.6.4	Explain the rules on personal account dealing (COBS 11.7)	7 – 7.7
Topic 8: The FSA's use of Principles and Outcomes Based Regulation Demonstrate an understanding of the FSA's use of principles and outcomes based regulation to promote ethical and fair outcomes		
8.1.1	Explain the application and purpose of the FSA's Principles for Businesses (PRIN 1.1.1 & 2)	8 – 1
8.1.2	Explain the consequences of breaching the FSA's Principles for Businesses (PRIN 1.1.7 to 9 and DEPP 6.2.14 & 15)	8 – 1.4
8.1.3	Identify the FSA's Principles for Businesses (PRIN 2.1.1 and PRIN 4)	8 – 1.2
8.1.4	Explain the importance of corporate culture and leadership	8 – 2
8.1.5	Explain the application and purpose of the Statements of Principle and Code of Practice for approved persons (APER)	8 – 3
Topic 9: Code of Ethics and Professional Standards Demonstrate an ability to apply the Code of ethics and professional standards to business behaviours of individuals		
9.1.1	Identify the elements of the CFA Code of ethics	9 – 1
9.1.2	Explain the professional principles and values on which the Code is based	9 – 1
9.1.3	Apply the Code to a range of ethical dilemmas	9 – 1
Topic 10: Ethical and Compliance Driven Behaviour Demonstrate an ability to critically evaluate the outcomes that distinguish between ethical and compliance driven behaviour		
10.1.1	Identify typical behavioural indicators	9 – 2

Syllabus Item	BPP Ref Chapter–Section
10.1.2 Critically evaluate the outcomes which may result from behaving ethically – for the industry, individual advisers and consumers	9 – 2
10.1.3 Critically evaluate the outcomes which may result from limiting behaviour to compliance with the rules – for the industry, firm, individual advisers and consumers	9 – 2
Topic 11: Retail Clients Demonstrate an understanding of how the retail customer is served by the financial services industry	
11.1.1 Explain the obligations of a firm towards consumers and their perceptions of financial services	10 – 1
11.1.2 Explain the main needs of consumers and how they are prioritised	10 – 1
11.1.3 Identify suitable investment solutions to suit different needs of consumers	10 –
Topic 12: Client Objectives and the Investment Advice Process Demonstrate an ability to apply the investment advice process	
Section 12.1: The Client's Financial Objectives	
12.1.1 Explain the importance of establishing and quantifying a client's objectives	10 – 2.3
12.1.2 Explain the need to prioritise objectives to accommodate a client's affordability	10 – 2.4
Section 12.2: The Client's Current Circumstances	
12.2.1 Explain the importance of the fact find process in establishing a client's current financial circumstances	10 – 2.5
12.2.2 Identify the factors shaping a clients' circumstances	10 – 2.5
Section 12.3: The Client's Attitude to Risk	
12.3.1 Analyse the main types of investment risk as they affect investors	10 – 2.6
12.3.2 Explain the role of diversification in mitigating risk	10 – 2.6
12.3.3 Analyse the impact of timescale on a client's attitude to risk	10 – 2.6
12.3.4 Explain the key methods of determining a client's attitude to risk	10 – 2.6
Section 12.4: Advice and Recommendations	
12.4.1 Explain why asset allocation always comes before investment or product selection	10 – 2.7
12.4.2 Explain the key roles of past performance, charges and the financial stability of the provider as criteria within the fund selection process	10 – 2.12
12.4.3 Explain the importance of stability, independence and standing of trustees, fund custodians and auditors in the fund selection process	10 – 2.12
12.4.4 Identify benchmarks and other performance measures	10 – 2.7
12.4.5 Explain the importance of reviews within the financial planning process	10 – 2.7

Syllabus Item	BPP Ref Chapter–Section
Section 12.5: The Objectives of Pension funds, Life Assurance and General Insurance Companies and the Factors that Impact Upon their Investment Decisions	
12.5.1 Explain the features and objectives of the following funds in the UK: – pension funds (defined benefit and defined contribution) – life assurance funds – general insurance funds	10 – 3
12.5.2 Distinguish among the typical asset allocations for the above funds	10 – 3
12.5.3 Explain the return objectives of the major fund types	10 – 3
12.5.4 Classify funds by their income/capital growth requirements	10 – 3
12.5.5 Explain the effect of each of the following on a fund's asset allocation: – time horizons – liability structure – liquidity requirements	10 – 3.7
12.5.6 Explain the taxation of the various types of funds in the UK	10 – 3.9
12.5.7 Explain the effect that tax legislation may have on the stock selection and asset allocation of a fund	10 – 3.9
12.5.8 Identify the other types of legal requirements that affect pension, insurance funds and private clients	10 – 3
Topic 13: Skills Required when Advising Clients Demonstrate an understanding of the range of skills required when advising clients	10 – 5
13.1.1 Communicate clearly, assessing and adapting to the differing capabilities of clients	10 – 5
13.1.2 Evaluate the factors shaping a clients' needs and circumstances	10 – 4
13.1.3 Apply suitable investment solutions to suit different types of circumstances	10 – 4
Topic 14: The UK Tax System Demonstrate an understanding of the UK tax system as relevant to the needs and circumstances of individuals and trusts	
14.1.1 Explain the principles of income tax applicable to earnings, savings and investment income in the UK	11 – 1
14.1.2 Explain in relation to income tax the system of allowances, reliefs and priorities for taxing income	11 – 1
14.1.3 Explain the taxation of the income of trusts and beneficiaries	11 – 1, 11 – 4
14.1.4 Explain the system of national insurance contributions	11 – 2
14.1.5 Explain the principles of capital gains tax in the UK	11 – 3
14.1.6 Explain the principles of inheritance tax	11 – 4
14.1.7 Explain the implications of residence and domicile in relation to liability to income, capital gains and inheritance tax	11 – 3, 11 – 4

Syllabus Item	BPP Ref Chapter–Section
14.1.8 Explain the system of UK tax compliance including self assessment, Pay As You Earn (PAYE), tax returns, tax payments, tax evasion and avoidance issues	11 – 5
14.1.9 Explain the principles of stamp duty land tax (SDLT) as applied to property transactions – buying/selling and leasing	11 – 6
14.1.10 Explain the principles of stamp duty reserve tax (SDRT)	11 – 6
14.1.11 Explain how companies are taxed in the UK	11 – 7
14.1.12 Explain in outline the principles of Value Added Tax (VAT)	11 – 8
Topic 15: The Taxation of Investments Demonstrate an ability to analyse the taxation of investments as relevant to the needs and circumstances of individuals and trusts	
15.1.1 Analyse the taxation of direct investments including cash and cash equivalents, fixed interest securities, equities and property	12 – 1
15.1.2 Analyse the taxation of indirect investments including pension arrangements, individual savings accounts (ISAs) , child trust funds(CTFs), onshore and offshore collective investment schemes and investment companies, onshore and offshore life assurance policies, real estate investment trusts and Venture Capital Trusts (VCTs) and Enterprise Investment Schemes (EISs)	12 – 2
Topic 16: Tax Planning Demonstrate an ability to analyse the role and relevance of tax in the financial affairs of individuals and trusts	
16.1.1 Explain the limitations of lifetime gifts and transfers at death in mitigating IHT	13 – 3
16.1.2 Analyse the key principles of income tax planning – spouse, civil partners, children, pension contributions, ISA allowances and other tax advantaged schemes (EIS and VCT's etc.)	13 – 1
16.1.3 Analyse how the use of annual CGT exemptions, the realisation of losses, the timing of disposals, and sale and repurchase of similar assets can mitigate CGT	13 – 2
Topic 17: Application of Personal Tax Planning to Investment Advice Demonstrate an ability to apply the knowledge of personal taxation to the provision of investment advice	
17.1.1 To carry out computations on the most common elements of income tax and NICs; CGT; IHT including the impact of lifetime transfers and transfers at death	11, 12, 13
17.1.2 To make elementary tax planning recommendations in the context of investments and pensions advice	13

1

The Financial Services Industry

INTRODUCTION

In this first chapter of the Study Text, we look at the place of the financial services industry within the economic system, and at the main institutions and markets within the industry. We examine also the roles of the national Government, and the status of EU legislation in the UK.

EU Directives have been influential on the UK regulatory system through the implementation of the Markets in Financial Instruments Directive (MiFID). The UCITS Directive enables funds to be marketed throughout Europe.

CHAPTER CONTENTS

BPP
LEARNING MEDIA

1

Chapter Learning Objectives

1   The UK financial services industry – a European and global context

Demonstrate an understanding of the UK financial services industry, in its European and global context

1.1   The financial services industry and the role of Government

1.1.1 Explain the functions of the financial services industry

1.1.2 Evaluate the role and impact of the main financial institutions

1.1.3 Explain the role of Government including economic and industrial policy, regulation, taxation and social welfare

1.2   The impact of EU Directives on the investment industry

1.2.1 Explain the legal status of EU Directives within the UK

1.2.2 Explain the purpose and scope of the Markets in Financial Instrument Directive (MiFID) with respect to:

– Passporting
– Roles of home and host state
– Core and non-core investment services
– Financial instruments covered by the legislation

1.2.3 Explain the purpose and scope of the UCITS Directives

1   Functions of the Financial Services Industry

Learning objective	1.1.1 **Explain** the functions of the financial services industry.

1.1 The monetary economy

Money is the main **medium of exchange** in our society. In a **barter economy**, goods and services are exchanged one for another. If someone works to harvest corn, and is given corn in payment for their labour, this is a barter exchange. The use of money as a medium of exchange creates much flexibility in economic transactions. If the harvester is paid in money instead of corn, he may be able to use that money to buy cooking pots and meat. He cannot subsist only on corn.

Most measures of 'money' include balances (eg at banks and building societies) as well as notes and coin. Money functions as a medium of exchange because:

- It is **divisible** into small units (pounds and pence, dollars and cents)
- There are **sufficient quantities of money** to use for transactions
- Money is **generally accepted** by all parties in transactions

The modern **monetary economy** involves a huge variety of types of transactions involving money. Because money is a recognised medium of exchange among people, it is accepted that debt relationships between people, and claims by one person or institution over another, can be expressed in monetary terms.

The **financial services industry** covers various activities within our monetary **economy**. At the national level, we have the economy of the United Kingdom, with its own currency, the pound sterling. The financial services industry also operates within an international framework, resulting from both the multinational nature of many financial services activities and from various international agreements and regulatory influences. As a member of the **European Union (EU),** the United Kingdom is subject to EU legislation.

1.2 The flow of funds in the economy

The **flow of funds** in an economy describes the movement of funds or money between one group of people or institutions in the economic system and other groups.

If we begin by ignoring the country's imports and exports of goods and services and foreign investments, we can start to build up a picture of the flow of funds by identifying three sectors in the economy.

- The **personal sector** – mainly individuals or households
- The **business sector** (or industrial and commercial sector) – ie companies and other businesses
- The **government sector** – ie central government, local government and public corporations

Within each of these three sectors, there are continual **movements of funds**.

- Individuals will give money or lend money to other individuals.

- Companies will buy goods and services from other companies, and may occasionally lend money direct to other companies.

- Central government will provide funds for local government authorities and loss-making nationalised industries.

As well as movements of funds within each sector, there are flows of funds between different sectors of the economy.

These flows of funds can be shown in a diagram.

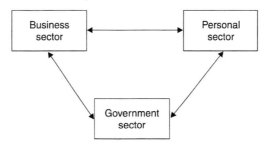

Flow of funds ignoring financial intermediation

But reality is not quite so simple, and our analysis of the flow of funds in the UK should also take account of two other main factors.

- The **overseas sector** comprises businesses, individuals and governments in other countries. The UK economy is influenced by trade with the foreign sector and flows of capital both from and to it.

- **Financial intermediaries** – see below.

1.3 Financial intermediation

An intermediary is a go-between, and a financial intermediary is an institution which **links lenders with borrowers**, by obtaining deposits from lenders and then re-lending them to borrowers. Such institutions can, for example, provide a link between savers and investors.

The role of **financial intermediaries** such as banks and building societies in an economy is to provide means by which funds can be transferred from **surplus units** (for example, someone with savings to invest in the economy) to **deficit units** (for example, someone who wants to borrow money to buy a house). Financial intermediaries develop the facilities and **financial instruments** which make lending and borrowing possible.

If no financial intermediation takes place, lending and borrowing will be direct.

If financial intermediation does take place, the intermediary provides a service to both the surplus unit and the deficit unit.

For example, a person might deposit savings with a bank, and the bank might use its collective deposits of savings to provide a loan to a company.

Financial intermediaries might also lend abroad or borrow from abroad, and a fuller version of a diagram depicting the flow of funds is thus as follows.

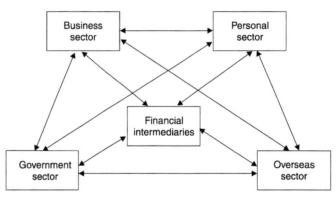

Flow of funds in an open economy, showing the role of financial intermediation

A **financial intermediary** is a party bringing together providers and users of finance, either as a broker facilitating a transaction between two other parties, or in their own right, as principal.

UK financial intermediaries include the following sectors of the financial services industry:

- Banks
- Building societies
- Insurance companies, pension funds, unit trust companies and investment trust companies
- The Government's National Savings & Investments (NS&I)

In spite of competition from building societies, insurance companies and other financial institutions, banks arguably remain the major financial intermediaries in the UK.

The clearing banks are the biggest operators in the retail banking market, although competition from the building societies has grown in the UK.

There is greater competition between different banks (overseas banks and the clearing banks especially) for business in the wholesale lending market.

Financial intermediaries can link lenders with borrowers, by obtaining deposits from lenders and then re-lending them to borrowers. But not all intermediation takes place between savers and investors. Some institutions act mainly as intermediaries between other institutions. Almost all place part of their funds with other institutions, and a number (including finance houses, leasing companies and factoring companies) obtain most of their funds by borrowing from other institutions.

1.4 Benefits of financial intermediation

Financial intermediaries perform the following functions.

- They provide obvious and **convenient** ways in which a **lender can save money** to spend in the future. Instead of having to find a suitable borrower for their money, lenders can deposit money. Financial intermediaries also provide a ready **source of funds for borrowers**.

- They can aggregate or 'package' the amounts lent by savers and lend on to borrowers in different amounts (a process called **aggregation**). By aggregating the deposits of hundreds of small savers, a bank or building society is able to package up the amounts and lend on to several borrowers in the form of larger mortgages.

- Financial intermediaries provide for **maturity transformation**, i.e. they bridge the gap between the wish of most lenders for liquidity and the desire of most borrowers for loans over longer periods. For example, while many depositors in a building society may want instant access to their funds, the building society can lend these funds to mortgage borrowers over much longer periods, by ensuring that it attracts sufficient funds from depositors over this longer term.

By pooling the funds of large numbers of people, some financial institutions are able to give small investors access to professionally managed **diversified portfolios** covering a varied range of different securities through collective investment products such as unit trusts and investment trusts.

Risk for individuals is reduced by **pooling**. Since financial intermediaries lend to a large number of individuals and organisations, losses suffered through default by borrowers or capital losses are pooled and borne as costs by the intermediary. Such losses are shared among lenders in general.

1.5 Management of risk

For most people, **risk** means the chance that something will go wrong. Taking a risk means doing something that could turn out to be damaging, or could result in a loss.

Individuals can face various risks, such as a risk of physical injury, ill health or death, a risk of damage to property or theft of property, a risk that an investment will lose money, a risk that their bank or other financial institution may fail, and so on.

Insurance, of various kinds, offers ways of reducing various risks, by transferring the risk to an insurer who bears risks for many others in exchange for premiums collected from each insured party.

Various financial instruments made available through the financial services industry allow individuals to expose themselves to **investment risks** that they may wish to run, in the hope of a positive return on their investment.

Businesses, likewise, face various risks. A business may lose customers or key staff, its products may fail, changes in the law may curtail its activities, and so on. A company is owned by its members – that is, its **shareholders**. When a company is exposed to risks, this will affect the value of the shareholders' stake in the company. However, there are other stakeholders in a company who may stand to lose from the risks that a company is exposed to: these other **stakeholder groups** that could be affected include providers of debt finance (often, banks), employees and directors. As with individuals, insurance offers a way in which businesses can manage various risks.

Financial products offer ways in which individuals and businesses can **manage** risk.

It is not the aim of **risk management** to eliminate risks entirely. The aims of risk management can be formulated as follows.

- Make an assessment of risk when taking decisions, and keep investment risk within acceptable limits

- Avoid unnecessary risks and prevent unnecessary losses

- Reduce the frequency of adverse outcomes when the risk probability is high, and reduce the impact of adverse outcomes where the severity of the risk is high

Risk cannot be totally eliminated, for either individuals or businesses. The Financial Services Authority (FSA), as regulator of the financial services industry, asserts that it sees it as both **impossible and undesirable to remove all risk** and failure from the financial system.

Exercise: Risk

Set out some reasons why it could be undesirable to remove all risk from the financial system.

Solution

If there were no risk in the financial system, companies would not be able to raise finance through the system for risky ventures such as developing new medicines or investing in innovative technologies.

People may wish to take risks with money that they can afford to lose, to give the possible prospect of high returns if an investment turns out well.

Many of the things that people would like to do, such as buy their own home, are subject to market forces that inevitably involve risks: house prices might fall, so that someone with a mortgage might find that the house comes to be worth less than the mortgage loan on the house.

Removing all risk from transactions could mean that excessive resources are spent on bureaucracy to regulate institutions and markets. Alternatively, a 'risk-free' financial system might involve the State effectively 'underwriting' all the risks that an individual might face: this suggests an economic system with a very high level of State control, which many would consider to be undesirable.

2 MARKETS AND INSTITUTIONS

Learning objective — **1.1.2 Evaluate** the role and impact of the main financial institutions.

2.1 Capital markets and money markets

The capital markets and the money markets are types of market for dealing in capital.

- **Capital markets** are financial markets for raising and investing largely **long-term** capital.
- **Money markets** are financial markets for lending and borrowing largely **short-term** capital.

2.2 Long-term and short-term capital

What do we mean by **long-term** and **short-term** capital?

- By **short-term capital**, we mean capital that is lent or borrowed for a period which might range from as short as overnight up to about one year, and sometimes longer.

- By **long-term capital**, we mean capital invested or lent and borrowed for a period of about five years or more, but sometimes shorter.

- There is a **grey area** between long-term and short-term capital, which is lending and borrowing for a period from about one to two years up to about five years, which is not surprisingly referred to as **medium-term** capital.

2.3 The London Stock Exchange

The **London Stock Exchange** (LSE) is an organised **capital market** which plays an important role in the functioning of the UK economy. The LSE provides the main way for larger companies to raise funds through the issue of **shares** (equity). It makes it easier for large firms and the government to raise long-term capital, by providing a market place for businesses seeking capital and investors to come together.

The **Alternative Investment Market** (AIM), which opened in 1995, is a market where smaller companies which cannot meet the more stringent requirements needed to obtain a full listing on the Stock Exchange can raise new capital by issuing shares. It is cheaper for smaller company to be on the AIM than to meet the requirements for a full listing. Like the Stock Exchange main market, the AIM is also a market in which investors can trade in shares already issued. The AIM is regulated by the Stock Exchange.

2.4 Banks

Banks can be approached directly by individuals (**retail** business) and businesses for medium-term and long-term loans as well as short-term loans or overdrafts.

The major clearing banks, many investment banks and foreign banks operating in the UK are often willing to lend medium-term capital, especially to well established businesses.

2.5 The gilt-edged market

The **gilt-edged market** is a further major capital market in the UK. The government borrows over the medium and longer term by issuing government stocks (called 'gilt-edged stock' or 'gilts'). Trade in second-hand gilts will continue until the debt eventually matures and the government redeems the stock.

The **primary** gilts market is the market for the sale of new gilt issues. There is an active **secondary** market in second-hand gilts with existing holders selling their holdings of gilts to other investors in the gilts market.

2.6 Providers of capital

Providers of capital include **private individuals** in the retail sector. This includes those who buy stocks and shares on the Stock Exchange, and those who deposit money with banks, building societies and National Savings & Investments (NS&I). NS&I is a government institution set up to borrow on behalf of the government, mainly from the non-banking private sector of the economy.

There are also important groups of **institutional investors** which specialise in providing capital and act as financial intermediaries between suppliers and demanders of funds. Many financial services organisations now have diversified operations covering a range of the following activities.

- **Pension funds**. Pension funds invest the pension contributions of individuals who subscribe to a pension fund, and of organisations with a company pension fund.

- **Insurance**. Insurance companies invest premiums paid on insurance policies by policy holders. Life assurance policies, including life-assurance based savings policies, account for substantial assets, which are invested in equities, bonds, property and other assets.

- **Investment trusts**. The business of investment trust companies is investing in the stocks and shares of other companies and the government. In other words, they trade in investments.

- **Collective funds. Unit trusts and Open-ended Investment Companies (OEICs)** are similar to investment trusts, in the sense that they invest in stocks and shares of other companies.

- **Venture capital**. Venture capital providers are organisations that specialise in raising funds for new business ventures, such as 'management buy-outs' (ie purchases of firms by their management staff). These organisations are therefore providing capital for fairly risky ventures.

2.7 Overview of capital markets

The role of financial intermediaries in capital markets is illustrated in the diagram below.

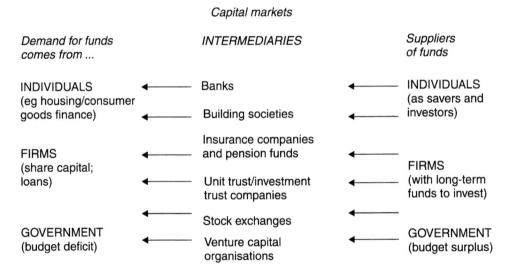

Capital markets

2.8 Changes in capital markets

Recent years have seen very big changes in the capital markets of the world.

- **Globalisation of capital markets.** The capital markets of each country have become internationally integrated. Securities issued in one country can now be traded in capital markets around the world. For example, shares in many UK companies are traded in the USA. The shares are bought by US banks, which then issue ADRs (American depository receipts) which are a form in which foreign shares can be traded in US markets without a local listing.

- **Securitisation of debt.** Securitisation of debt means creating tradable securities which are backed by less liquid assets such as mortgages and other long-term loans.

- **Risk management (and risk assessment).** Various techniques have been developed for companies to manage their financial risk such as swaps and options. These 'derivative' financial instruments may allow transactions to take place 'off-balance sheet' and therefore not easily evident from the company's financial statements. The existence of such transactions may make it more difficult for banks and other would-be lenders to assess the financial risk of a company that is asking to borrow money.

- **Increased competition.** There is much fiercer competition than there used to be between financial institutions for business. For example, building societies have become direct competitors to the retail banks, and foreign banks have also competed in the UK with the big clearing banks. Banks have made shifts towards more fee-based activities (such as selling advice and selling insurance products for commission) and away from the traditional transaction-based activities (holding deposits, making loans).

Securitisation of debt involves disintermediation. **Financial disintermediation** is a process whereby ultimate borrowers and lenders by-pass the normal methods of financial intermediation (such as depositing money with and borrowing money from banks) and find other ways of lending or borrowing funds; or lend and borrow directly with each other, avoiding financial intermediation altogether. Securitisation of debt provides firms with a method of borrowing from non-banks. Although banks might act as managers of the debt issue, finding lenders who will buy the securitised debt, banks are not doing the lending themselves.

2.9 The money markets

The UK **money markets** are operated by the banks and other financial institutions. Although the money markets largely involve **wholesale borrowing and lending** by banks, some large companies and the government are also involved in money market operations. The money markets are essentially shorter term debt markets, with loans being made for a specified period at a specified rate of interest.

The money markets operate both as a **primary market**, in which new financial claims are issued and as a **secondary market**, where previously issued financial claims are traded.

Amounts dealt in are relatively large, generally being above £50,000 and often in millions of pounds. Loans are transacted on extremely 'fine' terms – ie with small margins between lending and borrowing rates – reflecting the **economies of scale** involved. The emphasis is on liquidity: the efficiency of the money markets can make the financial claims dealt in virtually the equivalent of cash.

2.10 The banks and the banking system

There are different types of **banks** which operate within a banking system, and you will probably have come across a number of terms which describe them. **Commercial banks** make commercial banking transactions with customers. They are distinct from the country's **central bank**.

- **Clearing banks** are those that operate the clearing system for settling payments (eg payments by cheque by bank customers).

- The term **retail banks** is used to describe the traditional High Street banks. The term **wholesale banks** refers to banks which specialise in lending in large amounts to major customers. The clearing banks are involved in both retail and wholesale banking but are commonly regarded as the main retail banks.

- **Investment banks** offer services, often of a specialised nature, to corporate customers.

These categories are not mutually exclusive: a single bank may be a retail clearing bank, with wholesale and investment banking operations.

2.11 Building societies

The **building societies** of the UK are **mutual** organisations whose main assets are mortgages of their members. Among their liabilities are the balances of the investor members who hold savings accounts with the society. The **Building Societies Act 1986** requires that at least **50%** of a building society's funds must be raised from share accounts held by individual members.

The distinction between building societies and banks has become increasingly blurred, as the societies have taken to providing a range of services formerly the province mainly of banks, and banks have themselves made inroads into the housing mortgage market. Some building societies now offer cheque book accounts, cash cards and many other facilities that compete directly with the banks.

The building society sector has shrunk in size over the last twenty years or so as a number of the major societies have either converted to public limited companies and therefore become banks or have been taken over by banks or other financial institutions.

2.12 The central bank

A **central bank** is a bank which acts on behalf of the government. The central bank for the UK is the **Bank of England**. The Bank of England is a nationalised corporation.

Functions of the Bank of England

- It acts as **banker to the central government** and holds the 'public deposits'. Public deposits include the National Loans Fund, the Consolidated Fund and the account of the Paymaster General, which in turn includes the Exchange Equalisation Account.

- It is the **central note-issuing authority** in the UK – it is responsible for issuing bank notes in England.

- It is the **manager of the National Debt** – ie it deals with long-term and short-term borrowing by the central government and the repayment of central government debt.

- It is the manager of the Exchange Equalisation Account (ie the UK's **foreign currency reserves**).

- It acts as adviser to the government on **monetary policy**.

- The Bank's **Monetary Policy Committee (MPC)** acts as agent for the Government in carrying out its monetary policies. Since May 1997, the MPC has had operational responsibility for **setting short-term interest rates** at the level it considers appropriate in order to meet the Government's inflation target.

- It acts as a **lender to the banking system**. When the banking system is short of money, the Bank of England will provide the money the banks need – at a suitable rate of interest.

Supervision of the **banking system** is the responsibility of the Financial Services Authority (FSA).

2.13 The central bank as lender of last resort

In the UK, the **short-term money market** provides a link between the banking system and the government (Bank of England) whereby the Bank of England lends money to the banking system, when banks which need cash cannot get it from anywhere else.

- The Bank will supply cash to the banking system on days when the banks have a cash shortage. It does this by buying eligible bills and other short-term financial investments from approved financial institutions in exchange for cash.

- The Bank will remove excess cash from the banking system on days when the banks have a cash surplus. It does this by selling bills to institutions, so that the short-term money markets obtain interest-bearing bills in place of the cash that they do not want.

The process whereby this is done currently is known as **open market operations** by the Bank. This simply describes the buying and selling of short-term assets between the Bank and the short-term money market.

The Bank acted as lender of last resort to the bank Northern Rock, when the bank became unable to raise enough funds on the wholesale money markets during 2007.

3 UK FINANCIAL SERVICES AND THE EUROPEAN AND GLOBAL CONTEXT

3.1 The UK's position in financial services

The financial services industry is a key sector of the UK economy. The UK financial services industry employs over 1 million people and net overseas earnings from the industry amount to over 5% of national output or GDP.

With a long history going back to the time of merchant adventurers who sought finance for world-wide overseas trading, the 'Square Mile' of the **City of London** is the centre for the UK financial services industry. The City is the largest centre for many international financial markets, such as the currency markets. The UK has the world's largest share in the metals market (95%), Eurobond trade (70%), the foreign equity market (58%), derivatives markets (36%) and insurance (22%).

3.2 Banking

While there are over 300 **banking** groups and building societies operating in the UK, the ten largest UK-owned banking groups hold some 70% of UK households' deposits. Building societies hold over 20% of household deposits.

The UK has the greatest concentration of foreign banks, numbering around 500 compared with around 300 in the USA, in the world. London accounts for 19% of global cross-border bank lending, more than any other financial centre. The total assets of the UK banking system exceed £3,000 billion of which approximately 55% belongs to foreign banks. The assets of UK-owned banks, totalling around £1,300 billion, are dominated by around a dozen retail banks, with national branch networks serving domestic, personal and corporate customers.

The banks and building societies form a significant part of the market for financial services. A banking institution could maintain access to a full range of products and product providers by setting up an independent arm. However, few have maintained a wholly independent stance. Most have either formed tied links to life insurance companies ('life offices') or have acquired or set up their own insurance companies which mainly or wholly offer products to clients introduced through the bank or building society.

3.3 Insurance

UK **life insurance companies** sell various products within the UK retail market, including collective investment schemes such as unit trusts, OEICs and investment trusts, pension products and individual life insurance. The development of life assurance provision by **banks** is known as **bancassurance** or **all finanz**. The Association of British Insurers (ABI) defines **bancassurers** as 'insurance companies that are subsidiaries of banks and building societies and whose primary market is the customer base of the bank or building society'.

The UK has a major **general insurance** and **reinsurance** market ranging from personal motor insurance to insurance for space satellites. Reinsurance is a process by which a company – for example, a life office writing new business – can sell or pass on the risks on its policies to a third party **reinsurer**.

The UK insurance business generates premium income in the UK insurance market of over £170 billion annually. This makes the third largest such market in the world, exceeded only by the US and Japan. The

London market – centred on **Lloyds** of London – is the global market leader in aviation and marine insurance, with market shares of 31% and 19% respectively.

Lloyds acts as a major reinsurer for life assurance. Lloyds is a long-established market in which **underwriting syndicates** operate independently. Syndicates are made up of companies and individuals (**Lloyds 'names'**) who provide capital and assume the risk of liabilities they insure or reinsure. Syndicates are run by **managing agents** who appoint **underwriters** to write (assess) risks on behalf of the syndicate. Although the Financial Services Authority (FSA) has overall regulatory responsibility for Lloyds, much of the regulatory work is delegated to the Council of Lloyds.

3.4 Pensions

With a rapidly ageing population, there is a **pensions crisis** worldwide. Many countries are passing the burden for pensions provision from the state sector to the private sector.

Domestically, the UK pensions market is of great importance, and a higher proportion of pension payments are provided by the private sector in the UK than in nearly any other country.

3.5 Fund and asset management

Collective funds such as unit trusts and investment trusts need to be managed. In the **fund management** sector, the value of assets under management exceeds £4 trillion. Around one quarter of these funds were managed on behalf of overseas clients. The UK fund management sector offers liquid markets, with the opportunity to trade in large blocks of shares, and a relatively liberalised operating environment combined with protection against abuse. More funds are invested in the London than the ten top European centres combined. Edinburgh is the UK's second major fund management centre and is the sixth largest in Europe.

3.6 Securities and currency markets

As well as having a substantial domestic market in **equities** (company shares) and **bonds** (interest-bearing securities), the UK is a major international centre for trading in the Euromarket, which is the market for debt denominated in other currencies – not just the euro. Eurobonds account for the majority of all bonds issued and the UK issues 60% of them and has a 70% share of the secondary market.

More **foreign companies** are traded on the London Stock Exchange than on any other exchange. Turnover in these companies' shares in London represents approximately half of global turnover in foreign equities.

The UK has over 30% of the global market in **currency trading**, making London the leading world centre for foreign exchange ('forex') trading.

3.7 London as a financial centre

At the time of the introduction of the euro as a common European currency, it was suggested by many that London could lose its strong position as a leading world financial centre and might lose out to competing European centres such as Frankfurt.

There are a number of aspects favouring London as a financial centre.

- Its location in time zones: able to deal with US and Asian markets at either end of the day
- A workforce that is English-speaking – the international business language
- A varied pool of relatively well-educated labour
- Non-business activities making the City an attractive place to work
- Transport links (including air) and infrastructure

- A trend towards an increasingly cosmopolitan business environment
- The historical legacy and long tradition of supporting commerce
- Diversity in financial products available and traded
- Market transparency
- 'Fairness' of business environment, with relatively low incidence of corruption
- Government generally responsive to business needs
- Relatively 'light touch' regulatory environment, although being made less so

Against these potentially positive factors, it could be argued that London's institutional financial markets have a generally wholesale mentality.

There are other threats, as well as opportunities, affecting London's future.

- The potential for outsourcing operations to other countries has increased due to technological advances as well as some relaxation in regulatory regimes.

- Financial markets are showing increasing **virtuality**, so that with electronic communication, physical location becomes less significant.

- There are continuing trends towards consolidation in exchanges, clearing houses and central securities depositories.

- Firms are becoming increasingly likely to relocate processing centres and head offices wherever it is most beneficial.

- The financial turmoil of 2007 to 2009 and its aftermath is likely to lead to a markedly changed landscape for the financial sector for the future.

3.8 Aspects of finance in Europe

Germany and **Switzerland** both have a **universal banking** tradition. Under this system, any recognised bank can provide a full range of banking services, including retail banking services alongside wholesale and investment banking. This is different from the traditional structure of banking in the **UK**, the **USA** and **Japan**. Changes such as the repeal of the Glass-Steagall Act in the late 1990s removed some of the restrictions on the range of activities that individual banks could undertake (such as commercial banking alongside investment banking), although forthcoming banking reforms may reverse some of those changes. However, where it appears that a single bank provides such a range of services in the UK and the USA, this is generally managed by setting up separately capitalised subsidiaries with similar names to the parent company.

Spain, **France** and the **Netherlands** have banking traditions somewhere between the universal and segmented models.

Italy's financial system has been more based on banks than on markets, with firms raising funds mainly through the banking system. Equity involvement has been limited, with founding families continuing to play a lead role in firms.

In **Germany** and **France** as well as Italy, relatively little use has been made of equity finance by firms.

The financial systems of the smaller **Northern European (Scandinavian) countries** have been dominated by a few large domestic banks that have evolved into larger Nordic financial groups through cross-border mergers and acquisitions.

3.9 USA

3.9.1 Financial system

Although the US is often seen as similar to the UK in being a **market-based** financial system, with companies' finance deriving from the issue of securities, at some times the proportion of US company finance coming from bond and equity issues has been lower than in the UK.

Nevertheless, Wall Street, where the New York Stock Exchange is situated, remains at the centre of the system in people's perceptions. The importance of stocks to the average American grew with the growth of mutual funds (collective investments) and pension plans such as '401(k)' plans.

The size of the US economy and the dominance of the US dollar in international transactions has made the US financial system central to both the US economy and the global economy.

The US banking system is characterised by the large number of deposit-taking banks, which may be either state-chartered or national and federally licensed institutions. Non-depository institutions include securities firms, insurance companies, mutual funds, pension funds and finance companies.

3.9.2 Financial services

The term 'financial services' became more widely used in the USA following the Gramm-Leach-Bliley Act of the late 1990s. This legislation enabled different types of companies operating in the US financial services industry to merge.

For companies in the US, there are broadly two distinct approaches to this form of business.

- One approach is for a bank to buy an insurance company or an investment bank, keep the original brands of the acquired firm, and adds the acquisition to its holding company to diversify its earnings. Outside the U.S. (for example, in **Japan**), non-financial services companies are permitted within the holding company. Then, each company still appears independent, and has its own customers.

- A second approach is for a bank to create its own brokerage division or insurance division and attempt to sell those products to its own existing customers, with incentives for combining different services with one company.

3.10 Asian financial centres

3.10.1 Financial centres

Ranking after London and New York, the third and fourth largest financial centres are found in Asia – being **Tokyo** and **Singapore** respectively. Within China, **Shanghai** and **Hong Kong** are also key centres.

3.10.2 China

With a population of around 1.3 billion, **China** comprises approximately 20% of the world population, and so – with continued economic growth – represents substantial buying potential over the longer term. China will come to represent a significant pool of consumers of services as time goes on.

- In 2006, China's Gross Domestic Product (GDP) was broadly equivalent to that of the UK, at US$ 2.5 trillion.

- China's economic growth (increase in GDP) has been around 10% annually every year since 1978 – which is approximately four times the UK's growth rate over the same period.

- There is increasing foreign investment in China, particularly by European investment funds.

- In recent years, foreign banks and financial institutions have been able to establish a foothold in China through cash and share ownership, in spite of China's traditionally protectionist stance.

In a similar way to **India** and **Malaysia** in recent years, China could become a cost-effective focus for service provision in the **financial sector**. The experience of outsourcing into other emerging markets in recent years shows how security and reliability are key to the expansion of such service provision.

Against these factors in China's favour, it is likely to take some more time for China to build up to the 'critical mass' of other major world financial centres.

4 THE ROLE OF GOVERNMENT

ing objectives **1.1.3 Explain** the role of government including economic and industrial policy, regulation, taxation and social welfare.

1.2.1 Explain the legal status of EU Directives in the UK.

4.1 Overview

There are various ways in which Government actions impinge on people's lives and on the activities of businesses.

Legislation (laws) introduced by Parliament often gives authority for Government departments to introduce secondary legislation in the form of additional **regulations**.

Government agencies and local authorities affect our lives in many aspects, whether for example, through taxation or in the services and benefits they provide to us – including roads, and **social welfare services** such as healthcare, State pensions and elderly services.

The extent to which the Government influences what we do reflects the type of **economic system** we have. The economic system of the UK and of the wider European Union to which the UK belongs can be described as that of the **mixed economy**.

- A **mixed economy** involves some degree of State intervention in economic activity, while mostly markets are allowed to operate as freely as possible so long as intervention is not needed in the public interest.

- This type of economy stands between the two extremes of a *laissez-faire* **free market economy** in which market forces are allowed to reign, with minimal State intervention, and of a centrally planned **command economy**, such as that of the former Soviet Union and other Communist-ruled States, in which the government controls most industries and regulates many prices and wages, possibly with a rationing system to distribute scarce goods and services.

4.2 The UK and the EU

4.2.1 Overview

The **European Union (EU)**, formerly called the EEC or the European Community (EC), is one of several international economic associations. Its immediate aim is the integration of the economies of the member states. A more long-term aim is political integration. The association dates back to 1957 (the Treaty of Rome) and the EU now has 27 members including the UK.

The European Union has a **common market** combining different aspects, including **a free trade area** and a **customs union**.

- A **free trade area** exists when there is no restriction on the movement of goods and services between countries. This may be extended into a **customs union** when there is a free trade area between all member countries of the union, and in addition, there are common external tariffs applying to imports from non-member countries into any part of the union. In other words, the union promotes free trade among its members but acts as a protectionist bloc against the rest of the world.

- A **common market** encompasses the idea of a customs union but has a number of additional features. In addition to free trade among member countries there are also free markets in each of the **factors of production**. A British citizen has the freedom to work in any other country of the European Union, for example. A common market will also aim to achieve stronger links between member countries, for example by harmonising government economic policies and by establishing a closer political confederation.

4.2.2 UK sovereignty and EU membership

UK Statute law is made by Parliament (or in exercise of law-making powers delegated by Parliament). Until the United Kingdom entered the European Community in 1973, the UK Parliament was completely **sovereign**.

In recent years however, UK membership of the EU has restricted the previously unfettered power of Parliament. There is an **obligation**, imposed by the Treaty of Rome on which the EU is founded, to bring UK law into line with the Treaty itself and with EU Directives. Regulations, having the force of law in every member state, may be made under provisions of the Treaty of Rome.

4.2.3 Status of EU legislation

EU legislation takes the following three forms.

- **Regulations** have the force of law in every EU state without need of national legislation. Their objective is to obtain uniformity of law throughout the EU. They are formulated by the Commission but must be authorised by the Council of Ministers.

- **Directives** are issued to the governments of the EU member states requiring them within a specified period (usually two years) to alter the national laws of the state so that they conform to the directive. Until a Directive is given effect by a national (UK) statute, it does not usually affect legal rights and obligations of individuals.

- **Decisions** of an administrative nature are made by the European Commission in Brussels. A decision may be addressed to a state, person or a company and is immediately binding, but only on the recipient.

The Council and the Commission may also make recommendations and deliver opinions, although these are only persuasive in authority.

4.3 Monetary policy

4.3.1 Overview

Monetary policy is the area of government economic policy making that is concerned with changes in the **amount of money** in circulation – the **money supply** – and with changes in the **price of money** – **interest rates**. These variables are linked with **inflation** in prices generally, and also with **exchange rates** – the price of the domestic currency in terms of other currencies.

4.3.2 Setting interest rates

Since 1997, the most important aspect of monetary policy in the UK has been the influence over interest rates exerted by the **Bank of England**, the **central bank** of the UK. The **Monetary Policy Committee (MPC)** of the Bank of England was charged with the responsibility of setting interest rates with the aim of meeting the government's current inflation target which currently stands at **2%**, plus or minus 1% as measured by the **Consumer Prices Index (CPI)**, also known as the Harmonised Index of Consumer Prices (HCIP). Inflation below the target of 2% is judged by the Bank of England to be unsatisfactory, as is inflation above the target.

The **UK inflation objective** was originally formalised in the 1998 Bank of England Act. That Act states that the Bank of England is expected 'to maintain price stability, and, subject to that, to support the economic policy of HM Government including its objectives for growth and employment'.

The MPC decides the short-term **benchmark 'repo' rate** at which the Bank of England deals in the money markets. This will tend to be followed by financial institutions generally in setting interest rates for different financial instruments. However, a government does not have an unlimited ability to have interest rates set how it wishes. It must take into account what rates the overall market will bear, so that the benchmark rate it chooses can be maintained. The Bank must be careful about the signals it gives to the markets, since the effect of expectations can be significant.

The monthly minutes of the MPC are published. This arrangement is intended to remove the possibility of direct political influence over the interest rate decision.

The Bank of England **reducing** interest rates is an **easing** of monetary policy.

- Loans will be cheaper, and so consumers may increase levels of debt and spend more. Demand will tend to rise and companies may have improved levels of sales. Companies will find it cheaper to borrow: their lower interest costs will boost bottom-line profits.

- Mortgage loans will be cheaper and so there will be upward pressure on property prices.

- Values of other assets will also tend to rise. Investors will be willing to pay higher prices for gilts (government stock) because they do not require such a high yield from them as before the interest rate reduction.

- Interest rates on cash deposits will fall. Those who are dependant on income from cash deposits will be worse off than before.

The Bank of England **increasing** interest rates is a **tightening** of monetary policy.

- Loans will cost more, and demand from consumers, especially for less essential 'cyclical' goods and services, may fall. Companies will find it more expensive to borrow money and this could eat into profits, on top of any effect from reducing demand.

- Mortgage loans will cost more and so there will be a dampening effect on property prices.

- Asset prices generally will tend to fall. Investors will require a higher return than before and so they will pay less for fixed interest stocks such as gilts.

- Interest rates on cash deposits will rise, and those reliant on cash deposits for income will be better off.

4.3.3 Quantitative easing

Quantitative easing is the term given to a method by which the central bank (in the UK, the Bank of England) manipulates liquidity in the financial system. This allows adjustments to the **money supply** when the interbank interest rate is at or close to zero, and interest rates can therefore no longer be lowered.

Although this process is sometimes characterised as 'printing money', it actually involves the central bank purchasing mostly short-term financial assets using money it has created *ex nihilo* ('out of nothing') and has shown as a credit in the central bank's books. The new money is intended to increase the overall money supply through deposit multiplication, as the institutions receiving the money will be encouraged to lend and the cost of borrowing will be reduced. This is alternatively referred to as '**open market operations**'.

4.4 Exchange rate policy

The **exchange rate** of the national currency (pounds sterling) against other major currencies (such as the US dollar, the euro and the Japanese yen) is another possible focus of economic policy.

The Government could try to influence exchange rates by buying or selling currencies through its central bank reserves. However, Government currency reserves are now relatively small and so such a policy might have to be limited in scope.

Another way the Government might wish to influence exchange rates is through changes in **interest rates**: if UK interest rates are raised, this makes sterling a relatively more attractive currency to hold and so the change should exert upward pressure on the value of sterling. As we have seen, interest rate policy is now determined by the MPC. Interest rate policy is decided in the light of various matters apart from exchange rates, including the inflation rate and the level of house prices.

If the UK joined the **single European currency**, the **euro**, interest rates would effectively be determined at the European level, by the European Central Bank, instead of at the national level as now. It would not be possible for interest rates in different eurozone countries to be much out of line at any one time, since differences would encourage money flows to seek the higher rates available in a particular country, and borrowers would seek the best rates available. The forces of supply and demand would lead to an approximate equalisation of rates.

4.5 Fiscal policy

A government's **fiscal policy** concerns its plans for **spending, taxation and borrowing**.

These aspects of fiscal policy reflect the three elements in public finance.

- **Expenditure**. The government, at a national and local level, spends money to provide goods and services, such as a health service, public education, a police force, roads, public buildings and so on, and to pay its administrative work force. It may also, perhaps, provide finance to encourage investment by private industry, for example by means of grants.

- **Income**. Expenditure must be financed, and the government must have income. Most government income comes from taxation, but some income is obtained from direct charges to users of government services such as National Health Service charges.

- **Borrowing**. To the extent that a government's expenditure exceeds its income, it must borrow to make up the difference. The amount that the government must borrow each year is known as the **Public Sector Net Cash Requirement (PSNCR)** in the UK.

Government **spending is an injection** into the economy, adding to the level of overall demand for goods and services, whereas **taxes are a withdrawal**.

A government's '**fiscal stance**' may be **neutral, expansionary** or **contractionary**, according to its overall effect on national income.

- **Spending more money** and financing this expenditure by borrowing would indicate an expansionary fiscal stance. Expenditure in the economy will increase and so national income will rise, either in real terms, or partly in terms of price levels only: the increase in national income might be real, or simply inflationary.

- **Collecting more in taxes** without increasing spending would indicate a contractionary fiscal stance. A government might deliberately raise taxation to take inflationary pressures out of the economy

The impact of changes in fiscal policy is not always certain, and fiscal policy to pursue one aim (eg lower inflation) might for a while create barriers to the pursuit of other aims (eg employment).

Government planners need to consider how fiscal policy can affect savers, investors and companies.

(a)   The tax regime as it affects different savings instruments will affect **investors'** decisions.

(b)   **Companies** will be affected by tax rules on dividends and profits, and they may take these rules into account when deciding on dividend policy or on whether to raise finance through **debt** (loans) or **equities** (by issuing shares).

The formal planning of fiscal policy usually follows an annual cycle. In the UK, the most important statement is **the Budget**, which takes place in the Spring of each year. The Chancellor of the Exchequer also delivers a Pre-Budget Report each Autumn. The Pre-Budget Report formally makes available for scrutiny the Government's overall spending plans.

4.6 Industrial policy

4.6.1 Overview

While macroeconomic policy-making is concerned with the economy as a while, industrial policy is focused on particular sectors of the economy. The UK government current's approach to industrial policy aims to create an institutional framework that allows businesses to prosper, and individuals and households to improve steadily their living standards.

The institutional framework has the following aims.

- Promoting effective competition
- Flexibility in labour and capital markets
- Maintaining a legal system which gives confidence and trust to market participants
- Providing a stable macroeconomic framework

Other aspects of UK policy concentrate on the advance and commercial application of scientific knowledge, and investment in physical infrastructure, education and health. **Innovation policies** seek to balance the benefits of intellectual property protection with facilitating the widespread exploitation of new knowledge through, among other things, easing barriers to the widespread dissemination and adoption of ideas.

Underpinning this approach is a presumption that, as a whole, the effective operations of markets are a better way of bringing about improvements to business efficiency and the most economically beneficial allocation of capital, knowledge and employment. Government is however seen to have a role where **market failures** arise, for example, in the provision of public goods such as education and healthcare services, and overcoming externalities through policies on science, skills, innovation and regulation.

Responsibility for the various themes of industrial policy is spread across difference central Government departments, although the **Department for Business, Innovation and Skills** plays a key role.

4.6.2 Industry policy and the European Union

The UK works with the European Commission and other EU Member States to address from the European perspective issues that are confronting all industrialised countries – the challenges laid down by globalisation, including for example the intense competition from growing economies like China and India, the greater fragmentation and wider dispersion of supply chains and increased pressures on industrial and local adjustment in relation to our international competitiveness, and energy and climate change.

Actions under the EU Policy agenda

- A commitment to focus on economic growth and employment

- Shaping policies to allow businesses to create more and better jobs implemented in a way that balances and mutually reinforce economic, environmental and social objectives

- An integrated approach aimed at improving the coherence between different policy dimensions and increasing their relevance to business

- Bringing business directly into the process through the establishment of 'High Level Groups'

These High Level groups bring together members of the various European Commission Directorates General, Member State Governments and relevant stakeholders from industry, consumers/civil society, trade unions, Non-Governmental Organisations and regulators and are mandated to provide advice to policy makers at Community and national levels, industry and civil society organisations on issues effecting European industrial competitiveness.

4.7 Free movement of capital

Free international trade is generally associated with the free movement of goods (and services) between countries. Another important aspect of international trade is the **free movement of capital**.

- If a UK company (or investor) wishes to set up a business in a different country, or to take over a company in another country, how easily can it transfer capital from the UK to the country in question, to pay for the investment?

- Similarly, if a Japanese company wishes to invest in the UK, how easily can it transfer funds out of Japan and into the UK to pay for the investment?

Some countries (including the UK, since the abolition of exchange controls in 1979) have allowed a fairly free flow of capital into and out of the country. Other countries have been more cautious, mainly for one of the following two reasons.

- The free inflow of foreign capital will make it easier for foreign companies to take over domestic companies. There is often a belief that certain key industries should be owned by residents of the country. Even in the UK, for example, there have been restrictions placed on the total foreign ownership of shares in companies such as British Aerospace and Rolls Royce.

- Less developed countries especially, but other more advanced economies too, are reluctant to allow the free flow of capital out of the country. After all, they need capital to come into the country to develop the domestic economy.

4.8 Regulation of the financial services industry

4.8.1 Overview

While it is widely accepted that the **market mechanism** enables prosperity, there are aspects of unbridled free markets that can lead to exploitation, abuse of information and dishonest dealing to the detriment of the overall welfare. There is a need, given that such **market failures** have the potential to occur, to have certain protections in place to ensure that markets are conducted in accordance with principles of fairness and consumers in general are dealt with fairly.

Consumer protection in the financial services industry and other consumer markets became an increasingly important aspect of UK Governments' policy from the 1970s onwards. The Financial Services Act 1986 (FSA 1986) was brought in to replace the system of **self-regulation** which had previously prevailed in the UK financial sector.

The FSA 1986 brought a new system of **'self-regulation within a statutory framework'**, with financial services firms authorised by Self-Regulatory Organisations (SROs).

When the Labour Party gained power in 1997, it wanted to make changes to the regulation of financial services. A series of **financial scandals**, including those involving the Maxwell Group, Barings Bank, BCCI and pensions mis-selling, had added weight to the political impetus for change, leading to the establishment of the Financial Services Authority as the single statutory regulator of the financial services industry, under the **Financial Services and Markets Act 2000 (FSMA 2000)**. This Act brought together the regulation of investment, insurance and banking. Giving financial advice on investments became a regulated activity under the new statutory regime from 1 December 2001.

Although it is not a government agency, the FSA carries out the work of statutory regulation. The **Chancellor of the Exchequer** is ultimately responsible for the system of regulation for the financial services industry.

4.8.2 Voluntary codes and statutory regulation

In some areas, financial services providers are subject to **voluntary codes**, which an industry sector develops itself, rather than rules imposed through the law (statutory rules).

Clearly, if the Government chooses and Parliament agrees, it can extend statutory regulation to areas previously governed by voluntary codes. For example, **mortgage advice and selling**, previously governed by the voluntary Mortgage Code, came under FSA regulation in October 2004. **General insurance** regulation followed in January 2005.

The area of banking can be taken as another example. The FSA regulates banks' status as authorised deposit-taking institutions and supervises the banks' liquidity position and capital adequacy. (This supervisory role used to be undertaken by the Bank of England.) Until 2009, banks and building societies followed a voluntary code (the **Banking Code**) in their relations with personal customers in the UK. On 1 November 2009, responsibility for the regulation of deposit and payment products transferred to the FSA. A Lending Standards Board (LSB) continues to monitor and enforce compliance with a new **Lending Code** that replaces those elements of the Banking Code and Business Banking Code relating to lending.

4.9 International regulatory issues

4.9.1 The creation of a single European market

Passporting for firms operating across borders (explained further later in this Section of the Chapter) is an important concept in the creation of the single market but is only one of various tools in trying to encourage cross-border activities. In recognition of the need for a co-ordinated approach to the creation of a single market in Europe, the EU convened the Lisbon Conference which led, in 1999, to the announcement of the aim of creating a single market in financial services, they had hoped, by 2005. This process is known as the **Financial Services Action Plan (FSAP)**.

The stated aims of the FSAP are to create a single wholesale market, an open and secure retail financial services market and state-of-the-art prudential rules and regulation. The longer-term aim was that Europe would be the world's most competitive economy by 2010.

In order to achieve this, a committee of 'wise men' was set up, chaired by Alexandre Lamfalussy who is a senior European academic and adviser. This committee was charged with identifying targets for completing the single market for the investment industry by making the implementation of Directives more efficient and effective.

The proposal of the wise men was to use a four-level approach.

- **Level 1:** Legislation, in the form of **Regulations and Directives** is proposed by the European Commission following consultation with the European Parliament and European Council. Legislation should be based on broad framework principles and the detailed technical implementing measures should be decided at Level 2.

- **Level 2:** The **European Securities Committee (ESC)** assists the European Commission in adopting technical implementing measures. The ESC is made up of policy makers from the member states. Representatives from HM Treasury sit on the ESC.

- **Level 3:** The **Committee of European Securities Regulators (CESR)**, which has the objective of improving the consistent implementation of Level 1 and Level 2 legislation across member states, aims to ensure best practices and a consistent regulatory approach is taken and to provide technical advice to the Level 2 process. The CESR is made up of regulators from the member states, including representatives from the UK's FSA.

- **Level 4:** The European Commission, member states and supervisory authorities work to ensure the implementation and enforcement of EU law.

The FSAP consists of 42 new legislative measures, including 27 Directives. Some of the more debated Directives are as follows.

- The **Market Abuse Directive** sought to harmonise rules on abusive practices.

- The **Takeover Directive** aimed to harmonise the rules relating to takeovers within the EU. The experiences gleaned from the Takeover Directive are a good example of political, cultural and economic divergence of views throughout the EU. Twelve versions of the Directive were tabled and rejected. In 2004 agreement was finally reached but in order to obtain agreement many important provisions (such as those relating to frustrating action) were made optional in order to reach a consensus. Thus the effectiveness of the Directive is questionable, as it does not truly harmonise EU takeover practices.

- The **Markets in Financial Instruments Directive (MiFID)**, sometimes known as **Investment Services Directive II (ISD II)**, has expanded the reach of cross-border investment activity, which was limited under the first Directive (see later). There were fierce debates about the ability of Multilateral Trading Facilities (MTFs) to passport due, in part, to some member states wishing to maintain the dominant position of their domestic markets.

- The **Distance Marketing Directive** extended the requirement to provide cancellation rights and certain documentation to retail customers dealt with at a distance. Under the FSA's original rules, cancellation rights were only generally provided where private customers purchased packaged products such as life policies. Under the new Directive, cancellation rights and documentation must be provided in a wider range of cases such as for securities broking services provided at a distance. This required UK firms to significantly alter their documentation and cancellation procedures. These rules came into force in late 2004.

While the aims of Lamfalussy are to be applauded, the practicalities of creating a complete single market remain questionable. Arguably a large number of barriers have stood in the way of full and meaningful integration, including the following.

- Lack of proper implementation of Directives by some member states

- Delay in implementation of Directives by some member states

- Lack of real censures for non-compliant member states

- Too great a focus on meeting the now out-of-date 2005 FSAP deadline rather than producing good legislation

- Lack of consumer desire to deal with foreign service providers

- Lack of integration of cross-border settlement and clearing services

- Lack of full coverage of the FSAP measures

- A protectionist attitude of some member states to their domestic markets: for example, in some member states, market-makers must still have a local presence

- Differences in law, language and culture throughout the EU

- Lack of a clear view as to what a single market might ultimately look like

However, there have been some positive achievements.

- All of the 42 FSAP measures have been adopted by the EU.

- The two committees (ESC and CESR) created by the Lamfalussy process have been largely a success. Indeed this committee structure has since been implemented in the sphere of banking and insurance regulation. In the sphere of banking regulation, the committees are called the European Banking Committee (EBC) and Committee of European Banking Regulators (CEBR) respectively.

4.9.2 The financial markets crisis

The **Financial Stability Forum (FSF)** is a body made up of authorities from various major countries and international institutions. In April 2008, the FSF reported on the recent turmoil in financial markets.

The FSF's report noted that the turmoil that broke out in the summer of 2007 followed an exceptional boom in **credit growth** and **leverage** in the financial system. A long period of **benign economic and financial conditions** had increased the amount of risk that borrowers and investors were willing to take on. Institutions responded, expanding the market for securitisation of credit risk and aggressively developing the **'originate and distribute' model**: institutions originating loans then distributed them as packaged securities. The system became increasingly dependent on originators' underwriting standards and the performance of credit rating agencies.

By the summer of 2008, accumulating losses on US **subprime mortgages** were triggering widespread disruption to the global financial system. Large losses were sustained on complex structured securities. Institutions reduced leverage and increased demand for liquid assets. Many credit markets became illiquid, hindering credit extension.

Eight months after the start of the market turmoil, many financial institutions' balance sheets were burdened by assets that have suffered major declines in value and vanishing market liquidity. Market participants were reluctant to transact in these instruments, adding to increased financial and macroeconomic uncertainty.

4.9.3 Steps to re-establish confidence

To re-establish confidence in the soundness of markets and financial institutions the FSF authorities began to take exceptional steps with a view to facilitating adjustment and **dampening the impact on the real economy**. These steps have included **monetary and fiscal stimulus, central bank liquidity operations**, policies to **promote asset market liquidity** and actions to **resolve problems at specific institutions**. Financial institutions have taken steps to rebuild capital and liquidity cushions.

Even with these measures in place, the financial system and world economies remained under great stress. While national authorities may continue to consider short-term policy responses should conditions warrant it, the FSF has proposed the following **further steps** to restore confidence in the soundness of markets and institutions:

- Strengthened prudential oversight of capital, liquidity and risk management
- Enhancing transparency and valuation of financial instruments
- Changes in the role and uses of credit ratings
- Strengthening the authorities' responsiveness to risks
- More robust arrangements for dealing with stress in the financial system

Some would argue that the financial turmoil of 2007-2009 has revealed various shortcomings in the **oversight of financial markets and institutions**. There are likely to be changes at national and international levels along the lines proposed by the FSF to seek to address these issues.

4.9.4 Regulatory consequences in Europe

The turmoil in markets heightened focus on the debate about how European regulatory initiatives are organised, through the **Lamfalussy** four-step process. Some believe that too much is entrusted to its 'Level Three' committees which bring together regulators from each country to agree on the details of implementing directives and to coordinate wider efforts, such as the supervision of cross-border institutions such as investment banks. The changes under the **Financial Services Action Plan (FSAP)** have meant that the three committees, for banking, insurance and securities regulators, have wielded substantial power in how rules are applied. It seems unlikely that there will be major changes to the process however, and the idea of a single pan-European regulator does not appear to have gained any more traction.

During 2009, there was discussion of changes the EU had agreed to the structure of regulatory and supervisory cooperation, including a new **European Systemic Risk Board** which has been proposed. The ESRB will have representation from central banks across Europe, including the Bank of England, and will monitor threats to financial stability, such as property price bubbles or debt bubbles. Lord Turner of the FSA has observed that the success of the proposals will depend on 'the ability of the proposed ESRB to develop good quality risk analysis, and the willingness of politicians to take its warning seriously and to countenance potentially unpopular responses.'

5 MARKETS IN FINANCIAL INSTRUMENTS DIRECTIVE

Learning objectives

1.2.2 Explain the purpose and scope of the Markets in Financial Instrument Directive (MiFID) with respect to:

- passporting
- roles of home and host state
- core and non-core investment services
- financial instruments covered by the legislation

5.1 Introduction

The **Markets in Financial Instruments Directive (MiFID)** was adopted by the European Council in April 2004 and is part of the European **Financial Services Action Plan**. MiFID was originally due for implementation in April 2006. However, due to the number of changes that MiFID requires the industry to make, the deadline was deferred twice, delaying its effective date until **1 November 2007**.

MiFID replaces the previous Investment Services Directive (ISD), and it applies to all **investment firms**, e.g. investment and retail banks, brokers, assets managers, securities and futures firms, securities issuers and hedge funds. For more detail on the criteria for establishing whether a firm is subject to MiFID, see 'Scope of MiFID', section 5.4 below.

EU Directives require the law in each country to be changed by Parliament in accordance with the directive.

5.2 Implementation of MiFID

The MiFID **Level 1** Directive sets out a number of specific conduct of business 'principles' and a requirement that the European Commission impose more specific 'Level 2' requirements which flesh out the principles.

The MiFID **Level 2** Directive – similar to secondary legislation in the UK – was formally adopted in September 2006 and covers technical implementation measures in the form of **organisational requirements** and **operating conditions**. In addition, the European Commission aims to adopt 'Regulations' which deal with 'market' issues, e.g. transaction reporting and transparency, which will be directly applicable to the UK.

The provisions of the Level 1 and Level 2 Directives are being implemented in the UK through changes to UK law and FSA rules.

New regulation has been required on the basis of **'maximum harmonisation'**, which means that member states should not be able to add rules of their own or make amendments to the original text, a process called **'gold plating'**. The FSA has been accused of 'gold plating' in the past whilst implementing other European Directives.

The European Commission and the Committee of European Securities Regulators (CESR) has been focusing more recently on the delivery of convergent implementation of the MiFID requirements across Member States – this is **Level 3**.

5.3 Passporting within the EEA

The idea of a **'passport'**, which already existed under the ISD, enables firms to use their domestic authorisation to operate not only in their **home state**, but also in other **host states** within the **European Economic Area** (EEA) (EU plus Norway, Iceland and Liechtenstein).

An important aspect of MiFID is that, to make cross-border business easier, the home country principle has been extended. Under MiFID, investment firms which carry out specified investment services and activities (a wider range than under the ISD, as detailed below) are authorised by the member State in which they their registered office is located (the **home state**).

Where a **branch** is set up, **host state** rules will continue to apply. A **tied agent** established in the EEA will be able to act on behalf of a firm instead of the firm needing to set up a branch. (A **'tied agent'**, similarly to an **appointed representative** under FSMA 2000, acts on behalf of and under the authority of an investment firm and as a result does not require authorisation.)

Firms which have an **ISD** 'passport' should automatically be given a MiFID passport.

5.4 Scope of MiFID

MiFID applies to a specified range of 'core' **investment services and activities** in relation to specified categories of **financial instruments**, as summarised below.

- **Investment firms** are firms which provide such services or engage in such activities.

- Investment firms are also regulated in respect of various 'non-core' **ancillary services** they may provide (as also listed below).

- **Credit institutions** (which includes banks and building societies, in the UK) are regulated by the Banking Consolidation Directive. However, most MiFID provisions apply to these institutions when they engage in activities within MiFID's scope.

Investment services and activities

- Receiving and transmitting orders
- Execution of orders on behalf of clients
- Dealing on own account
- Managing portfolios on a discretionary basis
- Investment advice
- Underwriting of financial instruments
- Placing of financial instruments
- Operating a Multilateral Trading Facility (MTF)

Financial instruments covered by MiFID

- Transferable securities, e.g. shares and bonds

- Money market instruments

- Units in collective investment undertakings

- Derivatives relating to securities, currencies, interest rates and yields, financial indices and financial measures settled either physically or in cash, including: options, futures, swaps and forward rate agreements

- Commodity derivatives capable of being settled in cash, commodity derivatives capable of being physically settled on a regulated market or multilateral trading facility, and certain other commodity derivatives which are not for commercial purposes

- Derivative instruments for transferring credit risk

- Financial contracts for differences (CFDs)

- Derivatives relating to climatic variables, freight rates, emission allowances, inflation rates or other official economic statistics capable of being settled in cash

Ancillary services

- Safekeeping and administration of financial instruments, including: custodianship; collateral and cash management

- Granting credit or loans to an investor to enable him to carry out a transaction in which the firm is involved

- Advising undertakings on capital structure, industrial strategy

- Advising on mergers and acquisitions

- Foreign exchange services connected with providing investment services

- Investment research, financial analysis or other general recommendations relating to transactions in financial instruments

The broad range of UK firms falling under the rules as MiFID firms comprises: dealing and managing firms, MTFs, corporate finance firms, venture capital firms, commodity firms, oil and energy market participants, credit institutions carrying on MiFID business, exchanges, UCITS investment firms, and certain advisers and professional firms.

5.5 MiFID exclusions

Although MiFID has extended regulation beyond what was regulated under the ISD, there are a number of exclusions. These exclusions mean that a significant part of the **retail financial services sector** falls outside the scope of MiFID, as explained below.

MiFID's overall scope is narrower than the UK regulatory regime. However, a UK exclusion (in the Regulated Activities Order) will not apply if it conflicts with MiFID.

Note that MiFID applies to **EEA-domiciled firms** only. (However, the FSA rules extend MiFID requirements to 'MiFID equivalent activities of third country firms').

The following are **excluded** from the scope of MiFID.

- **Insurance companies** including reinsurers

- **Pension funds** and **collective investment schemes**, and their depositories or managers, although UCITS managers who provide advice or discretionary management to clients who are not funds will generally be subject to MiFID requirements

- **Group treasury activities**

- **Persons administering their own assets**

- **Professional investors** investing only for themselves

- **Commodity producers and traders**

- Investment services relating to administration of **employee share schemes**

- **Incidental business in the course of professional activity** bound by legal, ethical or regulatory provisions

- **Firms not providing investment services** or involved in investment activities

MiFID **Article 3** allows Member States **to exclude** from MiFID the activities of the firms whose investment services are limited to receiving and transmitting orders in transferable securities or collective investment schemes, plus related advice. Such firms may not hold client money or securities, nor put themselves in debt to the client. Orders must be transmitted only to investment firms, credit institutions, EEA-regulated collective investment schemes or closed-ended funds traded on a regulated market in the EEA. Many firms of **financial advisers** and other **retail investment product distributors** will meet these criteria, and the UK has enabled them to be excluded from MiFID regulation. Such firms may alternatively opt in, in order to benefit from **passporting**.

5.6 The 'common platform'

The organisational and systems and controls requirements of **MiFID** and the **Capital Requirements Directive (CRD)** are being implemented through a single set of high level rules: this is known as the 'common platform', since it applies to firms commonly, whichever of the Directives they are subject to.

- Firms subject to both **MiFID and CRD** include most banks and investment firms.

- Firms subject to **MiFID only** are those authorised to provide investment advice and/or receive and transmit orders without having permission to hold client money or securities.

- Firms subject to **CRD only** include banks that do not perform any investment services or other activities within the scope of MiFID.

The implementation of MiFID has led to the introduction of a new **Conduct of Business Sourcebook (COBS),** whose rules are shorter than the previous COB Sourcebook. Various other changes to the *FSA Handbook* have also been necessary.

5.7 Multilateral Trading Facilities and Systematic Internalisers

MiFID introduces the ability to passport **Multilateral Trading Facilities (MTFs)** as a 'core' investment service. MTFs are systems where firms provide services similar to those of exchanges by matching client orders. A firm taking proprietary positions with a client is not running an MTF. There has been debate about the requirements to be imposed on MTFs. The Committee of European Securities Regulators (CESR) has published standards they expect to be met by MTFs, including notifying the home state regulator of activities, fair and orderly trading, price transparency, clarity of systems and reduction of financial crime.

A **Systematic Internaliser** is an investment firm which deals on its own account by executing client orders outside a regulated market or a MTF. MiFID will require such firms to publish firm quotes in liquid shares (for orders below 'standard market size') and to maintain those quotes on a regular and continuous basis during normal business hours.

6 UCITS DIRECTIVES

Learning objective   **1.2.3 Explain** the purpose and scope of the UCITS Directive.

6.1 EU provisions on collective investment schemes

The EU has enacted a number of directives relevant to collective investment schemes (CISs). These are known as the **UCITS Directives**. **UCITS** stands for **Undertakings for Collective Investment in Transferable Securities**.

The aim of UCITS was to create a type of passport throughout the EEA for collective investment schemes that meet the UCITS criteria. The idea was to promote the free movement of services in the same way as investment firms can passport their services throughout the EEA.

The CIS must be authorised in its home State and receive confirmation from its home State regulator that the CIS complies with UCITS criteria. That confirmation is then provided to the host State regulator, who the fund manager notifies that they wish to market the fund in that EEA state. Although UCITS aims to make cross-border sales of CIS easier, the CIS must comply with the marketing rules of the host state and the documentation requirements of the directive.

The first **UCITS Directive** contained a number of limitations. The main limitation was that the definition of **permitted investments** was very narrow. This meant that generally schemes wanting to use UCITS to sell cross-border could only invest in transferable securities. Initially the permitted investments included securities funds (containing for example shares and bonds), warrant funds and umbrella funds, where each sub-fund is either a securities fund or a warrant fund. In addition, the first UCITS Directive contained various categories of scheme, e.g. a securities fund and an umbrella fund, with separate investment rules for each category.

UCITS was updated in 2002 by the **UCITS III Product Directive,** which expanded the range of assets which UCITS funds are able to invest in. It also made provision for a single UCITS scheme to replace all of the previous categories of fund which had separate rules.

6.2 UCITS schemes

As a result of the **UCITS Product Directive**, UCITS schemes are now able to invest in the following types of **permitted investment**.

- Transferable securities (see below)
- Money market instruments

- Forward contracts and financial derivatives
- Deposits
- Units in other Collective Investment Schemes

Transferable securities comprise shares, instruments creating or acknowledging indebtedness (e.g. debentures, loan stock, bonds, government and public securities) and certificates representing certain securities.

Although **commodity derivatives** are excluded, it would appear that derivatives based on commodity indices could be eligible as financial derivatives.

6.3 UCITS and non-UCITS schemes

Under FSA Handbook (COLL) rules, both UCITS and non-UCITS retail schemes can invest in a variety of types of instrument, including warrants and financial derivatives, within their overall investment objectives, provided that they apply a risk management procedure. A non-UCITS retail scheme can invest in an even wider range of assets, including gold or 100% investment in immovable property.

Non-UCITS schemes may also **borrow** up to 25% of the fund value on a **permanent** basis, while UCITS retail schemes are only permitted to borrow on a **temporary** basis, up to 10% of the fund value.

CHAPTER ROUNDUP

- Financial intermediaries such as banks and building societies take deposits from savers and re-lend to borrowers. Financial intermediation brings benefits from aggregation and maturity transformation.

- Financial services products can help people manage risk, for example by pooling risks (insurance) and by offering access to diversified portfolios of assets at relatively low cost.

- Capital markets, such as the Stock Exchange, are markets for long-term capital. Money markets are shorter term debt markets in which banks and other financial institutions deal mainly with each other, on a wholesale basis.

- The UK financial services industry employs over 1 million people in the UK and accounts for around 5% of national output. Key areas are banking, life insurance, general insurance, pensions, fund and asset management, currency markets and securities markets. London has various advantages which have enabled it to maintain its position as a leading global financial centre.

- The Government plays a role in economic and industrial policy, regulation, taxation and social welfare. Regulatory interventions seek to avoid or provide remedies for cases of market failure, thus protecting consumers and providing free and fair markets. Economic policy encompasses monetary policy (particularly through interest rates), fiscal policy (public spending and taxation) and exchange rate policy (occasional intervention ion currency markets).

- European Union legislation has an increasing importance, and takes precedence over UK law.

- The Markets in Financial Instruments Directive (MiFID) was implemented into the UK on 1 November 2007. The aim is to open up European markets by making it easier for firms to passport their activities across the European Economic Area (EEA).

- MiFID applies to a range of 'core' investment services and activities.

- The UCITS Directives allow for investment funds to passport across the EEA.

TEST YOUR KNOWLEDGE

1. Outline the benefits of financial intermediation.

2. What is meant by securitisation of debt?

3. What is a 'bancassurer'?

4. Explain the status of an EU Directive in relation to national law.

5. Explain what is meant by quantitative easing, and what is its intended effect.

6. List two MiFID exclusions.

7. Define a multilateral trading facility.

8. What does UCITS stand for?

TEST YOUR KNOWLEDGE: ANSWERS

1. **Benefits of financial intermediation**

   - Intermediaries provide ways in which a lender can deposit money to spend in the future, together with a ready source of funds for borrowers.

   - Financial intermediaries aggregate or 'package' the amounts lent by savers and lend on to borrowers in different amounts.

   - Financial intermediaries provide for maturity transformation: intermediation bridges the gap between the wish of many lenders for liquidity and the desire of many borrowers for loans over longer periods.

   - Risk is reduced by pooling. Since financial intermediaries lend to a large number of individuals and organisations, losses suffered through default by borrowers or capital losses are pooled.

   (See Section 1.4)

2. Securitisation of debt means creating tradable securities which are backed by less liquid assets such as mortgages and other long-term loans.

   (See Section 2.8)

3. The Association of British Insurers (ABI) defines bancassurers as 'insurance companies that are subsidiaries of banks and building societies and whose primary market is the customer base of the bank or building society'.

   (See Section 3.3)

4. EU Directives are issued to the governments of the EU member states requiring them within a specified period (usually two years) to alter the national laws of the state so that they conform to the directive. Until a Directive is given effect by a UK statute it does not usually affect legal rights and obligations of individuals.

   (See Section 4.2.3)

5. Quantitative easing is a method by which the central bank manipulates liquidity in the financial system. This allows adjustments to the money supply when the interbank interest rate is at or close to zero, and interest rates can therefore no longer be lowered. Ity involves the central bank purchasing mostly short-term financial assets using money it has created *ex nihilo* and has shown as a credit in the central bank's books. The new money is intended to increase the overall money supply through deposit multiplication, as the institutions receiving the money will be encouraged to lend and the cost of borrowing will be reduced.

   (See Section 4.3.3)

6. Any two from: credit institutions; insurance companies; collective Investment schemes; non-EEA domiciled firms.

   (See Section 5.5)

7. This is a system which may be operated by an investment firm that enables parties, who might typically be retail investors or other investment firms, to buy and sell financial instruments.

   (See Section 5.7)

8. Undertakings for Collective Investment in Transferable Securities.

   (See Section 6.1)

2

Financial Markets

INTRODUCTION

The London Stock Exchange operates a market place for trading bonds and other securities in the UK and has trading platforms including SETS and SETSqx.

The FSA operates as the UK Listing Authority (UKLA) to regulate company listings on the Exchange.

The creation of Multilateral Trading Facilities (MTFs) is a challenge to the mainstream exchanges, with MTFs taking a significant market share of transactions.

Diverse instruments are traded on the financial markets. The various types of derivative instruments, which are derivative in the sense that they are based on an underlying asset or price, include tailor-made 'over-the counter' (OTC) instruments as well as exchange traded instruments.

CHAPTER CONTENTS

CHAPTER LEARNING OBJECTIVES

2 **Financial markets**

Demonstrate an understanding of UK and international financial markets

2.1 **UK equity and fixed interest markets**

    2.1.1 **Identify** the main dealing systems and facilities offered in the UK equities market

    2.1.2 **Identify** the nature of the stocks that would be traded on each of the above systems and facilities

    2.1.3 **Explain** the structure and operation of the primary and secondary UK markets for gilts and corporate bonds

    2.1.4 **Explain** the motivations for and implications of dual listing of a company

2.2 **Types of market**

    2.2.1 **Compare** and **contrast** exchange trading and over-the counter (OTC) markets

    2.2.2 **Distinguish** between the following alternative trading venues:

        –   Multilateral Trading Facilities
        –   Systematic Internalisers
        –   Dark pools

    2.2.3 **Distinguish** between a quote-driven and order-driven market

    2.2.4 **Explain** the roles of the various participants in the UK equity market

2.3 **Settlement procedures in the UK**

    2.3.1 **Explain** the clearing and settlement procedures for UK exchange traded securities

2.4 **Regulation of UK investment exchanges**

    2.4.1 **Explain** the role of an investment exchange

    2.4.2 **Explain** the need for investment exchanges to be authorised

    2.4.3 **Explain** the relevance of investment exchanges being recognised by the FSA

    2.4.4 **Identify** the recognised investment exchanges and clearing houses in the UK

    2.4.5 **Identify** and distinguish the roles of:

        –   The London Stock Exchange (LSE)
        –   NYSE Liffe
        –   LCH.Clearnet

2.5 **The UK Listing Authority and prospectus requirements**

    2.5.1 **Explain** the role of the FSA as the UK listing authority

    2.5.2 **Identify** the source of the listing rules as FSMA 2000 and relevant EU directives

    2.5.3 **Explain** the main conditions for listing on the Official List, AIM and PLUS markets

2.5.4 Explain the purpose of the requirement for prospectus or listing particulars

2.4.5 Identify the main exemptions from listing particulars

2.6 Information disclosure and corporate governance requirements for UK equity markets

2.6.1 Explain the disclosures required under the FSA's disclosure and transparency rules relating to:

– Directors' interests
– Major shareholdings

2.6.2 Explain the purpose of corporate governance regulation

2.6.3 Explain, in outline, the scope and content of corporate governance regulation in the UK (the Combined Code)

2.6.4 Explain the LSE requirements for listed companies to disclose corporate governance compliance

2.6.5 Explain the continuing obligations of LSE listed companies regarding information disclosure and dissemination

2.6.6 Explain, in outline, the UK company law requirements regarding the calling of general meetings

2.6.7 Distinguish between extraordinary and annual general meetings

2.6.8 Distinguish between the types of resolution that can be considered at company general meetings

2.6.9 Distinguish between the voting methods used at company meetings

2.6.10 Explain the role and powers of a proxy

2.7 Regulation of derivatives markets

2.7.1 Identify the main features of the regulation of derivatives

2.7.2 Identify the main features of clearing and settlement on derivatives exchange and for over-the-counter derivatives trading

2.7.3 Explain the arrangements for market transparency and transaction reporting in the main derivative markets

2.7.4 Explain the impact of MiFID and International Accounting Standards on the regulation of derivative markets

2.8 International markets

2.8.1 Explain the mechanics of dealing in equities and fixed interest securities in each of the following specific countries:

– US
– Japan
– France
– Germany

2.8.2 Identify the participants in each of the above markets

2.8.3 Explain the structure and operation of the primary and secondary markets for Eurobonds

2.8.4 Explain the general principles of dealing in other markets, including energy markets, and settlement issues in those markets

2.9 International settlement and clearing

2.9.1 Explain the settlement and clearing procedures overseas including the role of international central securities depositories, an appreciation of different settlement cycles and issues in managing global assets

1 UK EQUITY AND FIXED INTEREST MARKETS

Learning objectives

2.1.1 Identify the main dealing systems and facilities offered in the UK equities market.

2.1.2 Identify the nature of the stocks that would be traded on each of the above systems and facilities.

2.2.3 Distinguish between a quote-driven and order-driven market.

2.2.4 Explain the roles of the various participants in the UK equity market.

2.1.4 Explain the motivations for and implications of dual listing of a company.

1.1 The role of the LSE

The **London Stock Exchange plc** is, above all else, a business. Its primary objective is to establish and run a market place in securities. In any economy there are savers and borrowers. The exchange acts as a place in which they can meet.

- Initially, the companies (the borrowers) issue shares to the investing public (the savers). This is known as the **primary market**.

- Investors would not be willing to invest their money unless they could see some way of releasing it in the future. Consequently, the exchange must also offer a **secondary market** trading in second-hand shares, this allows the investor to convert the shares into cash.

Overview of the Exchange's Activities

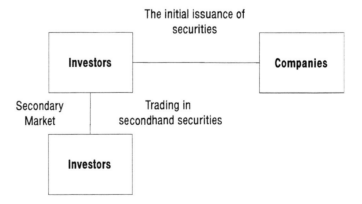

Primary Market

The initial issuance of securities

Investors ——————— **Companies**

Secondary Market

Trading in secondhand securities

Investors

1.1.1 The development of the UK stock market

On 27 October 1986 (**Big Bang** day), the UK stock markets went through a major transformation. Before this date, the market had been a physical market place. Customers appointed a broker to act as their agent to enter the market and buy or sell stock on their behalf. The principal to the trade, who operated from pitches on the floor of the exchange, was known as the jobber.

With Big Bang, the physical market place was abolished and replaced by screen systems which tried to recreate the atmosphere of an open outcry market. Dealing now takes place using these screen systems and telephones. In addition, all Stock Exchange members are now broker-dealers with **dual capacity**. This means that they can act as agents on behalf of customers or as principals dealing directly with the customers.

1.1.2 Trading methods of The London Stock Exchange

The LSE has taken the view that one single market structure for trading shares is inappropriate, given that the diversity and liquidity of shares on offer is so wide. Consequently different types of shares, with varying levels of liquidity, trade via a variety of market systems that are described in more detail below. (**AIM** is the LSE's junior market, the Alternative Investment Market.)

System	SETS	SETSqx	SEAQ
Nature	Order driven	Combined order and quote driven	Quote driven
Market makers?	**No** market makers	**At least one** market maker per stock	**At least two** market makers per stock
Full list stocks traded	All stocks classified as 'liquid' under MiFID, ie all FTSE All Share Index stocks, Exchange Traded Funds, Exchange Traded Commodities and the most actively traded Irish stocks	All stocks classified as 'illiquid' under MiFID, i.e. illiquid equities	None
AIM stocks traded	Most traded AIM stocks	All AIM stocks in AIM EURO sectors not traded on SETS	All remaining AIM stocks

Before the implementation of MiFID, less liquid shares were traded on SETSmm or SEAQ (the LSE historical quote driven system). In October 2007, SETSmm was absorbed into SETS and all SEAQ shares moved to SETSqx in preparation for MiFID. SEAQ is now only used for trading fixed interest products and highly illiquid AIM stocks.

1.1.3 Order-driven v quote-driven markets

Before we look at the detailed mechanics of each of the trading platforms, it is worth considering the fundamental differences between an **order-driven** and a **quote-driven** market.

- Where a market is **order-driven**, the relevant trading system will match buyers and sellers automatically, provided that they are willing to trade at prices compatible with each other. This is essentially the function which SETS performs. Prices of securities which trade on SETS are, therefore, purely driven by the buyers and sellers in the market themselves.

- A **quote-driven** market, such as SEAQ, requires certain market participants (market makers) to take responsibility for acting as buyers and sellers to the rest of the market so that there will always be a price at which a trade can be conducted. For such a market to operate efficiently, up-to-date prices at which market makers are willing to trade need to be made available to other market participants.

This is the function performed by SEAQ. Unlike SETS, SEAQ does not provide a mechanism for trades to be executed automatically: transactions are, therefore, normally conducted over the telephone.

SETSqx (discussed later in this Section) combines the market making quote-driven model and the order-driven model.

1.1.4 The Stock Exchange Electronic Trading Service (SETS)

The SETS system (known as the Order Book, as it is an order-driven system) is used for the most liquid domestic equities. Since these stocks are highly liquid, an **order matching** system (allowing buyers and sellers to deal with one another directly rather than going through dealers (market-makers) who would charge a spread) provides a cheap market structure for these shares.

The London Clearing House (known as LCH.Clearnet) acts as the central counterparty to all SETS trades. All automatically executed trades **novate** to LCH.Clearnet such that the buyer buys from LCH.Clearnet and the seller sells to LCH.Clearnet.

1.1.5 The order book

The SETS screen displays limit orders (orders to buy or sell shares with a maximum or minimum price stated). The limit orders are **automatically matched** by the electronic order book. If an order is not matched entirely, the **unmatched portion will remain on the order book**. Orders are prioritised in a strict sequence, with **price** first, then the **time of input** with the earlier orders first.

Below is an example order book for a SETS security.

Buy			Sell		
Time	Volume	Price	Price	Volume	Time
09:03	12,000	174	175	1,100	09:15
10:08	5,000	174	176	1,400	09:12
09:31	11,000	173	176	12,530	09:45
09:32	4,500	173	176	2,721	09:52
09:20	8,350	172	177	12,000	10:00
09:24	12,050	172	177	4,290	10:02
09:40	4,933	172			

In order to trade shares, market participants can then either:

- Match automatically with an order currently displayed on the screen, or
- Place their own order onto the screen and hope someone will match their order at a later time.

1.1.6 SETSqx

SETSqx ('Stock Exchange Electronic Trading Service-quotes and crosses') replaced the Stock Exchange Alternative Trading Service plus (SEATS plus) in June 2007 and in October 2007 it replaced SEAQ for all main market securities.

The SETSqx system combines committed principal quotes with periodic auctions where anonymous limit orders are placed. Market makers and non market makers can participate in auctions, these auctions take place at 08:00, 11:00, 15:00 and 16:35.

The market makers will provide a ready counterparty to market participants wishing to trade SETSqx shares (and bonds) in return for being able to make profits from a spread between buying and selling prices.

In order to act as a market maker, the relevant firm undertakes **an obligation** to **quote firm, two-way** prices in shares for which they register. Market makers must therefore quote **both buying and selling** prices (two-way prices) at which they **must deal** (firm prices) up to a predetermined transaction size dependent upon historic volumes. This is referred to as the **Exchange Market Size (EMS)**.

Each share is assigned an **Exchange Market Size (EMS)**, which is important as this gives the **Minimum Quote Size (MQS)**. This is the minimum amount of shares a market maker must be prepared to buy, or sell, at their quoted price. Market maker obligations – Mandatory Quotation Period from 08:00 until the end of closing auction Obligation to quote up to 1 × EMS.

1.1.7 The Stock Exchange Automated Quotations System (SEAQ)

SEAQ (known as a **quote display system**) is the secondary system used for fixed income securities and less frequently traded AIM stocks.

The SEAQ system is used to disseminate market maker quotes to all market makers simultaneously. Since at least two market makers are required for a share to trade on SEAQ, the system is referred to as a competing market maker system. Some AIM shares are traded on SEAQ, although the majority are traded on SETSqx.

1.2 Dual listing of a company

A company may list its shares on more than one exchange – for example, in both New York and London.

Consequences of dual listing

- The company will have access to a wider pool of investors

- Increased liquidity may reduce bid/offer spreads, lowering transaction costs for investors

- The company will face higher costs in maintaining each listing

- The company will generally suffer a greater compliance burden, e.g. the relatively onerous Sarbanes-Oxley Act provisions if there is a listing in the USA

1.3 Fixed interest markets

ng objective 2.1.3 **Explain** the structure and operation of the primary and secondary UK markets for gilts and corporate bonds.

1.3.1 Fixed interest securities

Fixed interest stocks, or 'bonds' are negotiable debt instruments issued by a borrower for a fixed period of time paying interest, known as the **coupon**. The coupon is fixed at the issue date and is paid regularly to the holder of the bond until it is redeemed at maturity when the principal amount is repaid.

Fixed interest covers **Government bonds** (called gilt-edged stocks, or **'gilts'**, in the case of UK Government issues) and debt instruments issued in the private sector – **corporate bonds**.

1.3.2 The Debt Management Office

A prime responsibility of the **Debt Management Office (DMO)** of the Treasury is to ensure that the government is able to borrow the money it requires to fund the **Public Sector Net Cash Requirement (PSNCR)**. The most important source of financing open to the government is the gilts market.

The DMO controls the issue of gilts into the market place and uses a variety of methods depending upon the circumstances it faces at any time.

1.3.3 Types of gilt issue

Issues by the DMO may be of an entirely new gilt with a coupon/maturity dissimilar to existing issues. Currently, the DMO believes that the range of issues in the market is, if anything, too large and may lead to excessive fragmentation of supply and demand.

In order to avoid the problem above, the DMO may issue a **tranche** of an existing stock. This entails issuing a given amount of nominal value on exactly similar terms to an existing gilt. The DMO refers to this as 'opening up an existing gilt'. The advantages of tranches are that they avoid adding further complexity to the gilt market and increase the liquidity of current issues. When a tranche is issued, it may be identified by the letter 'A' in order to indicate that when the tranche is issued a full coupon may not be paid on the next payment date, to reflect the fact that the gilt has only been in issue for part of the coupon period.

A small tranche may be referred to as a **tranchette**.

1.4 The secondary gilts market

1.4.1 Overview

As with the equities market, gilts used to be traded on the floor of the Stock Exchange. However, in 1986 they moved to a telephone-driven market supported by market makers.

The DMO is the lead regulator in the gilts market. Its objective is to ensure that the gilts market remains solvent, liquid and, above all, fair. The reason for this commitment is that the DMO is obliged to issue, on the government's behalf, gilts to fund the Public Sector Net Cash Requirement (PSNCR). In order to do this, the DMO must have access to the markets. It is the DMO that allows participants to enter the gilts market and, thereafter, it is the DMO that monitors their capital adequacy on a daily basis.

1.4.2 Gilt-Edged Market Makers (GEMMs)

The **Gilt-Edged Market Makers (GEMMs)** are the focus of the market place. Their role is to **ensure that two-way quotes exist at all times** for all gilts. Market makers are allowed to enter the market by the DMO. Once accepted as a gilt-edged market maker, the firm is obliged to make a market in **all conventional gilts**. For index-linked stocks, because the market is less liquid the DMO has authorised a more limited list of market makers. GEMMs make use of the LSE's SEAQ (Stock Exchange Automated Quotation system).

1.4.3 Inter-Dealer Brokers

The **Inter-Dealer Brokers (IDBs)** act as an escape valve for GEMMs. If a GEMM was to build up a large position in a particular stock and then decide to unwind it, it might be difficult to achieve without revealing to the rest of the market that he was long or short of a stock. This is obviously a dangerous position and would discourage Gilt-Edged Market Makers from taking substantial positions. The Inter-Dealer Brokers provide an anonymous dealing service, allowing GEMMs to unwind positions. IDBs are only accessible to market makers in the gilts market.

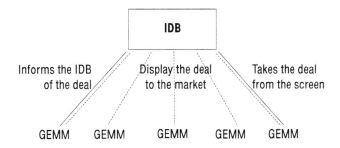

Equity market makers also have access to Inter– Dealer Brokers. The ability to unwind positions anonymously through the IDBs is also viewed as an important mechanism for ensuring equity market liquidity.

1.4.4 Stock Borrowing and Lending Intermediaries (SBLIs)

If market makers wish to take a short position in a stock, i.e. sell more than they currently have on their books, they will need to have stock in order to settle the trade. The **Stock Borrowing and Lending Intermediaries (SBLIs) provide access to large pools of unused stock**. The institutional investors in the UK buy large blocks of securities and often hold these blocks for a number of years. The SBLIs borrow stock on behalf of market makers from these dormant positions. The stock is passed to the market maker who uses it to settle the trade, and in effect, to go short.

Eventually, the market maker will be obliged to buy stock to cover the short position, and this stock will then be passed back to the institutional investor. The SBLI charges commission on the trade of around 0.5%. This commission is split between the intermediaries and the institution. This is a facility available to all market participants and provides them with vital access to stock positions enabling them to go short.

The SBLIs also act as a focus for surplus cash, enabling those who are long of funds to deposit money, and market makers who need to borrow money to obtain finance.

1.4.5 Broker-dealers

All member firms of the LSE are **broker-dealers**. Broker-dealers have dual capacity, giving them the choice to either act as agents (broker) on behalf of customers, or to deal for themselves as principal (dealer), dealing directly with customers. Acting as principle involves buying and selling on the firms account.

1.5 Exchange trading and OTC markets

An **exchange-traded instrument** is one that is packaged in a standardised way, in respect of the contract size and dates for example, facilitating the creation of a liquid market in the instrument, on an exchange.

An 'over the counter' or **OTC** instruments one that has been specially negotiated with a financial institution, generally to fit the needs of a particular client or group of clients

1.6 MTFs and 'dark pools'

g objective **2.2.2** **Distinguish** between the following alternative trading venues:

- Multilateral Trading Facilities
- Systematic Internalisers
- Dark pools

The **Markets in Financial Instruments Directive (MiFID)** has encouraged the development of many new trading and reporting systems.

Multilateral Trading Facilities (MTFs) are systems bringing together multiple parties to buy and sell financial instruments, which are encouraged by the more liberalised rules under MiFID.

MTFs may be crossing networks or matching engines that are operated by an investment firm or a market operator. Instruments traded on a MTF may include shares, bonds and derivatives. MiFID requires operators of MTFs to ensure their markets operate on a fair and orderly basis. It aims to ensure this by placing requirements on MTF operators regarding how they organise their markets and the information they give to users. Additionally, MiFID provides for the operators of MTFs to **passport their services** across borders.

Examples of MTFs include **Turquoise**, **Chi-X**, **PEX** (Portugal) and **Nordic MTF**. **BATS Europe**, operated by the US platform BATS Trading, and **Nasdaq OMX Europe**, an equities platform of the US-based NASDAQ OMX, were both launched in 2008. The European unit of Liffe partnered with HSBC and BNP Paribas to launch **Smartpool**, for large order execution of European stocks. **SIX Swiss Exchange** (formerly SWX Europe) has been in partnership with Nyfix Millennium of the US to create **Swiss Block**, for Swiss blue chip stocks. Nyfix also operates **Euro Millennium™**. **Equiduct** is another MTF.

This new generation of platforms offers the prospect of firms making use of internal crossing networks – more often now called **dark liquidity pools** or '**non-displayed liquidity venues**', whereby firms can buy and sell blocks of shares off-exchange, away from the public domain. This offers trading anonymity, without prices being displayed on the public order book usually found on exchanges. There are more than 40 dark pools operating in the US, the largest being Goldman Sachs' Sigma X and Credit Suisse's CrossFinder. By mid-2008, dark pools were estimated to account for 12% of US daily stock trading volume. In the past, **stock exchanges** have viewed off-exchange trading as their main source of competition. The moves by **Liffe** and **SIX Swiss Exchange** to form links with dark pools can be seen as a case of 'If you can't beat 'em, join 'em'.

Some exchanges have adapted their technology to handle the need for large orders to be hidden from the market: LSE and Liffe both offer an **iceberg facility** through which only a small part of a large order is displayed at one time. Meanwhile, sell-side brokers have been developing algorithms to help them to detect if an order is being traded away from the market.

More **regulatory attention** could be paid to the growing use of dark pools in the future, in case of any systemic risk that they might present.

1.7 Systematic Internalisers

A **Systematic Internaliser (SI)** is an investment firm which deals on its own account by executing client orders outside a regulated market or a MTF. MiFID requires such firms to publish firm quotes in liquid shares (for orders below 'standard market size') and to maintain those quotes on a regular and continuous basis during normal business hours.

2 SETTLEMENT PROCEDURES

Learning objective   2.3.1 **Explain** the clearing and settlement procedures for UK exchange traded securities.

2.1 Introduction

The usual settlement period is three business days after the day of the bargain (referred to as T + 3).

Rolling Settlement

˙Trade date   Settlement date

Three business days settlement period

Settlement of UK equities, corporate bonds, gilts and money market instruments occurs through Euroclear UK & Ireland (formerly known as CREST), which operates an **electronic dematerialised settlement system**.

Settlement in sterling or euros is made on a **Delivery versus Payment (DVP)** basis, where both parties are ready to settle with each other at the same time, known as real time gross settlement.

2.2 Advanced and delayed settlement

It is possible to negotiate special settlement periods. The ability to have special settlement periods, up to **260 business days** after the day of the trade, gives flexibility to investors.

2.3 Cum and ex status

Shares normally trade on the basis of **cum (with) dividend**. This means that any purchaser of the shares is entitled to expect to receive the next dividend. As a share approaches its dividend payment date, a company sets a **books closed date** (also known as the 'record date' or the 'on register date'). The company pays the next dividend to all shareholders who are on the register of shareholders, on the books closed date. The books closed date will be some time before the dividend payment date to make administration easy for the company.

If a shareholder buys a share cum dividend and fails to have his name entered on the register of shareholders by the books closed date, the company will send the dividend cheque to the previous shareholder. The new shareholder does not lose the dividend, since they are legally entitled to it, but the mechanics of arranging for the old shareholder to remit the dividend to the new shareholder are cumbersome and time consuming.

In order to avoid this problem, the Stock Exchange has developed a system whereby shares will commence trading ex-dividend on the Stock Exchange **two business days prior to the books closed date**. A purchaser of the share ex-dividend is not entitled to receive the next dividend as it belongs to the seller of the share. It is possible, by agreement, to carry out a transaction ex-dividend before the official ex-dividend date. This is only permitted by the Exchange for ten business days before the normal ex-div date.

The idea is that shareholders who buy the shares cum dividend will be able to get on the register of shareholders in time to receive the dividend. Those who buy the shares ex-dividend will not be entered on the register by the books closed date. This means that the appropriate person always receives the dividend from the company.

Marking a Share Ex-Dividend

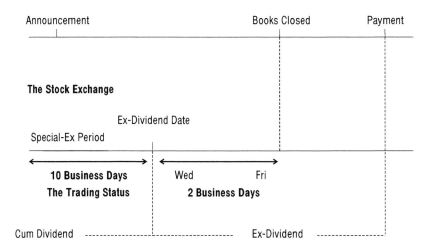

The ex-dividend date will usually be a Wednesday, and books closed date will, therefore, usually be a Friday.

3 UK REGULATION OF INVESTMENT EXCHANGES

3.1 Recognised Investment Exchanges (RIEs)

Learning objectives

2.4.1 Explain the role of an investment exchange.

2.4.2 Explain the need for investment exchanges to be authorised.

2.4.3 Explain the relevance of investment exchanges being recognised by the FSA.

2.4.4 Identify the recognised investment exchanges and clearing houses in the UK.

2.4.5 Identify and distinguish the roles of the London Stock Exchange (LSE), NYSE Liffe, LCH.Clearnet.

The act of running an investment exchange is, in itself, a regulated activity (arranging deals in investments) and therefore requires regulatory approval. However, **Recognised Investment Exchange** status exempts an exchange from the requirement. This status assures any parties using the exchange that there are reasonable rules protecting them.

Membership of an RIE does not confer authorisation to conduct regulated activities. Many firms are members of an RIE and also required to be authorised and regulated by the FSA. Membership of an RIE merely gives the member privileges of membership associated with the exchange, such as the ability to use the exchange's systems.

Exchanges with RIE status

- EDX London Ltd
- ICE Futures Europe
- LIFFE Administration and Management (NYSE Liffe)
- London Stock Exchange plc
- PLUS Markets plc
- The London Metal Exchange Limited (LME)

3.2 NYSE Liffe

The most important London market for financial futures and options is **NYSE Liffe**, formerly Euronext.liffe, and before that the London International Financial Futures and Options Exchange (LIFFE).

Euronext was formed in 2000 by the merger of the Amsterdam, Brussels and Paris securities and derivatives exchanges. In 2001 Euronext purchased Liffe. Trading takes place on an electronic order matching system known as Liffe.Connect. Only NYSE Liffe members are able to trade and clear contracts.

Once a trade has been matched it is registered with the LCH.Clearnet which becomes the central counterparty. To protect itself from the risk that firms default, LCH Clearnet requests margin is posted.

Initial margin is payable on opening a contact. It is a returnable good faith deposit required from all those entering 'risky' positions. The amount required by the LCH.Clearnet is usually linked to the worst probable (not possible) one-day loss that a position could sustain. Initial margin is payable in cash and various acceptable collateral. This amount will be returned as long as the investor honours his contractual obligations. However, should the investor default, this initial margin will be used by the LCH to offset the effect of default.

In addition to initial margin, variation margin is payable based on the profits and losses incurred on each position during the day. At the end of each day the positions are 'marked-to-market' to the daily settlement price, and profits and losses are calculated. Variation margin is essentially 'pay as you go' profits and losses on a daily basis. Variation margin is normally payable in cash only.

The day to day supervision of the rules on Euronext.life is carried out by the 'Market Supervision Department'.

NYSE Liffe members are subject to a comprehensive set of **membership rules** that focus particularly on trading conduct. As such, they focus primarily on the relationship between members rather than between members and customers. It should be remembered that membership of NYSE Liffe does not convey any kind of authorisation to conduct investment business in the UK. It allows access to the market place.

Infringements of the rules will lead initially to an investigation by the Market Supervision Department, which may ultimately lead to a disciplinary hearing for the member concerned. Penalties may be imposed on its members by NYSE Liffe, such as fines, trading suspensions and, ultimately, expulsion from exchange membership.

3.3 Recognised Overseas Investment Exchanges (ROIEs)

As well as the above UK exchanges that are permitted to operate under the RIE status, certain **Recognised Overseas Investment Exchanges (ROIEs)** are permitted to operate in the UK.

ROIEs

- Chicago Board of Trade (CBOT)
- Eurex (Zurich)
- ICE Futures U.S., Inc
- NASDAQ
- New York Mercantile Exchange Inc. (NYMEX Inc.)
- SIX Swiss Exchange AG
- Sydney Futures Exchange Limited
- The Chicago Mercantile Exchange (CME)

A ROIE is also granted exemption from the requirement to seek authorisation under FSMA 2000.

3.4 Recognised Clearing Houses (RCHs)

This recognition permits the organisation to carry out the clearing and settlement functions for an exchange.

At present there are four **RCHs**:

- Euroclear UK & Ireland Limited (formerly CRESTCo)
- LCH.Clearnet Limited
- European Central Counterparty Ltd
- ICE Clear Europe Limited

3.5 Designated Investment Exchanges (DIEs)

In addition to those RIEs in the UK and overseas which the FSA recognises as being effectively run, there are also overseas exchanges that have been given a form of approval yet are unable to conduct regulated activities in the UK.

Designated Investment Exchange (DIE) status assures any UK user of the overseas market that the FSA believes there are appropriate forms of local regulation that guarantee the investor's rights.

The term 'designated' does *not* mean exempt from the requirement to seek authorisation.

There are currently thirty **Designated Investment Exchanges** and they include, for example:

- Tokyo Stock Exchange
- New York Stock Exchange
- New York Futures Exchange
- International Capital Markets Association
- Hong Kong Exchanges and Clearing Limited

(A full list is available in the **FSA Register** on the FSA's website.)

4 UKLA AND PROSPECTUS REQUIREMENTS

4.1 The London Stock Exchange and the FSA (UKLA)

Learning objective   2.5.1 **Explain** the role of the FSA as the UK listing authority.

The **London Stock Exchange (LSE)** is a company whose aim is to run an **orderly market place in securities**. The Financial Services Authority (FSA) regulates the LSE, and has granted it the status of a Recognised Investment Exchange (RIE). The LSE publishes rules governing the trading in securities in the secondary markets, and to some extent in the primary markets.

In May 2000, the FSA took on the statutory role of **Competent Authority**. This obliges the FSA to maintain the **Official List** – the list of companies whose securities are admitted to the LSE. Through a division called the UK Listing Authority (UKLA), it determines which companies may be listed on the LSE, monitors their continuing eligibility, and imposes strict standards of conduct for companies and their advisers in the UKLA Listing Rules.

The UKLA's role also includes the implementation of certain EU Directives and the listing of gilts.

There are two levels of entry into the stock market, namely through the **Official List** and traded on the **main market**, or through the **Alternative Investment Market (AIM)**. Of the two, the Official List (or 'Full

List') is the senior market, and membership demands the most onerous responsibilities. Although UKLA regulates the Full List, LSE regulates AIM (see later), publishing the AIM Rules and monitoring compliance with them.

4.2 The criteria for listing

2.5.2 Identify the source of the listing rules as FSMA 2000 and relevant EU directives.

2.5.3 Explain the main conditions for listing on the Official List, AIM and PLUS markets.

2.5.4 Explain the purpose of the requirement for prospectus or listing particulars.

The UKLA's rules for admission to listing are contained in the **Listing Rules**. The Listing Rules are found within the FSA Handbook. These detail the requirements that a company must meet prior to being admitted to the Full List. The basic conditions you are required to know for your exam are as follows.

- The expected market value of shares to be listed by the company must be at least **£700,000**. If the company is to issue **debt**, the expected market value of any such debt is to be at least **£200,000**.

- All securities issued must be **freely transferable**.

- The company must have a trading record of at least **three years**. Its main business activity must have been continuous over the whole three-year period. In addition, there should be three years of audited accounts. This requirement is waived for innovative high growth companies, investment companies and in certain other situations.

- The shares must be sufficiently marketable. A minimum of **25% of the company's share capital being made available for public purchase** (known as the **free float**) is normally seen to satisfy this requirement. The lower the free float, the fewer shares are available in the market, potentially leading to higher share price volatility.

These are the basic entry conditions which must be met prior to admission to the Full List. In addition, the company will be required to pay a fee.

All applicants for listing must appoint a UKLA-approved **sponsor** whose role is to:

- Ensure the company and its directors are aware of their obligations
- Ensure the company is suitable for listing and satisfy UKLA of this fact
- Liaise with UKLA and submit documentation to them as required
- Co-ordinate the listing process

Companies must also produce a prospectus containing full details on the company's past and present activities and performance, directors, capital structure and future prospects.

Once listed, a company must produce interim (six-monthly) accounts within 90 calendar days and annual accounts within six months.

4.2.1 Continuing obligations

All applicants for membership agree to be bound by the **continuing obligations** of the Listing Rules which require the company to:

- Notify the LSE of any **price-sensitive information**

- Publish information about important transactions undertaken by the company under the Class Tests Rule

- Inform the LSE of any changes in the important registers of ownership of the shares, such as notifiable interests and directors' shareholdings

- Notify the LSE of **dividends**

- Issue reports. Annual financial statements must be available within **six months** of the year-end, and in addition, companies are obliged to produce half-yearly results within **90 calendar days** of the half-year. This is an improvement on the rules contained within the Companies Act, which require plcs to produce accounts within seven months (private companies have ten months).

All of these disclosures must be made through an official **Regulatory Information Service (RIS)** or other UKLA-approved **Primary Information Provider (PIP)** service.

When an announcement is lengthy, guidance is that prominence should be given to **current and future trading prospects**.

If price-sensitive information is inadvertently released to analysts or journalists, a company must take immediate steps to provide the information to the whole market.

A company should correct their public forecasts as soon as it becomes aware that the outcome is significantly different. However, companies are not obliged to tell analysts their forecasts are wrong.

4.2.2 Documentation and advertising

All applicants must have a **sponsor** to guide them through the process of applying for a hearing and submitting documentation to the UKLA, the Competent Authority. Documentation in its final form must be submitted **48 hours prior to the hearing** (the '48-hour rule').

Companies are obliged to produce and include in that documentation a statement by the directors confirming that the working capital of the business will be adequate. This letter must be submitted and approved by the sponsor.

Fully listed companies are generally required to produce a **prospectus** under the **Listing Rules**. This contains detailed information and a report given by the company's accountants on the information produced. The level of detail and the requirement for verification makes a prospectus under the listing rules much more expensive to produce than an ordinary prospectus produced by an unlisted company issuing shares.

4.3 Alternative Investment Market (AIM)

The LSE introduced the second-tier **Alternative Investment Market (AIM)** in 1995. This forum for trading a company's shares enables companies to have their shares traded through the LSE in a lightly regulated regime. Thus smaller, fast-growing companies may obtain access to the market at a lower cost and with less regulatory burden.

4.3.1 Conditions for admission to AIM

A summary of the main conditions that companies must meet in order to secure admission to AIM is as follows.

- All securities must be **freely transferable**.

- AIM companies must have an LSE-approved **Nominated Advisor (NOMAD)** to advise the directors on their responsibilities, and guide them through the AIM process. The NOMAD is retained to advise the directors once an AIM listing is granted. Should the company lose its NOMAD, it must appoint a new one (otherwise the listing will be suspended).

- AIM companies must also have a **broker** to support trading of the company's shares.

- AIM companies must comply with **ongoing obligations** to publish **price-sensitive information** immediately and to disclose details of **significant transactions**. The NOMAD has a duty to ensure the AIM company meets its ongoing obligations.

- Companies with a track record of less than **two years** must agree to a **'lock-in'**, whereby the directors, significant shareholders and employees with 0.5% or more of their capital, agree **not to sell their shares for a year** following admission.

For AIM companies, there is no minimum level of free float (shares available for purchase by the public), no minimum market value for their securities and no minimum trading history.

However, they must produce a prospectus, which is considerably less detailed than for a full listing, and is known as an **Admission Document**.

4.3.2 Summary of UKLA and AIM rules

	Full List	AIM
Trading record	Three years	None
Percentage in public hands	25%	None
Minimum market value	£700,000 for equity £200,000 for debt	None
Free transferability	Yes	Yes
Requirement to produce a prospectus	Yes	Yes*
Applicable rules	UKLA	LSE

* Remember, AIM companies produce a simplified version called an Admission Document.

4.4 PLUS

PLUS Markets Group (PMG) is an independent FSA-regulated UK provider of primary and secondary equity market services and currently trades over 7,000 small and mid-cap company shares under MiFID rules.

- The PLUS primary market specialises in smaller companies, domestic and international, representing a wide range of sectors and all stages of development. There are currently circa 180 companies quoted on the primary market with a combined market capitalisation of over £2.4 billion.

- The PLUS secondary market trading platform is based on a quote-driven trading model, which PMG believes is the most efficient and effective system by which shares in small and mid-cap companies may be traded. Market makers commit their own capital to the market, playing a key role in providing both price formation and liquidity.

There is no requirement for a company to have had a trading record, and no minimum capitalisation and no minimum free float.

To gain admission to PLUS, a company must appoint a PLUS Markets corporate adviser.

Companies on PLUS must maintain appropriate corporate governance arrangements. There must be at least one independent director and there must be published audited reports and accounts within the nine-month period before admission of the company to the market. The company must have adequate working capital, and there must be no restrictions on transferring shares, which must be eligible for electronic settlement.

4.5 The Prospectus Directive and cross-border prospectuses

2.5.5 Identify the main exemptions from listing particulars.

The **Prospectus Directive** is an EU directive which came into force in December 2003. It was implemented in the UK by the Prospectus Regulations 2005, which amended Part IV FSMA 2000, and by the Prospectus Rules in the FSA Handbook.

The Directive requires that a prospectus is produced whenever there is a public offer of securities or where securities are admitted to trading on a regulated market. The Directive specifies the content of prospectuses and requires that they are approved by the relevant **competent authority** – in the UK, this is the **FSA**.

These requirements are designed to increase protection of investors by ensuring the quality of prospectuses and to enhance international market efficiency through the issue of single approved prospectuses for use throughout the EEA.

The Directive identifies two types of situation where prospectuses are required:

- An offer of securities to the general public
- Admission of securities to trading on a regulated market

Under the Prospectus Directive, there is a **'single passport'** for issuers, with the result that a prospectus approved by one competent authority can be used across the EEA without any further approval or burdensome administrative procedures in other member states. If the competent authority in the relevant member state approves the prospectus, it will be accepted throughout the EEA.

A prospectus is required on admission of a company's transferable securities to a **regulated market** in the EEA: the London Stock Exchange is such a regulated market.

London's **Alternative Investment Market (AIM)** was deregulated in 2004, and there are some exemptions which may apply to AIM IPOs (Initial Public Offers), takeovers and fund raising.

The overall position is that a prospectus is required in the case of an offer of transferable securities to the public in the EEA, unless an exemption applies. An 'offer' is defined broadly and covers any communication in any form and by any means which presents sufficient information about the terms of the offer and the securities offered such as to enable an investor to decide to buy or subscribe to those securities.

The main **exemptions** are as follows.

- Offers made only to qualified investors, which includes regulated institutions and investment companies, as well as some UK-resident persons and small and medium-sized enterprises who meet specified criteria and are registered as qualified investors with the FSA

- Cases where the total consideration for the offer over a 12-month period is less than €100,000

- Offers made to fewer than 100 persons per EEA state other than qualified investors

- Documents where securities are offered in connection with a takeover or merger, if they contain information similar to that in a prospectus: such documents will not require formal approval

5 INFORMATION DISCLOSURE AND CORPORATE GOVERNANCE

ng objective **2.6.1 Explain** the disclosures required under the FSA's disclosure and transparency rules relating to:
- Directors' interests
- Major shareholdings

5.1 Directors' dealings

The **Listing Rules (LR)** set out requirements for issuers seeking a listing on the official list of the LSE.

LR 9 Annex 1 also contains the **Model Code** for **directors' dealings**. The Model Code restricts dealings by directors on their own account in the company's shares at certain times and governs the approval process and disclosure of such dealings at all times: clearance to deal must be sought from a designated director. The Model Code is intended to ensure that shareholder-directors demonstrate to other shareholders that they will not abuse their position for unfair advantage. No trades should be undertaken in a listed company by its directors in the **close period**. The close period is the 60 days before the company publishes either a preliminary statement of its annual results or its annual report. The close period before publication of the half-yearly report is from the end of the six-month period up to publication. For quarterly results, the close period is one month prior to the announcement. If, as provided by the **Disclosure and Transparency Rules (DTR)**, **Interim Management Statements** are issued instead of quarterly reports, there is no close period and companies must exercise discretion.

Directors and senior executives are **persons discharging managerial responsibilities (PDMRs)**. PDMRs other than directors must not deal in any securities of the company without first notifying the company secretary or a designated director and receiving clearance to deal from him. PDMRs must also seek to prohibit dealings during a **close period** by investment managers or connected persons on behalf of himself or connected persons.

A PDMR must take reasonable steps to prevent any dealings by or on behalf of any connected person of his in any securities of the company on considerations of a short-term nature.

Since March 2009, a **PDMR** is however permitted to enter into a **trading plan** (for example, with an independent investment manager)in order to deal in securities of the issuer during both open and prohibited periods without breaching the Model Code and without suspicion of dealing on the basis of inside information.

- The trading plan must be entered into in an open period when the PDMR is not in possession of inside information, and cannot be amended in a prohibited period.

- Cancellation of a trading plan is not permitted during a prohibited period except in exceptional circumstances and provided the PDMR does not have inside information at the time of cancellation.

The **Prospectus Rules (PR)** set out the requirements for, and contents of, prospectuses. These are required where securities are offered to the public.

DTR requires issuers of securities to control inside information and make timely disclosures of price-sensitive information to the market.

DTR also covers notifications of holdings in a company's shares. The rules require those who discharge managerial responsibilities to make notifications to the issuer and the market via a Regulatory Information Service.

DTR additionally requires issuers to maintain **lists of insiders**.

5.2 Notification requirements: interests in a company

5.2.1 Rules

DTR requires that, where a person's holding of financial instruments, including interests held through Contracts for Differences (CfDs), in a UK company on the relevant market:

- Reaches or falls below 3% of the **voting rights**, or
- Increases or reduces **across one full percentage point** above 3% (e.g. 4.9% to 5.2%),

then they must, within **two business days**, notify the company, which must make the notifications public by the end of the following trading day.

For certain voting rights, the thresholds that apply are 5%, 10% and each whole percentage figure above 10%. The holdings involved include holdings of authorised **unit trusts** and **open-ended investment companies**, of EEA qualifying **investment managers**, and of registered US investment managers.

EEA issuers (ie, companies issuing shares) incorporated and with their registered office in another EEA Member State are instead required to comply with their home State's requirements.

Those holding **short positions** are those who have transacted to sell shares, only to buy later, thus gaining if the price falls in the intervening period. Short positions in publicly quoted financial sector companies (that is, UK banks or insurers, or their UK-incorporated parent companies) are required to disclose a net short position representing **0.25% or more of the issued capital** of the relevant company at the market close on the previous day, and if the holding crosses **0.1% bands** above that level (i.e. at 0.35%, 0.45% etc), either increasing or decreasing. This was introduced as an emergency measure during the financial crisis in 2008, but the rule was left in place with no proposed expiry date.

5.2.2 Connected parties

For the purposes of this rule, a stake comprises

- The stakeholder's own position.

- Any shares owned by the stakeholder's spouse or infant child (< 18 years old).

- Shares owned by a connected/controlled company: under the definitions of the Companies Act **a controlled company is one where the stakeholder owns 33⅓% of the capital**.

- Any **concert parties**. A concert party is an organisational grouping, whether bound by a contract or not, which agrees to act together. For example, five individuals may each obtain a 2% stake in a company which does not in itself require disclosure, however, they are in effect acting as one unit with a 10% stake.

5.2.3 Notifiable interests

An additional requirement requires any holders of **non-beneficial** holdings in a company's stock, of **at least 10%** are obliged to notify the company of their stake **within two business days**.

5.3 Registers of interests

A company is obliged to maintain two registers of interests in the shares of that company. The first relates to the disclosure of substantial holdings – **material and notifiable interests** – in the company's share capital. This record is open to public inspection and **any changes** in it must be **notified to the market via a Regulatory Information Service (RIS) or Primary Information Provider (PIP) without delay (not later than the end of the next business day)**. It is this register that contains all the information required under the disclosure of **3%** interests.

The second register relates to the **directors' share interests** and again, any changes must be notified to the company within four days and the company must notify **a Regulatory Information Service or PIP without delay (not later than the end of the next business day).** Under the **Model Code**, which is a set of rules enforced by the UK Listing Authority, directors are placed under a number of 'voluntary' controls. The most important of these is that directors should **not buy or sell shares** in their own company in the **two months immediately preceding the announcement of results**, the close or prohibited period. It should be noted that this does not constitute insider dealing, it is simply an infringement of a series of UK Listing Authority rules and regulations.

A further restriction is that directors are **not** permitted to deal in futures and options on the shares of their company.

Following rule changes that came into force on 6 March 2009, directors are permitted to enter into a **trading plan** (for example, with an independent investment manager) in order to deal in their company's securities during both open and prohibited periods without breaching the Model Code and without suspicion of dealing on the basis of inside information, subject to the following conditions.

- The trading plan must be entered into in an open period when the director is not in possession of inside information, and cannot be amended in a prohibited period.

- Cancellation of a trading plan is not permitted during a prohibited period except in exceptional circumstances and provided the director does not have inside information at the time of cancellation.

5.4 Corporate governance

objectives

2.6.2 Explain the purpose of corporate governance regulation.

2.6.3 Explain, in outline, the scope and content of corporate governance regulation in the UK (the Combined Code).

2.6.4 Explain the LSE requirements for listed companies to disclose corporate governance compliance.

2.6.5 Explain the continuing obligations of LSE listed companies regarding information disclosure and dissemination.

Issues of **corporate governance** are concerned with how companies are directed and controlled. Institutional shareholders have abandoned their traditional 'back seat' role and show an increasingly pro-active approach to holding directors of the company to account. The change in attitude has been fuelled by some notable corporate failures and the perception that directors may be improving their own pay and conditions at the expense of the shareholders.

The UKLA requires listed companies to disclose in their annual report both how they have applied the principles of good governance. This first requirement requires the company to explain how both the **main and the supporting principles** of the **Combined Code on Corporate Governance** have been applied. Secondly, the company also has to disclose whether they have complied with the **provisions of the code of best practice**. Any departures from the Code's provisions should be explained. This 'comply or explain' approach has been retained in the updated version of the Code. The way it operates is widely supported by companies and investors as allowing flexibility while ensuring sufficient information for investors to come to their own conclusions.

5.5 Combined Code on Corporate Governance

The revised **June 2008 edition** of the Combined Code, published by the **Financial Reporting Council**, came into effect for accounting periods beginning on or after 29 June 2008. The revised code has been implemented simultaneously with new FSA Part 6 Rules, which include the Listing Rules and implement new EU requirements on corporate governance. The Code is likely to be reviewed periodically, and the next such **review** is likely to be in **2010**.

5.5.1 Overall aims

The Combined Code aims to promote confidence in corporate reporting and governance, and to promote good governance so as to support the following outcomes.

- Contribute to better company performance by helping a board discharge its duties in the best interests of shareholders

- Avoid the consequence of vulnerability or poor performance, which can result if good governance is ignored

- Facilitate efficient, effective and entrepreneurial management that can deliver shareholder value over the longer term.

The Code does not set out to be a rigid set of rules. Rather, it aims to be 'a guide to the components of good board practice distilled from consultation and widespread experience over many years'.

The main principles underlying each Section of the Code are outlined below.

5.5.2 Section A: Directors

The Code sets out the principle that every company should be headed by an **effective board**, which is collectively responsible for the success of the company.

There should be a clear division of responsibilities at the head of the company between the running of the board (**Chairman**) and the executive responsibility for the running of the company's business (**Chief Executive**). No one individual should have unfettered powers of decision.

The board should include a **balance** of **executive and non-executive directors** (and in particular **independent** non-executive directors) such that no individual or small group of individuals can dominate the board's decision taking.

There should be a **formal, rigorous and transparent** procedure for the **appointment of new directors** to the board.

All directors should receive induction on joining the board and should regularly update and refresh their **skills and knowledge**.

The board should undertake a formal and rigorous **annual evaluation** of its own performance and that of its committees and individual directors.

All directors should be submitted for **re-election** at regular intervals, subject to continued satisfactory performance. The board should ensure **planned and progressive refreshing** of the board.

5.5.3 Section B: Remuneration

This Section seeks to ensure that levels of **directors' remuneration** are sufficient to attract, retain and motivate directors of the quality required to run the company successfully, with the proviso that a company should avoid paying more than is necessary for this purpose.

The Code states that a significant proportion of executive directors' remuneration should be structured so as to link rewards to corporate and individual performance.

There should be a formal and transparent procedure for developing policy on executive remuneration and for fixing the remuneration packages of individual directors. No director should be involved in deciding his or her own remuneration.

5.5.4 Section C: Accountability and audit

This Section of the Code seeks to ensure that the board:

- Presents a balanced and understandable assessment of the company's position and prospects (**financial reporting**)

- Maintains a sound system of **internal control**, to safeguard shareholders' investment and the company's assets.

Audit committee and auditors: there should be formal and transparent arrangements for applying financial reporting and internal control principles and for maintaining the relationship with the company's auditors.

5.5.5 Section D: Relations with shareholders

There should be a **dialogue with institutional shareholders** based on the mutual understanding of objectives.

The board should use the **AGM** to communicate with investors and to encourage their participation.

5.5.6 Section E: Institutional shareholders

Section E of the 2008 Combined Code recommends an approach for institutional shareholders to take in the governance of portfolio firms whose shares they hold on behalf of beneficiaries. (The aims of other Sections of the Code are outlined later in this Section.)

Section E has no formal status. What it does do is to develop an idea of what good corporate governance might look like for an institutional shareholder and to propose that institutional shareholders perform it.

Section E.1 of the Combined Code (2008) recommends that;

'Institutional shareholders should enter into a dialogue with companies based on the mutual understanding of objectives [and] apply the principles set out in the Institutional Shareholders' Committee's "The Responsibilities of Institutional Shareholders and Agents – Statement of Principles", which should be reflected in fund manager contracts'.

Section E.3 of the 2008 Combined Code states

'Institutional shareholders have a responsibility to make considered use of their votes'

5.6 Information disclosure and dissemination

** g objective** **2.6.5 Explain** the continuing obligations of LSE listed companies regarding information disclosure and dissemination.

A listed company has a **continuing obligation** to keep holders of securities and the wider market properly informed. The company must also publicise to the market profit announcements, dividend declarations, material acquisitions, changes of directors, and other information to enable holders of securities and members of the public to appraise the company's position and avoid a false market being created in the company's securities. The company's forecasts should be corrected as soon as possible if the actual outcome is significantly different: downward profit revisions in such cases are generally called '**profits warnings**'.

Companies should maintain consistent procedures to determine what information is price-sensitive and should therefore be released. If price-sensitive information is inadvertently released to analysts, journalists or others, the company should take immediate steps to publicise the information to the whole market.

DTR provides that an issuer may **delay** the **public disclosure** of inside information, such as not to prejudice its legitimate interests, provided that the public would not be likely to be misled and the issuer is able to ensure the confidentiality of the information. For example, public disclosure of information may be delayed for a limited period if the firm's financial viability in 'grave and imminent danger' to avoid undermining negotiations to ensure the firm's long-term financial recovery.

The various items of required information described above must be provided through an official **Regulatory Information Service (RIS)** or other UKLA-approved **Primary Information Provider (PIP)** service.

Approved RISs include:

- Regulatory News Service (RNS) of the LSE
- FirstSight.
- PR Newswire Disclose
- Business Wire Regulatory Disclosure

5.7 Meetings and resolutions

Learning objectives

2.6.6 Explain in outline, the UK company law requirements regarding the calling of general meetings.

2.6.7 Distinguish between extraordinary and annual general meetings.

2.6.8 Distinguish between the types of resolution that can be considered at company general meetings.

2.6.9 Distinguish between the voting methods used at company meetings.

2.6.10 Explain the role and powers of a proxy.

The Companies Acts include provisions on the conduct and structure of company meetings which will apply in the absence of any provisions to the contrary in the company's Memorandum and Articles.

The owners of a company are the shareholders. There are a number of key events and decisions which can only be taken by the shareholders, and these decisions are taken in a General Meeting. If a shareholder is unable to attend they are able to appoint a **proxy**, or ask the Chairman to vote on their behalf.

Every calendar year (although there can be 15 months between each meeting) a company must hold **an Annual General Meeting (AGM). The Companies Act states that 21 calendar days' notice** must be given prior to this meeting, although this notice period may be waived if **all** the shareholders agree (100%).

The AGM will at least consider the following.

- Approving the accounts
- Reappointing directors
- Reappointing auditors and giving power to the directors to fix their remuneration
- Approval or rejection of the dividend

If any other meeting has to be called during the year in order to obtain specific approval for an event, this is termed an **Extraordinary General Meeting (EGM)**. (Additionally, for traded companies, members with at least 5% of voting rights, or 100 members, can require the company to consider a matter in an AGM)

- Following implementation of the **EU Shareholder Rights Directive**, the general position is that **21 calendar days' notice** is required for an EGM.

- However, traded (listed) companies may require a minimum of **14 days'** notice, provided that they pass a **special resolution** annually and offer all shareholders the ability to appoint proxies electronically.

A company may now communicate notice of a meeting electronically. Electronic communication may include email, notification on a website or any other electronic method. A notice is deemed to have been sent when first transmitted and delivered 48 hours after being sent. Therefore, for notification periods regarding the AGM or EGM, the notice period commences from the delivery date of the electronic communication.

There are a number of detailed rules within the Companies Act concerning the appointment of the Chairman of the meeting and quorum. In general, a **quorum** is achieved when two members (shareholders) are present (this is the minimum number required).

5.8 Voting and proxies

Voting procedures with respect to resolutions can be done by a show of hands, or by a poll vote (one vote per share). **Proxies may only vote by way of a poll**.

There are two different types of proxy. A **general proxy** is used to appoint another person to vote as he thinks, considering anything that is discussed at the meeting. A **special proxy** is used to appoint another person to vote in a particular way, either for or against a resolution. This is sometimes referred to as a 'two-way proxy'. **A proxy is valid for the meeting and any adjournment**.

A poll may be demanded by shareholder(s) **representing 10% or more of the voting rights** in the company. Alternatively, five members, or the Chairman, can demand a poll vote.

6 REGULATION OF DERIVATIVES MARKETS

6.1 Scope of regulation

objectives

2.7.1 Identify the main features of the regulation of derivatives.

2.7.4 Explain the impact of MiFID and International Accounting Standards on the regulation of derivative markets.

The UK **derivatives exchanges**, which include NYSE Liffe and the London Metals Exchange, are Recognised Investment Exchanges. Accordingly, the exchanges mainly regulate the market, with the FSA being responsible for the financial soundness and conduct of business of exchange members.

6.2 MiFID

In Europe the most important source of regulation for the derivatives market is the Market in Financial Instruments Directive (MiFID). MiFID harmonised the day-to-day regulation of dealings in the securities and derivatives markets, making it easier for firms to conduct their business in financial instruments all around the European Economic Area (EEA) without having to seek specific authorisation in each state.

MiFID applies to investment firms who are carrying out activities in relation to the following derivative instruments:

- Derivatives relating to securities, currencies, interest rates and yields, financial indices and financial measures settled either physically or in cash, including: options, futures, swaps and forward rate agreements

- Commodity derivatives capable of being settled in cash, commodity derivatives capable of being physically settled on a regulated market or multilateral trading facility, and certain other commodity derivatives which are not for commercial purposes, indeed **MiFID introduced commodity derivatives into the list of regulated investments**

- Derivative instruments for transferring credit risk

- Financial contracts for differences (CFDs)

- Derivatives relating to climatic variables, freight rates, emission allowances, inflation rates or other official economic statistics capable of being settled in cash

A UK based firm would normally receive its authorisation to trade in derivatives from the Financial Services Authority. There are similar bodies in other EEA states.

6.3 USA

In the USA, there are two main relevant regulatory bodies, the **Securities and Exchange Commission (SEC)** and the **Commodity Futures Trading Commission (CFTC)**. US regulations governing derivatives trading originally stem from the Wall Street crash of 1929 and are contained in the **Commodity Exchange Act 1936** which have been updated through the **Commodity Futures Modernization Act 2000**. The SEC primarily regulates derivatives on securities whereas the CFTC primarily regulates commodities.

6.4 Regulatory objectives

The purpose of regulators around the world are broadly similar whether they are incorporated into law or just on a self-regulatory basis.

These objectives are achieved through a variety of measures that seek to control the firms and the individuals who work in the derivatives markets and the exchanges on which they trade. Another common characteristic is a greater level of protection for less sophisticated investors than for large corporates or the banks dealing on the exchanges for their own account. The main activities of derivatives regulators is, therefore

- Regulation of individuals
- Regulation of companies
- Regulation of exchanges
- Supervision
- Sanction processing
- Passporting regulated status
- Classifications/exemption

6.5 International Accounting Standards

Under International Accounting Standard 39 (IAS39), derivatives must be recognised in the **balance sheet at fair value** (except those that are used as a hedge). Fair value is defined as the value at which a contract could be exchanged, or a liability settled between two parties in an arm's length transaction. All (non-hedge) derivatives must, therefore, be 'marked to market' and stated at their current market value.

The treatment of gains and losses depends on whether or not the derivative can be recognised as a hedging instrument. However, assuming this is not the case (i.e. usual situation), **gains and losses from changes in market value will be recognised as income or expenses** in the company's income statement.

6.6 Market transparency

Learning objective

2.7.3 **Explain** the arrangements for market transparency and transaction reporting in the main derivative markets.

Trading on a derivatives exchange is subject to transparency rules of the exchange, as governed by regulatory provisions. MiFID is backed up by the **Transparency Directive** in its efforts to create a single capital market for the EEA.

The Transparency Directive requires pre- and post-trade transparency in the markets so that investors can easily compare execution venues and therefore select the best market to trade financial instruments in, rather than having to use their own monopolistic national exchange.

6.7 Clearing and settlement

g objective **2.7.2 Identify** the main features of clearing and settlement on derivatives exchanges and for over-the-counter derivatives trading.

6.7.1 Exchange trading

For the **London International Financial Futures and Options Exchange (NYSE Liffe)**, the main international derivatives exchange of the NYSE Euronext group, trading is undertaken on LIFFE CONNECT, an electronic order matching system.

LCH.Clearnet (LCH) acts as a **central counterparty** on behalf of Liffe for all trades. LCH receives a feed from Liffe of trades from its LIFFE CONNECT trading system. These are agreed trades and the Trade Registration System (TRS) and the Clearing Processing System (CPS) permit clearing members to confirm business into the correct clearing accounts.

The LCH then acts as principal to all trades which have been transacted. Hence every exchange member who buys or sells a contract ends up with a position with the LCH either directly, if they themselves are clearing members, or indirectly through the clearing member of the exchange who clears their trades.

The LCH thus takes all the risk of counterparties' failing to honour obligations. The LCH reduces its risk by requiring cash or collateral deposits (initial margins) for the clearing members' positions.

Only NYSE Liffe members can trade on Liffe and anyone else wishing to trade a Liffe contract must do so through such a member who takes responsibility for the registration, margining and settlement of the trade.

Individuals using the services of NYSE Liffe members

- **Traders** – people acting on their own behalf, known as 'locals' or their company's behalf. Traders make a profit from the positions taken.

- **Brokers** – people acting for a third party and making profits by charging commission

Day-to-day supervision on Liffe is carried out by the Market Supervision Department (MSD) of the exchange.

6.7.2 OTC derivatives

With **over-the-counter (OTC) derivatives**, settlement is direct with the counterparty rather than through an exchange or clearing broker. Confirmations need to be sent out by counterparties, who will need to make the necessary amendments for corporate actions, instead of this being dealt with by a broker.

During 2009 and 2010, there have been moves in both the USA and Europe to have **OTC derivatives** cleared through **clearing houses** in the future. This should increase transparency and reduce the risk of counterparty default, and may thus help to reduce systemic risks arising from OTC derivatives trading.

7 INTERNATIONAL MARKETS

Learning objectives

2.8.1 Explain the mechanics of dealing in equities and fixed interest securities in each of the following countries: US; Japan; France; Germany.

2.8.2 Identify the participants in each of the above markets.

2.8.4 Explain the general principles of dealing in other markets, including emerging markets, and settlement issues in these markets.

7.1 Government bonds comparison

Government bonds of other countries share some of the features of gilts. Below is a summary of the major foreign government bonds and their key features.

Government bonds: country comparison

	Japan (JGB)	US T-Bond	French OAT**	German Bund	Eurobonds	UK Corporates	UK Gilt
Coupon Frequency	Semi-annual	Semi-annual	Annual	Annual	Annual	Annual	Semi-annual
Settlement	3 business days	Same/ Next day	1 business day	3 business days	3 business days	3 business days	Same/ Next day
Registered or bearer	R or B	R	B	B	B	R	R
Normal life	10 years, some super longs with life of 40 years	Life of over 10 years	Issued with lives of between 6 and 30 years	Mostly 10 years	Varied		Varied
Withholding tax	25%, but bilateral agreement reduces to 10%	None	None	None	None	20%	None
Medium-term debt	–	T-Note life of 2 to 10 years*	BTAN life of 2 to 5 years	BOBLs with lives of up to 5 years and Schatz with lives of 2 to 6 years	–	–	–
Settlement agencies	Japanese Government Bond Clearing Corporation	Federal Reserve	Relit, Sicovam, Euroclear and Clearstream	Euroclear and Clearstream	Euroclear and Clearstream	CREST	CREST, Clearstream, Euroclear and Bank of New York
Accrued interest convention	$\frac{\text{Actual}}{365}$	$\frac{\text{Actual}}{\text{Actual}}$	$\frac{\text{Actual}}{\text{Actual}}$	$\frac{\text{Actual}}{\text{Actual}}$	$\frac{\text{Actual}}{\text{Actual}}$	$\frac{\text{Actual}}{\text{Actual}}$	$\frac{\text{Actual}}{\text{Actual}}$

*   All types of US government bond are issued by Dutch Auction.

**   The French government also has an inflation-linked bond, the OATi. All French Government bonds settle T + 1

7.2 ADRs and GDRs

American Depository Receipts (ADRs) are the conventional form of trading UK and other countries' equities in the US on the NYSE. In order to encourage US investors to buy UK shares, the shares are lodged with an American bank which then issues a receipt for the shares. This receipt is in bearer form and denominated in dollars.

It is possible to trade ADRs in what is known as **pre-release form**. Here, the holding bank releases the receipt to the dealer prior to the deposit of shares in its vaults. The dealer may then sell the ADRs in the market. However, the cash raised through this trade must then be lodged with a holding bank as collateral for the deal. This situation may exist for a maximum of three months, at the end of which the broker must purchase shares in the cash market and deposit them with the holding bank which then releases the collateral.

ADRs, whilst being designated for the American market, also trade in London. These securities are traded in the normal way through the International Order Book. In line with the domestic American markets, settlement for ADRs takes place in three business days.

The ADR holder has all the transferability of the American form document with no stamp duty, other than a one-off fee on creation of 1½%. Dividends are received by the bank which holds the shares. They are then converted into dollars and paid to the holders. The holder of the ADR has the right to vote at the company's meeting in the same way as an ordinary shareholder.

The only right which they do not possess is that of participation in rights or bonus issues. In the case of such an issue, the bank holding the shares will sell the bonus shares or rights nil paid and distribute the cash proceeds to the ADR holders. Any ADR holder who wishes to participate in the rights issue will have to convert their ADR back into share form.

A **Global Depositary Receipt (GDR)** is very similar to an ADR. Like an ADR, a GDR is a security, which bundles together a number of shares of a company listed in another country. It is a term used to describe a security primarily used to raise dollar-denominated capital either in the US or European markets. The name GDR is a generic term describing structures deployed to raise capital either in dollars and/or euros.

7.3 Markets: USA

7.3.1 Equities

The United States is home to the world's largest stock market with its constituent parts being the New York Stock Exchange, the American Stock Exchange, NASDAQ OMX, the Philadelphia Stock Exchange, the Boston Stock Exchange, the Chicago Stock Exchange, the Cincinnati Stock Exchange and the Pacific Exchange.

The **New York Stock Exchange** was established in 1792 and is an order-driven floor dealing market. NASDAQ OMX is a screen-based, quote driven market which is owned and operated by NASDAQ OMX group, the stock of which was listed on its own stock exchange in 2002, and is monitored by the Securities and Exchange Commission.

Trading on the NYSE revolves around **specialists** who receive and match orders via a limit order book. Specialists will also act as market makers where an order cannot be matched via the order book to ensure continuous liquidity in a stock. The primary regulator of the US equities market is the Securities and Equities Commission (SEC).

Orders can be passed to specialists via the telephone or by means of an automated system known as **superDOT** (super designated order turnaround system). Most small trades will be brought to the market via superDOT, and will benefit from a speedy turnaround (typically within around 20 seconds of entering the order).

7.3.2 US Government bond market

The **US Government bond market** is the largest Government bond market in the world. This size is evident in both the quantity of issuance in the primary market and volumes of activity in the secondary market.

The US Treasuries market is not dissimilar in structure from the UK gilts market. This is due to the UK reforms that have been designed to bring the two markets into line. Indeed, the general direction of all government bond markets has been towards greater '**fungibility**' or similarity, with the US being seen as the role model.

The key player in the market is the **Federal Reserve** (the 'Fed'). As the US central bank, it operates in much the same way as the Bank of England in the UK.

The **US Treasury** is part of government and responsible for the issuance of debt in order to fund the deficit.

Central to the operation of the market are the **primary dealers**. These firms are the market makers. They are authorised to conduct trades by the Fed and are obliged to make markets in all issues. As with the UK, there are inter-dealer brokers (IDBs) to facilitate the taking and unwinding of large positions. There are no money brokers, but there is a full repo market.

While the stocks are listed on the New York Stock Exchange, the market is effectively an over-the-counter market. The market operates 09:00 to 16:00 locally, but is perhaps the most truly global market. The market has deep liquidity across the maturity range and prices are quoted in decimals.

There are three main types of instrument issued.

- **Treasury bills (T-bills)** – with a maturity of 3 - 12 months, at a discount to face value
- **Treasury notes (T-notes)** – coupon securities, issued with initial maturities of 2 -10 years
- **Treasury bonds (T-bonds)** – coupon securities, issued with an initial life of over 10 years

The **US Treasury** is responsible for the **issuance** of new securities. Issuance takes place on a regular calendar with weekly issues of three or six-month Treasury bills, monthly issues of one-year bills and two and five-year notes, and quarterly issues in set cycles of longer dated stocks.

The **competitive auction** in the US is basically the system that was introduced into the UK in 1987. The principal differences are that, in the US, the primary dealers are obliged to bid for stock and bids are on a yield basis (rather than price in the UK).

7.3.3 US domestic corporate bond markets

Unlike the UK, the US corporate sector has been able to borrow substantial sums via the issue of debt securities. In part, this has been forced upon them by the highly fragmented nature of the domestic banking market. Equally, however, investors are willing to hold corporate debt as part of their portfolios in a way in which UK investors are not.

Under **rule 144A**, corporates are allowed to issue bonds into the **private placement market** without seeking full Securities and Exchange Commission (SEC) registration. This access to the market is not restricted to overseas issuers, and the market is dominated by US domestic issuers who have chosen not to enter the public market.

7.3.4 Yankee bonds

Ever since 1945, the dollar has been the key international currency. Prior to the emergence of the Eurodollar market (and to a limited extent after this), there has been substantial interest from non-US firms in raising dollar finance. A **Yankee bond** is a dollar-denominated bond issued in the US by an overseas borrower. Given that Eurodollar bonds may not be sold into the US markets until they have **seasoned** (a period of 40 days), there is still a divide between the Euromarket and the domestic market.

7.4 Markets in Japan

7.4.1 Equities

The Tokyo Stock Exchange is order driven through the CORES dealing system. Settlement is on T+3 by book entry transfer through the JSCC (Japanese Securities Clearing Corporation).

7.4.2 JGBs

The **bond market** in **Japan** is dominated by Government bonds. This domination is not in terms of volume, where **Japanese Government Bonds (JGBs)** account for only half of the market, but in the secondary market where they account for over 80% of the secondary market trading. Within this, there tends to be a strong focus on the 'benchmark' bond. This has in the past caused wide discrepancies between the benchmark and other 'side issues'.

The **issue process** is complex with a monthly auction/syndicate issue. In Japan, the syndicate (still dominated by the large investment banks) is allocated 40% of the issue, with 60% sold via public auction. The terms of the issue are set by the Ministry of Finance having taken soundings in the market from the syndicate.

JGBs trade on both the Tokyo Stock Exchange (**TSE**) and the Broker-Broker (OTC) market. The market does tend to focus on the 'benchmark' issues, with occasionally 90% of the volume taking place in that stock. However, any issues that are deliverable into the JGB future will possess a fair degree of liquidity.

TSE transactions settle after three days (T+3) with the OTC taking nine days or more, following a complicated settlement timetable. Settlement is conducted through book entry systems.

7.4.3 Other markets in Japan

In Japan, there are a number of important issuers other than the government. In the form of 'quasi-government' there are the agencies and municipal stocks.

International borrowers are able to access the domestic pool of savings through the issue of Samurai (publicly issued yen bonds) and Shibosai (yen bonds issued via private placement).

7.5 Markets in France

7.5.1 Equities

There is one stock market in France: Euronext. It operates a computerised order book known as the NSC. Settlement is on T+3 through the systems of Euroclear France, the central securities depository.

7.5.2 Bonds

The French bond market developed into one of the key international bond markets, mainly due to the economic transformation that took place since the introduction of the 'Franc fort' policy in 1985. In 1993, plans were announced to move towards a more independent central bank in line with the obligations of the Maastricht Treaty. This commitment made the French market the most efficient bond market within the first wave of European Economic and Monetary Union (EMU), with a transparent, liquid and technologically strong market.

The development of MATIF (the French financial futures market, now part of Euronext) and the trading of the 'Notional' future into the French long bond were also a vital component in the reform of the market.

The French Government issues three **types of bond**, each with a different maturity.

- **Bons du Trésor à Taux Fixe (BTFs)** are the French T-bills, issued at a discount to face value and with maturities of 13, 26 and 52 weeks.

- **Bons du Trésor à Taux Fixe et Intéret Annuel (BTANs)** are fixed rate Treasury notes issued with maturities of between two and five years and an annual coupon. New issues are made on a six-monthly basis and, in between these new issues, existing issues are reopened on a monthly basis.

- **Obligations Assimilables du Trésor (OATs)** are the conventional Government bonds that have become the key funding instruments used by the Government. They are issued with maturities of between 6 and 30 years.

All French Government issues are now in book entry form with no physical delivery.

Over half the market is made up of debt issues from the **public corporations**. These stocks are not, for the most part, guaranteed by the Government, but the corporations concerned do possess strong credit ratings. They have established their own market structure in order to facilitate trading in their stocks. All issues are by way of a placing through a syndicate of mainly local banks.

7.6 Markets in Germany

7.6.1 Equities

The Deutsche Börse is a fierce competitor with the LSE. Trading takes place through a computerised order book called XETRA. Settlement is on T+2. Clearing, settlement and custody take place through Clearstream.

7.6.2 Bonds

The German bond market, including Government bonds, domestic bonds and Eurobonds, is the third largest in the world and one of the largest in Europe (the second largest after Italy).

Unlike the UK, Germany has a strong **corporate debt market** and a relatively weak equity market. The bulk of finance for industry is provided through the banks, either as lenders or shareholders, with debt securities other than Eurobonds being less significant. Within the context of debt issuance, it is the banks that issue bonds and then lend on the money to the corporate sector.

The German financial markets have undergone a process of liberalisation and modernisation. These have gradually removed the residual capital controls and allowed the development of a market in futures and options. With the adoption of the Euro, the German bond market emerged as the benchmark for Government bonds of the Eurozone.

The bulk of the banking sector bond issuance comes in the form of Pfandbriefe. These are effectively bonds collateralised against portfolios of loans. Offenliche Pfandbriefe are backed by loans to the public sector and Hypotheken Pfandbriefe are backed by mortgages.

There is a variety of **types of issue**.

- **(Bundesanleihen)** are the conventional bonds in the market, with normal maturities of ten years. Special bonds have been issued to fund the reunification process and are referred to as unity bonds.

- **Bobls (Bundesobligationen)** are medium-term issues with lives of up to five years.

- **Bundesschatzanweisungen (Schatze) and Kassenobligationen** are a second type of medium-term finance: these were issued with maturities of between two and six years.

- **BU-Bills** are six-month bills issued by the Bundesbank.

Settlement date for domestic bond deals is three banking days after the day of dealing. This now matches to the Eurobond three-day settlement period, allowing Government or bank bonds held outside Germany to settle via Euroclear and Clearstream.

7.7 Emerging markets

There are various **bond and equity markets in growing and emerging markets**, each with its own unique characteristics.

In many of these markets, bond and equity trading is OTC and is restricted to locally registered participants. Settlement systems in such markets tend to be run by central banks with no counterparty guarantees. In addition, non-electronic settlement systems and physical delivery are not uncommon. These characteristics make participation both difficult and risky for the UK investor.

In an effort to achieve some international harmonisation, the larger (G30) economies have published some recommendations of good practice including T + 3 settlement for equities.

7.8 Eurobonds

ig objective   **2.8.3 Explain** the structure and operation of the primary and secondary markets for Eurobonds.

7.8.1 The market

The Eurobond market is, in effect, an international market in debt. Companies issuing debt in the Eurobond market have their securities traded all around the world and are not limited to one domestic market place.

The market only accepts highly rated companies, since Eurobonds themselves are unsecured debt.

7.8.2 The instruments

In essence, a Eurobond is simply a debt instrument issued by a borrower (typically a government or a large company) normally or predominantly **outside of the country in whose currency it is denominated**. For example, a US dollar Eurobond could be issued anywhere in the world except for the US. As such, a better name for it might be an 'international bond'. As mentioned above, Eurobonds frequently carry no security other than the high name and credit rating of the issuer. Another important feature of bonds issued in this market is that, for the most part, they are issued in **bearer form**, with no formal register of ownership held by the company.

For a number of pragmatic reasons, the clearing houses in the Euromarkets do maintain a form of register of ownership, but that this register is not normally open either to government or tax authorities. Combined with the feature of being bearer documents, a vital aspect of the Eurobond is that unlike most government bonds it does not attract withholding tax. **Eurobonds pay coupons gross and usually annually**.

Most Eurobonds are issued in **bullet form**, redeemed at one specified date in the future. However, a number of issues have alternative redemption patterns. Some bonds are redeemed over a number of years with a proportion of the issue being redeemed each year. Whilst Eurobonds are not issued in registered form, each will have an identifying number. A **drawing** of numbers is made every year from the pool of bonds in issue, the numbers drawn are published and the bonds are called in and redeemed. This redemption process is known as a drawing on a Eurobond.

7.8.3 Dealing and settlement

There is no formal market place for Eurobond trading. The market is telephone driven and the houses are based in London. The market is regulated by the **International Capital Market Association (ICMA)** which operates rules regulating the conduct of dealers in the market place.

Settlement is conducted for the market by two independent clearing houses, **Euroclear and Clearstream**. These clearing houses immobilise the stocks in their vaults and then operate electronic registers of ownership.

Settlement in the Eurobond market is based on a **three business day** settlement system. Once again, the important feature about the registers maintained by the two clearing houses is that they are not normally available to any governmental authority, thereby preserving the bearer nature of the documents.

7.8.4 Eurobond issuance

New Issues in the Eurobond Market

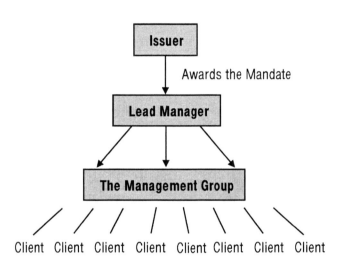

The most common form of issue used in the Eurobond market is a **placing**. A traditional method of issuing a Eurobond is for an issuer to appoint a lead manager and award them the mandate. The mandate gives the lead manager the power and responsibility to issue the bond on the issuer's behalf. The lead manager may then create a management group of other Eurobond houses. Each house then receives a portion of the deal and places it with its client base. The lead manager may elect to run the entire book alone, and miss out the other members of the management group.

A **bought deal** is where the lead manager agrees detailed terms with the issuer including the coupon and the maturity. In normal issues the lead manager has the ability to amend the terms of the issue as market conditions dictate. It is also common for the lead manager to place the entire deal themselves in these circumstances without forming a syndicate.

There are a number of variations on these methods of issue. Under a **fixed price reoffer**, the members of the management group are prohibited from selling the bonds in the secondary market at below the issue price until the syndicate has been broken. The syndicate will break when the lead manager believes the bulk of the issue has been placed.

8 INTERNATIONAL SETTLEMENT AND CLEARING

g objective **2.9.1 Explain** the settlement and clearing procedures overseas including the role of international central securities depositories, an appreciation of different settlement cycles and issues in managing global assets.

8.1 International markets settlement

8.1.1 Overview

	Order or quote driven	Settlement period: equities	Settlement period: Govt. bonds	Settlement agency
USA	NYSE – order* NASDAQ – quote	T + 3	T + 0	DTC DTC
Japan	TSE – order	T + 3	T + 3	TSE
Germany	Xetra – order	T + 2	T + 2	Clearstream
France	Order	T + 3	T + 3	Euroclear
UK	SETS – order SETSqx – quote and order SEAQ – quote	T + 3	T + 1	Euroclear UK & Ireland

* International trading on the NYSE is largely made up of American Depository Receipts (ADRs). ADRs will help facilitate the trading of non-US company shares within the US. ADRs settle T+3, are dominated in dollars and pay a dollar dividend.

8.2 Central securities depositories (CSDs)

8.2.1 Establishment of CSDs

In 1989, the Group of 30 (G30) recommended that each domestic market should establish a **Central Securities Depository (CSD)** to hold securities. The fundamental objectives for the establishment of a CSD are for gains in efficiencies and for reduction in risk. Efficiency gains are achieved through the elimination of manual errors, lower costs and increased speed of processing through automation, which all translate into lower risks. Most markets that did not already have established CSDs in 1989 have organised one or more CSDs and centralised local settlement through them.

8.2.2 Alternative holding systems

Almost all countries have some form of central depository where the securities are either immobilised or dematerialised.

- In a **'dematerialised' system**, there is no document which physically embodies the claim. The system relies on a collection of securities accounts, instructions to financial institutions which maintain those accounts, and confirmations of account entries.

- **Immobilisation** is common in markets that previously relied on physical share certificates, but the certificates are now immobilised in a depository, which is the holder of record in the register. Access by investors to the depository is typically through financial institutions which are members of the depository.

Through the establishment of CSDs, investors are able to reduce risks of loss, theft and illiquidity costs substantially by holding securities through one or more tiers of financial intermediaries such as banks or brokers.

There can be several types of holding systems. For example, some professional investors and financial intermediaries have direct contractual relationships with CSDs. They hold interests in securities through accounts on the records of the CSDs. Other investors, particularly retail investors, generally hold their interests through brokers or other financial intermediaries at a lower tier in the multi-tiered structure.

8.2.3 ICSDs and CSDs

International Central Securities Depositories (ICSDs) have established linkages with several domestic **CSDs** and have created a sub-custodian network.

The roles of ICSDs and CSDs are distinguished in the following Table.

ICSDs	CSDs
International client base	Domestic/local client base
Cross-border activity	Domestic activity only
All securities	Local securities only
Settlement	Settlement
Custody	Custody
Collateral management	
Other services	
Securities lending	

The principal ICSDs – **Euroclear** and **Clearstream** – have traditionally provided clearance and custody of Eurobonds and other Euromarket instruments. In recent years however they have increasingly become involved in settlement and custody of international equities.

CHAPTER ROUNDUP

- Equities may be listed on the primary markets (such as the LSE), and may be dual-listed in more than one country. The Alternative Investment Market (AIM) is the UK's less regulated second-tier market.

- The Debt Management Office (DMO) takes responsibility for issuing gilts on behalf of the Treasury.

- Secondary markets now include new competition from various Multilateral Trading Facilities.

- Where a market is order-driven, the relevant trading system will match buyers and sellers automatically, provided that they are willing to trade at prices compatible with each other. A quote-driven market requires certain market participants (market makers) to take responsibility for acting as buyers and sellers to the rest of the market so that there will always be a price at which a trade can be conducted.

- On the LSE, the SETS system (known as the Order Book, as it is an order-driven system) is used for the most liquid domestic equities. The London Clearing House (known as LCH.Clearnet) acts as the central counterparty to all SETS trades.

- SETSqx ('Stock Exchange Electronic Trading Service-quotes and crosses') has replaced SEAQ for all main market securities. SETSqx combines the market making quote-driven model and the order-driven model.

- In the gilts market, Gilt-Edged Market Makers (GEMMs) have the role of ensuring that there are two-way quotes at all times for all gilts.

- A Systematic Internaliser (SI) is an investment firm which deals on its own account by executing client orders outside a regulated market or a MTF.

- Settlement of UK equities, corporate bonds, gilts and money market instruments occurs through Euroclear UK & Ireland (EUI), which operates an electronic dematerialised settlement system.

- Operating an investment exchange is a regulated activity (arranging deals in investments) and therefore requires regulatory approval.

- The most important London market for financial futures and options is NYSE Liffe.

- Companies must release required information to the market through an official Regulatory Information Service (RIS) or other UKLA-approved Primary Information Provider (PIP) service.

- The Prospectus Directive requires that a prospectus is produced whenever there is a public offer of securities or where securities are admitted to trading on a regulated market. The Directive specifies the content of prospectuses and requires that they are approved by the relevant competent authority (FSA).

- The Combined Code on Corporate Governance aims to promote confidence in corporate reporting and governance, and to promote good governance.

- Companies legislation makes provisions on the conduct and structure of company meetings which will apply in the absence of any provisions to the contrary in the company's Memorandum and Articles.

- The UK derivatives exchanges, which include Liffe and the London Metals Exchange, are Recognised Investment Exchanges. Accordingly, the exchange mainly regulates the market, with the FSA being responsible for the financial soundness and conduct of business of exchange members.

- In the USA, there are two main relevant regulatory bodies, the Securities and Exchange Commission (SEC and the Commodity Futures Trading Commission (CFTC). There are plans to move OTC derivatives trading within clearing houses.

- Under IAS 39, derivatives must be recognised in the balance sheet at fair value (except those that are used as a hedge).

- The markets in major developed economies internationally share many features of the UK equity and bond markets. In many emerging economy markets however, bond and equity trading is OTC and is restricted to locally registered participants. Settlement systems in such markets tend to be run by central banks with no counterparty guarantees.

- The Eurobond market is an international market in debt. Companies issuing debt in the Eurobond market have their securities traded all around the world and are not limited to one domestic market place.

- Domestic markets have established Central Securities Depositories (CSDs) to hold securities. In a 'dematerialised' system, the system relies on a collection of securities accounts, instructions to financial institutions which maintain those accounts, and confirmations of account entries. With the alternative of immobilisation, certificates are immobilised in a depository, which is the holder of record in the register. International Central Securities Depositories (ICSDs) have established linkages with several domestic CSDs and have created a sub-custodian network.

TEST YOUR KNOWLEDGE

1. What role does the LCH.Clearnet play in SETS orders?

2. What is a GEMM?

3. What is the standard settlement for UK equities?

4. When do equities go ex-dividend?

5. Give two examples of Designated Investment Exchanges.

6. Explain the role of a NOMAD.

7. What is the main requirement of IAS 39?

8. Outline the main recommendation of Section E (Institutional shareholders) of the Combined Code on Corporate Governance.

9. How are US government bonds issued?

10. Explain what is meant by 'immobilisation' in the context of central depositories.

TEST YOUR KNOWLEDGE: ANSWERS

1. The LCH.Clearnet acts to guarantee all trades and so remove counterparty risk. This process is known as novation.

    (See Section 1.1.4)

2. A gilt-edged market maker. They provide liquidity for the gilt market.

    (See Section 1.4.2)

3. T + 3.

    (See Section 2.1)

4. Two business days prior to the books closed date.

    (See Section 2.3)

5. There are currently thirty Designated Investment Exchanges and they include, for example:

    - Tokyo Stock Exchange
    - New York Stock Exchange
    - New York Futures Exchange
    - International Capital Markets Association
    - Hong Kong Exchanges and Clearing Limited

    (See Section 3.5)

6. AIM companies must have an LSE-approved Nominated Advisor (NOMAD) to advise the directors on their responsibilities, and guide them through the AIM process. The NOMAD is retained to advise the directors once an AIM listing is granted. Should the company lose its NOMAD, it must appoint a new one (otherwise the listing will be suspended).

    (See Section 4.3.1)

7. The key requirement of IAS39 is that all derivatives held by an institution, except those designated as a hedge, must be stated in accounts at their fair value.

8. Section E of the 2008 Combined Code recommends an approach for institutional shareholders to take in the governance of portfolio firms whose shares they hold on behalf of beneficiaries.

    (See Section 5.5.6)

9. They are issued by Dutch Auction.

    (See Section 7.1)

10. Immobilisation is common in markets that previously relied on physical share certificates. The certificates are now immobilised in a depository, which is the holder of record in the register. Access by investors to the depository is typically through financial institutions which are members of the depository.

    (See Section 8.2.2)

3

Legal Concepts

INTRODUCTION

In this chapter, we cover some key legal concepts, whose meanings are quite precise. An important concept in law and business is that a company is a 'legal person' separate from its owners (its shareholders).

From time to time, a client of a financial adviser might run into financial difficulties, and face bankruptcy or, in the case of a corporate client, insolvency proceedings. It is important for the adviser to have a broad understanding of the legal and financial implications for the client in these circumstances.

We also gain an understanding of powers of attorney, the law on which was changed by the Mental Capacity Act 2005, and of trusts and trusteeship.

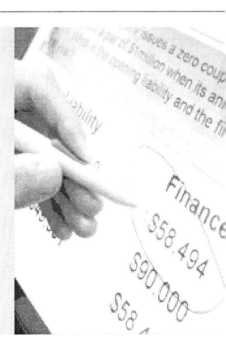

3　Legal concepts

Demonstrate an understanding of legal concepts relevant to financial advice

- **3.1.1 Explain** legal persons and power of attorney
- **3.1.2 Explain** basic law of contract and agency
- **3.1.3 Explain** the types of ownership of property
- **3.1.4 Explain** insolvency and bankruptcy
- **3.1.5 Explain** Wills and intestacy
- **3.1.6 Identify** the main types of trusts and their uses

1　LEGAL PERSONS AND POWER OF ATTORNEY

Learning objective	3.1.1 **Explain** legal persons and power of attorney.

1.1 Legal personality

A **legal person** possesses legal rights and is subject to legal obligations. In law, the term **person** is used to denote two categories of **legal person**.

- An individual human being is a **natural person**.
- The law also recognises **artificial persons** in the form of corporations.

A corporation, such as a limited company, is distinguished from an unincorporated association. An **unincorporated association** (for example, a partnership) is not a separate legal entity; it does not have a legal identity separate from that of its members.

1.2 Companies and limited liability

The most important consequence of registration of an enterprise as a company is that a company becomes a **legal person distinct from its owners**. The owners of a company are its members, or shareholders.

A significant consequence of the fact that the company is distinct from its members is that its members therefore have **limited liability**.

The **company** itself is **liable without limit for its own debts**. If the company buys plastic from another company, for example, it owes the other company money.

The members (shareholders) own the business, so they might be the people who the creditors logically asked to pay the debts of the company if the company is unable to pay them itself. Limited liability prevents this by stipulating the creditors of the company cannot demand the company's debts from members of the company, for example if the company fails.

Although the creditors of the company cannot ask the members of the company to pay the debts of the company, there are some amounts that members are required to pay, in the event of a winding-up.

Type of company	Amount owed by member at winding up
Company limited by shares	Any outstanding amount from when they originally purchased their shares. If the member's shares are fully paid, they do not have to contribute anything in the event of a winding-up.
Company limited by guarantee	The amount they guaranteed to pay in the event of a winding-up.

Liability is usually limited by **shares**. Companies limited by guarantee are appropriate to **non-commercial activities**, such as a charity or a trade association which aims to keep income and expenditure in balance but also have the members' guarantee as a form of reserve capital if it becomes insolvent.

A company, as a separate legal entity, may also have liabilities in tort (eg to pay damages for negligent acts) and crime. Criminal liability of companies is a topical area following events such as the Paddington train disaster.

It is currently extremely difficult to prosecute a company on criminal charges, as it is necessary to show a '*mens rea*', or controlling mind. Unless a company is very small it is difficult to show that the mind controlling the company was connected with the criminal act.

A company may be identified with those who control it, for instance to determine its residence for tax purposes. The courts may also ignore the distinction between a company and its members and managers if the latter use that distinction to **evade** their **legal obligations**.

1.3 Power of attorney

A **power of attorney** is a document made by a person ('the donor') which appoints another person ('the attorney' or 'the donee') or persons, to act for the donor in legal matters. An example of the use of a power of attorney is where the donee is given power to sign documents on behalf of the donor.

The power of attorney may be a **general** power, to allow the donee to act for the donor in all matters, or restricted to a **specific** act, for example to execute a specific document. In either case, the donor can still act himself. The donor is liable for the acts of the donee, for example, the donor would be bound by a document signed by the donee, provided that the donee has acted within the terms of the power of attorney.

1.4 Making a power of attorney

A general power of attorney may be set out in the form set out in s10 of the Powers of Attorney Act 1971. This shows the names of the donor and donee and states that the donee is appointed as attorney for the donor. The document must be executed as a deed. In general, this form cannot be used by trustees to delegate trustee powers. However, under s1 of the Trustee Delegation Act 1999, it can be so used in the case where the trustee is a co-owner of land and also has a beneficial interest in the land eg where land is held in joint ownership, whether as tenants in common or joint tenants.

A limited form of power of attorney should be drawn up by a lawyer and specify exactly the powers being given to the donee. It should be formally executed (as a deed).

A **trustee** may delegate his powers by executing a power of attorney under the terms of the Trustee Act 1925 (as amended). The delegation can be for a period up to twelve months in length. Notice of the execution of the power of attorney must be given within seven days to any person who has power to appoint trustees and to the other trustees.

1.5 Length of a power of attorney

An ordinary power of attorney (whether given as an individual or as a trustee) is only valid while the donor is capable of giving instructions. It can be revoked by the donor.

The power will also cease at the end of a time specified in it or when a specific act has been carried out, or if the donee dies or becomes incapacitated. Therefore it will cease to have effect if the donor becomes mentally incapacitated. For this reason, a **lasting power of attorney (LPA)** – explained below – may be advisable for many people, and it is probably a good idea to consider this at the same time as executing a **will**.

1.6 Mental Capacity Act 2005

The **Mental Capacity Act 2005** sets out a single **'decision-specific' test** for assessing whether a person lacks capacity to take a particular decision at a particular time. A lack of capacity cannot be established merely by reference to a person's age, appearance, or any aspect of a person's behaviour. Carers and family members have a right to be consulted.

The Act deals with two situations where a designated decision-maker can act on behalf of someone who lacks capacity.

- **Lasting powers of attorney (LPAs).**This is similar to the previous Enduring Power of Attorney (EPA), except that the Act also allows people to let an attorney make health and welfare decisions.

- **Court appointed deputies.** The Act provides for a system of court appointed deputies to replace the previous system of receivership in the Court of Protection.

1.7 Lasting power of attorney (LPA)

Lasting powers of attorney were established under the **Mental Capacity Act 2005**.

An LPA is a legal document that the Donor makes using a special form available from the **Office of the Public Guardian (OPG)**. It allows the Donor to choose someone now (the Attorney) that he or she trust to make decisions on the Donor's behalf about things such as the Donor's property and affairs or personal welfare at a time in the future when the Donor no longer wishes to make those decisions or may lack the mental capacity to make those decisions for himself or herself.

An LPA **can only be used** after it is registered with the **Office of the Public Guardian (OPG)**.

Where there is no power of attorney, the Court of Protection may make orders concerning the person's property and may appoint a **receiver** with specified powers to manage the person's affairs with the authority of the court.

Anyone aged 18 or over, with the capacity to do so, can make an LPA appointing one or more Attorneys to make decisions on their behalf. Someone cannot make an LPA jointly with another person; each person must make his or her own LPA.

If no lasting power of attorney is made before a person becomes incapable, it may be necessary to apply to the **Court of Protection** – a more cumbersome and possibly expensive procedure. The Court of Protection is intended to protect the finances of people who are no longer able to manage their own affairs.

There are two different types of LPA:

- **Personal Welfare LPA**
- **Property and Affairs LPA**

1.8 Personal Welfare LPA

A **Personal Welfare Lasting Power of Attorney (LPA)** allows a person to plan ahead by choosing one or more people to make decisions on their behalf regarding personal healthcare and welfare.

These personal welfare decisions can only be taken by somebody else when the person lacks the capacity to make them for himself or herself – for example, if the person is unconscious or because of the onset of a condition such as dementia.

The **Personal Welfare Attorney(s)** will only be able to use their power once the LPA has been registered and provided that the person cannot make the required decision for himself or herself.

A person can decide to give the Attorney the power to make decisions about any or all of their personal welfare matters, including healthcare matters. This could involve some significant decisions, such as:

- Giving or refusing consent to particular types of health care, including medical treatment decisions, or

- Whether the person continues to live in their own home, perhaps with help and support from social services, or whether residential care would be more appropriate

There is provision on the LPA form to give the Attorney(s) the power to make decisions about 'life-sustaining treatment', but this power must expressly be given.

The person can also give the Attorney(s) the power to make decisions about day-to-day aspects of their personal welfare, such as diet, dress or daily routine.

1.9 Property and Affairs LPA

A **Property and Affairs Lasting Power of Attorney (LPA)** allows someone to plan ahead by choosing one or more people to make decisions on their behalf regarding their property and financial affairs.

Someone can appoint a **Property and Affairs Attorney** to manage their finances and property while they still have capacity as well as when they lack capacity. For example, it may be easier to give someone the power to carry out tasks such as paying bills or collecting benefits or other income.

This might be easier for lots of reasons: someone might find it difficult to get about or to talk on the telephone, or they might be out of the country for long periods of time.

The Property and Affairs LPA does not allow the Attorney to make decisions about the person's personal welfare: this requires a **Personal Welfare LPA**.

1.10 Pre-existing Enduring Power of Attorney (EPA)

The Mental Capacity Act 2005 replaced the former Enduring Powers of Attorney (EPA). It is not possible to make any changes to an **existing EPA** or make a new one. However, an unregistered EPA can still be used and the Attorney will still need to register it with the OPG if they have reason to believe the person is, or is becoming, mentally incapable in the future.

Someone can also make an LPA to run alongside an EPA if they wish. For example, someone may have an existing EPA that makes provision for decisions about their property and affairs, and decide to make a Personal Welfare LPA to run alongside that, to provide for decisions concerning their healthcare and welfare.

Someone may also consider replacing your an unregistered EPA with a Property and Affairs LPA. An unregistered EPA can be revoked at any time while the person has the mental capacity to do so. However, if the EPA has been registered, it cannot be revoked except by permission of the Court of Protection.

The best way to revoke an unregistered EPA is to sign a formal document (called a 'Deed of Revocation').

1.11 Registering an LPA

An LPA can be registered at any time after it is made, with OPG. The Donor can register their own LPA providing they are able to make these sorts of decisions for themselves. Alternatively, the Attorney can register the LPA if they believe that the Donor is no longer able to make these decisions themselves.

To register the LPA, the applicant must complete a form to notify the people the Donor has said they want to be informed (the named persons) of the registration. If any of the named persons have concerns about the registration of the LPA – for example, if they feel that the Donor was put under pressure to make it – then they can object to the LPA being registered.

The OPG will check the LPA and the application form. If there are no problems, the OPG will set a registration due date. This date will be six weeks from the date that the OPG gives notice of the application to register to either the Donor or the Attorney(s), depending on who has made the application (for example, if the Donor applies to register the OPG will give notice of the application to the Attorneys). This is because everyone who is entitled to notice is also entitled to object to the application for registration. If there are any objections, it may not be possible to register the LPA until these have been resolved.

If there are no objections or problems with the application, the registered copy of the LPA will be sent within five working days of the end of the six-week waiting period.

The **Public Guardian** is responsible for establishing and maintaining a **register of LPAs**, as well as a **register of EPAs**.

2 CONTRACT AND AGENCY

Learning objective   3.1.2 **Explain** basic law of contract and agency.

2.1 Elements of a valid contract

A contract is a legally binding agreement between mutually consenting two parties who intend to enter into a legal relationship.

There are **three essential elements** to look for in the formation of a valid contract: **agreement, consideration** and **intention**.

The first essential element of a binding contract is **agreement**. To determine whether or not an agreement has been reached, the courts will consider whether one party has made a firm **offer** which the other party has **accepted**.

In most contracts, offer and acceptance may be made **orally** or in **writing**, or they may be implied by the conduct of the parties. The person making an offer is the offeror and the person to whom an offer is made is the offeree.

In life assurance, the **proposal form** makes up the offer which the life assurance company can either accept at standard rates or on special terms, or reject. If the assurance company accepts on special terms, it is effectively rejecting the proposal and making a counteroffer, which the proposer then either accepts or rejects.

The second of the three essential elements of a contract is **consideration**. The promise which a claimant seeks to enforce must be shown to be part of a bargain to which the claimant has himself contributed.

Third, an agreement is not a binding contract unless the parties **intend to create legal relations**. What matters is not what the parties have in their minds, but the inferences that reasonable people would draw from their words or conduct.

The requirements of standardisation in business have led to the **standard form contract**. The **standard form contract** is a document prepared by many large organisations setting out the terms on which they contract with their customers. The individual must usually take it or leave it.

2.2 Contract law and consumer protection

Many contracts are made between experts and ordinary consumers. The law will intervene only where the former takes unfair advantage of his position. The law seeks to protect the idea of '**freedom of contract**', although **contractual terms** may be regulated by **statute**, particularly where the parties are of unequal bargaining strength.

In the second half of the 20th century, there was a surge of interest in consumer matters. The development of a mass market for often complex goods has meant that the consumer can no longer rely on his own judgement when buying sophisticated goods or services.

Consumer interests are now served by two main areas.

- **Consumer protection agencies**, which include the Financial Services Authority, government departments (including the Office of Fair Trading) and independent bodies (including the Consumers' Association)

- **Legislation**, for example, Financial Services and Markets Act 2000, Consumer Credit Acts 1974 and 2006; Unfair Contract Terms Act 1977 and Unfair Terms in Consumer Contracts Regulations 1999

2.3 Form of a contract

As a general rule, **a contract may be made in any form**. It may be written, or oral, or inferred from the conduct of the parties. For example, a customer in a self-service shop may take his selected goods to the cash desk, pay for them and walk out without saying a word.

However, certain contracts must be in **writing**, such as for the purchase of land and property. Also bear in mind that specific consumer legislation or regulations may require certain agreements to be in a specified form, such as in writing or transmitted through a website.

2.4 Capacity to contract

Capacity to contract is the legal ability to enter into a contract.

- Someone who is **insane** may have their capacity to contract limited by law.
- **Minors** – that is, those under 18 – do not have unrestricted capacity to enter into contracts.

2.5 Legality of object

If you enter into an agreement with an accomplice to steal property, such a contract would be **illegal** and the contract would **not be valid**.

2.6 Utmost good faith

If you buy a used car from a private seller and find that it falls apart soon after you bought it, that usually is your problem. Provided that the seller answered honestly any questions that you asked, they were not obliged to volunteer information that you did not seek. The general principle here is: *caveat emptor* – 'let the buyer beware'.

However, if you make a proposal for insurance, including life insurance, you are expected to give to the insurance company **all relevant information** which will enable the company to assess the risk, eg if you are seriously ill or in a dangerous occupation or have a risky lifestyle, or whether you are a normal risk for which the company would issue a contract on standard terms.

This requirement to **disclose all relevant information** is fundamental to an insurance contract. If the rule is not observed the policy can be treated by the insurer as **voidable**. The requirement is termed **'utmost good faith'** or *uberrimae fidei.*

2.7 The agency relationship

'**Agents**' are engaged by '**principals**' generally in order to perform tasks which the principals cannot or do not wish to perform themselves, because the principal does not have the time or expertise to carry out the task. In normal circumstances, the agent discloses to the other party that he (the agent) is acting for a principal whose identity is also disclosed.

Agency is a relationship which exists between two legal persons (the **principal** and the **agent**) in which the function of the agent is to form a contract between his principal and a third party.

The relationship of principal and agent is usually created by mutual consent. The consent need not generally be formal nor expressed in a written document. **It is usually an 'express' agreement**, even if it is created in an informal manner.

When an agent agrees to perform services for his principal for reward there is a contract between them.

2.8 Examples of agency relationships

There are many examples of agency relationships which you are probably accustomed to, although you may not be aware that they are examples of the laws of agency. Some examples are as follows.

- **Partnerships.** A feature of partnerships is that the partners are agents of each other.

- **Brokers.** Any broker is essentially a middleman or intermediary who arranges contracts in return for commission or brokerage. For example, an **insurance broker** is an agent of an insurer who arranges contracts of insurance with the other party who wishes to be insured. However, in some contexts (for example, when the broker assists a car owner to complete a proposal form) he is also treated as the agent of the insured. Insurance, especially marine insurance, has complicated rules applicable to the relationship (insurer-broker-insured).

- **Appointed representatives of product providers.** A financial adviser who works as an appointed representative (tied adviser) for a product provider firm (such as a life office) is an **agent of the product provider firm**, while the firm is principal. The firm, as principal, is responsible for the acts and omissions of its appointed representatives (its agents) and must ensure that its agents comply with FSA rules.

- An **independent financial adviser (IFA)**, who offers advice on products from a full range of providers, is the **agent of his client** in respect of the advice or recommendations offered to the client. This is the case whether or not the IFA is a member or appointed representative of a

network. The insurer or other product provider is not liable for the acts or omissions of the IFA, and the IFA owes no duty to the product provider. The IFA owes a duty of care to his or her client.

2.9 Obligations of an agent

Even if the agent undertakes his duties without reward, the agent has obligations to his principal.

- **Performance and obedience.** The agent must **perform** his obligations, following his principal's instructions with **obedience**, unless to do so would involve an illegal act.

- **Skill and accountability.** The agent must act with the standard of **skill and care** to be expected of a person in his profession and to be **accountable** to his principal to provide full information on the agency transactions and to account for all moneys arising from them.

- **No conflict of interest.** The agent owes to his principal a duty not to put himself in a in a situation where his own interests conflict with those of the principal; for example, he must not sell his own property to the principal (even if the sale is at a fair price).

- **Confidence.** The agent must keep in **confidence** what he knows of his principal's affairs even after the agency relationship has ceased.

- **Any benefit** must be handed over to the principal unless he agrees that the agent may retain it. Although an agent is entitled to his agreed remuneration, he must account to the principal for any other benefits. If he accepts from the other party any commission or reward as an inducement to make the contract with him, it is considered to be a bribe and the contract is fraudulent.

2.10 Authority of the agent

The **contract** made by the agent is **binding** on the principal and the other party **only if** the **agent was acting within the limits of his authority** from his principal.

3 OWNERSHIP OF PROPERTY

g objective | 3.1.3 **Explain** the types of ownership of property.

3.1 Real property

In legal terminology, **land** includes buildings and anything else which is permanently attached to the land.

Real property (also called 'realty') is land owned in perpetuity – in other words, **freehold property.** The mediaeval common law courts granted special remedies: the right of the dispossessed owner to have the land returned to him. For that historical reason, land in freehold ownership is in a category (real property) of its own.

Freehold property is distinguished from **leasehold property**. With leasehold property (in legal terminology, 'chattels real'), the right of a tenant (or lessee) will come to an end either by expiry of a fixed period (which may be as much as 999 years) or by termination by notice (and in other more unlikely events). When it terminates the landlord (or lessor) resumes possession from the tenant. The landlord is therefore said to have a 'reversion' which becomes possession when the lease terminates. While the lease continues, the tenant has possession but is usually required to pay a rent to the landlord.

A **lease** is a form of **contract**. If granted for a term of more than three years it must generally be in the form of a **deed**.

3.2 Personal property

Personal property – or **'personalty'** – is anything owned that is not **realty**, ie **real property** (freehold land). It is so called because the owner's claim could be satisfied by payment of the value instead of returning the property – his claim was against the wrongdoer personally and he could not automatically recover the property or thing.

Personal property comprises:

- **Leasehold land**, and
- Pure **personalty** (including chattels and things in action)

Banknotes and coins are 'things in action'.

These technical legal terms can be significant. For example, someone (the **testator**) may by his **will** give his 'real estate' to A and his 'chattels' to B and his remaining personalty to C.

Moveable tangible property – generally called **chattels** – are literally those items of property of which ownership and possession can be transferred simply by delivery, such as furniture, books and jewellery.

3.3 Forms of co-ownership of land

It is possible for more than one person to own **land**. If land is purchased or transferred to two or more persons, these persons become either **joint tenants** or **tenants in common**. (Note that this applies to owning freehold land outright, even though the word 'tenant' is used.)

- **Joint tenancy** is where two or more people acquire land but no words of 'severance' are used. This means that the transfer does not state what share in the land each person has. The land is merely 'held by X and Y'. It is both legal and equitable co-ownership. **Joint tenancy** is a convenient and commonly used way for a husband and wife to own the matrimonial home. If one of the couple dies, the other will have title to the whole property.

- **Tenants in common** have shares in the land. For instance, a conveyance may state that the land should go to 'P, Q and R equally' – each then owns one-third part of the interest. It is equitable ownership. If P subsequently dies, his or her one-third share goes into P's estate: Q and R still own a one-third share each.

3.4 Significance of the type of ownership

The importance of the distinction is that if a **joint tenant** dies his interest lapses and the land is owned wholly by the survivor(s). He may not pass his interest on by **will**. The advantage is that only a limited number of interests can exist. The disadvantage is the fact that survival decides ownership. With tenants in common, each tenant can bequeath his interest which means that a house owned by tenants in common (A, B and C equally) will, if C dies and leaves his interest to D, E, F and G, be owned by A, B, (one-third part each) D, E, F and G (one-twelfth part each). While perhaps being fairer, this can be cumbersome!

The Law of Property Act 1925 achieved a compromise by providing that, where land is owned by two or more persons, no more than four of those persons hold the **legal estate** as joint tenants and trustees, for the benefit or **equitable interest** of themselves and other co-owners. Thus transfers can be effected by four signatures but the sale proceeds are subject to trusts so that all the owners get fair shares.

4 BANKRUPTCY AND INSOLVENCY

g objective **3.1.4 Explain** insolvency and bankruptcy.

4.1 Bankruptcy

Bankruptcy occurs when an individual's financial affairs are taken over by a court. The individual's assets are transferred into a **trust** which is used to repay as much debt as possible.

The term 'bankruptcy' applies to individuals, not to companies. A sole trader or partner who owes money (a debtor) and is unable to pay the debt could be faced with bankruptcy proceedings.

Inability to pay a debt will occur when the individual cannot find the money. Inadequate cash flow, rather than a loss-making business, may be the problem. Typically, the business will have insufficient cash coming in to meet its various payment obligations, and will be unable to borrow more money. In this situation, the individual's business will have more current liabilities than liquid assets.

The current legislation dealing with bankruptcy is the **Insolvency Act 1986**, as amended by the **Insolvency Act 2000** and the **Enterprise Act 2002**.

4.2 Creditors' petition for a bankruptcy order

Bankruptcy proceedings against an individual begin with the presentation of a petition for a **bankruptcy order** to the court. (This could be the High Court or a County Court with power to deal with such proceedings.)

The petitioner is usually a creditor, or several creditors acting jointly. (However, a debtor may petition to have himself/herself declared bankrupt.) The court will not entertain a petition from a creditor unless the creditor is owed at least £750 (currently) on an unsecured debt.

A creditor's petition must allege that the debtor is unable to pay the debt or has very little prospect of being able to pay it. This inability to pay must be demonstrated in court by showing one of the following:

- That a **'statutory demand'** (in the prescribed form) has been served on the debtor, requiring him or her to pay, and this demand has not been satisfied within three weeks

- That a **judgement debt** (ie a payment ordered by a court or judge) has been returned unsatisfied, in whole or in part

In the time between the presenting of a petition for a bankruptcy order and the court's decision, the debtor may be tempted to dispose of some of his or her property, in order to put it outside the reach of the creditors. Under the Insolvency Act 1986, however, any disposal of property or payment of money after a petition has been presented will be **void** if the debtor is subsequently judged to be bankrupt, **unless** the court approves the disposal or payment.

When a petition for a bankruptcy order has been presented, the court may decide to make a bankruptcy order, i.e. declare the individual bankrupt. The bankruptcy of the individual begins on the day this order is made.

When a bankruptcy order has been made, the Official Receiver takes control of the debtor's assets, as **receiver and manager**. The Official Receiver is an official of the Department of Business, Innovation and Skills and an officer of the court.

The duty of the receiver and manager is to protect the bankrupt's property until a **trustee in bankruptcy** has been appointed.

4.3 Trustee in bankruptcy

The function of the **trustee in bankruptcy** is to get possession of and realise the value of the bankrupt's assets, and distribute them to the creditors, in accordance with the Insolvency Act.

Every bankruptcy is under the general control of the court, which has wide powers to control the trustee.

All property owned by the debtor on the date of the bankruptcy order, and any property acquired subsequently, passes to the trustee. The only items of property the debtor is allowed to retain are:

- The tools of his/her trade
- A vehicle, if one is needed for his/her trade or employment
- Clothing, bedding and furniture belonging to the debtor and his/her family

4.4 Income payments order

As regards the income of a bankrupt person, the trustee is entitled only to the excess income above what is needed to support the bankrupt and his/her family. Income includes income from employment or holding office and profits from carrying on a business. The trustee can apply to the court, claiming for all such excess income to belong to the bankrupt's estate.

The court may then make an **income payments order**, permitting the debtor to receive an income from his/her trade or employment. However, the trustee may take any income in excess of what is considered reasonable.

4.5 Disposal of matrimonial homes

If the debtor owns his/her own **home**, and lives alone, lives with a co-habitee and/ or lives with adult children, the debtor's interest in the home passes to the trustee. The trustee will immediately obtain a court order for sale of the property.

If the **matrimonial home** is owned by the bankrupt's spouse or former spouse, the trustee should not normally have an interest in the property for the bankrupt's estate. However, if the property has been transferred by the bankrupt to the spouse under suspicious circumstances, the trustee can apply to the court to have a claim on the property for the bankrupt's estate.

After one year from the date of the bankruptcy order, it is presumed that the needs of the creditors outweigh all other considerations, unless there are exceptional circumstances. As a consequence, after that time a court order can probably be obtained for the eviction of the debtor and his/her family, and for the sale of the home.

Under the Enterprise Act 2002, there is a limit of three years during which the trustee in bankruptcy can deal with the bankrupt's interest in the home. After this period it will revert back to the bankrupt.

Banks and other **lenders of mortgage finance** to buy a matrimonial home need to be aware of the potential problems in the event of the borrower's bankruptcy. Before granting a mortgage, the lender will ask about any potential legal or beneficial interest in the property of a person other than the borrower. The lender might insist that the mortgage should be in joint names. If one person is declared bankrupt, the other person remains subject to the mortgage, and is responsible for the mortgage payments in full.

4.6 Distribution of assets following a bankruptcy order

The job of the trustee is to dispose of the bankrupt's assets, and distribute the proceeds to the creditors.

The debts of the bankrupt person must be paid by the trustee in the following order of priority:

- The costs of the bankruptcy (including the professional fees of the trustee)
- Preferential debts. Preferential debts include:
  - Accrued holiday pay owed to employees
  - Wages and salaries of employees due in the last four months before the bankruptcy order, subject to a maximum amount per employee (currently £800).
- Ordinary unsecured creditors. These can only be paid once the other categories of debt have been paid in full. If the proceeds from selling the bankrupt's assets are insufficient, these creditors are treated equally. For example, if there is £50,000 left over from the disposal of assets to pay ordinary unsecured creditors of £100,000, each unsecured creditor will receive 50p in the £1 on their unpaid debt.

Example: Creditors

A bankruptcy order was made against Peter Wilton. The trustee eventually disposed of his home, which was subject to a £170,000 mortgage, for £250,000. His other assets realised £200,000. Preferential debts were £25,000, the costs of bankruptcy were £15,000 and unsecured creditors totalled £500,000.

How much did unsecured creditors receive?

Solution

Realisation of:

	£
Home	80,000
Other assets	200,000
	280,000
Bankruptcy costs	(15,000)
Preferential debts	(25,000)
	240,000

Unsecured creditors will receive £240,000/£500,000 = 48p in the pound.

4.7 Voidable transactions by the bankrupt

A trustee in bankruptcy has a duty to obtain the most money possible in order to pay the bankrupt's creditors. If the bankrupt undertakes certain transactions that harm the interests of the creditors (or harm some creditors at the expense of others), the trustee can apply to the court for the transactions to be declared void.

4.8 Automatic discharge of bankruptcy order

Following the enactment of the Enterprise Act 2002, a bankruptcy order is normally discharged automatically **one year** after the date of the order. This means that the individual is no longer a bankrupt, and is free of debts, even if these have not been paid in full. Once the bankruptcy order has been discharged, any property subsequently obtained by the ex-bankrupt belongs to him/her, and does not vest in the trustee.

4.9 Bankruptcy Restriction Orders

Bankruptcy Restriction Orders (BROs) are designed to protect the public from a bankrupt whose conduct has been irresponsible or reckless. A BRO imposes restrictions that apply after a bankrupt has been discharged. The restrictions can apply for between two and fifteen years.

4.10 Insolvency

The law on **corporate insolvency** in the UK is similar in many respects to the law on bankruptcy. The courts responsible for administering corporate insolvency law are the High Court (Chancery Division) and the county courts. (This section deals with the law in England and Wales. The law in Scotland differs in some respects.) The **Insolvency Act 2000** and the **Enterprise Act 2002** introduced major changes to corporate insolvency laws.

4.11 Aims of insolvency law

The purpose of insolvency law is to govern what should happen to the property of a company that is insolvent. The basic aims of the law are to:

- **Protect** the creditors of the company
- **Balance** the interests of competing groups
- **Control or punish** directors responsible for the company's financial collapse
- **Encourage** 'rescue' operations

4.12 Tests of corporate insolvency

There are two tests of corporate insolvency as follows.

- **Inability to pay debts when they fall due.** A company can be the subject of a winding-up petition if it fails to pay an undisputed debt, currently of more than £750.

- A **'balance sheet test'.** A company can be deemed insolvent if its liabilities exceed its assets.

It is important to be able to establish whether a company is solvent or insolvent.

- It is often a requirement for a company to be deemed insolvent for insolvency proceedings to be started.

- In the case of a voluntary liquidation, the liquidation cannot be initiated by the members (company shareholders) if the company is insolvent.

4.13 Types of insolvency proceeding

There are three types of corporate insolvency 'officials', depending on whether a company goes into **administration, receivership** or **liquidation**.

- **Administration. Administrators** are officers of the court. They may be appointed under an administration order or may be appointed by companies and directors without a court order. The purpose of an administration is to provide a better way of realising the company's assets than could be achieved by a liquidation or receivership (see below), when the company is in financial difficulties.

- **Receivership.** In most cases, **a receiver is appointed out of court by a debenture holder (usually a bank)** in pursuance of powers to do so contained in the debenture. A receiver is concerned principally with the interests of the secured creditors who appointed him and will try to take control of the charged assets. If the receiver is appointed under a debenture giving a general floating charge over the company's assets, he will be an **administrative receiver** and take over the management.of the company's property. The Enterprise Act 2002 largely abolished administrative receivership, in favour of a more streamlined procedure than there used to be for appointing an administrator.

- **Liquidation**. A **liquidator** acts mainly in the interests of **unsecured creditors** and **members** (shareholders) of the company. Liquidators of insolvent companies might be appointed either:

    - Under a voluntary liquidation arrangement, or
    - Following an unsecured creditor's petition to the court for liquidation of the company

    Liquidation means that the company must be dissolved and its affairs 'wound up', or brought to an end. The assets are realised, debts are paid out of the proceeds, and any surplus amounts are returned to members. Liquidation leads on to dissolution of the company.

4.14 Fraudulent and wrongful trading

If, when a company is wound up, it appears that its business has been carried on with **intent** to **defraud creditors** or others, the court may decide that the persons (usually the directors) who were knowingly parties to the fraud shall be **personally responsible** for debts and other liabilities of the company: s213 Insolvency Act 1986.

5   WILLS AND INTESTACY

g objective   **3.1.5 Explain** wills and intestacy.

5.1 Wills and administration of an estate

A **will** is a legal document which gives effect to the wishes of an individual (the **testator**, if male, the **testatrix** if female) as to how their estate should be distributed after their death. It appoints the persons who will have the responsibility for dealing with the estate (the **executors**, also called **personal representatives**) and gives instructions as to how the estate should be distributed.

A will must be signed in the presence of two witnesses. A **witness** or the **spouse of a witness** cannot benefit from a will. If a witness or the spouse of a witness is named as a beneficiary, the will is not made invalid, but that person will not be able to inherit under the will.

The executors need to obtain a **Grant of Probate** from the Probate Registry to show they are entitled to **administer the estate**. Then they can collect the assets of the estate. The executors are responsible for settling all liabilities of the estate before paying out the money to the beneficiaries. The liabilities include funeral expenses, inheritance tax (in respect of which the executors must submit an account and pay any IHT due before obtaining the **Grant of Probate**), liabilities incurred while the testator was alive and expenses incurred during the period of administration (ie while the estate is under the control of the executors). The estate cannot be paid out to the beneficiaries until all liabilities have been settled and the executors are satisfied that no claims will be made against the estate.

The assets comprising the estate are held by the executors on trust for the beneficiaries until they are distributed to them. Usually this will only last as long as it takes to administer the estate. However, longer term trusts are frequently created by wills. The trustees of these can be separate individuals to the executors and the trust terms can be the same as those of lifetime (*inter vivos*) trusts. Trusts are typically created to cater for minors. Another common use is the creation of a **discretionary trust** to use the inheritance tax nil rate band of the first of a married couple to die.

An important reason to effect a will is for a parent to indicate whom they would like as **guardians** to care for minor children. If this is not done (or if there are objections to the parent's choice), the guardians will be appointed by a court.

A will is made **invalid** if the testator **marries**, unless the testator expressly stated that the will was made in contemplation of marriage. If the testator **divorces**, bequests in favour of the **ex-spouse** no longer have effect.

5.2 Reasons for making a will

There are the following reasons for making a will.

- To arrange for beneficiaries other than those appointed under the intestacy rules to benefit. Unmarried partners and stepchildren cannot benefit other than by a will. Children of a previous marriage might also lose out if the testator remarries.

- To use tax reliefs and allowances

- To create trusts to cater for the long-term needs of the beneficiaries or to enable capital to skip generations

- To choose executors and trustees and to extend their statutory powers

- To specify funeral arrangements

5.3 Intestacy

An individual who dies without a will is known as an **intestate**. The estate of an intestate individual is dealt with under the Administration of Estates Act 1925 and the Intestates Estates Act 1952 as follows. What is stated about **spouses** below applies also to same-sex **civil partners** who have formed a civil partnership under the **Civil Partnership Act 2004**.

- Where the intestate leaves:

    A surviving spouse (or civil partner) but no issue (children, grandchildren and so on) and no parent, brother or sister of the whole blood or issue thereof, the surviving spouse takes the whole estate absolutely.

    A surviving spouse and issue: the surviving spouse take the personal chattels plus a statutory legacy of £250,000 (with interest up to payment). The residue, if any, is held 50% on trust for the benefit of the surviving spouse for life and thereafter on statutory trusts for the issue and 50% immediately on statutory trusts for the issue.

    A surviving spouse, no issue but one or more of: parent, brother or sister of the whole blood or their issue; the surviving spouse takes the personal chattels plus the remainder up to £450,000 (with interest up to payment) plus 50% of the residue absolutely. The other half is taken by the parents in equal shares and if none to the brothers and sisters of the whole blood or their issue on statutory trusts.

    Issue but no surviving spouse: the whole estate is held on statutory trusts for the benefit of the issue.

No surviving spouse or issue: the estate is distributed as follows.

Relatives surviving	Interest taken
Both parents	The whole in equal shares
One parent	The whole
Brothers and sisters of the whole blood (same two parents)	The whole on statutory trusts
Brothers and sisters of the half blood (one parent in common)	The whole on statutory trusts
Grandparents	The whole in equal shares
Uncles and aunts of the whole blood (same two parents as deceased's parent)	The whole on statutory trusts
Uncles and aunts of the half blood (one parent in common with deceased's parent)	The whole on statutory trusts
If no relative takes an absolute interest	The Crown takes the whole

- Issue means children, grandchildren and so on. Adopted children are treated as children of their adoptive parents, not their natural parents. If a child predeceases the intestate person, that child's children takes his share, if more than one, equally.

- A surviving spouse is one still legally married to the deceased. An ex-spouse has no rights under the rule of intestacy nor has an unmarried partner.

- Under the statutory trusts, the entitlements of minor children are held on trust until they attain the age of eighteen years.

The **Law Reform (Succession) Act 1995** provides that a spouse must survive the deceased by 28 days in order to be entitled to a share. If the spouse dies within 28 days, distribution takes place as if there were no surviving spouse.

5.4 Mirror and mutual wills

A husband and wife or an unmarried couple may make wills in similar terms. For example, the husband may make a will which leaves his estate to his spouse, if she survives him, failing that to their children. The wife's will leaves her estate to her husband, if he survives her, failing that to their children. Such wills are called **mirror or reciprocal wills**.

Under general legal principles, a will may be revoked at any time. This also applies to mirror/reciprocal wills. In particular, after one of the spouses has died, the other may alter his or her will, for example in favour of a new spouse.

Under the doctrine of **mutual wills**, two persons (often husband and wife) **make an agreement** that their property is to devolve in a certain way. For example, the agreement may specify that on the first of them to die the deceased's property passes to the survivor, and after his or her death, the property of both of them passes to nominated beneficiaries, such as their children. The agreement must amount to a contract, not merely an understanding.

Clearly, this is very similar to the creation of mirror wills and it will be important to show that there was indeed an agreement to create mutual wills (which are effectively irrevocable dispositions), not merely mirror wills.

If it is decided that mutual wills have been made, the law will allow the ultimate beneficiaries to enforce the agreement.

6 TRUSTS AND THEIR USES

3.1.6 **Identify** the main types of trusts and their uses.

6.1 What is a trust?

A **trust** is an equitable obligation (see below for an explanation of 'equitable') in which certain persons (the **trustees**) are bound to deal with property over which they have control (the **trust property**) for the benefit of certain individuals (the **beneficiaries**).

The trustees may also be beneficiaries of the trust. An individual who transfers assets into a trust during his lifetime is known as a **settlor** and such trusts are known as **settlements**. A settlor may also be a trustee and/or a beneficiary. A trust may also be set up in a **will** and is then usually called a **will trust**. Where the trust is set down in writing, this document is called the '**trust instrument**'.

6.2 Trustees and beneficiaries: equitable interest

The word **'equity'** derives from the Latin word meaning justice or fairness.

Trusts are an invention of the law of equity. Originally the law of England was made up primarily of ancient customs which varied from one region to another. This was eventually compiled into a law which was uniform throughout England and known as the **common law**.

Over time, common law attained a definite shape but it did not tend to evolve sufficiently fast to cater for the changing needs of society. In particular, it tended to look at the form of a transaction (e.g. in a land purchase whose name appeared on the title deeds) rather than the substance (e.g. who provided the purchase money). It therefore became customary for individuals to appeal to the King's Chancellor in circumstances where the enforcement of common law would have been unduly harsh. The King's Chancellor was empowered by the King to give redress and relief from the full effects of common law where conscience indicated that this was appropriate.

Eventually definite principles were evolved and these were compiled into a system of rules. These rules became known as **Equity**. For example, equity would recognise the interest of the provider of purchase monies whether or not that person's name appeared on the title deeds.

Equity and common law frequently conflicted and in 1873 the Judicature Act provided that equity should override common law. The Act also provided that all courts could administer both types of law. The two types of law, however still remain distinct. Legal rights (those derived under common law) and equitable rights (those derived under equity) therefore need to be distinguished from each other.

Trusts encompass both types of interest. The **legal title** (ie legal ownership) to the property in a trust will be held by the **trustees** whereas the **equitable (or beneficial) interest** will belong to the **beneficiaries**. For example, land could be transferred to the trustees and the legal title would be in their names. Equity would recognise that the land was not transferred to the trustees for their own benefit but to be held for the benefit of the beneficiaries in accordance with the terms of the trust. If the trustees do not act in accordance with the terms of the trust, the beneficiaries may apply to the Court to enforce the trust.

6.3 Types of trust

A trust may be a **bare trust**, also known as a **simple trust**, where there is a sole beneficiary. In such a trust, the trustee has no discretion over payment of income or capital to the beneficiary, who has an immediate and absolute right to both capital and income. The beneficiary of the trust can instruct the trustee how to manage the trust property, and has the right to take actual possession of the trust property at any time.

An **interest in possession trust** arises where a beneficiary, known as an 'income beneficiary' or a 'life interest', has a legal right to the income or other benefit derived from the trust property as it arises. For example, the **life interest** may have the right to occupy a house during his or her lifetime, or an **income beneficiary** the right to receive income from the trust property for a specified period or until death. On the death of the life interest/income beneficiary, the assets of the trust will be held for the benefit of the second class of beneficiary, known as the **remainderman** or the reversionary interest. A trustee of an interest in possession trust has the duty to safeguard the interests of both classes of beneficiary.

A trust may be a **discretionary trust** where the trustees exercise their discretion as to which beneficiaries will be entitled to receive income or capital from the trust. The exact rights of each beneficiary are not determined in advance. This can be of use in family situations. First of all, it may enable the settlor to control the conduct of the beneficiaries by the trustee's use of discretionary powers. Second, it keeps the trust flexible. For example, the settlor can constitute a discretionary trust for the benefit of a class of people, such as his grandchildren. If a new grandchild is born after the trust is set up, the grandchild will automatically rank as a beneficiary.

For **inheritance tax (IHT)** purposes, there is a **chargeable lifetime transfer (CLT)** when a discretionary trust or an interest in possession trust is set up. The trust suffers an IHT **principal charge** once every ten years and an **exit charge** when property leaves the trust.

Charitable trusts are those set up for the purpose of charitable deeds, defined as the relief of poverty, the advancement of religion, the advancement of education or purposes beneficial to the community. Such trusts enable the settlor to give some degree of individuality to a gift, specifying how it may be used and, as **charities**, are basically free from tax.

6.4 Uses of trusts

6.4.1 Overview

Trusts are useful vehicles for non-tax reasons such as to preserve family wealth, to provide for those who are deemed to be incapable (minors, and the disabled) or unsuitable (due to youth or poor business sense) to hold assets directly.

6.4.2 Will trusts

A discretionary trust may be set up by will. The rate of inheritance tax on principal charges and exit charges within the trust will then depend on the settlor's cumulative transfers in the seven years before his death and the value of the trust property. The discretionary trust allows the transferee flexibility about who is to benefit from the trust and to what extent. This can be useful if there are beneficiaries of differing ages and whose financial circumstances may differ.

6.4.3 Lifetime trusts

Although gifts to trusts during lifetime can lead to an IHT charge (a CLT), there can be tax benefits from setting up trusts during the settlor's lifetime. As long as the cumulative total of CLTs in any seven-year period does not exceed the nil rate band there will be no lifetime IHT to pay on creation of the trust. The trust will be subject to IHT at 0% on the ten-year anniversary and later advances, unless the value of the trust property grows faster than the nil rate band.

If a discretionary trust is used, the settlor can preserve the maximum flexibility in the class of beneficiaries and how income and capital should be dealt with.

If the settlor is included as a beneficiary of the trust the gift will be treated as a gift with reservation.

6.4.4 Family settlements

As mentioned above, the purpose of many trusts is to enable the wealthy to retain their wealth. Trusts will tie up wealth within the family and will often be constructed to minimise tax liabilities. They may be created through a will but will often be set up when the settlor is alive, to make tax planning easier.

Key benefits to the family

- Controlling who owns and receives benefit from the property
- Potential reduction of tax liabilities
- Giving someone the benefit of property while preventing them from wasting it through careless actions

For example, a house may be left on trust so that one member of the family can use it during their lifetime (i.e. have a **life interest in possession**), while another member can receive the house when the person with the life interest dies (i.e. the **remainderman**).

6.4.5 Those who cannot hold property on their own behalf

Unincorporated associations (for example, some charities, trade unions or clubs) are unable to own property, since they are not legally recognised as persons. In such a case, the property can be held on behalf of the association by a trustee.

Children under the age of 18 are not allowed to have legal ownership of land. In order to give land to a child, a trust will need to be set up for the benefit of the child, who can receive legal ownership of the land on reaching his or her majority.

6.4.6 Marriage

Whereas most of the trusts mentioned above will be expressly made, a trust in the context of marriage or cohabitation will often be a **resulting trust**. An example would be a situation where a house is held in the name of one of the two partners (X) but the other partner (Y) has contributed money to purchase the house. Since the house is intended to be occupied jointly, X may have legal ownership of the house but is holding part of the interest on trust for Y, even if this were not stated explicitly.

6.4.7 Confidentiality

Leaving property through a trust can protect the identity of the beneficial owner, who will only be known to the trustee. Such a trust will be referred to as a '**secret trust**'.

CHAPTER ROUNDUP

- In law, an individual human being is a natural person, while a corporation, such as a limited company, is also a legal person: a legal entity separate from the natural persons connected with it, for example its members or shareholders.

- A power of attorney is a document made by a person ('the donor') which appoints another person ('the attorney' or 'the donee') or persons, to act for the donor in legal matters. With Lasting Powers of Attorney, established under the Mental Capacity Act 2005, an attorney can make health and welfare decisions, or the attorney may be limited to making decisions about property and affairs of the person.

- A contract is a legally binding agreement between mutually consenting two parties who intend to enter into a legal relationship. Elements to look for in the formation of a valid contract are: agreement, consideration and intention. As a general rule, a contract may be made in any form.

- An insurance contract requires the proposer of the contract to disclose all relevant information, as it is an 'utmost good faith' (*uberrimae fidei*) contract.

- Agency is a relationship which exists between two legal persons (the principal and the agent) in which the function of the agent is to form a contract between his principal and a third party.

- Real property ('realty') is land owned in perpetuity – freehold property. Personal property ('personalty') –is any property that is not realty.

- When an individual is declared bankrupt, his or her financial affairs are taken over by a court and the individual's assets are transferred into a trust used to repay debt.

- The basic aims of the law on corporate insolvency are to: protect the creditors of the company; balance the interests of competing groups; control or punish directors responsible for the company's financial collapse; and encourage 'rescue' operations.

- A will is a legal document giving effect to the wishes of the testator (male), or the testatrix (female) on how their estate should be distributed after their death. It also appoints the executors (or 'personal representatives'), who have responsibility for dealing with the estate.

- The estate of an intestate individual who dies intestate (leaving no will) is dealt with under rules laid down by the Administration of Estates Act 1925 and the Intestates Estates Act 1952.

- A trust is an equitable obligation in which the trustees are bound to deal with the trust property for the benefit of the beneficiaries of the trust. Typical ways in which trusts are applied include: will trusts; lifetime trusts; family settlements; unincorporated associations; land gifted for children; protecting the identity of a beneficial owner.

TEST YOUR KNOWLEDGE

1.   What types of legal person does the law recognise?

2.   What types of power of attorney may be set up under the Mental Capacity Act 2005?

3.   What are the three essential elements of a valid contract?

4.   Give two cases or persons who do not have the legal capacity to enter into a contract.

5.   Outline what is meant by an agency relationship.

6.   'A leasehold interest is a form of real property': True or False?

7.   Mr W and Mrs W own their house in such a way that, if one of the couple dies, the other will own it in full. What form of joint ownership is this?

8.   Outline the function of the Trustee in Bankruptcy.

9.   Outline what a will is, and what it does.

10.   Outline what a trust is.

11.   What would be the likely purpose of a secret trust?

TEST YOUR KNOWLEDGE: ANSWERS

1. An individual human being is a natural legal person. The law also recognises artificial legal persons in the form of corporations.

    (See Section 1.1)

2. Two types of Lasting Power of Attorney (LPA) are possible:

    - Personal Welfare LPA
    - Property and Affairs LPA

    (See Section 1.7)

3. The three essential elements to look for in the formation of a valid contract are: agreement, consideration and intention.

    (See Section 2.1)

4. Someone who is insane; someone who is under 18 years of age.

    (See Section 2.4)

5. Agency is a relationship which exists between two legal persons (the principal and the agent) in which the function of the agent is to form a contract between his principal and a third party.

    (See Section 2.7)

6. False. Leasehold property is a form of personalty.

    (See Section 3.2)

7. A joint tenancy.

    (See Section 3.3)

8. The job of the trustee in bankruptcy is to get possession of and realise the value of the bankrupt's assets, and distribute them to the creditors, in accordance with the Insolvency Act.

    (See Section 4.3)

9. A will is a legal document giving effect to the wishes of an individual (the testator, if male, the testatrix if female) as to how their estate should be distributed after their death. It appoints the persons who will have the responsibility for dealing with the estate (the executors, also called personal representatives) and gives instructions as to how the estate should be distributed.

    (See Section 5.1)

10. A trust is an equitable obligation (see below for an explanation of 'equitable') in which certain persons (the trustees) are bound to deal with property over which they have control (the trust property) for the benefit of certain individuals (the beneficiaries).

    (See Section 6.1)

11. Leaving property through a 'secret' trust can protect the identity of the beneficial owner, who will only be known to the trustee.

    (See Section 6.4.7)

4

Regulation of Financial Services

INTRODUCTION

The FSA, HM Treasury and the Bank of England act as the 'tripartite authorities' in respect of ensuring financial stability. The Treasury has some specific responsibilities regarding the FSA. Future changes will see the FSA abolished and the Bank of England will have much wider regulatory powers.

The Takeover Panel regulates takeovers in the UK and acts independently of the FSA. We also look in this Chapter at some other bodies that play a role in the regulatory system.

Other issues to cover in this section of the syllabus include the Trustee Act 2000, the Pensions Act 2004 and the Statement of Investment Principles.

CHAPTER LEARNING OBJECTIVES

4 **Regulation of financial services**

Demonstrate an understanding of the regulation of financial services

4.1.1 **Distinguish** between the regulatory bodies of the Financial Services Authority (FSA), HM Treasury and the Bank of England

4.1.2 **Explain** the function of the following bodies/persons

- The Panel for Takeovers and Mergers
- The Department for Business, Innovation and Skills
- The Office of Fair Trading
- The Competition Commission
- The Information Commissioner

4.1.3 **Explain** the make-up of the Panel on Takeovers and Mergers (the takeover panel) and how it is financed

4.1.4 **Explain** the regulatory power of the City Code on Takeovers and Mergers

4.1.5 **Explain** the main provisions of the City Code including the bid timetable

4.1.6 **Explain** the scope of the Financial Services and Markets Act 2000

4.1.7 **Explain** the scope of the Regulated Activities Order 2001 (as amended) in terms of:

- Regulated activities
- Regulated investments

4.1.8 **Explain** the purpose and scope of the FSA's rules regarding Senior Management Arrangements, Systems and Controls (SYSC)

4.1.9 **Explain** the purpose and scope of the Trustee Act 2000

- The rights and duties of the parties involved
- The nature of the trust deed
- Investment powers of trustees

4.1.10 **Explain** the significance of the Pensions Act 2004

- Scheme-specific funding requirement
- The Pensions Regulator
- The Pension Protection Fund

4.11 **Explain** the purpose of a Statement of Investment Principles

1 THE TRIPARTITE AUTHORITIES

4.1.1 Distinguish between the regulatory bodies of the Financial Services Authority (FSA), HM Treasury and the Bank of England.

1.1 FSA as the UK statutory regulator

The creation of the FSA as the UK's main **statutory regulator** for the industry brought together regulation of investment, insurance and banking.

With the implementation of FSMA 2000, the FSA took over responsibility in 2001 for:

- Prudential supervision of all firms, which involves monitoring the adequacy of their management, financial resources and internal systems and controls, and

- Conduct of business regulations of those firms doing investment business. This involves overseeing firms' dealings with investors to ensure, for example, that information provided is clear and not misleading

Arguably, the FSA's role as rule-maker has been diminished by the requirements of EU Single Market Directives – in particular, the far-reaching **Markets in Financial Instruments Directive (MiFID)**, implemented in November 2007 – as the FSA has increasingly needed to apply rules which have been formulated at the **European level**.

1.2 The Bank of England

The responsibility of the **UK's central bank**, the **Bank of England**, for banking supervision was transferred to the **Financial Services Authority (FSA)** as part of the **Bank of England Act 1998**. Despite losing responsibility for banking supervision, the Bank of England ('the Bank') gained the role in 1998 of **setting official UK interest rates**, a role carried out by the Bank's **Monetary Policy Committee (MPC)**.

The Bank also seeks to maintain stability in the financial system by analysing and promoting initiatives to strengthen the financial system.

The Bank is able to make interventions in the currency markets, to the extent that its currency reserves enable it to do so.

The Bank of England also undertakes **open market operations** in the money markets to implement monetary policy. (including **'quantitative easing'**, termed more colloquially **'printing money'**, although it generally refers to creating balances rather than actually printing banknotes). In addition, the Bank operates the wholesale payments system, the real-time gross settlements system.

The Bank is also the financial system's '**lender of last resort**', being ready to provide funds in exceptional circumstances, as occurred when the bank Northern Rock got into financial difficulties in 2007.

1.3 HM Treasury

The **Treasury** is the United Kingdom's economics and finance ministry. It is responsible for formulating and implementing the UK Government's financial and economic policy. The Chancellor of the Exchequer has overall responsibility for the work of the Treasury.

The Treasury's aim is to raise the rate of sustainable growth and achieve rising prosperity and a better quality of life, with economic and employment opportunities for all.

It has various objectives and performance targets including maintaining a stable macroeconomic environment with low inflation and sound public finances. It is the Treasury that have determined that the Bank of England should target at inflation level of 2%, as measured by the 12 month increase in the Consumer Price Index.

The Debt Management Office is an agency of the Treasury. The DMO takes responsibility for issuing government debt.

1.4 Financial stability: Bank of England, Treasury, FSA

A **Memorandum of Understanding (MOU) on financial stability**, which was revised in 2006, seeks to address the issue of maintaining confidence and stability in the financial system. The MOU divides responsibility between the '**Tripartite Authorities**' – the Bank of England, HM Treasury and the FSA.

The Memorandum sets out a framework for monitoring and assessing, and co-ordinating the authorities' responses to, financial stability risks, including business continuity issues. The process is overseen by the **Tripartite Standing Committee**, comprising the Chancellor of the Exchequer, the Governor of the Bank of England and the Chairman of the FSA. The Committee regularly reviews the key systemic risks to the UK's financial intermediaries and infrastructure and co-ordinates the three authorities' response and contingency planning.

The Memorandum sets out the roles and responsibilities of each authority.

- The **Bank of England** contributes to the maintenance of the stability of the financial system as a whole, drawing on its macro-economic and financial analysis and on its operational involvement in markets, payment systems and other elements of market infrastructure.

- The **FSA** is responsible for the authorisation and supervision of financial institutions, for supervising financial markets and securities clearing and settlement systems, and for regulatory policy in these areas.

- **HM Treasury** has responsibility for the overall institutional structure of regulation and the legislation that governs it.

1.5 HM Treasury responsibility for the regulatory system

With the FSA Board being appointed by the **Treasury** and, being the minister with overall responsibility for the Treasury, the Chancellor of the Exchequer is ultimately responsible for the regulatory system for financial services under FSMA 2000.

HM Treasury, to which the FSA is accountable, will judge the FSA against the requirements laid down in FSMA 2000 which includes a requirement to ensure that the burdens imposed on the regulated community are **proportionate** to the benefits it will provide. In delivering against this, the FSA has undertaken a cost/benefit analysis whenever it has increased the burden of a rule.

HM Treasury also requires that the FSA submit an **annual report** covering such matters as the discharge of its functions and the extent to which the regulatory objectives have been met. HM Treasury also has powers to commission and publish an independent review of the FSA's use of resources and commission official enquiries into serious regulatory failures.

1.6 Future changes

The regulation of the UK financial services industry continues to evolve and react to new circumstances as they develop. There was criticism of the FSA for failing to be aware of the weakness of banks such as **Northern Rock**, which required emergency assistance and had to be nationalised. The financial turmoil in the period 2007 to 2009 stemmed in large part from excessive lending by banks, particularly to sub-prime borrowers, and from the 'securitisation' or packaging of mortgages by lenders for selling on to investors who were insufficiently aware of the risks attached to the securities, This period of turmoil has highlighted the need for continuing review and reform of regulatory arrangements.

In **June 2010**, with a new Conservative–Liberal Democratic coalition Government in power, it was announced that **the Financial Services Authority in its current form would be abolished**. The FSA would lose much of its role to a new **Consumer Protection and Markets Authority**. The rump of the organisation would, as a subsidiary of the Bank of England, become a prudential regulator responsible for ensuring the safe operation of individual banks, building societies and insurance companies. There would be a sweeping increase in the powers of the **Bank of England**, which would have a new remit of preventing a build-up of risk in the financial system, Mervyn King, the Bank's Governor, said that his new role in enforcing financial stability would be to 'turn down the music when the dancing gets a little too wild'.

2 OTHER BODIES

4.1.2 Explain the function of the following bodies/persons

- The Panel for Takeovers and Mergers
- The Department for Business, Innovation and Skills
- The Office of Fair Trading
- The Competition Commission
- The Information Commissioner

4.1.3 Explain the make-up of the Panel on Takeovers and Mergers (the takeover panel) and how it is financed.

2.1 The Panel for Takeovers and Mergers

The **Panel on Takeovers and Mergers** (the **Takeover Panel**) is an independent body established in 1968, whose main functions are to issue and administer the **City Code on Takeovers and Mergers** and to supervise and regulate takeovers and other matters to which the Code applies. Its central objective is to ensure fair treatment for shareholders in takeover bids.

The regulation of takeovers and mergers was the last aspect of the UK regulatory environment left almost exclusively to practitioner self-regulation. However, there was change when the **Takeover Directive (Interim Implementation) Regulations 2006** were implemented as Part 28 of the Companies Act 2006 (CA 2006).

Before the implementation of the Takeover Directive on 20 May 2006, the Panel did not have, nor did it seek to have, the force of law. Its only direct disciplinary powers were censures and withdrawing the facilities of the market from anybody who broke its rules.

The **Takeover Panel** was given **statutory authority** in the **Companies Act 2006**, with effect from January 2007. CA 2006 gives the Panel this authority in respect of all bids subject to the Takeover Code and not only those to which the Takeover Directive applies. The Panel has statutory powers under CA 2006 to make rules on takeover regulation, to require disclosure of information and to impose sanctions on those who breach its rules. In practical terms however, these changes are likely to make little difference to how the Panel operates.

The **City Code on Takeovers and Mergers** may be variously referred to as the City Code, the Blue Book, the Takeover Code or simply the Code. The **Code** has been developed since 1968 to reflect the collective opinion of those professionally involved in the field of takeovers as to appropriate business standards and as to how fairness to shareholders and an orderly framework for takeovers can be achieved. The rules set out in the Code, which are derived from the Takeover Directive, now have a statutory basis.

The **Takeover Panel** comprises up to 34 members which include a Chairman, up to two Deputy Chairmen, and up to twenty members and other individuals appointed by various industry bodies.

The Takeover Panel assumes overall responsibility for the policy, financing and administration of the Panel's functions and for the functioning and operation of the Code. The Panel operates through a number of committees and is directly responsible for those matters which are not dealt with through one of its committees.

- The day-to-day work of takeover supervision and regulation is carried out by the **Executive**. In carrying out these functions, the Executive operates independently of the Panel. The Executive may be approached for general guidance on the interpretation or effect of the Code, or in relation to a specific issue on a 'no names' basis.

- The **Code Committee** carries out the rule-making functions of the Panel and is responsible for keeping the Code under review and for proposing, consulting on, making and issuing amendments to the Code.

- The **Hearings Committee** reviews rulings of the Executive and hears disciplinary proceedings instituted by the Executive when the Executive considers that there has been a breach of the Code.

- The **Takeover Appeals Board** is an independent body which hears appeals against rulings of the Hearings Committee. The Board may confirm, vary, set aside, annul or replace the contested ruling of the Hearings Committee.

The **Panel** is **financed** by:

- A £1 levy on the buyers and sellers of share transactions in certain securities over £10,000 (the 'PTM levy')

- Document charges (payable on offer documents), and

- Exemption charges (£5,000 per review, payable by groups enjoying exempt status)

2.2 The Office of Fair Trading (OFT)

2.2.1 The role of the OFT

The **Office of Fair Trading (OFT)** has the goal of helping make markets work well for consumers. Markets work well, the OFT states, 'when fair-dealing businesses are in open and vigorous competition with each other for custom'.

The OFT offers advice, support and guidance to businesses on competition issues and on consumer legislation. It also seeks to promote good practice in business by granting 'approved status' to Consumer Codes of Practice meeting set criteria. The OFT will pursue businesses that rig prices or use unfair terms in contracts.

Under the **Control of Misleading Advertising Regulations**, the OFT works with bodies including the Advertising Standards Authority in exercising its powers to seek injunctions to stop advertising that is deceptive or misleading.

The OFT also regulates the consumer credit market with the aim of ensuring fair dealing by businesses in the market. It operates a **licensing system** through which checks are carried out on consumer credit businesses and issues guidelines on how the law will be enforced.

2.2.2 The OFT and the FSA

The OFT has specific responsibilities under FSMA 2000.

It is part of the role of the OFT to keep under review the activities and rules of the FSA with respect to competition issues.

If the OFT believes that FSA rules will impact adversely on competition, then it will report this to the FSA, the Treasury and the **Competition Commission (CC).** The CC is required to report on the matter to the Treasury, the FSA and the OFT. The Treasury must then decide on any further action, which could include requiring the FSA to change the rules concerned.

2.3 The Competition Commission

The **Competition Commission (CC)** has a general function in ensuring that the operation of the regulatory regime set up under FSMA 2000 and the exercise by the FSA of its powers under the Act cannot be considered anti-competitive and that there are no adverse effects on competition.

More specifically, the CC has the following two roles under FSMA 2000.

- The first role (under **s162** FSMA 2000) concerns the FSA's rules, guidance and statements of principle, which the **Office of Fair Trading (OFT)** is responsible for keeping under review.

- The second role (under **s306** FSMA 2000) relates to the regulatory provisions and practices of **Recognised Investment Exchanges** and **Recognised Clearing Houses**. The OFT is also required to keep these regulatory provisions and practices under review.

In both cases, the **OFT** must make a **report** if it considers that rules, guidance and principles, or regulatory provisions and practices, have a significantly adverse effect on competition. The OFT may also make a report if it considers that there is no such effect on competition.

Any such report made by the OFT must be sent to the CC. The **CC** must **investigate** the subject matter of the OFT's report. If that report concludes that there is a significant adverse effect on competition and the OFT has asked the CC to consider the report, the CC must make its own report, unless it considers – giving reasons – that no useful purpose would be served by a report.

If the CC makes a report and concludes that there is an adverse effect on competition, it must also state whether it considers that the effect is justified and if not, state what action the Treasury ought to direct the FSA to take. The Treasury will then consider whether to direct to the FSA to take action.

2.4 The Information Commissioner

Under the **Data Protection Act 1998 (DPA 1998)**, where persons process personal data, whether electronically or manually, they must (unless exempt) be registered with the **Information Commissioner** (who maintains a **public registry of data controllers**) and must comply with the DPA provisions. The requirements apply to most organisations and cover all personal data whether it relates to clients, employees, suppliers or any other person.

3 THE CITY CODE

Learning objectives

4.1.4 Explain the regulatory power of the City Code on Takeovers and Mergers.

4.1.5 Explain the main provisions of the City Code including the bid timetable.

3.1 Overview of competition regulation

Statutory Merger Control

Office of Fair Trading

Looks at current takeovers and mergers
to ascertain if there has been a
substantial lessening of competition

May clear (i.e. bid can go ahead) or refer
the bid to Competition Commission

↓

Competition Commission

Commission investigates the bid and
recommends whether there has been a
substantial lessening of competition

Bid is block   **Bid is cleared**

UK competition regulations are designed to ensure mergers and acquisitions are not going to result in uncompetitive practices or a **substantial lessening of competition**.

Competition investigations have a two-tier approach involving Office of Fair Trading (OFT) investigation followed by possible reference to the Competition Commission for a second-stage, in-depth investigation where necessary.

The only exception to this is where **Secretary of State for Business, Innovation and Skills** intervenes in cases of national security. The Secretary of State is head of the Department for Business, Innovation and Skills (BIS).

The main statutory rules on competition are within the **2002 Enterprise Act**.

As guidance, the following scenarios will qualify for investigation.

- The combined enterprise **controls at least 25%** of the goods or services in the sector in the UK, or
- The turnover of the entity being acquired **exceeds £70 million**.

While the Panel is swift in making its decisions, the CC is not. The OFT can investigate **four months** from when the transaction is made public. Cases referred to the Competition Commission must normally be investigated **within 24 weeks** of the date of reference.

The Competition Commission has the power to **impose fines** for failure to comply with any request for information.

The Competition Commission will publish preliminary findings prior to its final decision and will consult on, and give reason for, its conclusion. Appeals against this decision may be made to the **Competition Appeal Tribunal,** a separate judicial body.

3.2 City Code: application

3.2.1 UK, Channel Islands and Isle of Man registered and traded companies

The City Code (or '**Takeover Code**') applies to all offers for public companies which have their registered offices in the **United Kingdom, the Channel Islands or the Isle of Man** if any of their securities are admitted to trading on a regulated market in the United Kingdom (UK RIE) or on any stock exchange in the Channel Islands or the Isle of Man.

3.2.2 Other companies

The City Code also applies to all offers for public (plc) and private companies (Ltd) which have their registered offices in the United Kingdom, the Channel Islands or the Isle of Man and which are considered by the Panel to have their place of central management and control in the United Kingdom, the Channel Islands or the Isle of Man, but in relation to private companies only when:

- The company's equity share capital has been listed on the LSE during the last ten years before the offer or proposed offer is announced

- Dealings or prices in the company's shares have been advertised on a regular basis for at least six continuous months in the last ten years

- The company's shares have been dealt in on the AIM or subject to any other marketing arrangement in the last ten years

- The company has filed a prospectus to issue equity shares in the last ten years

The objective of these rules is to cover any company where the public may have had an opportunity to purchase shares in the recent past.

Takeovers and other matters to which the Code applies may from time to time be subject to the dual jurisdiction of the Panel and an overseas takeover regulator. In such cases, early consultation with the Panel is advised so that guidance can be given on how any conflicts between the relevant rules may be resolved.

3.2.3 Statutory basis of the Code

Under the **Companies Act 2006**, the City Code on Takeovers and Mergers has **statutory effect** with regard to transactions to which it applies, except in the Channel Islands and the Isle of Man where the Takeover Panel claims jurisdiction as previously, but on a non-statutory basis.

3.3 Application of the Code: transactions

3.3.1 Mergers and takeovers

The City Code applies to all takeover and merger transactions, including partial offers for less than 100% of a company's shares and situations where control of a company is to be obtained or consolidated. However, it does not usually relate to offers for non-voting, non-equity shares.

3.3.2 Control

Control is defined in the definitions section as where at least 30% of the company's voting rights are held. Although, strictly speaking, control only passes when more than 50% of the voting rights are held. The Panel believes that effective control can be achieved at this much lower percentage.

When a shareholding, including that of parties acting in concert, exceeds **30%**, the shareholder **must make a takeover offer**.

3.3.3 Definition of 'concert party'

A **concert party** comprises persons who, pursuant to an agreement or understanding (whether formal or informal), co-operate to obtain or consolidate control of a company or to frustrate the successful outcome of an offer for a company.

3.4 Structure of the City Code

The City Code starts with six general principles governing the conduct of takeover activity in the UK. These are followed by a series of detailed rules adding guidance and indication to the principles laid out before. These are the guiding principles of the Code. Adherence to the principles is treated more seriously than adherence to the detailed rules, which simply supplement those principles.

3.5 General Principles of the Code

The City Code is intended to ensure fair treatment for all shareholders. It is recognised that it is impossible to devise rules that cover every situation.

The Panel accordingly states the following six **General Principles** to assist companies and the Panel in **interpreting** and **applying the spirit of** the City Code.

1	**All holders of the securities of an offeree company of the same class must be afforded equivalent treatment. If a person acquires control of a company, the other holders of securities must be protected.** This principle is central to the spirit of the Takeover Code. It aims to protect shareholders from abusive transfers of control to shareholders or groups of shareholders without the payment of a premium for the transfer of this control. It also protects against abuse of the position of significant shareholders compared to that of minority shareholders.
2	**The holders of the securities of an offeree company must have sufficient time and information to enable them to reach a properly informed decision on the bid. Where it advises the holders of securities, the board of the offeree company must give its views on the effects of implementation of the bid on employment, conditions of employment and the locations of the company's places of business.** This principle is reflected in the specific Code rules relating to the contents of offer and defence documents, on requirements for announcements, and on the offer timetable.
3	**The board of an offeree company must act in the interests of the company as a whole and must not deny the holders of securities the opportunity to decide on the merits of the bid.** This principle will be of key importance in situations where offeree directors are going to continue their involvement in the company after the transaction. This may occur with a recommended offer, where the offeree company's directors are to keep their seats on the Board and receive an incentive scheme to make the company perform. It will also be very relevant for management buyouts.
4	**False markets must not be created in the securities of the offeree company, of the offeror company or of any other company concerned by the bid in such a way that the rise or fall of the prices of the securities becomes artificial and the normal functioning of the markets is distorted.** This principle is reiterated in the market abuse provisions of the Financial Services and Markets Act 2000. It is reflected in specific Code rules requiring adequate information for investors, prompt announcements and documents, and also in the prohibitions on manipulative dealings in securities.

5	An offeror must announce a bid only after ensuring that he/she can fulfil in full any cash consideration, if such is offered, and after taking all reasonable measures to secure the implementation of any other type of consideration.
	Any firm offer made for an offeree company is binding on the bidder once announced. This principle emphasises the importance of ensuring that any offer made is capable of being implemented, thereby providing shareholders with certainty that the offer can proceed and that finance is available for consideration.
6	An offeree company must not be hindered in the conduct of its affairs for longer than is reasonable by a bid for its securities.
	The Takeover Directive provides that shareholders must be given reasonable time to consider their options in relation to a bid. However, if too much time is allowed, then there can be considerable uncertainty as to final outcomes as well as a diversion of valuable management time away from the core business of running the company. The rules therefore stipulate deadlines in relation to all stages of the bid process.

3.6 Rules

3.6.1 The pre-bid environment

The most important rules governing the pre-bid environment relate to the **secrecy** of negotiations. It is important to ensure the bid does not leak out to the public before it has been announced and organised. This is important for both the predator and target company. Should the market become volatile in a stock, the directors of that company may choose to suspend the bid and the Panel may investigate the reasons for that volatility. It is within the Panel's powers to force potential bidders into the open rather than to allow a **false market** to continue.

Before any announcement is made publicly that a bid is to take place, the predatory company must first talk to the target company's board. In a hostile takeover bid this will not be far in advance of the announcement, and may be just minutes before the press receive details of the bid.

3.6.2 Bid timings

The Bid Timetable

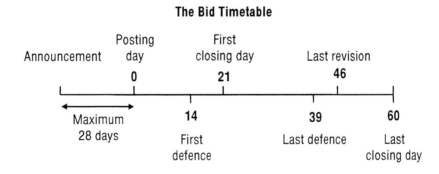

Once a bid has been announced, takeovers in the UK fit into a detailed and fixed time frame.

Announcement day

Once a bid has been publicly announced, the bidding company has **28 days** in which to post the details of its offer. If the bid is hostile, it is unlikely that the bidder will take the full 28-day allowance. All days throughout the City Code are **calendar days**.

Posting day

The posting day is the day on which the offer and its terms are fully revealed to the public. This counts as Day Zero for all other reference points.

Day 14: Posting of first defence document

Once the offer documents have been posted, the defending company's directors must, **within 14 days**, give their opinion on the bid. The directors must act in the best interests of the shareholders and that may mean the directors will recommend the bid.

Day 21: The first closing day

The first day that the bid can close is Day 21. At this point the offeror company will review the number of acceptances they have received. In the offer document they will have stated a level of acceptances at which the offer becomes unconditional. Only once acceptances go through this level, be it 50%, 60% or 70%, will the acceptances be taken up by the offeror.

If the company has reached its acceptance level it must declare that the offer has gone 'unconditional with regard to acceptances'. Any offer will then remain open for **14 days** to allow those shareholders who have been resisting the takeover to take the opportunity to sell their shares and leave the company.

If the bid has not been accepted by Day 21, the offeror company may, at its discretion, increase the level of the bid and extend the offer period. If, at any time during the takeover timetable, the offeror states that this is the final bid, or that no extension will be made, the offeror must abide by that decision unless another party enters the bid race.

Day 39: Last defence documents

On Day 39 the defending company may issue its **last formal defence documentation**.

Day 46: Last offer amendment

On Day 46 the offeror company may **amend its price** for the **final time**. From this point on it is not able to buy shares in the market place at above this offer price.

Day 60: The final closing

A bid can remain open for 60 days. By Day 60 it must be unconditional with regard to acceptances or the bid will lapse. If a bid lapses, the offeror company will be unable to launch another offer for **12 months**.

If, during the course of a bid, a new bid emerges the offeror company will automatically move to the new bid timetable.

One way to delay the bid is to refer a bid, via the Office of Fair Trading and the Secretary of State for Trade and Industry, to the Competition Commission. If this happens the bid is suspended and will restart at Day 37 in the timetable or the timetable will be cancelled altogether to restart only if the bid is cleared.

3.6.3 Mandatory bids

General principle 10 details the situation where an individual who gains control is being forced to launch a bid for the remaining shares in the company. In reality, legal control is achieved when a shareholder breaks through the 50% barrier. However, as far as the Panel is concerned, effective control is achieved at 30% and, under the rules of the Panel, **if a shareholder takes their stake to a 30% level or more, then they will be required to make a mandatory offer**. In some circumstances, a shareholder may already have a stake of between 30% and 50%. Such shareholders will be required to make a mandatory offer if they increase their holding without Panel consent.

It should be noted that there are only very limited circumstances in which a person is permitted to acquire 30% or more of a company anyway. In most circumstances, a person is forbidden to acquire 30% or more.

Under the terms of a mandatory offer, much of the offeror's discretion is removed. A mandatory bid must be at the **highest price** at which the offeror has purchased shares **within the last 12 months**. In addition, the offer must be for cash or have a cash alternative. For an ordinary bid, the bid need only be at the best price the offeror has paid in the past three months unless the Panel feels, at its discretion, that 12 months would be more appropriate. In addition, cash or a cash alternative is not usually required.

In an ordinary offer, the offeror sets the acceptance level and may specify an acceptance level of 90% prior to the bid going unconditional (it cannot, however, usually be less than **50%**). In a mandatory bid, the only acceptable level is 50%, which may mean that the offeror acquires a company with a substantial minority interest that may, to an extent, limit the offeror's powers of control.

3.6.4 The post-bid environment

As we have seen above, should the bid fail the offeror is prohibited from bidding again for 12 months, and any offer declared unconditional must remain open for a further 14 days after the date on which it went unconditional. In addition, if the offeror company achieves an **acceptance level of 90%** or above, it may be able to invoke the **compulsory purchase procedures** contained within the Companies Act which will enable it to force any minority shareholders to sell their shares to the offer company.

4 FSMA 2000 AND REGULATED ACTIVITIES

objectives | **4.1.6 Explain** the scope of the Financial Services and Markets Act 2000.

4.1.7 Explain the scope of the Regulated Activities Order 2001 (as amended) in terms of:

–   Regulated activities
–   Regulated investments

4.1 Primary and secondary legislation

Before looking at some key aspects of the Financial Services and Markets Act 2000 (FSMA 2000), the legislation under which the FSA was established, it is important to understand the legislative structure. FSMA 2000 itself only provides the skeleton of the regulatory system, much of the detail being provided by secondary legislation.

The **secondary legislation** links into various sections of the Act, fleshing out the requirements and, thus, requiring the two to be read in conjunction. An example of this is with regard to the authorisation requirement. FSMA requires that any firm undertaking a regulated activity must be authorised or exempt from authorisation. Whilst the routes that a firm may follow to obtain authorisation are contained in FSMA, the meaning of the term 'regulated activity' and the exemptions are found in secondary legislation –

namely the Regulated Activities Order. Both FSMA and the secondary legislation are drafted by HM Treasury.

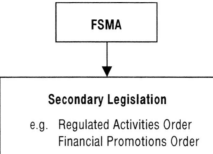

4.2 The general prohibition

4.2.1 Overview

FSMA 2000 establishes the regime of **authorisation of firms** to carry out **regulated activities. Section 19** FSMA 2000 contains what is known as the **general prohibition**.

The general prohibition states that no person can carry on a regulated activity in the UK, nor purport to do so, unless they are either **authorised or exempt**.

The definition of person here includes both **companies and individuals**. The list of exemptions and exclusions are set out in the regulations. There is no right to apply for an exemption from S19 if you do not fall into the existing categories.

4.2.2 Sanctions and defence

The sanctions for breaching S19 are fairly severe, namely: criminal sanctions, unenforceability of agreements, compensation, and actions by the FSA to restrain such activity.
Breach of the general prohibition is an offence punishable in a court of law.

The maximum penalties for conducting unauthorised regulated activities are set out in S23 FSMA 2000:

- **Magistrates' Court:** six months' imprisonment and/or a £5,000 fine
- **Crown Court:** two years' imprisonment and/or an unlimited fine

It is a **defence** for a person to show that all reasonable precautions were taken and all due diligence exercised, to avoid committing the offence.

4.3 Unenforceable agreements

As a consequence of the general prohibition, an agreement made by an **unauthorised** firm will be **unenforceable** against the other party.

FSMA 2000 makes it clear that agreements are not illegal or invalid as a result of a contravention of the general prohibition: they are merely '**voidable**'. This ensures that the innocent party to the agreement may still be able to enforce the agreement against the other party, even though the performance may be a criminal offence.

The innocent party will be entitled to recover **compensation** for any loss sustained if the agreement is made unenforceable.

4.4 The requirement for authorisation

As stated above, no person can carry on a regulated activity in the UK, nor purport to do so, unless they are either **authorised** or **exempt**.

The **Perimeter Guidance Manual (PERG)** in the FSA Handbook gives guidance about the circumstances in which authorisation is required, or exempt person status is available, including guidance on the activities which are regulated under FSMA 2000 and the exclusions which are available.

The following decision chart indicates the questions to be asked in establishing **whether a firm needs to be authorised**.

Does My Firm Need Authorisation?

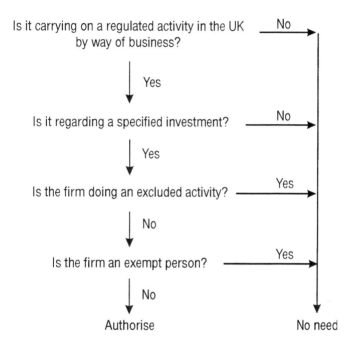

4.5 Exempt persons

The following are the types of person that are **exempt** from the requirement to seek authorisation under FSMA 2000.

- **Appointed representative.** In markets such as life assurance, the bulk of sales takes place through self-employed individuals who act on behalf of the companies. As the companies do not employ them, if this exemption were not in place, such persons would need separate authorisation. The exemption removes them from the scope of authorisation so long as they act solely on behalf of one firm and that firm takes complete responsibility for their actions.

- **Members of professions.** Solicitors, accountants and actuaries have been giving investment advice for many years. As long as giving such advice does not constitute a major proportion of their business (i.e. is incidental) and they are not separately paid for those activities, they are exempt from the requirement to seek authorisation. However, they will still be governed by their professional bodies (e.g. the Law Society, for solicitors). These professional bodies are known as **Designated Professional Bodies (DPBs)** and are subject to scrutiny by the FSA.

- **Certain persons listed in the Financial Services and Markets Act (Exemption) Order 2001**, including supranational bodies, municipal banks, local authorities, housing associations, the national grid, trade unions, the Treasury Taskforce, the English Tourist Board, government organisations (such as Bank of England, other central banks, an enterprise scheme, the International Monetary Fund and the UK's National Savings & Investments). In addition, charities and the Student Loans Company are exempt in respect of deposit-taking activities. The Financial Services and Markets Act (Exemption) Order 2001 is written by HM Treasury under powers set out in s38 FSMA 2000.

- **Members of Lloyd's.** The requirement to seek authorisation is disapplied for members of Lloyd's writing insurance contracts. The Society of Lloyd's, however, is required to be authorised. This exemption covers **being** a Lloyd's member but does not cover the activities of **advising** on Lloyd's syndicate participation or **managing** underwriting activities.

- **Recognised Investment Exchanges (RIEs), Recognised Overseas Investment Exchanges (ROIEs)** and **Recognised Clearing Houses (RCHs).**

Exam tip

> The word **APRIL** can be used to help learn the five types of exempt persons.
>
> **A**ppointed representatives
> **P**rofessional people, e.g. solicitors, accountants and actuaries
> **R**IE, ROIEs and RCHs
> **I**nstitutions who are exempt, e.g. the Bank of England
> **L**loyd's members

4.6 List of activities regulated

What range of activities are **regulated activities**? The activities regulated by FSMA 2000 are set out in the **Regulated Activities Order** (as amended).

Regulated activities

- **Accepting deposits.** These must be accepted by way of business to be covered.

- **Issuing electronic money.** Some banks and building societies issue 'e-money' which is a form of electronic money that can be used (like notes and coins) to pay for goods and services.

- **Effecting or carrying out contracts of insurance as principal.** After date 'N2' (30 November 2001), the FSA took responsibility for regulating all insurers for capital adequacy purposes and life insurance firms for Conduct of Business Rules. Since January 2005, the FSA has regulated the sales and administration of general insurance as well as life insurance.

- **Dealing in investments as principal or agent.** This covers buying, selling, subscribing for or underwriting investments.

- **Arranging deals in investments.** This covers making, offering or agreeing to make any arrangements with a view to another person buying, selling, subscribing for or underwriting investments.

- **Arranging regulated mortgage contracts.** This covers most mortgages, but generally does not cover buy-to-let or second charge loans.

- **Arranging home reversion plans.** Home reversion plans are one of two types of equity release product, the other being lifetime mortgages.

- **Arranging home purchase plans.** A home purchase plan serves the same purpose as a normal mortgage, in that it provides consumers with finance to buying a home. But it is structured in a way that makes it acceptable under Islamic law. As interest is contrary to Islamic law, a home purchase plan is in essence a sale and lease arrangement. The plan provider buys the property, which is then sold to the home purchaser by instalments.

- **Operating a multilateral trading facility (MTF)**. An MTF is a system which may be operated by an investment firm that enables parties, who might typically be retail investors or other investment firms, to buy and sell financial instruments.

- **Managing investments**. Managing investments belonging to another person where there is exercise of discretion by the manager.

- **Assisting in the administration and performance of a contract of insurance** (see above).

- **Safeguarding and administering investments** or arranging such activities.

- **Sending dematerialised instructions**. This relates to the use of computer-based systems for giving instructions for investments to be transferred.

- **Establishing a collective investment scheme.** This would include the roles of the trustee and the depository of schemes.

  Sections 235 and 236 FSMA 2000 define 'Collective Investment Schemes' to mean arrangements regarding property of any description where the participants and profits or income are pooled and the property in the scheme is managed by an operator.

- **Establishing, operating or winding-up a personal pension scheme or a stakeholder pension scheme**. Personal pension schemes include Self-Invested Personal Pensions (SIPPs), as their name implies. A stakeholder pension scheme follows similar rules to a personal pension plan, with caps on charges in addition.

- **Advising on investments**.

- **Advising on regulated mortgage contracts**.

- **Advising on regulated home reversion plans**.

- **Advising on regulated home purchase plans**.

- **Lloyd's market activities**. Lloyd's is the UK's largest insurance market.

- **Entering funeral plan contracts**.

- **Entering into and administering a regulated mortgage contract**.

- **Entering into and administering a home reversion plan**.

- **Entering into and administering a home purchase plan**.

- **Agreeing to carry on most regulated activities**. This is itself a regulated activity and so a firm must get the appropriate authorisation before agreeing to undertake business such as dealing or arranging for clients.

As you can see from the above list, the activities regulated cover the investment industry, banking, insurance and mortgage lending industries, and Lloyd's.

4.7 Activities carried on 'by way of business'

Note that the regulated activity must be carried on '**by way of business**' for the regulations to apply. Whether something is carried on by way of business is, ultimately, a question of judgement: in general terms it will depend on the degree of continuity and profit. HM Treasury has also (via secondary legislation) made explicit provisions for certain activities, such as accepting deposits. This will not be regarded as carried on by way of business if a person does not hold himself out as doing so on a day-to-day basis, i.e. he only accepts deposits on particular occasions. An example of this would be a car salesman accepting a down payment on the purchase of a car.

4.8 Territorial scope

Broadly speaking, a person will be covered by **FSMA 2000** if they carry on the activity:

- In the UK, e.g. has an establishment in the UK.

- Into the UK from overseas, e.g. providing cross-border dealing services (subject to certain limited exclusions for overseas persons).

- In another European Economic Area (EEA) state, if his registered office is in the UK and he is passporting services into that state under one of the single market directives.

- In another EEA state, if his registered office is in UK and the day-to-day management of the activity is the responsibility of that UK office.

4.9 Prohibition Order

S56 FSMA 2000 allows the FSA to prohibit individuals from carrying out specified functions in relation to regulated activities within the investment industry. A **Prohibition Order** under this Section may be issued in respect of anyone, whether they are an **approved person** or not.

4.10 Excluded activities

The **Perimeter Guidance Manual (PERG)** in the FSA Handbook gives guidance about the activities which are regulated under FSMA 2000 and the exclusions which are available.

As set out in the Regulated Activities Order and reiterated in PERG, the following activities are **excluded** from the requirement for authorisation.

- **Dealing as principal** where the person is not holding themselves out to the market as willing to deal. The requirement to seek authorisation does not apply to the personal dealings of unauthorised individuals for their own account, i.e. as customers of an authorised firm. It would also exclude companies issuing their own shares.

- **Trustees, nominees and personal representatives**. These persons, so long as they do not hold themselves out to the general public as providing the service and are not separately remunerated for the regulated activity, are excluded from the requirement to seek authorisation.

- **Employee share schemes**. This exclusion applies to activities which further an employee share scheme.

- **Media**, e.g. TV, radio and newspapers. Many newspapers and other media give investment advice. However, provided this is not the primary purpose of the newspaper, then under the exceptions granted within FSMA 2000, it need not seek formal authorisation. On the other hand, the publication of '**tip sheets**' (written recommendations of investments) will require authorisation.

- **Overseas persons**. Overseas persons are firms which do not carry on regulated activity from a permanent place within the UK. This exception covers two broad categories: first, where the activity requires the direct involvement of an authorised or exempt firm and, second, where the activity is carried on as a result of an unsolicited approach by a UK individual. Thus, if a UK individual asks a fund manager in Tokyo to buy a portfolio of Asian equities for them, the Japanese firm does not need to be authorised under FSMA 2000.

Exam tip	The word **DEMOTE** can help you to learn the five excluded activities.
	Dealing as principal, where the person is not holding themselves out to the market as willing to deal
	Employee share schemes
	Media
	Overseas persons
	Trustees
	Nomin**E**es and personal representatives

4.11 Specified investments

Only activities relating to **specified investments** are covered by FSMA 2000. Specified investments are also defined in the **Regulated Activities Order** (as amended).

Specified investments

- **Deposits**. Simply defined, this is a sum of money paid by one person to another under the terms that it will be repaid on a specified event (e.g. on demand).

- **Electronic money**. This is defined as monetary value, as represented by a claim on the issuer, which is stored on an electronic device, is issued on receipt of funds and is accepted as a means of payment by persons other than the issuer.

- **Rights under a contract of insurance**. Included in this category are general insurance contracts (such as motor insurance, accident or sickness), long-term insurance contracts (such as life and annuity) and other insurance contracts (such as funeral expense contracts).

- **Shares** or stock in the capital of a company wherever the company is based.

- **Debentures, loan stock and similar instruments**, e.g. certificate of deposit, Treasury bills of exchange, floating rate notes, bulldog bonds and unsecured loan stock (but not cheques or other bills of exchange, banker's drafts, letters of credit, trade bills or Premium Bonds).

- **Government and public securities**, e.g. gilts, US Treasury bonds (not National Savings & Investments products, such as Premium Bonds and Savings Certificates).

- **Warrants**. A warrant gives the right to buy a new share in a company.

- **Certificates representing certain securities**, e.g. American Depository Receipts.

- **Units in a Collective Investment Scheme** including shares in, or securities of, an Open-ended Investment Company (OEIC). A collective investment scheme is a specified investment whatever underlying property the scheme invests in.

- **Rights under a personal pension scheme or a stakeholder pension scheme**. These are pension plans which are not employment-based (occupational) schemes. As indicated above, a SIPP is a personal pension scheme.

- **Options** to acquire or dispose of any specified investment or currencies, gold, silver, platinum or palladium.

- **Futures** on anything for investment purposes. This differs from the treatment of options as it will cover all futures regardless of the underlying investment, provided it is for investment purposes.

  The definition of 'investment purposes' is complex. In general terms, any futures contract traded either on an exchange, or in an over-the-counter market or form similar to that traded on an exchange, will constitute an investment. The type of future, in effect, excluded by this definition would be a short-term contract between a producer and a consumer of a good to purchase that good in the future, e.g. a wheat buyer buying from a farmer. This can sometimes be referred to as a 'commercial purpose future'.

> As a rule of thumb, unless the examiner indicates otherwise, you should assume that a future *is* for investment purposes.

- **Contracts for differences (CfDs)**. A CfD is a contract whose price tracks the price of an underlying asset, while the CfD holder does not take ownership of the asset. The underlying asset might be a company's shares, a bond, a currency, a commodity or an index. Investors can use CfDs to take a short position – and thus gain from price declines, but lose if the price rises.

- **Lloyd's syndicate capacity and syndicate membership**. Lloyd's is an insurance institution specialising in risks such as aviation and marine insurance. Insurance is provided by members and syndicates.

- **Rights under a funeral plan contract**. These are contracts whereby someone pays for their funeral before their death.

- **Rights under a regulated mortgage contract**. Note that not all mortgages are covered, only regulated mortgages. In a regulated mortgage the loan is secured by a first legal mortgage or property located in the UK, which will be occupied (at least 40% of the time) by the borrower or their family.

- **Rights under a home reversion plan**.

- **Rights under a home purchase plan**.

- **Rights to or interests in anything that is a specified investment listed** (excluding 'Rights under regulated mortgage contracts'). 'Repos' (sale and repurchase agreements) in relation to specified investments (e.g. a government bond) are specified investments.

Spot currency ('forex') trades, general loans (e.g. car loans), property deals and National Savings & Investments products are *not* specified investments.

When applying for authorisation to carry out a regulated activity regarding a specified investment, the firm will specify on the application form which regulated activities relating to which specified investments it wishes to conduct.

5 SENIOR MANAGEMENT ARRANGEMENTS SYSTEMS AND CONTROLS

4.1.8 **Explain** the purpose and scope of the FSA's rules regarding Senior Management Arrangements, Systems and Controls (SYSC).

5.1 Overview

The FSA's **PRIN 3** (Principle for Businesses 3) states as follows.

Management and control
A firm must take reasonable care to organise and control its affairs responsibly and effectively, with adequate risk management systems. Note: it would not be a breach of this Principle if the firm failed to prevent unforeseeable risks.

This emphasis comes from a desire to avoid a repetition of the collapse of Barings Bank, where it was clear that management methods and the control environment were deficient.

The FSA suggests that, in order to comply with its obligation to maintain appropriate systems, a firm should carry out a regular review of the above factors.

There is a section of the *FSA Handbook* called **Senior Management Arrangements, Systems and Controls (SYSC)**. As the name suggests, the main purpose of this part of the *FSA Handbook* is to encourage directors and senior managers of authorised firms to take appropriate responsibility for their firm's arrangements and to ensure they know their obligations.

Exam tip

The examiner may refer to this *Handbook* section by its abbreviation as **SYSC**.

5.2 Purpose of SYSC

The purposes of SYSC are:

- To encourage firms' directors and senior managers to take appropriate practical responsibility for their firms' arrangements on matters likely to be of interest to the FSA because they impinge on the FSA's functions under the Act

- To increase certainty by amplifying Principle 3, under which a firm must take reasonable care to organise and control its affairs responsibly and effectively, with adequate risk management systems

- To encourage firms to vest responsibility for effective and responsible organisation in specific directors and senior managers

- To create a **common platform** of organisational and systems and controls requirements for firms subject to the CRD and/or MiFID (a **common platform** firm).

5.3 Organisational requirements

A firm must have robust **governance arrangements**, which include a clear **organisational structure** with well defined, transparent and consistent lines of responsibility, effective processes to identify, manage, monitor and report the risks it is or might be exposed to, and **internal control mechanisms**, including sound administrative and accounting procedures and effective control and safeguard arrangements for information processing systems.

Firm must establish, implement and maintain an adequate **business continuity policy**.

Firm must establish, implement and maintain **accounting policies and procedures** that enable it, at the request of the FSA, to deliver in a timely manner to the FSA financial reports which reflect a true and fair view of its financial position and which comply with all applicable accounting standards and rules.

Firm must **monitor and evaluate** the adequacy and effectiveness of its systems, internal control mechanisms and arrangements established and take appropriate measures to address any deficiencies.

Depending on the nature, scale and complexity of its business, it may be appropriate for a firm to form an audit committee with formal terms of reference. An **audit committee** could typically examine management's process for ensuring the appropriateness and effectiveness of systems and controls, examine the arrangements made by management to ensure compliance with requirements and standards under the regulatory system, oversee the functioning of the internal audit function (if applicable) and provide an interface between management and external auditors.

The senior personnel of a common platform firm must be of sufficiently good repute and sufficiently experienced as to ensure the sound and prudent management of the firm

A common platform firm, when allocating functions internally, must ensure that senior personnel and, where appropriate, the supervisory function, are responsible for ensuring that the firm complies with its obligations under the regulatory system. In particular, senior personnel and, where appropriate, the supervisory function must assess and periodically review the effectiveness of the policies, arrangements and procedures put in place to comply with the firm's obligations under the regulatory system and take appropriate measures to address any deficiencies.

5.4 Employees, agents and other relevant persons

Firm must employ personnel with the **skills, knowledge and expertise** necessary for the discharge of the responsibilities allocated to them.

Firm must have arrangements concerning the **segregation of duties** within the firm and the prevention of conflicts of interest. The effective segregation of duties is an important element in the internal controls of a firm in the prudential context.

Firm must ensure that its relevant persons are **aware of the procedures** which must be followed for the proper discharge of their responsibilities.

The systems, **internal control mechanisms** and arrangements established by a firm in accordance with this chapter must take into account the nature, scale and complexity of its business and the nature and range of investment services and activities undertaken in the course of that business.

The firm must monitor and, on a regular basis, evaluate the adequacy and effectiveness of its systems, internal control mechanisms and arrangements established in accordance with this chapter, and take appropriate measures to address any deficiencies.

5.5 Compliance, internal audit and financial crime

A common platform firm must establish, implement and maintain **adequate policies and procedures** sufficient to ensure compliance of the firm including its **managers, employees and appointed representatives** (or where applicable, tied agents) with its obligations under the regulatory system and for countering the risk that the firm might be used to further financial crime

A common platform firm must, where appropriate and proportionate in view of the nature, scale and complexity of its business and the nature and range of investment services and activities undertaken in the course of that business, establish and maintain an internal audit function which is separate and independent from the other functions and activities of the firm

A common platform firm must ensure the policies and procedures established include systems and controls that

- Enable it to identify, assess, monitor and manage money laundering risk
- Are comprehensive and proportionate to the nature, scale and complexity of its activities

5.6 Conflicts of interest

A common platform firm must establish, implement and maintain a written conflicts of interest policy and ensure that it

- Takes all reasonable steps to identify conflicts of interest
- Details arrangements to prevent conflicts of interest
- Discloses any conflicts where they may remain

5.7 Other requirements

Other SYSC requirements include

- A common platform firm to have effective processes to identify, manage, monitor and report the risks it is or might be exposed to

- Management cannot delegate responsibility where operational functions are outsourced

- A firm must ensure record keeping is adequate to ensure that the FSA can monitor its regulatory compliance

- Management and prudential requirements relating to **banks and insurance companies** relating to risk management systems for liquidity risk, operational risk, group risk, credit risk, market risk, insurance risk and prudential requirements.

Furthermore, the **compliance function** must be designed for the purpose of complying with regulatory requirements and to counter the risk that the firm may be used to further financial crime.

Depending on the nature, scale and complexity of the business, it may be appropriate for the firm to have a separate compliance function although this is not an absolute requirement. The organisation and responsibilities of the compliance department should be properly recorded and documented and it should be staffed by an **appropriate number of persons** who are sufficiently **independent** to perform their duties objectively. The compliance function should have unfettered access to relevant records and to the governing body of the firm. The MiFID requirements here are broadly in line with the FSA's existing rules.

5.8 Whistleblowing

SYSC also sets out guidance on **whistleblowing** where an employee blows the whistle on breaches of regulations or laws by their employer. This guidance reflects general legislation set out in the **Public Interest Disclosure Act 1998 (PIDA)**.

SYSC suggests that authorised firms should have appropriate internal procedures to implement PIDA. Under PIDA, firms may not exclude contractually an employee's right to 'blow the whistle'. PIDA also protects employees from unfair dismissal in such circumstances.

6 THE TRUSTEE ACT 2000

g objective **4.1.9 Explain** the purpose and scope of the Trustee Act 2000

- The rights and duties of the parties involved
- The nature of the trust deed
- Investment powers of trustees

6.1 Overview

The main aim of the **Trustee Act 2000** was to widen the investment powers and powers of delegation for trusts. Trustees and their advisers need to follow the Act unless the trust deed overrules the Act.

The Trustee Act 2000 has implications in five important areas.

- Investment powers
- The power to delegate
- A statutory duty of care
- Trustee remuneration
- The power to insure trust property

6.2 Investment powers

The earlier Trustee Investment Act 1961 authorised trustees to invest in certain permitted investments and obliged them to split trust funds between different types of investments. Under the Trustee Act 2000, trustees can make any investment of any kind that they could as if the funds were their own, except for investment in overseas land. Trustees are however subject to a fundamental duty to act in the best interests of all the beneficiaries. They are also subject to a **statutory duty of care** in exercising new investment powers, and under the Trustee Act 2000 must also:

- Keep aware of the need for diversification and suitability of the investments of the trust
- Obtain and consider 'proper advice' when making or reviewing investments
- Keep investments under review

The investment provisions of the Trustee Act 2000 do not apply to occupational pension schemes (which are governed by the Pensions Act 1995), authorised unit trusts or to certain schemes under the Charities Act 1993.

6.3 Power to delegate

The Act allows trustees to **delegate** functions to agents, including their **powers of investment**. Where delegation occurs to agents who provide asset management services, there must be a **Policy Statement**.

6.4 Duty of care

The Act imposes a **statutory duty of skill and care**, which applies when trustees carry out certain functions such as exercising their powers of investment, employing agents, using nominees and custodians and insuring trust properties. This is a subjective test that takes into account the knowledge, experience and professional status of the trustee. Generally, higher standards will be expected of investment professionals than of lay persons.

6.5 Professional charging

The Trustee Act 2000 reversed a rule that previously prevented professional trustees from benefiting from their office. The Act provides that, where there is more than one trustee, they should have powers to authorise one or more of their number to charge for services to the trust if they are acting **in a professional capacity**.

6.6 Power to insure

The Act gives to trustees the **power to insure** in full any property that is subject to the trust against risk of loss or damage due to any event as if the property were their own, where in the past, they could only insure up to 75% of the value. The premiums may be paid out of income or capital funds of the trust. The purchase of investment products with capital guarantees would normally fall within these powers.

7 PENSIONS ACT 2004

Learning objective	**4.1.10 Explain** the significance of the Pensions Act 2004
	– Scheme-specific funding requirement
	– The Pensions Regulator
	– The Pension Protection Fund

7.1 Types of pension scheme

Pension schemes invest money during a person's working life in order to provide a source of income when that person retires.

Schemes may be categorised into two types:

- Defined contribution or money purchase schemes
- Defined benefit or final salary schemes

Defined contribution schemes will tend to collect a stable amount of money or stable proportion of an employee's salary each month for investment. However, whilst the contributions into the scheme may be defined, the ultimate amount to be received as a pension is unknown. The ultimate pension benefits will depend on, amongst other things, the amount of money contributed and the investment performance.

Defined benefit schemes aim to provide a known benefit for employees. This will typically be a pre-specified proportion of final salary on retirement, with the proportion being dependent on the number of years' service an employee has provided to their employer. Whilst the ultimate amount to be received by way of pension is therefore defined, the level of contributions into the scheme cannot be known in advance with any certainty. For example, if investments perform poorly, contributions may have to be increased in order to ensure sufficient funds will be available to pay the pension as originally promised.

Approved pension schemes receive tax relief on contributions made.

7.2 The Pensions Regulator

The **Pensions Regulator** is the regulatory body for work-based pension schemes in the UK. It replaced OPRA as the regulator on 6 April 2005. A work-based pension scheme is any scheme that an employer makes available to employees. This includes all occupational schemes, and any stakeholder and personal pension schemes where employees have direct payment arrangements.

The Pensions Regulator has a defined set of statutory objectives, and wide **powers** to investigate schemes and to take action where necessary. The Regulator takes a proactive, risk-focused approach to regulation.

The Pensions Act 2004 gives the Pensions Regulator a set of specific objectives.

- To protect the benefits of members of work-based pension schemes

- To promote good administration of work-based pension schemes

- To reduce the risk of situations arising that may lead to claims for compensation from the Pension Protection Fund

7.3 The Pension Protection Fund

The **Pensions Act 2004** has introduced a **Pension Protection Fund (PPF)** to protect employees in the event their company scheme is not able to meet its obligations. Where a sponsoring employer becomes insolvent and unable to pay its liabilities the PPF will provide compensation up to 100% of benefits to existing pensioners and up to 90% of benefits to those who have not yet retired. The PPF is funded by a levy on all benefit pension schemes. The greater the deficit of a company's pension fund between the present value of its future liabilities and the current fund size, the greater the amount that must be contributed into the scheme. This works as an incentive to firms to reduce down their deficits.

The funding provisions of this new scheme requires trustees to:

- Prepare a statement of funding principles specific to circumstances of each scheme. This sets out how the statutory funding objective will be met. This statement must be reviewed every three years.

- Obtain periodic actuarial valuations and actuarial reports.

- Prepare a schedule of contributions.

- Put in place a recovery plan where the statutory funding requirement is not met.

8 STATEMENT OF INVESTMENT PRINCIPLES

Learning objective   4.1.11 **Explain** the purpose of a Statement of Investment Principles.

8.1 Overview

Members of work-based pension schemes must be given specific information regarding the investment of money held within the pension scheme and the investment returns received. This will be set out in the **Statement of Investment Principles (SIP)** which must be provided to members, generally each year, and which must include specific information required by legislation and regulations.

This follows recommendations of the institutional investment review (**Myners Report**, 2001) that pension funds should set out in their **SIP** what they are doing to implement each of their principles. Where pension funds choose not to meet a given principle, they should explain publicly, and to their members, why not.

The following series of **principles that codify the model of best practice** which was the most important outcome of the review. It is hoped that these proposals will positively encourage diversity in investment approaches: the principles constitute a **framework for good practice**.

8.2 Effective decision-making

Decisions should be taken only by persons or organisations with the skills, information and resources necessary to take them effectively.

Trustees should ensure that they have sufficient in-house staff to support them in their investment responsibilities. Trustees should also be paid, unless there are specific reasons to the contrary.

It is good practice for the trustee boards to have an investment subcommittee to provide appropriate focus.

8.3 Clear objectives

Trustees should set out an overall investment objective for the fund that:

- Represents their best judgement of what is necessary to meet the fund's liabilities
- Takes account of their attitude to risk

Objectives for the overall fund should not be expressed in terms that which have no relation to the fund's liabilities, such as performance relative to other pension funds, or to a market index.

8.4 Focus on asset allocation

Strategic asset allocation decisions should receive a level of attention that fully reflect the contribution that they can make towards achieving the fund's investment objective. Decision-makers should consider a full range of investment opportunities, not excluding from consideration any major asset class, including private equity.

8.5 Expert advice

Contracts for actuarial services and investment advice should be opened to separate competition. The fund should be prepared to pay sufficient fees for each service to attract a broad range of kinds of potential providers.

8.6 Explicit mandates

Trustees should agree with both internal and external investment managers an explicit written mandate covering agreement between trustees and managers on:

- An objective, benchmark(s) and risk parameters
- The manager's approach in attempting to achieve the objective
- Clear timescale for measurement and evaluation

8.7 Appropriate benchmarks

Trustees should:

- Explicitly consider whether the index benchmarks they have selected are appropriate

- Where they believe active management has the potential to achieve higher returns, set both targets and risk controls that reflect this, giving managers the freedom to pursue genuinely active strategies

8.8 Performance measurement

Trustees should arrange for measurement of the performance of the fund and make formal assessment of their own procedures and decisions as trustees. They should also arrange for a formal assessment of performance and decision-making delegated to advisers and managers.

8.9 Transparency

A strengthened Statement of Investment Principles should set out:

- Who is taking which decisions and why this structure has been selected

- The fund's investment objective

- The fund's planned asset allocation strategy, including projected investment returns on each asset class, and how the strategy has been arrived at

- The mandates given to all advisers and managers

- The nature of the fee structures in place for all advisers and managers, and why this set of structures has been selected.

8.10 Regular reporting

Trustees should publish their Statement of Investment Principles and the results of their monitoring of advisers and managers and send them annually to members of the fund. The SIP should explain why a fund has decided to depart from any of these principles.

CHAPTER ROUNDUP

- With the implementation of FSMA 2000, the FSA took over responsibility in 2001 for prudential supervision of all firms and conduct of business regulations of those firms doing investment business.

- The Bank of England plays a role in setting interest rates and in seeking to maintain financial stability. Its role will expand following the future proposed abolition of the FSA.

- The national inflation target is set by HM Treasury, who have responsibilities over the FSA in the regulatory system.

- The Panel on Takeovers and Mergers, funded by a levy on larger share transactions, regulates takeovers through the City Code on Takeovers and Mergers, with statutory force since Companies Act 2006 changes.

- The Office of Fair Trading seeks to promote good practice in business, and has a role in ascertaining whether proposed takeovers will lessen competition. The OFT is empowered to refer bids to the Competition Commission, which may block a takeover.

- The City Code is designed to ensure that shareholders are treated fairly and are not denied an opportunity to decide on the merits of a takeover and that shareholders of the same class are given equivalent treatment by an offeror.

- Detailed rules in the City Code dictate the timetable of a bid and the practices and procedures before and during a takeover.

- FSMA 2000 establishes the regime of authorisation of firms to carry out regulated activities relating to specified investments.

- The SYSC section of the FSA Handbook seeks to encourage directors and senior managers of authorised firms to take appropriate responsibility for their firm's arrangements and to ensure they know their obligations.

- The Trustee Act 2000 gives wide investment powers and powers of delegation for trusts where the trust deed does not already specify otherwise.

- The Pensions Regulator is the regulatory body for work-based pension schemes in the UK.

- The Pensions Act 2004 has introduced a Pension Protection Fund to protect employees in the event their company scheme is not able to meet its obligations.

- Members of work-based pension schemes must be given specific information regarding the investment of money held within the pension scheme and the investment returns received. This will be set out in the Statement of Investment Principles which must be provided, generally each year, and which must include specific information required by legislation and regulations.

TEST YOUR KNOWLEDGE

1. What are the 'Tripartite Authorities'?

2. How is the Panel on Takeovers and Mergers financed?

3. What is a 'concert party', in the context of the City Code?

4. Outline the main purposes of the City Code.

5. Which of the following is not a specified investment – Share warrant; NS&I Savings Certificate; Contract for Differences?

6. What is the full name of SYSC, within the FSA Handbook?

7. All trustees must follow the rules on investment powers in the Trustee Act 2000, as these take precedence over anything to the contrary in the trust deed. True or False?

8. What is the name of the regulator of pensions?

9. What is the purpose of the Pension Protection Fund?

10. What is the normal medium for providing periodically to members of work-based pension schemes information regarding the investment of money held within the pension scheme and the investment returns received?

TEST YOUR KNOWLEDGE: ANSWERS

1. In the context of monitoring financial stability, the authorities are the FSA, HM Treasury and the Bank of England.

   (See Section 1.4)

2. A flat £1 levy on all transactions dealt on the LSE above £10,000, plus document charges and exemption charges.

   (See Section 2.1)

3. A concert party comprises persons who, pursuant to an agreement or understanding (whether formal or informal), co-operate to obtain or consolidate control of a company or to frustrate the successful outcome of an offer for a company.

   (See Section 3.3.3)

4. To ensure that shareholders are treated fairly and are not denied an opportunity to decide on the merits of a takeover, and that shareholders of the same class are afforded equivalent treatment by the predator/offeror.

   (See Section 3.5)

5. Warrants and CfDs are specified investments, but the products of National Savings & Investments (a Government agency) are not.

   (See Section 4.11)

6. Senior Management Arrangements, Systems and Controls.

   (See Section 5.1)

7. False. Trustees and their advisers need to follow the Act only if the trust deed does not overrule the Act.

   (See Section 6.1)

8. The Pensions Regulator.

   (See Section 7.2)

9. To protect employees in the event that their work-based pension scheme is not able to meet its obligations.

   (See Section 7.3)

10. The Statement of Investment Principles (SIP).

    (See Section 8.1)

5

The Financial Services Authority

INTRODUCTION

The FSA has objectives that are set in legislation.

The FSA Handbook is the main source of rules that must be followed by any firms engaged in regulated activities. The rule book is continuing to evolve and recent moves from 'rules-based' regulation to 'principles-based' regulation are intended to lead to less emphasis on detailed rules.

The FSA's strategy on supervision has been undergoing some change following the financial crisis of 2007-2009, with a more 'intrusive' approach being adopted.

CHAPTER CONTENTS

CHAPTER LEARNING OBJECTIVES

5 The role of the Financial Services Authority (FSA)

Demonstrate an understanding of the FSA's responsibilities and approach to regulation

5.1.1 Explain the role and statutory objectives of the FSA

5.1.2 Identify and distinguish among the blocks of the FSA Handbook

5.1.3 Explain, in outline, the procedure for authorisation of firms, including knowledge of the threshold conditions

5.1.4 Explain the FSA's risk based approach to supervision and the enforcement and disciplinary powers of the FSA relating to:

- – Information gathering (EG 3)
- – Variation and cancellation of Part IV permission (EG 8)
- – Prohibition of individuals (EG 9)
- – Restitution and redress (EG 11)
- – Statutory notices (DEPP 1&2)

1 FSA ROLE AND OBJECTIVES

Learning objective   **5.1.1 Explain** the role and statutory objectives of the FSA.

1.1 Status of the Financial Services Authority (FSA)

The FSA is an unusually large and powerful regulator although arguably, following the implementation of **MiFID** with effect from November 2007, its role as a legislator is now somewhat diminished as a substantial portion of the FSA rules are determined at European level. Furthermore, the FSA is due to be abolished when the new 2010 Government re-organises regulation, giving more power to the Bank of England, as we have already noted.

The FSA regulates investment, banking and insurance businesses and is the sole authorising body. The FSA is not, however, regarded as acting on behalf of the Crown. Its members, officers and staff are, therefore, not Crown or civil servants. In fact, the FSA is a **private limited company** given powers by FSMA 2000.

Under Schedule 1 FSMA 2000, the FSA has **statutory immunity** from prosecution other than where it can be shown to be acting in bad faith, or in breach of human rights legislation. The concept of bad faith has been tested in recent years, notably by the House of Lords in *Three Rivers DC and others v. Governor and Company of the Bank of England*. This case opened the way for the liquidators of BCCI to bring a claim for 'misfeasance in public office' against the Bank of England for its handling of the BCCI affair, which ultimately failed in 2005.

1.2 Functions of the FSA

Under **s2(4) FSMA 2000**, the **general functions** of the FSA are to:

- Make rules (under FSMA 2000)

- Prepare and issue codes (under FSMA 2000)
- Give general guidance
- Determine policy and principles

The FSA's **principal powers** more specifically include the following.

- Granting **authorisation** and permission to firms to undertake regulated activities
- **Approving** individuals to perform controlled functions
- The right to issue under **S138 FSMA 2000:**
  - General rules (such as the *Conduct of Business* rules) for authorised firms which appear to be necessary or expedient to protect the interests of consumers
  - Principles (such as the *Principles for Businesses*)
  - Codes of conduct (such as the *Code of Practice for Approved Persons*)
  - Evidential provisions and guidance
- The right to **investigate** authorised firms or approved persons
- The right to take **enforcement** action against authorised firms and approved persons
- The right to **discipline** authorised firms and approved persons
- The power to take action against any person for **market abuse**
- The power to **prosecute** for the criminal offences of money laundering, insider dealing and market manipulation
- The right to authorise **collective investment scheme**s, which include unit trust schemes and Open Ended Investment Companies (OEICs)
- The power to **recognise** investment exchanges and clearing houses
- As the **UK Listing Authority**, approval of companies for stock exchange listings in the UK

Note that the term '**firm**' is used generally in the FSA regulations to apply to an authorised person, whether the person is an individual, a partnership or a corporate body.

1.3 The FSA's statutory objectives

1.3.1 Overview

The Financial Services and Markets Act 2000 (FSMA 2000) gives to the FSA five **statutory objectives** (previously four, before the Financial Services Act 2010):

- **Market confidence**: maintaining confidence in the financial system
- **Public awareness**: promoting public understanding of the financial system
- **Financial stability**: contributing to the protection and enhancement of the stability of UK financial system
- **Consumer protection**: securing the appropriate degree of protection for consumers
- **Reduction of financial crime**: reducing the extent to which it is possible for a business to be used for a purpose connected with financial crime

We now look at the regulatory objectives in turn.

1.3.2 Market confidence

A major aspect of this objective is maintaining market confidence by ensuring that the market is not distorted by insiders exploiting privileged information or by persons conducting artificial transactions. It is hoped that the civil offence of market abuse will deliver the confidence that this objective implies. This objective will also embrace requirements regarding recognition of exchanges and ensure reliable price mechanisms.

However, the objective talks of confidence in the UK financial system, which is a broader concept than just market confidence. This links more broadly to how the regulatory regime will deal with systemic risks such as those evident in the Barings and BCCI failures and, more recently, the financial crises of 2007 and 2008.

1.3.3 Public awareness

This objective is seeking to correct an information imbalance that exists between the firms that market the products and consumers, many of whom are unaware of the simplest financial concepts. The regime seeks to correct this information imbalance by requiring firms to disclose key information about products.

It has been argued in recent years that the complexity of financial products such as pensions and life assurance means that the doctrine of disclosure cannot be practically applied. The regulatory regime, therefore, seeks to supplement the disclosure requirement with a stipulation on the regulator to educate consumers of key areas and risks.

> **Changes to FSA objectives**. The FSA was given its public awareness objective on its creation in 2001. The Financial Services Act 2010 requires the FSA to create an independent **Consumer Financial Education Body (CFEB)** with a specific mandate from Parliament to take forward consumer financial education in the UK. **The FSA's public awareness objective will be removed in due course.** In the meantime, the FSA retains its public awareness objective, but its responsibilities in this area in practice must be viewed in the light of Parliament's mandate to the CFEB.

1.3.4 Financial stability

The financial stability objective was given to the FSA by the Financial Services Act 2010 (amending FSMA 2000).

As the supervisory authority, the FSA's principal contribution is ensuring that individual firms and groups are well supervised and that the Authority identifies industry-wide and business model risks.

The FSA seeks to identify relationships between potential macro-prudential (at the level of the economy and the financial services sector and sub-sectors) and micro-prudential risks (at the level of the firm), taking into account conduct and market issues. The FSA aims to feed those insights into our discussions with its 'Tripartite' partners (HM Treasury and the Bank of England).

The FSA seeks to ensure that the regulatory framework in the UK, the EU and globally, supports the overall stability of the financial system.

The Authority provides appropriate information and market data to the Treasury and the Bank of England. The FSA also has a role to play in determining the degree to which the Tripartite Authorities intervene in macro-prudential matters.

1.3.5 Securing the appropriate degree of protection for consumers

The key to considering the scope of the FSA's obligation to protect consumers is the term 'appropriate'. In deciding what this term means, FSMA 2000 requires the FSA to take into account the need that consumers may have for advice and accurate information. In short, therefore, FSMA 2000 tries to strike a balance between what is reasonable for consumers to expect from the FSA and their responsibility for decisions.

1.3.6 The reduction of financial crime

The objective of reducing the extent to which it is possible for financial services business to be used for **financial crime** links closely with the other objectives, as reduction of financial crime will clearly increase confidence in the financial system and ensure protection for consumers.

Financial crime is defined by FSMA 2000 as meaning fraud or dishonesty, misconduct or misuse of information relating to a financial market or handling the proceeds of crime. Thus, the civil offence of market abuse links to this objective, as does the FSA's increased role in the prevention of money laundering.

2 THE FSA HANDBOOK

objective   5.1.2 **Identify** and distinguish among the blocks of the FSA Handbook.

2.1 The role of the FSA Handbook

Financial services regulation derives centrally from the Financial Services and Markets Act 2000 (FSMA 2000), with additional secondary legislation (Statutory Instruments) providing more detail. In the day-to-day running of a regulated firm, it will not generally be necessary to consult the legislation and secondary legislation directly. The principles, rules and regulations to which a firm must adhere when running the business are generally found in the **FSA Handbook.** Even where standards are imposed by FSMA 2000 itself, such as in the case of market abuse and financial promotion, the FSA Handbook is used to provide additional requirements. A **consultation process** generally takes place before new rules are added to the Handbook, which goes some way to alleviating concerns regarding accountability of the FSA and practitioner involvement under FSMA 2000.

The FSA derives its power to make rules in the *FSA Handbook* from FSMA 2000. The Handbook includes the over-arching **Principles for Businesses** as well as various detailed rules such as those contained in the **Conduct of Business Sourcebook**.

Given the range of financial services activities covered, it is hardly surprising that the FSA Handbook is a lengthy document. However, the Handbook has been undergoing a process of simplification, in line with the move towards principles-based regulation. This process was partly carried out in conjunction with the implementation of the Markets in Financial Instruments Directive (MiFID), which resulted in major changes to the content of the *Handbook* with effect from 1 November 2007.

2.2 Structure of the FSA Handbook

The *FSA Handbook* is split into seven main blocks, as follows.

High Level Standards	Prudential Standards
Principles for Businesses (PRIN)	General Prudential Sourcebook (GENPRU)
Statements of Principle and the Code of Practice for Approved Persons (APER)	Prudential Sourcebooks for Banks, Building Societies and Investment Firms (BIPRU), for Insurers (INSPRU), for UCITS Firms (UPRU) and for Mortgage and Home Finance Firms and Insurance Intermediaries (MIPRU)
Threshold Conditions (COND)	
Senior Management Arrangements, Systems and Controls (SYSC)	
Fit & Proper Test for Approved Persons (FIT)	Interim Prudential Sourcebooks (for Banks, Building Societies, Friendly Societies, Insurers and Investment Businesses) (IPRU)
General Provisions (GEN)	
Fees Manual (FEES)	

Business Standards
Conduct of Business (COBS)
Banking Conduct of Business (BCOBS)
Insurance: New Conduct of Business Sourcebook (ICOBS)
Mortgages and Home Finance: Conduct of Business (MCOB)
Client Assets (CASS)
Market Conduct (MAR)
Training & Competence (TC)

Regulatory Processes	Redress
Supervision (SUP)	Dispute Resolution: Complaints (DISP)
Decision Procedure and Penalties Manual (DEPP)	Compensation (COMP)
.	Complaints against the FSA (COAF)

Specialist Sourcebooks
Building Societies (BSOCS)
Collective Investment Schemes (COLL)
Credit Unions (CRED)
Electronic Money (ELM)
Professional Firms (PROF)
Recognised Investment Exchanges and Recognised Clearing Houses (REC)
Regulated Covered Bonds (RCB)

Listing, Prospectus and Disclosure
Listing Rules (LR)
Prospectus Rules (PR)
Disclosure Rules and Transparency Rules (DTR)

2.3 Handbook Guides and Regulatory Guides

Additional **Handbook Guides** point particular kinds of firm in the direction of material relevant to them in the Handbook. These include guides for Energy Market Participants, for Oil Market Participants, and for Service Companies.

There are also **Regulatory Guides** on certain topics, including the Enforcement Guide, and the Perimeter Guidance Manual (PERG) which gives guidance about the circumstances in which authorisation is required or exempt person status is available.

2.4 Types of provision in the FSA Handbook

The *FSA Handbook* contains a number of different kinds of provisions, indicated by letters as follows.

R	This indicates a **rule** and means that it places a binding duty on a firm.
E	This indicates an **evidential provision**. If a firm complies with an evidential provision, this will tend to establish compliance with the linked rule. If a firm breaches an evidential provision, this will tend to establish that a breach of the linked rule has occurred.
G	This indicates **guidance**, which is not binding on a firm but is used to flesh out particular issues arising from rules.
D	The letter **D** indicates **directions** and **requirements** given under various powers conferred by FSMA 2000 and relevant statutory instruments. Directions and requirements are **binding** upon the persons or categories of person to whom they are addressed.
UK	The **UK** flag icon is used to indicate directly applicable, non-FSA, UK legislative material, such as Acts of Parliament and statutory instruments, regulations and orders. Cross-references to this material will use the letters UK.
EU	An **EU** flag icon indicates EU legislative material, such as EU Directives and directly applicable EU Regulations. Cross-references to this material will use the letters **EU**.
P	The letter **P** is used to indicate the **Statements of Principle for approved persons** made under s64 of FSMA 2000. The Statements of Principle are **binding** on approved persons.
C	The letter **C** is used for paragraphs made under s119(2)(b) of FSMA 2000 which specify descriptions of behaviour that, in the opinion of the FSA, **do not amount to market abuse**. These descriptions are conclusive because such behaviour is to be taken, for the purposes of the Act, as not amounting to market abuse.

2.5 Industry guidance

Industry Guidance includes Codes of Practice and similar Statements generated by **trade associations and professional bodies** to help their members understand and follow good practice in meeting regulatory requirements.

As well as not taking action against a person for behaviour that it considers to be in line with **guidance**, the FSA will similarly not take action that is in line with **other materials** published by the FSA in support of the Handbook or **FSA-confirmed Industry Guidance** which were current at the time of the behaviour in question.

However, as **Industry Guidance** is not mandatory (and is one way, but not the only way, to comply with requirements), the FSA does not presume that because firms are not complying with it they are not meeting FSA requirements.

3 AUTHORISATION OF FIRMS

Learning objective 5.1.3 **Explain**, in outline, the procedure for authorisation for firms, including knowledge of the threshold conditions.

FSMA 2000 has created a single authorisation regime for the regulated activities within its scope. This contrasts with the previous financial services regulation arrangements, which contained a variety of separate regulatory regimes.

A firm may be authorised by one of two main routes:

- Authorisation by the FSA
- Passporting under the Markets in Financial Instruments Directive (MiFID)

3.1 Passporting within the EEA

The concept of a **passport** enables firms to use their domestic authorisation to operate not only in their **home state**, but also in other **host states** within the **European Economic Area** (EEA) (EU plus Norway, Iceland and Liechtenstein).

An important aspect of MiFID is that, to make cross-border business easier, the home country principle has been extended. Under MiFID, investment firms which carry out specified investment services and activities (a wider range than under the ISD, as detailed below) are authorised by the member State in which they their registered office is located (the **home state**).

Where a **branch** is set up, **host state** rules will continue to apply. A **tied agent** established in the EEA will be able to act on behalf of a firm instead of the firm needing to set up a branch. (A '**tied agent**', similarly to an **appointed representative** under FSMA 2000, acts on behalf of and under the authority of an investment firm and as a result does not require authorisation.)

3.2 Authorisation by the FSA

By far the most common route to authorisation is to obtain permission from the FSA to carry out one or more regulated activities.

The permission that a firm receives will play a crucial role in defining the firm's business scope. This permission is sometimes referred to as **Part IV permission** as it is set out in Part IV of FSMA 2000.

Where a firm obtains permission to do one or more regulated activities, it is then authorised to do those activities. In the application, the applicant must set out which regulated activities and specified investments it requires permission for. The permission will set out what activities and investments are covered and any limitations and requirements that the FSA wishes to impose.

It is not a criminal offence for a firm to go beyond its permission but doing so may give rise to claims from consumers. Furthermore, the FSA will be able to use the full range of disciplinary sanctions, such as cancelling or varying permission.

3.3 Threshold conditions

Before it grants permission, the FSA must be satisfied that the firm is **fit and proper**. In accordance with FSMA 2000, the firm must meet and continue to satisfy the **'threshold conditions'** for the activity concerned in order to be deemed fit and proper. These link closely with the statutory objective of protecting consumers in that they all go towards ensuring that the business will be operated effectively and supervised by the FSA.

There are five threshold conditions (set out in the **COND** part of the FSA Handbook) as follows.

- **Condition 1** sets out the **legal status** that the applicant must have to carry on certain regulated activities, i.e. the legal structure of the business.

- **Condition 2** relates to the **location of the offices** of the applicant. If the applicant is a UK company, its head and registered offices must be located in the UK. For an applicant that is not a company, if it has its head office in the UK, then it must carry on business in the UK.

- **Condition 3** relates to the effect of **close links** of the applicant with other entities, e.g. other members of the same group.

- **Condition 4** requires that the applicant for authorisation must have **adequate resources** for the activities they seek to undertake. Such resources would not only include capital, but also non-financial resources such as personnel.

- **Condition 5.** The final condition relates to the **suitability** of the applicant. The firm must be considered to be 'fit and proper', i.e. it must have integrity, be competent and have appropriate procedures in place to comply with regulations. The management and staff of the firm must also be **competent**.

Exam tip

> Use the word **CALLS** to help you to learn the five threshold conditions.
>
> > **C**lose links
> > **A**dequate resources
> > **L**egal status
> > **L**ocation of offices
> > **S**uitability

The FSA provides guidance on the threshold conditions in the *FSA Handbook*. The guidance is unsurprisingly very general, as satisfaction of the threshold conditions is considered on a case-by-case basis in relation to each regulated activity that the firm wishes to carry on.

Note that suitability to carry on **one** regulated activity does not mean that the applicant is suitable to carry on **all** regulated activities.

In determining whether the applicant satisfies and will continue to satisfy the threshold conditions under FSMA 2000, the FSA will consider whether the applicant can demonstrate that the firm is ready, willing and organised to comply with the regulatory obligations that will apply if it is given permission to conduct those regulated activities.

Linking closely to Condition 4 is the requirement that the firm demonstrates that it has adequate **financial resources** to meet the financial resources requirement for its type of firm.

3.4 Outline of the authorisation process

Where a firm wishes to obtain permission from the FSA to do a regulated activity, it will be sent an application pack requiring detailed information from the firm. The amount of detailed information that the applicant will have to submit will be related to the risks posed to the four statutory objectives. Therefore, although some applicants will have to complete all sections of the pack, other sections are specific to certain types of business.

In order to get permission, the applicant must show that it is **fit and proper**. This means a number of things.

- Firstly, the applicant must satisfy the **threshold conditions**.

- Secondly, the FSA will operate a risk assessment process. This allows the FSA to be proportional in terms of the information required and the allocation of FSA resources.

In order to assess the above, the applicant will need to detail such matters as the precise scope of the permission it wishes to apply for; the impact of the FSA Handbook on its activities, systems and controls needed and prepare a full business plan setting out its resources (human, systems and capital). The FSA may require applicants to attend meetings to discuss the application before the application documents are submitted.

The initial determination of the application is taken by FSA staff. When the firm is given permission to do a regulated activity it will be recorded on the **public register** of authorised persons maintained by the FSA.

If the FSA staff decide to refuse the application or impose a limit on it, they must give this recommendation to the **Regulatory Decisions Committee (RDC),** who will consider the facts and decide whether to proceed with the staff recommendation or grant the application.

Where an application is refused or limited by the RDC, the applicant may appeal to the **Financial Services and Markets Tribunal**.

4 FSA's Approach to Supervision

Learning objective | **5.1.4 Explain** the FSA's risk based approach to supervision.

4.1 Supervision policy and ARROW

The FSA's approach to supervision is designed to reflect a number of important concepts.

- The FSA's **regulatory objectives**

- The responsibility of **senior management** to ensure that it takes reasonable care to organise and control the affairs of the firm effectively and develops and maintains adequate risk management systems. It is the responsibility of the management to ensure the firm complies with its regulatory requirements.

- The principle that the burden or restriction on firms should be **proportionate** to the benefits to be provided

The FSA's policy on supervision is grouped under the **four** headings:

- **Diagnostic**
- **Monitoring**
- **Preventative**
- **Remedial**

The FSA's overall approach is one of **risk-based supervision**. The Authority has developed a system known as the **A**dvanced **R**isk-**R**esponsive **O**perating Frame**W**ork ('**ARROW**'), which involves the FSA looking at particular risks posed by individual firms and also risks to consumers and to the industry as a whole.

ARROW II is a revised model introduced in 2006 and designed to allow FSA supervisors more accurately to reflect their assessment of risk in individual firms or through cross-firm 'thematic' work.

The aim is to focus the FSA's resources in the most efficient and economic way. The FSA will, therefore, undertake an **impact and probability** assessment on each firm to determine the risks that the firm poses to the five regulatory objectives. In terms of impact, this assesses the effect on the five regulatory objectives. In terms of probability, this is analysed in terms of **risk groups** arising from the firm's strategy, business risks, financial soundness, type of customers, systems and controls and organisation of the firm. The FSA will place firms into risk categories and communicate with them the outcome of the assessment.

The general procedure for this categorisation is as follows.

1.   **Preliminary assessment** of the firm's impact on the regulatory objectives
2.   **Probability assessment** – the detail will depend on the impact rating and complexity of the firm
3.   A sample of various firm's categorisations are then reviewed by a **validation panel**
4.   A **letter** is sent to the firm outlining category
5.   The FSA ensures **ongoing review** of risk assessment

In terms of the supervisory process, the FSA will use a broad **range of tools**, including:

- Desk-based reviews
- Meetings with the firm
- On-site inspections
- Issuing public statements
- Imposing conditions on the firm

4.2 From principles based regulation to 'intrusive' supervision

In the wake of the recent financial crisis, the Chief Executive of the FSA, Hector Sants, commented in a March 2009 speech that 'a principles-based approach does not work with individuals who have no principles'.

Mr Sants said: 'In future, we will seek to make judgements on the judgements of senior management and take actions if, in our view, those actions will lead to risks to our statutory objectives'.

This was a fundamental change in the FSA's approach to supervision, moving from **evidence based regulation** (based on observable facts) to regulation based on judgements about the future.

The new 'intrusive and direct' approach proposed by the FSA would, Mr Sants continued, 'carry significant risk and our judgements will necessarily not always be correct'. It did however appear that society expected regulators to behave in this way.

4.3 Turner Review (March 2009)

The regulatory role of the FSA had come under heavy criticism, from the House of Commons Treasury Committee as well as more widely, following the run on the **Northern Rock** bank in the autumn of 2007. While the directors of the mortgage lender had 'pursued a reckless business model', in the words of the Committee, the FSA had, the Committee asserted, 'systematically failed in its regulatory duty to ensure that Northern Rock would not pose a systemic risk'.

In the light of this and other aspects of the financial turmoil of 2007 and 2008, Lord Adair Turner, Chairman of the FSA, prepared a report commissioned by the Chancellor of the Exchequer to review the events that had led to the financial crisis and to recommend reforms. The **Turner Review** was published in March 2009 as a *'Regulatory response to the global banking crisis'*, and extended to approximately 120 pages.

The FSA's regulatory and supervisory approach, before the crisis, was based on a philosophy that was sometimes characterised – although not by the FSA itself – as a '**light touch**' regulatory regime.

This philosophy seemed to have been broadly based on the beliefs that:

- **Markets are in general self-correcting**, with market discipline a more effective tool than regulation or supervisory oversight through which to ensure that firms' strategies are sound and **risks** contained

- The **primary responsibility for managing risks lies with the senior management** and boards of the individual firms, who are better placed to assess business model risk than bank regulators, and who can be relied on to make appropriate decisions about the balance between risk and return, provided appropriate systems, procedures and skilled people are in place

- **Customer protection is best ensured** not by product regulation or direct intervention in markets, but **by ensuring that wholesale markets** are as **unfettered** and **transparent** as possible, and that the **way in which firms conduct business** is appropriate

The philosophy resulted in a **supervisory approach** which involved:

- A **focus**, evident also in supervisory systems across the world, on the supervision of individual **institutions** rather than on the whole **system**

- A focus on ensuring that **systems and processes** were correctly defined, rather than on challenging **business models and strategies**. (Risk mitigation programmes set out after ARROW reviews – explained later – therefore tended to focus more on organisation structures, systems and reporting procedures, than on overall risks in business models.)

- A focus within the FSA's oversight of '**approved persons**' (eg those proposed by firms for key risk management functions) on checking that there were **no issues of probity** raised by past conduct, **rather than assessing technical skills**, with the presumption that management and boards were in a better position to judge the appropriateness of specific individuals for specific roles

- A balance between conduct of **business regulation** and **prudential regulation** which, with the benefit of hindsight, now appeared **biased towards the former** in most sectors

The Review emphasised the importance of regulation and supervision being based on a '**macro-prudential' (system-wide) approach** rather than focusing solely on specific firms.

The **Turner Review recommendations** included:

- Fundamental changes to **bank capital and liquidity regulations** and to banks' published **accounts**

- National and international action to ensure that **remuneration policies** are designed **to discourage excessive risk-taking**

- Major **changes in the FSA's supervisory approach**, with a focus on business strategies and system-wide risks, rather than internal processes and structures

- Major reforms in the regulation of the European banking market, combining a **new European regulatory authority** and **increased national powers** to constrain risky cross-border activity

4.4 Regulatory response

Writing in the Chief Executive's Overview to the FSA's **2009/10 Business Plan**, Hector Sants complained that the regulatory philosophy of **more principles-based regulation** had often been misunderstood. The focus of the Authority's philosophy, he wrote, is not *per se* on our principles, but rather on judging the consequences of the actions of the firms and the individuals we supervise. Given this philosophy, Sants argued, a better 'strapline' would be **outcomes-focused regulation**. This theme was also discussed in the FSA's Discussion Paper 09/2 *A regulatory response to the global banking crisis.*

An example of this developing emphasis on **outcomes** is found in the FSA's approach to the principle of treating customers fairly (TCF): later in this Study Text, we explain the TCF **consumer outcomes** against which firms are expected to measure their progress in meeting the TCF principle.

As well as other initiatives, the FSA's supervisory operating model has been revised to deliver '**Intensive Supervision**' – a more 'intrusive' and direct regulatory style, requiring the supervisor to have a more integrated or 'holistic' and 'macro-' view of firms and the markets in which they operate.

These changes are being put in place through the '**Supervisory Enhancement Programme**' (**SEP**).

Key features of Intensive Supervision model

- Enhanced analysis and risk identification focusing on business model risk and macro-prudential analysis

- Greater focus on outcome testing over ensuring firms have the appropriate systems and controls

The Intensive Supervision model will be underpinned by the delivery of what the FSA calls its '**credible deterrence**' **philosophy**.

The **SEP** seeks to provide better, more effective and consistent supervision through:

- Relationship management, and an integrated and consistent supervisory process across all relationship managed firms

- A focus on big picture risks: business models and strategy

- A balanced approach to prudential and conduct risks

- An increased focus on macro-prudential and cross-sector risks

- A willingness to make judgements on future risks and to require firms to mitigate them in advance of them crystallising

The new model has required a significant increase in the FSA's supervisory **resource** (200 additional supervisors by mid-2009). Other changes within the Authority include enhanced training requirements for supervisors and strengthened technical support.

4.5 Financial Services Act 2010

Under significant time pressure prior to the dissolution of Parliament, the outgoing Labour Government passed the **Financial Services Act 2010**, which omitted the establishment of a proposed Council for Financial Stability, but included the following measures.

- A requirement for the FSA to make general rules about remuneration policies of regulated firms

- Extension of the company law disclosure regime, under which companies disclose details of directors' remuneration, including executive remuneration reports

- A requirement for the FSA to make rules requiring financial institutions to create and maintain recovery and resolution plans (often called 'living wills') so as to reduce the probability of, and the systemic risks associated with, such institutions failing

- Wider powers for the FSA to regulate short selling, by giving it powers to make rules binding on all investors which are not limited to cases of possible market abuse;

- Increased disciplinary and information gathering powers for the FSA as part of the SEP

5 ENFORCEMENT AND DISCIPLINE

5.1.4 Explain the enforcement and disciplinary powers of the FSA relating to:

- – Information gathering (EG 3)
- – Variation and cancellation of Part IV permission (EG 8)
- – Prohibition of individuals (EG 9)
- – Restitution and redress (EG 11)
- – Statutory notices (DEPP 1&2)

5.1 Overview

The FSA's powers on enforcement are extensive. FSMA 2000 Part XI and the Decision Procedures and Penalties manual (**DEPP**) set out the FSA's powers in this area.

5.2 Information gathering and investigatory powers

The FSA has wide powers under ss165–176 FSMA 2000.

- **Information and documents.** The power to require an authorised firm (or any person connected with it), appointed representatives or certain other persons, e.g. RIEs, to provide it with information, reports or other documents it needs to carry out its duties. The FSA can require the information or documents to be provided within a specified reasonable timescale and at a specified place. The FSA may also require that the information provided is verified and documents are authenticated. The FSA can require a firm to appoint accountants, actuaries and other professionals to carry out a one-off investigation into the firm's activities and report back to the FSA. This is known as a skilled person's report, which the firm must pay for.

- **Investigators.** The FSA may appoint investigators to investigate possible regulatory breaches. This power covers authorised firms, approved persons, appointed representatives and, indeed in some cases such as market abuse, all persons. In some cases, such as money laundering and insider dealing, the FSA may share investigatory powers with the Department for Business, Innovation and Skills (BIS) and other bodies. Under s169 FSMA 2000, the FSA may also launch an investigation in support of an overseas regulator.

  The FSA can require a person under investigation or a connected person to attend for questioning by an investigator and can require a person to produce documents and answer questions. This effectively removes the right to silence. In order to ensure that the regime is compliant with human rights legislation, such answers will not be admissible in criminal or market abuse proceedings.

- **Entry to premises.** The FSA may seek access to an authorised firm's premises on demand. Where this is refused, a court warrant may be obtained.

Under s177 FSMA 2000, it is a criminal offence to falsify, conceal, destroy or dispose of a document that the person knows or suspects would be relevant to the investigation, or knowingly or recklessly provide false or misleading information. The maximum penalty for breaching s177 is two years' imprisonment and an unlimited fine in the Crown Court.

The FSA will not normally make public the fact that it is or is not investigating a particular matter unless it is in the interests of consumers. In addition, the FSA must use its powers in a way that is transparent, proportionate, consistent and fair.

5.3 Varying or cancelling permission and withdrawing authorisation

Under s45 FSMA 2000, the FSA has a general power to vary or cancel a firm's 'Part IV' permission to undertake a regulated activity or withdraw authorisation entirely. This will generally take place where:

- The FSA has serious concerns regarding the firm's business activities

- A firm fails to continue to satisfy the Threshold Conditions Sourcebook (set out in the High Level Standards block of the FSA Handbook) on an ongoing basis

- The firm has not carried out a regulated activity for which it has a Part IV Permission for at least twelve months

- It is desirable to protect consumers

More commonly, the FSA will vary a firm's permission by placing tailored requirements on the firm. For example, the FSA may use the power to stop the firm seeking a particular class of client or selling particular investments. Such action is normally taken to protect consumers, but the FSA may vary permission for other reasons, such as the fact that a firm has changed its controller or stops using its permission. The process requires referral to the Regulatory Decisions Committee (RDC). The firm must be able to refer the matter to the Financial Services and Markets Tribunal.

5.4 Varying or withdrawing approval of individuals

Variation or withdrawal of approval applies to certain individuals who work within an authorised firm and require approval. Approval to perform a **controlled function** may be removed if the individual is no longer fit and proper to conduct that controlled function. To withdraw approval, the FSA must refer the matter to the RDC who will give the individual (copied to their employer) a warning notice followed by a decision notice. The individual must be able to refer the matter to the Financial Services and Markets Tribunal.

In deciding whether to withdraw approval, the FSA will take into account the controlled functions being performed and a variety of factors including: qualifications and training; the fit and proper criteria, e.g. honesty, integrity, reputation, competence, capability, financial soundness; and whether the approved person has breached a statement of principle or been involved in their firm breaching a rule. The FSA will also consider the severity of the risk posed to consumers and confidence in the financial system and look at the individual's disciplinary record. Final notices of withdrawal of approval are normally published, unless this would prejudice the interests of consumers.

5.5 Prohibition of individuals

Section 56 FSMA 2000 allows the FSA to prohibit individuals from carrying out specified functions in relation to regulated activities within the investment industry. As already mentioned, this is called a **Prohibition Order** and may be issued in respect of anyone whether they are approved or not: such an order could be imposed on a trader, a director, an IT staff member or a secretary, for example.

An unapproved person breaching a prohibition order is subject to a maximum fine of £5,000. Final notices of the issue of prohibition orders are normally published on the FSA website.

5.6 Restitution and redress

There are two types of **restitution powers** available to the FSA – those that require a court order, and those the FSA can impose itself. These are set out at ss382–386 FSMA 2000.

The FSA will be able to apply to the court to require any person who has breached a rule or other requirement of FSMA 2000 to provide compensation or restitution to those who have suffered loss as a result. This will be particularly important where the FSA seeks to enforce rules such as market abuse against non-authorised persons.

In determining whether to exercise its powers, the FSA will have regard to the circumstances of the case and also other facts including other ways the consumer might get redress and whether it would be more effective or cost effective for the FSA to require redress. It should therefore be borne in mind that while the FSA has these powers, it will only exercise powers of redress for consumers in very limited circumstances. More commonly, a person who has suffered a loss will seek redress themselves directly from the firm and, if unsuccessful, from the Financial Ombudsman Service or the courts.

Where an authorised firm has breached a rule or other requirement of FSMA 2000, the FSA may require the firm to provide compensation or restitution without a court order.

Where there is evidence of industry-wide rule breaches (such as that seen in the pensions misselling scandal) the FSA may ask HM Treasury to make an order authorising an industry-wide review or enquiry.

5.7 Injunctions

The FSA may also (under s380 FSMA 2000) apply to a court for an injunction to restrain or prohibit persons from breaking a rule or other requirement of FSMA 2000.

5.8 Fines and censure

The FSA may discipline firms or approved persons for acts of misconduct. Traditional disciplinary measures available are private warnings, public statements of misconduct or censures and fines.

In certain cases, the FSA may determine that it is not appropriate to bring **formal disciplinary proceedings**, for example, if the conduct is minor or where full remedial action was taken by the firm or approved person themselves (although these facts are not necessarily conclusive that the FSA will not bring formal proceedings). If the FSA thinks it would be beneficial for the approved person or firm to know that they are close to being the subject of formal proceedings then the FSA can issue a private warning. A private warning will state that while the FSA has cause for concern, the FSA does not intend to take formal proceedings. This warning will form part of the firm or approved person's compliance history and may be relevant when determining future proceedings. The recipient of the private warning is asked to acknowledge receipt and may comment on the warning if they so wish.

For more serious breaches, a public statement of misconduct or censure will be appropriate, often combined with a fine. There is no limit on the monetary amount of the fine the FSA can award. Fines must be applied for the benefit of the regulated community.

5.9 Enforcement criteria

The primary responsibility for ensuring compliance with regulatory obligations rests with the authorised firm. The FSA's focus will thus primarily be on the firm when considering disciplinary action. Firms can be disciplined for breaches of rules and principles. However, where an approved person is personally culpable (covering deliberate or negligent conduct) the FSA may also take disciplinary action against an approved person.

The focus for an approved person will be whether they have breached the Statements of Principle for Approved Persons or have knowingly been concerned in a rule breach by the firm. Note that simply because a failure has occurred in an area for which an approved person is responsible does not automatically mean they will be disciplined, only if the person's conduct was below the standards expected.

If a breach involves one of the various regulators (such as the FSA, overseas regulators, exchanges, the Takeover Panel or another relevant body) the FSA will consult with the most appropriate bodies to consider the matter. The FSA has Memoranda of Understanding with various other organisations.

In determining whether or not to take any disciplinary action, the FSA will consider the full circumstances of the case. Some of the factors they may consider are as follows.

- **The nature and seriousness of the breach.** This includes: whether the breach was deliberate or reckless; the duration/frequency of the breach; the amount of any benefit obtained by the firm; whether the breach reveals serious or systemic weaknesses of the firm's management systems or internal controls of a firm; the loss or risk of loss to consumers and market users; and the nature and extent of any financial crime facilitated.

- **The conduct of the firm or approved person after the breach.** How quickly, effectively and completely the firm or approved person brought the breach to the attention of the FSA; how co-operative they were during the investigation and any remedial steps the firm or approved person has taken since the breach, e.g. compensating consumers and any internal disciplinary action.

- **The previous regulatory record of the firm.**

In determining whether to issue a censure or give a financial penalty, the FSA will consider all the relevant circumstances including:

- Whether the accused made a profit or avoided a loss as a result of the misconduct. If so, a financial penalty may be more appropriate

- More serious breaches are more likely to receive a financial penalty

- Whether the accused has admitted the breach, co-operated with the FSA and compensated consumers. If so, a censure/statement of misconduct may be more appropriate

- The disciplinary record/compliance history of the accused. A poor record or history may make a financial penalty more appropriate

In determining the size of any penalty, the FSA must have regard to:

- The seriousness of the misconduct
- The extent to which the misconduct was deliberate or reckless
- Whether the person on whom the penalty is to be imposed is an individual

5.10 Enforcement and the RDC

The FSA's **Enforcement Division** investigates when firms breach FSA rules or the provisions of FSMA 2000. Enforcement staff prepare and recommend action in individual cases. For more significant decisions (called **statutory notice decisions**) the FSA passes the case to another body which is a separate Committee of the FSA, called the **Regulatory Decisions Committee (RDC)**.

The RDC will look at the case and decide whether or not to take action. This would cover the giving of fines, censures, restitution orders, and withdrawing, varying or refusing authorisation or approval. For less serious disciplinary actions, e.g. requesting the firm to provide reports, the FSA may act itself under its 'executive procedures'.

The RDC is appointed by the FSA Board to exercise certain regulatory powers on its behalf. It is accountable to the board of the FSA for the decisions. However, the RDC is outside the FSA management structure and apart from the Chairman of the RDC, none of the RDC's members are FSA employees. The RDC members comprise practitioners and suitable individuals representing the public interest.

If the RDC decide to take action:

- A **Warning Notice** will be sent, containing details of the proposed action. The person concerned then has access to the material which FSA is relying on and may make **oral or written representations** to the RDC.

- The RDC will then issue a **Decision Notice** detailing the reasons for the decision, proposed sanction and a notice of the right to refer the matter to the Financial Services and Markets Tribunal, which undertakes a complete rehearing of the case.

- When a decision notice is accepted, or appeals finalised, a **Final Notice** is sent to the person.

A Final Notice only contains FSA/RDC/Tribunal discipline, not any disciplinary action the firm has taken itself internally. The process is summarised in the following table.

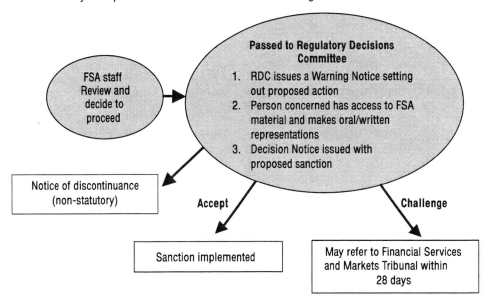

Under Part V of FSMA 2000, the FSA must commence disciplinary action within **two years** of first being aware of the misconduct.

The FSA must be proportionate in its use of regulatory enforcement measures: 'the punishment must fit the crime'. The disciplinary process has been designed to ensure that it is compliant with human rights legislation. Therefore, while FSA staff will investigate the matter and decide whether they feel enforcement action is appropriate, they will not take the final decision on matters of such regulatory significance.

The FSA can take decisions themselves under their own **executive procedures** for matters of lesser regulatory impact to the firms, such as imposing a requirement on a firm to submit regular reports covering activities such a trading, complaints or management accounts.

The different types of notice are summarised below.

5.11 Statutory notices

In summary, these are as follows.

- **Warning notice**: gives the recipient details about action the FSA/RDC proposes to take and the recipient's right to make representations.

- **Decision notice**: gives the recipient details of the action the FSA/RDC has decided to take subject to the RDC going through its formal procedures.

- **Further decision notice**: gives the recipient details of different action the FSA/RDC has decided to take subsequent to giving the original Decision Notice. This can only be given where the recipient consents.

- **Supervisory notice**: gives the recipient details about action the FSA/RDC has taken or proposes to take, normally with immediate effect, i.e. prior to formal procedures. In the FSA's Decision Procedure and Penalties Manual (DEPP), the supervisory notice about a matter first given to the recipient is referred to as the **first supervisory notice** and the supervisory notice given after consideration of any representations is referred to as the **second supervisory notice**.

5.12 Non-statutory notices

- **Notice of discontinuance**: is issued where proceedings set out in a decision or warning notice are being discontinued

- **Final notice**: sets out the terms of the action the FSA/RDC has decided to take and the date it takes effect from

5.13 Factors influencing enforcement action

In determining whether or not to take enforcement action, the FSA will consider the full circumstances of the case. Some of the factors they may consider are as follows.

- The **nature and seriousness** of the breach, including:
  - Whether the breach was deliberate or reckless
  - Whether the breach reveals serious or systemic weaknesses of the firm's management systems or internal controls of a firm
  - The loss or risk of loss to consumers and market users
- The **conduct** of the firm or approved person after the breach, including:
  - How quickly, effectively, and completely, the firm or approved person brought the breach to the attention of the FSA
  - Any remedial steps the firm or approved person has taken since the breach, e.g. compensating consumers, and any internal disciplinary action
- The **previous regulatory record** of the firm

In certain cases, the FSA may determine that it is not appropriate to bring formal enforcement proceedings, for example, if the conduct is minor or where full remedial action was taken by the firm or approved person themselves (although these facts are not necessarily conclusive that the FSA will not bring formal proceedings).

If the FSA think it would be beneficial for the approved person or firm to know that they were close to being the subject of formal proceedings, then the FSA can issue a **Private Warning**.

- A Private Warning will state that, while the FSA has cause for concern, it does not intend to take formal proceedings.

- A Private Warning will form part of the firm or approved person's compliance history and may be relevant when determining future proceedings.

- The recipient of the Private Warning is asked to acknowledge receipt and may comment on the warning if they wish to.

5.14 Recent FSA record on enforcement: 'credible deterrence'

The FSA's Annual Report for the year to 31 March 2009 showed that the FSA levied £27.3 million in financial penalties during the year, compared to £4.4 million in the previous year, and prohibited a record 58 individuals from carrying out regulated activities compared to 30 the year before. The Authority commented that this reflected its more proactive approach to enforcement – its **'credible deterrence philosophy'**.

5.15 Right to refer to the Tribunal

FSMA 2000 states that the FSA may not publish information if it would be unfair to the person to whom it relates. The effect of this is that no Warning Notice or Decision Notice may be published by the FSA or the person to whom it is given until reference to the Tribunal has been dealt with and it is clear of further appeals. Therefore, it will be the details of the Final Decision Notice which will be published by the FSA, not the original Decision or Warning Notice.

A person who receives a Decision Notice or Supervisory Notice (including a third party who has been given a copy of the Decision Notice) has the right to refer the decision to the **Financial Services and Markets Tribunal**.

The Tribunal is not bound by earlier proceedings, it can increase or reduce the penalty and can look at new evidence.

CHAPTER ROUNDUP

- The statutory objectives that are stated in FSMA 2000spell out the purpose of the regulatory framework under the FSA as overall regulator.

- The FSA has rule-making powers, and the power to determine policy and principles.

- The FSA handbook is divided into seven blocks. Within each block there are various sourcebooks.

- There is a single authorisation regime for the various types of regulated activity. To be authorised, the firm must be deemed fit and proper, and must satisfy the threshold conditions.

- The FSA's approach to supervision is 'risk-based', meaning that supervisory effort is directed at higher risk areas. The FSA has aimed to strike a balance between principles and rules with various corrective mechanisms being adopted to try to prevent any problems creating unacceptable levels of difficulty.

- ARROW, the Advanced Risk-Responsive Operating FrameWork, involves the FSA looking at particular risks posed by individual firms and also risks to consumers and to the industry as a whole.

- The 2009 Turner Review acknowledged that there are limits to the degree to which risks can be identified and offset at the level of the individual firm. As well stressing a more intensive and direct regulatory style in its Supervisory Enhancement Programme, the FSA has been seeking to focus regulatory effort on emphasising outcomes.

- The general prohibition (S19 FSMA 2000) states that no person may carry on a regulated activity in or into the UK by way of business or purport to do so, unless they are authorised or exempt.

- The FSA has wide powers to visit firms' premises without notice and to require documents to be produced.

- Regulatory enforcement measures include public censure, unlimited fines, restitution orders and cancellation of authorisation or approval. Various Statutory Notices may be issued in cases involving the FSA's Regulatory Decisions Committee.

- The Financial Services and Markets Tribunal can re-hear FSA enforcement and authorisation cases.

TEST YOUR KNOWLEDGE

1. Outline the FSA's statutory objectives.

2. List the seven blocks of the FSA Handbook.

3. Outline what is meant by 'passporting'.

4. What is 'ARROW II'?

5. Explain briefly the FSA's move away from 'evidence-based' regulation.

6. How much notice must the FSA give if it wants to seek entry to a firms' premises?

7. What is the role of the Regulatory Decisions Committee in enforcement cases?

8. What are the types of Statutory Notice in enforcement cases?

TEST YOUR KNOWLEDGE: ANSWERS

1.
   - **Market confidence**: maintaining confidence in the financial system

   - **Public awareness**: promoting public understanding of the financial system (an objective expected to be removed in due course)

   - **Financial stability**: contributing to the protection and enhancement of the UK financial system

   - **Consumer protection**: securing the appropriate degree of protection for consumers

   - **Reduction of financial crime**: reducing the extent to which it is possible for a business to be used for a purpose connected with financial crime

   (See Section 1.3.1)

2.
   - High level standards
   - Prudential standards
   - Business standards
   - Regulatory processes
   - Redress
   - Specialist sourcebooks
   - Listing, prospectus and disclosure

   (See Section 2.2)

3. The idea of a 'passport' enables firms to use their domestic authorisation to operate not only in their home state, but also in other host states within the EEA.

   (See Section 3.1)

4. ARROW (Advanced Risk-Responsive Operating FrameWork) is the risk-based supervision model which involves the FSA looking at particular risks posed by individual firms and also at risks to consumers and to the industry as a whole. ARROW II is a revised model which is designed to allow FSA supervisors more accurately to reflect their assessment of risk in individual firms or through cross-firm 'thematic' work.

   (See Section 4.1)

5. In future, the Authority would seek to make judgements on the judgements of senior management and take actions if it took the view that those actions would lead to risks to the statutory objectives.

   This was a fundamental change in the FSA's approach to supervision, moving from evidence based regulation, which is regulation based on observable facts, to regulation based on judgements about the future.

   (See Section 4.2)

6. None. The FSA may seek access to an authorised firm's premises on demand. Where this is refused, a court warrant may be obtained.

   (See Section 5.2)

7. The RDC is an FSA committee. It will examine and reach a decision on enforcement cases that are statutory notice decisions.

   (See Section 5.10)

8. Warning notice; decision notice; further decision notice; supervisory notice.

   (See Section 5.11)

6

The Regulatory Framework

INTRODUCTION

The rules we outline in this chapter cover various areas.

The approved persons regime is designed to ensure that employees undertaking certain roles meet specified levels of competence. A firm must have systems to ensure that staff stay appropriately trained and competent.

The regulator is required by law to seek to reduce financial crime, and the financial services industry must keep in place measures to help prevent and stop such crime.

An aggrieved customer may pursue an unresolved complaint against a firm with the Financial Services Ombudsman or, ultimately, the court. When firms do fail, the Financial Services Compensation Scheme offers some limited protection.

CHAPTER CONTENTS

CHAPTER LEARNING OBJECTIVES

6 The regulatory framework

Demonstrate an ability to apply the principles and rules as set out in the regulatory framework

6.1 Approved persons, controlled functions, training and competence

6.1.1 Define an approved person

6.1.2 Define a controlled function

6.1.3 Identify the types of controlled function defined within the FSA Handbook (SUP 10)

6.1.4 Identify the main assessment criteria in the FSA's Fit and Proper Test for approved persons (FIT)

6.1.5 Explain the application procedure for approved persons (SUP 10)

6.1.6 Explain the procedure for an approved person moving within a group (SUP 10)

6.1.7 Explain the requirements relating to training and achieving and maintaining competence

6.2 Record keeping and reporting information

6.2.1 Apply the rules relating to record keeping

6.2.2 Apply the rules relating to occasional reporting to client

6.2.3 Apply the rules relating to periodic reporting to clients

6.3 Market conduct and financial crime

6.3.1 Explain the various sources of money laundering and counter terrorism regulation and legislation

- FSA rules
- Money Laundering Regulations
- Proceeds of Crime Act 2002

6.3.2 Explain the role of the Joint Money Laundering Steering Group (JMLSG)

6.3.3 Explain the main features of the guidance provided by the JMLSG

6.3.4 Explain the three stages involved in the money laundering process

6.3.5 Explain the four offence categories under UK money laundering legislation

6.3.6 Explain the meaning of 'insider information' covered by CJA 1993

6.3.7 Explain the offence of insider dealing covered by the CJA

6.3.8 Identify the penalties for being found guilty of insider dealing

6.3.9 Explain the FSA's powers to prosecute insider dealing

6.3.10 Understand the nature of behaviours defined as market abuse (MAR 1.3, 4.5, 6, 7, 8 & 9)

6.3.11 Explain the enforcement powers of the FSA relating to market abuse (MAR 1.1, 4, 5 & 6)

6.4 Complaints handling, the Financial Ombudsman Service and the Financial Services Compensation Scheme

6.4.1 Explain the FSA rules relating to handling of complaints (DISP 1.3)

6.4.2 Explain the role of the Financial Ombudsman Service (DISP Introduction and DISP 2)

6.4.3 Distinguish compulsory from voluntary jurisdiction (DISP Introduction)

6.4.4 Explain the procedure and time limits for the resolution of complaints (DISP 1.4, 1.5 & 1.6)

6.4.5 Explain the rules relating to record keeping and reporting (DISP 1.9, 1.10)

6.4.6 Explain the rules relating to determination by the Ombudsman (DISP 3)

6.4.7 Explain the purpose of the Financial Services Compensation Scheme (FSCS) (COMP 1.1.7)

6.4.8 Explain the circumstances under which the FSCS will pay compensation (COMP 1.3.3, 3.2.1 (1) & (2), 4.2.1 & 2(1) to (6))

6.4.9 Identify the limits on the compensation payable by the FSCS (COMP 10.2.1, 2 & 3)

1 APPROVED PERSONS AND CONTROLLED FUNCTIONS

1.1 Procedure for obtaining approval

objectives

6.1.1 Define an approved person.

6.1.4 Identify the main assessment criteria in the FSA's Fit and Proper Test for approved persons (FIT).

6.1.5 Explain the application procedure for approved persons (SUP 10).

6.1.6 Explain the procedure for an approved person moving within a group (SUP 10).

Certain **individuals** within an authorised firm will require **approval** from the FSA because they carry out **controlled functions**. We explain what the controlled functions are below.

It is important to appreciate that the process of an **individual** obtaining **approved person** status is different from the process of a **firm** obtaining **authorisation**.

To obtain approval, a person must satisfy the FSA that they are **fit and proper** to carry out the controlled function. The suitability of a member of staff who performs a controlled function is covered in the **Fit and Proper Test for Approved Persons** (part of the High Level Standards section of the FSA Handbook).

The most important considerations are as follows.

- **Honesty, integrity and reputation.** The FSA will examine whether the person's reputation might have an adverse impact on the firm they are doing a controlled function for. This will include looking at a number of factors including whether they have had any criminal convictions, civil claims, previous disciplinary proceedings, censure or investigations by any regulator, exchange, governing body or court; any other previous contraventions of regulations; any complaints which have been upheld; any connection with any body which has previously been refused a registration, authorisation or licence or had such registrations, authorisations or licences revoked or been expelled by a regulatory or governmental body; whether they have had any management role within any entities which have gone into liquidation; whether they have been dismissed or asked to resign from a similar position or position of trust; any disqualifications as a director, and finally whether they have been candid and truthful in their dealings with all regulatory bodies and demonstrated a willingness to comply with the regulatory and legal standards applicable to them. When looking at previous convictions, even old (i.e. spent) convictions, as defined in the Rehabilitation of Offenders Act 1974, can be taken into account.

- **Competence and capability.** The FSA will examine whether the Training and Competence requirements in the FSA Handbook have been complied with and whether they have demonstrated by training and experience that they are able to perform the controlled function. If a person has been convicted of, or dismissed or suspended from employment due to drug or alcohol abuse this will be considered in relation only to their continuing ability to perform that function. In addition, S61 FSMA 2000 emphasises that the fit and proper test for approved persons includes assessing qualifications, training and competence. It is not a requirement that a person has experience in order to be approved.

- **Financial soundness.** The FSA will look at whether the applicant has any outstanding judgement debts, has filed for bankruptcy or been involved in any similar proceedings. The fact that a person is of limited financial resources will not in itself affect their suitability to perform a controlled function.

These criteria must be met on a continuing basis. Individuals performing a controlled function must obtain approval **before** they take up the role.

To apply for approval the firm must complete **Form A**. It is the responsibility of the firm and not the individual candidate to submit the application. Where a firm outsources a controlled function it must take reasonable care to ensure that no person performs a controlled function regarding the firm's regulated activities without FSA approval. FSMA 2000 allows the FSA **three months** from the time it receives a properly completed application form to come to a decision.

A firm must take reasonable care to ensure that a member of staff does not perform a controlled function unless he has prior approval from the FSA. The firm has a duty to send a notice to withdraw approval on **Form C** within **seven** business days to the FSA if an approved person ceases to perform a controlled function. If the individual is determined to be fit and proper, the FSA will grant the application for approval and provide written notification of this to the firm and will update its register of approved persons. Where the FSA staff decide to refuse a person approved person status, the matter is passed on to the RDC who will deal with the decision. If the applicant is not satisfied by the RDC's decision they can refer the matter to the Financial Services and Markets Tribunal.

The firm has a duty to send a **Form E** to the FSA where an approved person transfers internally.

1.2 Controlled functions

Learning objectives	**6.1.2 Define** a controlled function.
	6.1.3 Identify the types of controlled function defined within the FSA Handbook (SUP 10).

Section 59 FSMA 2000 and the **Supervision Manual (SUP)** state that a person cannot carry out a **controlled function** in a firm unless that individual has been **approved** by the FSA.

Note that we are now referring to the individual members of staff of an authorised firm. When a person is performing a controlled function and is not approved, there is a breach of statutory duty. In such a case, a private person has the right to sue their firm for damages if they have suffered loss, using **S71** FSMA 2000.

The FSA may specify a function as a **controlled function** if the individual performing it is:

- Exerting a significant influence on the conduct of the firm's affairs
- Dealing directly with customers
- Dealing with the property of customers

The *FSA Handbook* (specifically, the **Supervision Manual**) has identified specific controlled functions which are split into the following groups. (The numbering is discontinuous because of re-categorisation of functions.)

Group	Function
Governing functions	1. Director function 2. Non-executive director function 3. Chief executive function 4. Partner function 5. Director of an unincorporated association function 6. Small Friendly Society function
Required functions	8. Apportionment and oversight function 9. EEA investment business oversight function 10. Compliance oversight function 11. Money Laundering Reporting Officer function 12. Actuarial function 12A. With-profits actuary function 12B. Lloyd's actuary function
Systems and controls function	28. Systems and controls function
Significant management function	29. Significant management function
Customer functions	30. Customer function

Individuals who fall within all of the above categories **except** customer functions would be considered to be exerting a **significant influence** on the conduct of the firm's affairs.

In **July 2009**, the FSA made the following changes to the approved person regime:

- Extended the scope and application of director function and Non- Executive Director to include persons employed by an unregulated parent undertaking or holding company, whose decisions or actions are regularly taken into account by the governing body of a regulated firm

- Extended the definition of the significant management controlled function to include all proprietary traders who are not senior managers but who are likely to exert significant influence on a firm

2 TRAINING AND COMPETENCE

g objective 6.1.7 **Explain** the requirements relating to training and competence.

Principle 3 of the **Principles for Businesses** requires firms to take reasonable care to organise and control its affairs responsibly and effectively, with adequate risk management systems. This implies having appropriate systems of control, including ensuring employees maintain and enhance competence.

SYSC states that a firm's systems and controls should enable it to satisfy itself of the suitability of anyone who acts for it. A requirement under **MiFID** is that firms must employ personnel with the skills, knowledge and expertise necessary for the discharge of the responsibilities allocated to them.

Requirements relating to Training and Competence (TC) for employees are set out in the *FSA Handbook*, as summarised below.

A contravention of the TC rules does not give rise to a right of action by a private person under section 150 of FSMA 2000.

2.1 The competent employees rule

Competence means having the skills, knowledge and expertise needed to discharge the responsibilities of an employee's role. This includes achieving a good standard of **ethical behaviour**.

- The **competent employees rule** is now the main *Handbook* requirement relating to the competence of employees. The purpose of the TC sourcebook is to support the FSA's supervisory function by supplementing the competent employees rule for **retail activities**.

- The **competent employees rule** is that firms must employ personnel with the skills, knowledge and expertise necessary for the discharge of the responsibilities allocated to them. This rule applies to non-MiFID firms as well as **MiFID** firms.

2.2 Assessment of competence and supervision

Appropriate examination requirements apply to **designated investment business** carried on for a **retail client**, except that they do not apply to providing basic advice on non-deposit-based stakeholder products. There are also appropriate examination requirements for **regulated mortgage activity**, and home reversion schemes, carried on for customers.

Employees must not carry out these activities without first passing the relevant **regulatory module** of an appropriate examination.

Firms may choose to impose time limits on the time by which examinations must be passed, or on the number of times examinations can be attempted.

In respect of these activities, firms must not allow employees to carry them on without **appropriate supervision**.

The **level and intensity** of supervision should be significantly greater in the period before the firm has assessed the employee as competent, than after. A firm should, therefore, have clear criteria and procedures relating to the **specific point** at which the employee is **assessed as competent** in order to be able to demonstrate when and why a reduced level of supervision may be considered appropriate. At all stages, firms should consider the **level of relevant experience** of an employee when determining the level of supervision required.

Those providing the supervision should have the necessary **coaching and assessment skills**, as well as **technical knowledge**. Firms should consider whether supervisors should themselves pass **appropriate examinations**.

Employees' **training needs** should be assessed at the outset and at regular intervals, including when their role changes. Firms must review employees' competence on a regular and frequent basis, and should take action to ensure that they **remain competent** in their role, taking into account:

- Technical knowledge and its application
- Skills and expertise
- Changes in markets, products, legislation and regulation

2.3 Appropriate examinations

The FSA maintains a list of **appropriate examinations**, for the activities for which they are required, from which firms may choose. Although a firm may set its own examinations, choosing examinations from the FSA list may be relied on as 'tending to establish compliance' with the TC rules.

An employee with three years of 'up-to-date' **relevant experience outside the UK** may be exempted from modules of an appropriate examination, but the regulatory module must still be taken. However, this type of exemption will not apply to those advising retail clients on packaged products, broker fund advising, advising on syndicate participation at Lloyd's or acting as a pension transfer specialist.

2.4 T&C record-keeping

A firm must make appropriate records to demonstrate compliance with the rules in TC and keep them for the following periods after an employee stops carrying on the activity:

- At least five years for MiFID business
- Three years for non-MiFID business, and
- Indefinitely for a pension transfer specialist

3 RECORD KEEPING AND REPORTING INFORMATION

3.1 Record keeping

6.2.1 **Explain** the rules relating to record keeping.

Firms are required to arrange for orderly records to be kept, which must be sufficient to enable the FSA (or other competent authority) to:

- Monitor compliance with the requirements under the regulatory system
- Ascertain that the firm has complied with all obligations with respect to clients and potential clients

A firm must take reasonable care to make and retain adequate records of matters and dealings (including accounting records) which are the subject of requirements and standards under the regulatory system.

Records should be capable of being reproduced in English, on paper, or alternatively in the official language of a different country for records relating to business done there.

MiFID requires firms to keep records for **five years**, for MiFID business generally.

For **non-MiFID business**, a retention period of five years also commonly applies, but note the following exceptions.

Record retention periods

- Indefinitely, for pension transfers, pension opt-outs and FSAVCs (Free-Standing Additional Voluntary Contributions arrangements, for pensions)

- Five years, for life policies and pension contracts, but six years for financial promotions for these products

- Three years for some non-MiFID requirements, such as suitability reports for products other than those mentioned above

- Three years, for copies of confirmations and periodic statements, in respect of non-MiFID business

- Three years, for periodic statements provided to participants in collective investment schemes

- Six months for records of telephone conversations and electronic communications

3.2 Reporting executions

Learning objective **6.2.2 Apply** the rules relating to occasional reporting to clients (COBS 16.2).

In respect of **MiFID** and equivalent third country business, a firm must ensure that clients receive **adequate reports** on the services provided to it by the firm and their costs.

A firm must provide promptly in a durable medium the **essential information** on **execution of orders** to clients in the course of **designated investment business**, when it is not managing the investments. The information may be sent to an agent of the client, nominated by the client in writing.

For retail clients, a notice confirming execution must be sent as soon as possible and no later than the first business day following receipt of confirmation from the third party.

Firms must supply information about the **status of a client's order** on request.

For **series of orders** to buy units or shares in a collective undertaking (such as a **regular savings plan**), after the initial report, further reports must be provided at least at six-monthly intervals.

Where an order is executed in tranches, the firm may supply the price for each tranche or an average price. The price for each tranche must be made available on the request of a retail client.

For business that is not MiFID or equivalent third country business, confirmations need **not** be supplied if:

- The client has agreed not to receive them (with informed written consent, in the case of retail clients), or

- The designated investment is a life policy or a personal pension scheme (other than a SIPP), or

- The designated investment is held in a CTF and the information is contained in the annual statement

Copies of confirmations dispatched must be **kept** for at least **five years**, for MiFID and equivalent third country business, and for at least **three years** in other cases.

Information to be included in trade confirmations to a retail client

- Reporting firm identification

- Name / designation of client

- Trading day and time

- Order type (e.g. limit order / market order)

- Venue identification

- Instrument identification

- Buy / sell indicator (or nature of order, if not buy/sell)

- Quantity

- Unit price

- Total consideration

- Total commissions and expenses charged with, if requested, itemised breakdown

- Currency exchange rate, where relevant

- Client's responsibilities regarding settlement, including time limit for payment or delivery, and appropriate account details where not previously notified

- Details if the client's counterparty was in the firm's group or was another client, unless trading was anonymous

3.3 Periodic reporting

6.2.3 Apply the rules relating to periodic reporting to clients (COBS 16.3).

A firm **managing investments** on behalf of a client must provide a periodic statement to the client in a durable medium, unless such a statement is provided by another person. The statement may be sent to an agent nominated by the client in writing.

Information to be included in a periodic report

- Name of the firm

- Name / designation of retail client's account

- Statement of contents and valuation of portfolio, including details of:

    - Each designated investment held, its market value or, if unavailable, its fair value
    - Cash balance at beginning and end of reporting period
    - Performance of portfolio during reporting period

- Total fees and charges, itemising total management fees and total execution costs

- Comparison of period performance with any agreed investment performance benchmark

- Total dividends, interest and other payments received in the period

- Information about other corporate actions giving rights to designated investments held

For a **retail client**, the **periodic statement** should be provided once every **six months**, except that:

- In the case of a leveraged portfolio, it should be provided at least **once a month**

- It should be provided every **three months** if the client requests it (The firm must inform clients of this right.)

- If the retail client elects to receive information on a transaction-by-transaction basis and there are no transactions in derivatives or similar instruments giving rise to a cash settlement, the periodic statement must be supplied at least once every **twelve months**

A firm managing investments (or operating a retail client account that includes an uncovered open position in a contingent liability transaction – involving a potential liability in excess of the cost) must report to the client any **losses** exceeding any **predetermined threshold** agreed with the client.

Periodic statements for **contingent liability transactions** may include information on the **collateral value** and **option account valuations** in respect of each option written by the client in the portfolio at the end of the relevant period.

For **non-MiFID business**, a firm need not provide a periodic statement to a client habitually resident outside the UK if the client does not wish to receive it, nor in respect of a **CTF** if the annual statement contains the periodic information.

4 MONEY LAUNDERING AND COUNTER TERRORISM

Learning objective **6.3.1 Explain** the various sources of money laundering and counter terrorism regulation and legislation:

- FSA rules
- Money Laundering Regulations
- Proceeds of Crime Act 2002

4.1 Overview

Money laundering is the process by which money that is illegally obtained is made to appear to have been legally obtained. By a variety of methods, the nature, source and ownership of these criminal proceeds are concealed.

- Criminal conduct is any crime that constitutes an offence in the UK, or any act abroad that would constitute an offence if it had occurred in the UK.

- Property is criminal property if it constitutes a person's benefit from criminal conduct and the alleged offender knows or suspects that it constitutes this benefit.

This means that UK anti-money laundering legislation applies to the proceeds of all crimes no matter how small.

4.2 Terms and definitions

Learning objective **6.3.4 Explain** the three stages involved in the money laundering process.

There are three typical phases in the laundering of money: **placement**, **layering** and **integration**.

- · If the money launderer is able to deposit illicit proceeds within an institution or a state (**placement**), which requires little or no disclosure concerning the ownership of those funds, it may be difficult, if not impossible, to trace the property back to its criminal source.

- In the second instance, if property is passed through a complicated series of transactions (**layering**), involving legitimate as well as illegitimate enterprises, it may again be impossible to identify the owner or origin of that property.

- If the ownership or origin of the funds cannot be ascertained, it is virtually impossible to establish that they are the product of criminal activity. The funds can then be reused in legitimate activity (**integration**).

The following are the definitions of money laundering employed in the European Union Council Directive of 1991. They have, in the main, been adopted in subsequent UK legislation.

- The conversion or transfer of property for the purpose of concealing or disguising the origin of the property.

- The concealment or disguise of the true nature, source, location, disposition, movement, rights with respect to, or ownership of, illicitly gained property.

- The acquisition, possession or use of property derived from criminal activity or participation in criminal activity.

4.3 Action to combat money laundering

In recognition of the scale and impact of money laundering globally, various national governments have in recent years collaborated on an international scale to combat money laundering. Action taken has concentrated not only on the law enforcement process, but also on recommendations to banks and financial institutions to put in place practices and procedures that will assist in the detection of money laundering activity.

In the **EU**, it has been envisaged that the **Money Laundering Directives** would enable the financial sector to play a powerful role in combating money laundering and, consequently, criminal activity. Additionally, it was anticipated that regulation of this kind would maintain public confidence in the soundness and stability of the European financial system.

4.4 EU Money Laundering Directives

In 1991, the EU adopted Council Directive 91/308 (**First EU Money Laundering Directive**) on the prevention of the use of the financial system for the purpose of money laundering.

- The Directive required all EU Member States to create criminal offences applicable to individuals to prohibit money laundering activity. This was enacted into UK legislation via the **Criminal Justice Act 1993 (CJA 1993).** More recently the money laundering offences within CJA 1993 have been repealed and replaced with the **Proceeds of Crime Act 2002 (POCA 2002)** which we shall discuss in detail later.

- The Directive also stated that all EU Member States should ensure that all financial and credit institutions located within the Member States should implement certain internal procedures and controls.

The aim of these internal procedures is threefold.

1. **Deterrence:** to prevent credit and financial institutions being used for money laundering purposes

2. **Co-operation:** to ensure that there is co-operation between credit and financial institutions and law enforcement agencies

3. **Detection:** to establish customer identification and record-keeping procedures within all financial and credit institutions which will assist the law enforcement agencies in detecting, tracing and prosecuting money launderers

In 2001, a **Second EU Money Laundering Directive** was adopted to cure some of the deficiencies in the first Directive. Then, a **Third Money Laundering Directive** came into force on **15 December 2007**. The Third Directive more fully incorporates into EU law the **Forty Recommendations** of the international **Financial Action Task Force (FATF)**.

The latest **Money Laundering Regulations 2007 (MLR 2007)** repeal earlier regulations and implement the Third Directive.

The main changes brought about by the Third Directive are as follows.

- The term '**occasional transaction**' (with a monetary limit of transactions of a value below €15,000) is now used, instead of 'one-off' transaction as in earlier Regulations.

- A **risk-based approach** is mandatory, in respect of risk management generally, and in applying customer due diligence

- There is detailed coverage of **customer due diligence** in the 2007 Regulations, with substantial guidance on how firms should meet their obligation of identifying customers, and mandatory monitoring of customer relationships

- There is **enhanced** due diligence on a **risk-sensitive basis**, including for 'politically exposed persons' ('PEPs') from outside the UK

- There is additional scope for **relying on other appropriately qualified regulated firms**, although the 'relying firm' retains ultimate responsibility for meeting the obligations under the Regulations

4.5 Money Laundering Regulations 2007: Institutional liability

Under MLR 2007, there are a number of **supervising agencies** with whom businesses of different types are required to register.

- For the purposes of the Regulations, the FSA is responsible for the supervision of FSA-authorised firms and also certain other firms including leasing companies, commercial finance providers and safe custody services. FSA-authorised firms are automatically supervised by the FSA but other such businesses must register with the FSA under MLR 2007.

- Various other types of business falling under the regulations are supervised by other authorities: for example, auctioneers accepting cash of €15,000 or more and foreign exchange bureaux must register with HMRC, estate agents must register with the Office of Fair Trading and casinos must register with the Gambling Commission.

- Members of Designated Professional Bodies not conducting mainstream FSA-regulated activities are supervised by their professional bodies.

The **Money Laundering Regulations 2007 (MLR 2007)** relate to institutional liability generally. They require internal systems and procedures to be implemented to deter criminals from using certain institutions to launder money. They also aim to enable money laundering to be more easily detected and prosecuted by the law enforcement agencies.

The following 'risk-sensitive' policies and procedures must be established.

- Customer due diligence measures and ongoing monitoring

- Internal reporting

- Record-keeping procedures (for five-year period)

- Internal control

- Risk assessment and management

- Compliance monitoring, management and communication of the policies and procedures

- Recognition of suspicious transactions and reporting procedures (including appointing a Money Laundering Reporting Officer)

- Staff training programmes

The offence

Failure to implement these measures is a **criminal offence**. The **FSA** may institute proceedings (other than in Scotland) for money laundering regulation breaches. This power is not limited to firms or persons regulated by the FSA. Whether a breach of the Money Laundering Regulations has occurred is not dependent on whether money laundering has taken place: firms may be sanctioned for not having adequate **anti-money laundering (AML) /counter-terrorism financing (CTF)** systems.

Penalty

Failure to comply with any of the requirements of the ML Regulations constitutes an offence punishable by a maximum of two years' imprisonment, or a fine, or both when tried in a Crown Court. If this case was tried in a Magistrates Court the maximum penalty is 6 months plus a £5,000 fine.

Note that, where a UK business **outsources** certain operations to an overseas jurisdiction, the business is still effectively carried on in the UK. For example, if an investment bank moved its call centre to India, it would still have to comply with money laundering requirements and staff in India would need proper training.

4.6 The Proceeds of Crime Act 2002: Individual liability

6.3.5 **Explain** the four offence categories under UK money laundering legislation.

The four main offences are:

- **Assistance**
- **Failure to report**
- **Tipping off**
- **Failure to comply – covered above**

4.6.1 Assistance (POCA S327, S328, S329)

The offence

If any person knowingly helps another person to launder the proceeds of criminal conduct, he or she will be committing an offence. This covers obtaining, concealing, disguising, transferring, acquiring, possessing, investing or using the proceeds of crime. The legislation historically covered the laundering of the proceeds of **serious crime**, however as a result of the POCA it now covers the proceeds of **all crimes**, no matter how small. This could include evasion of tax.

The possible defences

- It is a defence to the above offence that a person **disclosed** his knowledge or belief concerning the origins of the property either to the police or to the appropriate officer in his firm.

- Under changes made by the **Serious Organised Crime and Police Act 2005 (SOCPA)**, there may also be a defence if the person knew or believed on reasonable grounds that the relevant criminal conduct occurred outside the UK and the conduct was not at the time unlawful in the overseas jurisdiction.

The penalty

The maximum penalties for any offence of assisting a money launderer are **14 years' imprisonment and/or an unlimited fine** when tried in a Crown Court. If tried in a Magistrates Court the maximum penalty is reduced to 6 months' imprisonment and a £5,000 fine.

4.6.2 Failure to report

The offence

If a person discovers information during the course of his employment that makes him **believe or suspect** money laundering is occurring, he must inform the police or the appropriate officer (usually the Money Laundering Reporting Officer (MLRO)) of the firm as soon as possible. If he fails to make the report as soon as is reasonably practicable, he commits a criminal offence.

For those working in the **regulated sector** (for an authorised firm), this offence covers not only where the person had actual suspicion of laundering (i.e. subjective suspicions) but also where there were **reasonable grounds for being suspicious**. The grounds are when a hypothetical **reasonable person** would in the circumstances have been suspicious (i.e. **objective suspicions**).

The possible defences

The only defences to this charge are if a person charged can prove one of the following.

- He had a **reasonable excuse** for failing to disclose this information. Whether an excuse is reasonable will depend on the circumstances of the case, but it is noteworthy that the person charged has the burden of proving that he had a reasonable excuse for his failure to disclose.

- Where the person had no subjective suspicion but is deemed to have objective suspicions, they had not been provided by their employer with appropriate **training** to recognise and report suspicions.

- Under changes made by the Serious Organised Crime and Police Act 2005 (SOCPA), there may also be a defence if the person knew or believed on reasonable grounds that the relevant criminal conduct occurred outside the UK and the conduct was not at the time unlawful in the overseas jurisdiction.

The relevant legislation specifically provides that any person making a disclosure of this kind will not be in breach of any **duty of confidentiality** owed to a customer.

The penalty

This offence is punishable with a maximum of **five years' imprisonment** and/or an **unlimited fine** when tried in a Crown Court. If tried in a Magistrates Court the maximum penalty is reduced to 6 months' imprisonment and a £5,000 fine.

4.6.3 Tipping off (POCA s333A)

The offence

Even where suspicions are reported, the parties must generally be careful not to alert the suspicions of the alleged launderer since, within the regulated sector, this can itself amount to an offence.

Under s333A, a person within the regulated sector commits an **offence** if, based on information they acquire in the course of business that is likely to prejudice any investigation, they disclose:

- That information has been passed to the police, HMRC, a Nominated Officer (generally, the firm's MLRO) or the Serious Organised Crime Agency, or

- That an investigation into money laundering allegations is being contemplated or carried out

The mischief that s333A seeks to prevent is the mischief of acting so as to frustrate an investigation, and there are a number of **exceptions**. An offence is **not** committed for disclosures within the EEA or territories with anti-money laundering regimes, broadly if the disclosure is:

- Within an EEA financial institution or credit institution or its group

- Between professional advisers within the same group

- Between financial and credit institutions or between advisers generally, for disclosure with the purpose of preventing a money laundering offence

- To the supervisory authority under the Money Laundering Regulations – which, for FSA-authorised firms, is the FSA

- By a professional adviser to their client if for the purpose of dissuading the client from committing an offence

Possible defence

It is a defence if the person charged can prove that he neither knew nor suspected that the disclosure would be likely to prejudice an investigation.

Penalty

Tipping off is punishable with a maximum of **five years' imprisonment** and/or an **unlimited fine** in the Crown Court, or three months' imprisonment and a maximum fine of £5,000 in the Magistrates' Court.

4.7 Senior management arrangements, systems and controls (SYSC)

4.7.1 Systems and controls in relation to compliance, financial crime and money laundering

SYSC provides that a firm must take reasonable care to establish and maintain effective systems and controls for compliance with applicable regulations and for countering the risk that the firm might be used to further financial crime. Applicable regulations include the Proceeds of Crime Act 2002, the Money Laundering Regulations 2007 and the Terrorism Act 2000.

The systems and controls laid down should enable the firm to identify, assess, monitor and manage **money laundering risk**, which is, the risk that a firm may be used to further money laundering. In addition, the systems and controls should be **comprehensive** and **proportionate** to the **nature**, **scale** and **complexity** of its activities and be regularly assessed to ensure they remain adequate. Failure by a firm to manage money laundering risk will effectively increase the risk to society of crime and terrorism.

In identifying its **money laundering risk** and in establishing the nature of the systems and controls required, a firm should consider a range of factors, including:

- Its customer, product and activity profiles
- Its distribution channels
- The complexity and volume of its transactions
- Its processes and systems
- Its operating environment

The SYSC rules require firms to ensure that their systems and controls include:

- Allocation to a director or senior manager (who may also be the money laundering reporting officer MLRO) overall responsibility within the firm for the **establishment** and **maintenance** of effective anti-money laundering systems and controls
- Appropriate provision of information to its governing body and senior management, including a report at least annually by that firm's **money laundering reporting officer (MLRO)** on the operation and effectiveness of those systems and controls
- **Appropriate training** for its employees in relation to money laundering
- Appropriate **documentation** of its risk management policies and risk profile in relation to money laundering, including documentation of its application of those policies
- Appropriate measures to ensure that **money laundering risk** is taken into account in its day-to-day operation e.g. in the development of new products, the taking on of new customers and changes in its business profile
- Appropriate measures to ensure that **identification procedures** for customers do not unreasonably deny access to its services

4.7.2 The Money Laundering Reporting Officer (MLRO)

The MLRO which each authorised firm must appoint has responsibility for oversight of its compliance with the FSA's SYSC rules on money laundering.

The MLRO:

- Must act as the focal point for all activity within the firm relating to anti-money laundering
- Must have a level of authority and independence within the firm
- Must have access to sufficient resources and information to enable them to carry out that responsibility
- Should be based in the UK

4.7.3 The nominated officer

A **nominated officer** is someone who has been nominated by their employer to receive reports of suspected money laundering. In practice this will be the **MLRO** or **his deputy**.

Employers will have reporting processes in place for staff with suspicions to disclose to the MLRO. The nominated officer will act as a filter for reporting, and is placed under a duty to disclose to the **Serious Organised Crime Agency (SOCA)**, if he knows or suspects, or has reasonable grounds to suspect, that another person is engaged in money laundering.

4.7.4 The compliance function

Depending on the nature, scale and complexity of its business, it may be appropriate for a firm to have a separate **compliance function**. The organisation and responsibilities of the compliance function should be documented.

The compliance function should:

- Be staffed by an appropriate number of competent staff who are sufficiently independent to perform their duties objectively
- Have unrestricted access to the firm's relevant records
- Have ultimate recourse to its governing body

A firm which carries on designated investment business with or for customers must allocate to a director or senior manager the function of having responsibility for oversight of the firm's compliance and reporting to the governing body in respect of that responsibility. This will be the person carrying out the controlled function '**Compliance oversight**' under the FSA's approved persons regime. As a minimum, this individual will have to oversee compliance with COB, CASS and COLL, however, firms are free to give additional responsibilities to this person.

4.8 Joint Money Laundering Steering Group Guidance 2007

Learning objectives   **6.3.2 Explain** the role of the Joint Money Laundering Steering Group (JMLSG).

6.3.3 Explain the main features of the guidance provided by the JMLSG.

4.8.1 Status

The JMLSG is made up of representatives of trade bodies such as the British Bankers Association. The purpose of the guidance notes is to outline the requirements of the UK money laundering legislation, provide a practical interpretation of the MLR 2007 and provide a base from which management can develop tailored policies and procedures that are appropriate to their business.

The latest **2007 version** of the JMLSG Guidance Notes enables the UK financial services industry to take the required **risk-based approach** to the international fight against crime.

The courts must take account of industry guidance, such as the Joint Money Laundering Steering Group (JMLSG) Guidance Notes, which have been approved by a Treasury Minister, when deciding whether:

- A person has committed the offence of failing to report money laundering under POCA 2002
- A person has failed to report terrorist financing under the Terrorism Act 2000, or
- A person or institution has failed to comply with any of the requirements of the Money Laundering Regulations 2007

When considering whether to take disciplinary action against an FSA authorised firm for a breach of SYSC, the FSA will have regard to whether a firm has followed relevant provisions in the JMLSG Guidance Notes. The guidance will therefore be significant for individuals or companies subject to regulatory action.

The Guidance Notes provide a sound basis for firms to meet their legislative and regulatory obligations when tailored by firms to their particular business risk profile. Departures from good industry practice, and the rationale for so doing, should be documented and may have to be justified to the FSA.

4.8.2 Directors' and senior managers' responsibility for money laundering precautions

Senior management of FSA authorised firms must provide direction to, and oversight of, the firm's **anti-money laundering (AML)** and **combating the financing of terrorism (CFT)** systems and controls.

Senior management in FSA-authorised firms have a responsibility to ensure that the firm's control processes and procedures are appropriately designed, implemented and effectively operated to manage the firm's risks. This includes the risk of the firm being used to further financial crime.

Senior management of FSA-authorised firms must also meet the following specific requirements.

- Allocate to a director or senior manager (who may or may not be the MLRO) overall responsibility for the establishment and maintenance of the firm's AML/CTF systems and controls;

- Appoint an appropriately qualified senior member of the firm's staff as the MLRO

4.8.3 High level policy statement and risk-based approach

The FSA requires authorised firms to produce adequate documentation of its risk management policies and risk profile in relation to money laundering, including documentation of the application of those policies.

A statement of the firm's AML/CFT policy and the procedures to implement it will clarify how the firm's senior management intend to discharge their legal responsibility. This will provide a framework of direction to the firm and its staff, and will identify named individuals and functions responsible for implementing particular aspects of the policy. The policy will also set out how senior management makes its assessment of the money laundering and terrorist financing risks the firm faces, and how these risks are to be managed.

The **policy statement** should be tailored to the circumstances of the firm as the use of a generic document might reflect adversely on the level of consideration given by senior management to the firm's particular risk profile.

The policy statement might include, but is not limited to, the following.

Guiding principles
An unequivocal statement of the culture and values to be adopted and promulgated throughout the firm towards the prevention of financial crime
A commitment to ensuring that customers' identities will be satisfactorily verified before the firm accepts them
A commitment to the firm 'knowing its customers' appropriately at acceptance and throughout the business relationship – through taking appropriate steps to verify the customer's identity and business, and his reasons for seeking the particular business relationship with the firm
A commitment to ensuring that staff are trained and made aware of the law and their obligations under it, and to establishing procedures to implement these requirements
Recognition of the importance of staff promptly reporting their suspicions internally
Risk mitigation approach
A summary of the firm's approach to assessing and managing its money laundering and terrorist financing risk
Allocation of responsibilities to specific persons and functions
A summary of the firm's procedures for carrying out appropriate identification and monitoring checks on the basis of their risk-based approach
A summary of the appropriate monitoring arrangements in place to ensure that the firm's policies and procedures are being carried out

4.8.4 The risk-based approach

A **risk-based approach** is mandatory under MLR 2007. The approach requires the full commitment and support of senior management, and the active co-operation of business units. The risk-based approach needs to be part of the firm's philosophy, and as such reflected in its procedures and controls. There needs to be a clear communication of policies and procedures across the firm, together with robust mechanisms to ensure that they are carried out effectively, any weaknesses are identified and improvements are made wherever necessary.

There are the following **steps** in adopting the required risk-based approach to money laundering.

- Identify the money laundering and terrorist financing risks that are relevant to the firm

- Assess the risks presented by the firm's particular customers, products, delivery channels and geographical areas of operation

- Design and implement controls to manage and mitigate these assessed risks

- Monitor and improve the effective operation of these controls, and

- Record appropriately what has been done, and why

What is the **rationale** of the risk-based approach? To assist the overall objective to prevent money laundering and terrorist financing, a risk-based approach:

- Recognises that the money laundering/terrorist financing threat to firms varies across customers, jurisdictions, products and delivery channels

- Allows management to differentiate between their customers in a way that matches the risk in their particular business

- Allows senior management to apply its own approach to the firm's procedures, systems and controls, and arrangements in particular circumstances, and

- Helps to produce a more cost effective system

4.8.5 Risk assessment and 'Know Your Customer'

Firms are expected to 'know their customers'. The **Know Your Customer (KYC)** requirements:

- Help the firm, at the time customer due diligence is carried out, to be reasonably satisfied that customers are who they say they are, to know whether they are acting on behalf of others, whether there are any government sanctions against serving the customer, and

- Assist law enforcement with information on customers or activities under investigation.

Based on an **assessment of the money laundering / terrorist financing risk** that each customer presents, the firm will need to:

- **Verify the customer's identity (ID)** – determining exactly who the customer is

- **Collect additional 'KYC' information**, and keep such information **current and valid** – to understand the customer's circumstances and business, and (where appropriate) the sources of funds or wealth, or the purpose of specific transactions

Many customers, by their nature or through what is already known about them by the firm, carry a **lower** money laundering or terrorist financing **risk**. These might include:

- Customers who are employment-based or with a regular source of income from a known source which supports the activity being undertaken; (this applies equally to pensioners or benefit recipients, or to those whose income originates from their partners' employment)

- Customers with a long-term and active business relationship with the firm

- Customers represented by those whose appointment is subject to court approval or ratification (such as executors)

Firms should not, however, judge the level of risk solely on the nature of the **customer** or the **product**. Where, in a particular customer/product combination, either or both the customer and the product are considered to carry a higher risk of money laundering or terrorist financing, the overall risk of the customer should be considered carefully. Firms need to be aware that allowing a higher risk customer to acquire a lower risk product or service on the basis of a verification standard that is appropriate to that lower risk product or service, can lead to a requirement for further verification requirements, particularly if the customer wishes subsequently to acquire a higher risk product or service.

4.9 Due diligence

One of the most important ways in which money laundering can be prevented is by establishing the identity of clients, thus making it difficult for those trading under assumed names or through bogus companies to gain access to the financial markets. This emphasises, again, the obligation to 'know your customer'.

In the context of **conduct of business rules**, the firm may generally accept at face value information which customers provide. The **money laundering regulations**, however, require that the firm takes positive steps to verify the information that they receive. The **JMLSG** Guidance Notes lay down some basic, but not exhaustive, procedures that can be followed.

4.10 CDD, EDD and SDD

MLR 2007 regulations require detailed **customer due diligence (CDD)** procedures and these are explained in the **JMLSG** guidance.

CDD involves:

- Identifying the customer and verifying his identity

- Identifying the beneficial owner (taking measures to understand the ownership and control structure, in the case of a company or trust) and verifying his identity

- Obtaining information on the purpose and intended nature of the business relationship

A firm must apply CDD when it:

- Establishes a business relationship
- Carries out an occasional transaction, of €15,000 or more
- Suspects money laundering or terrorist financing
- Doubts the veracity of identification or verification documents

As well as standard CDD there is:

- **Enhanced due diligence (EDD)** – for higher risk situations, customers not physically present when identities are verified, correspondent banking and **politically exposed persons** (PEPs)

- **Simplified due diligence (SDD)** – which may be applied to certain financial sector firms, companies listed on a regulated market, UK public authorities, child trust funds and certain pension funds and low risk products

Firms' information demands from customers need to be '**proportionate, appropriate and discriminating**', and to be able to be **justified to customers**.

4.10.1 Enhanced due diligence

EDD measures when a customer is not present include obtaining additional documents, data or information to those specified below, requiring certification by a financial services firm, and ensuring that an initial payment is from a bank account in the customer's name.

The category '**politically exposed persons**' (**PEPs**) comprises higher-ranking **non-UK** public officials, members of parliaments other than the UK Parliament, and such persons' immediate families and close associates. Prominent PEPs can pose a higher risk because their position may make them vulnerable to corruption. Senior management approval (from an immediate superior) should be sought for establishing a business relationship with such a customer and adequate measures should be taken to establish sources of wealth and of funds.

4.10.2 Simplified due diligence

SDD means not having to apply CDD measures. In practice, this means not having to identify the customer, or to verify the customer's identity, or, where relevant, that of a beneficial owner, nor having to obtain information on the purpose or intended nature of the business relationship.

4.10.3 Evidence of identity

How much identity information to ask for in the course of CDD, and what to verify, are matters **for the judgement of the firm**, based on its **assessment of risk**.

Documents offering evidence of identity are seen in the JMLSG Guidance Notes as forming the following broad hierarchy according to who has issued them, in the following order:

- Government departments or a court
- Other public sector bodies
- Regulated financial services firms
- Other firms subject to MLR or equivalent legislation
- Other organisations

For **private individuals**, the firm should obtain full name, residential address and date of birth of the personal customer. Verification of the information obtained should be based either on a document or documents provided by the customer, or electronically by the firm, or by a combination of both. Where business is conducted face-to-face, firms should request the original documents. Customers should be discouraged from sending original valuable documents by post.

Firms should therefore obtain the following in relation to **corporate clients**: full name, registered number, registered office in country of incorporation, and business address.

The following should also be obtained for private companies:

- Names of all directors (or equivalent)
- Names of beneficial owners holding over 25%

The firm should verify the identity of the corporate entity from:

- A search of the relevant company registry, or
- Confirmation of the company's listing on a regulated market, or
- A copy of the company's Certificate of Incorporation

4.10.4 Ongoing monitoring

As an obligation separate from CDD, firms must conduct ongoing **monitoring of the business relationship**, even where SDD applies. Ongoing monitoring of a business relationship includes scrutiny of transactions undertaken including, where necessary, sources of funds.

CDD and **monitoring** is intended to make it more difficult for the financial services industry to be used for money laundering or terrorist financing, but also helps firms guard against fraud, including impersonation fraud.

4.10.5 Reporting of suspicious transactions

All institutions must appoint an 'appropriate person' as the **Money Laundering Reporting Officer (MLRO)**, who has the following functions.

- To receive reports of transactions giving rise to knowledge or suspicion of money laundering activities from employees of the institution

- To determine whether the report of a suspicious transaction from the employee, considered together with all other relevant information, does actually give rise to knowledge or suspicion of money laundering

- If, after consideration, he knows or suspects that money laundering is taking place, to report those suspicions to the appropriate law enforcement agency, the Serious Organised Crime Agency (SOCA)

For the purpose of each individual employee, making a report made to the MLRO concerning a transaction means that the employee has fulfilled his statutory obligations and will have **no criminal liability** in relation to any money laundering offence in respect of the reported transaction.

4.11 Terrorism

4.11.1 Terrorist activities

Acts of terrorism committed since 2001 have led to an increase in international efforts to locate and cut off funding for terrorists and their organisations.

There is a considerable overlap between the movement of terrorist funds and the laundering of criminal assets. Terrorist groups are also known to have well-established links with organised criminal activity. However, there are two major differences between terrorist and criminal funds.

- Often only small amounts are required to commit a terrorist atrocity, therefore increasing the difficulty of tracking the funds.

- Whereas money laundering relates to the proceeds of crime, terrorists can be funded from legitimately obtained income.

The **Terrorism Act 2000** defines **terrorism** in the UK as the use or threat of action wherever it occurs, designed to influence a government or to intimidate the public for the purpose of advancing a political, religious or ideological cause where the action:

- Involves serious violence against a person, or

- Involves serious damage to property, or

- Endangers a person's life, or

- Creates a serious risk to the health or safety of the public, or

- Is designed seriously to interfere with, or seriously to disrupt an electronic system, e.g. a computer virus

4.11.2 Offences

The Terrorism Act 2000 sets out the following terrorist offences.

- **Fund raising**, which covers inviting another to provide money or other property to fund terrorism

- **Use and possession**, which covers using money or other property for the purposes of terrorism

- **Funding arrangements**, which covers involvement in funding arrangements as a result of which money or other property is made available for terrorism

- **Money laundering**, which covers any arrangement which facilitates the retention or control by any person of terrorist property by means of concealment, removal from the jurisdiction, transfer to nominees or in any other way

An offence will be committed if the action or possession of terrorist funds occurs in the UK. It will also be an offence if the action or possession occurs outside the UK but would have constituted an offence in the UK if it had occurred here.

4.11.3 Terrorist property

Terrorist property is defined as money or other property which is likely to be used for the purposes of terrorism, proceeds of the commission of acts of terrorism and proceeds of acts carried out for the purposes of terrorism.

4.11.4 Preventative measures

Although **MLR 2007** focuses on firms' obligations in relation to the prevention of money laundering, **POCA 2000** updated and reformed the obligation to report to cover involvement with any criminal property, and the **Terrorism Act 2000** extended this to cover terrorist property.

The JMLSG Guidance states that the risk of terrorist funding entering the financial system can be reduced if firms apply satisfactory money laundering strategies and, in particular, **know your customer** procedures. Firms should assess which **countries** carry the highest risks and should conduct careful scrutiny of transactions from countries known to be a source of terrorist financing.

For some countries, public information about known or suspected terrorists is available. For example, terrorist names are listed on the US Treasury website.

4.11.5 Sanctions and the Consolidated List

There are certain customers and organisations who may not be dealt with and whose assets must be frozen, as specified in anti-terrorism legislation and sanctions.

A **Consolidated List** of all targets to whom financial sanctions apply is maintained by HM Treasury, and includes all individuals and entities that are subject to financial sanctions in the UK. This list can be found at: www.hm-treasury.gov.uk/financialsanctions.

There is a range of **financial sanctions** applying against specific **countries or regimes**. HM Treasury directions can be found on the web sites of HM Treasury and JMLSG (www.jmlsg.org.uk). The obligations under the UK financial sanctions regime apply to all firms, and not just to banks.

4.11.6 Duty to report terrorism

A **duty to report** occurs where a person believes or suspects that another person has committed a terrorist offence and where the belief or suspicion has arisen in the course of a trade, profession, business or employment.

An individual commits an offence of failing to report if he does not disclose the suspicion and the information on which it is based to a constable (i.e. the police) as soon as is reasonably practicable.

The following are possible defences to the offence of the failure to report.

- The firm has an established procedure for making disclosures, and the individual properly disclosed the matters in accordance with this procedure.

- The person had a reasonable excuse for not making the disclosure.

A person guilty of failing to report will face a **maximum penalty** of **six months in jail** and/or **£5,000 fine** in the **Magistrates Court** and **five years in jail** and/or an **unlimited fine** in the **Crown Court**.

4.12 Failure to disclose: regulated sector (s21A Terrorism Act 2000)

In addition to the offences in POCA 2002, there is specific UK legislation relating to terrorism. The main legislation is the **Terrorism Act 2000** which is supplemented by the **Anti-Terrorism Crime and Security Act 2001** and the **Terrorism Act 2000 and Proceeds of Crime Act 2000 (Amendment Regulations) 2007**.

The offence

Under s21A Terrorism Act 2000 (as amended), it is an offence for those working in the **regulated sector** to fail to report (as soon as practicable) knowledge, suspicion or reasonable grounds for suspicion of offences or attempted offences relating to the following.

- Terrorist fund raising
- Use and possession of funds for terrorism
- Arrangements facilitating the retention or control of terrorist property

Thus, as with POCA 2002, there is an objective test for reporting. Reports should be made to the police or MLRO as soon as practicable.

Defences

There is a **defence** where person had a **reasonable excuse** for not making such a disclosure, and also where a professional adviser (i.e. a lawyer, accountant or auditor) receives the information in privileged circumstances.

Penalty

The offence is punishable (as in POCA 2002) with a maximum of **five years' imprisonment and/or an unlimited fine**, or 6 months' imprisonment and a fine of £5,000 in the Magistrates' Court.

4.12.1 Protected disclosures

There is clearly a concern that where a disclosure is made in accordance with the above requirements the client may claim this is a breach of client confidentiality. However, the rules state that where disclosures are made in accordance with the reporting rules there will not be a breach of client confidentiality.

4.13 Counter-Terrorism Act 2008

4.13.1 Overview

The **Counter-Terrorism Act 2008 (CTA 2008)** received royal assent and took effect on **26 November 2008**. This legislation is intended to provide further tools in the range of legislation addressing the risks of money laundering, terrorist financing and the proliferation of nuclear, biological, biological or chemical weapons.

4.13.2 Directions

Schedule 7 of CTA 2008 gives powers to the Treasury to issue **directions** to **firms in the financial sector**, which may relate to:

- Customer due diligence
- Ongoing monitoring
- Systematic reporting
- Limiting or ceasing business

The requirements to carry out CDD and ongoing monitoring build on similar obligations under the MLR. The requirements for **systematic reporting** and **limiting or ceasing business** are introduced by CTA 2008.

A Treasury direction under CTA 2008 must relate to a non-EEA country. A **direction** may be given only if the Financial Action Task Force advises that measures be taken, **or** if the Treasury reasonably believes that production or facilitation of nuclear, radiological, biological or chemical weapons, or terrorist financing or ML activities are being carried on in the country, **and** that this poses a significant risk to UK national interests.

A direction may impose an obligation to carry out EDD, or to undertake **ongoing monitoring** of a business relationship, which may involve retention of documentation or scrutiny of transactions.

Systematic reporting of **prospective transactions** may be required. A firm may also be required not to enter into a specified transaction or business relationship (**limiting or ceasing business**).

4.13.3 Penalties

A failure to comply with a direction could lead to a **civil penalty** (fine) imposed by the FSA as the enforcement authority, or to **criminal prosecution** (carrying a prison term of up to two years and/or a fine) – but not both for the same failure. No civil penalty will be applied and no criminal offence is committed if the firm took all reasonable steps and exercised all due diligence.

5 INSIDER DEALING

5.1 Introduction

objective **6.3.6 Explain** the meaning of 'inside information' covered by CJA 1993.

Insider dealing is the offence of acting with information that is not freely and openly available to all other participants in the market place. This became an offence in 1980 but the current legislation making it a criminal offence is found in **Part V** of the **Criminal Justice Act 1993**. HM Treasury is responsible for insider dealing legislation.

The Act makes it a **criminal offence** for connected persons who receive inside information to act on that information.

The legislation (Schedule 2) covers the following instruments.

- Shares
- Debt securities issued by the private or public sector
- Warrants
- Depository receipts
- Options, futures or contracts for a difference on any of the above

5.2 Insider

An insider is defined under CJA 1993 as an individual who has **information** in his possession that he **knows** is **inside information** and **knows** is from an **inside source**.

Inside information in this context refers to **unpublished price-sensitive information** that is **specific or precise** and **relates to a security or its issuer**.

What is **published** information? The following information is deemed to be 'published'.

- Information published via a regulated market, e.g. an RIE
- Information contained in public records
- Information which can otherwise be readily acquired by market users, e.g. in the financial press
- Information derived from public information
- Information which can only be acquired by expertise or by payment of a fee
- Information which is published only to a section of the public, rather than the public in general, or published outside the UK
- Information which can be acquired by observation, e.g. a factory burning down

An inside source is **an individual** and would include a **director, employee** or **shareholder** of an issuer of securities or a person having access to the information by virtue of their employment, office or profession.

A person will also be an inside source if he receives the information directly or indirectly from one of the above and satisfies the general definition above.

5.3 Offences

Learning objective 6.3.7 **Explain** the offence of insider dealing covered by the CJA.

If a person satisfies the definition of an insider, it is an offence for that person to:

- **Deal** in the affected securities either on a regulated market or through a professional intermediary
- **Encourage another** person to deal with reasonable cause to believe that dealing would take place on a regulated market or through a professional intermediary
- **Disclose the information** to another person other than in the proper performance of their duties

5.4 General defences

Learning objective 6.3.8 **Identify** the penalties for being found guilty of insider dealing.

An individual is not guilty of insider **dealing** if he can show that:

- He did not, at the time, expect the dealing to result in a profit attributable to the fact that the information was price sensitive
- At the time, he believed on reasonable grounds that the information had been disclosed widely enough to ensure that none of those taking part in the dealing would be prejudiced by not having the information
- He would have done what he did even if he had not had the information

A similar series of defences are available to the charge of **encouraging** another to deal in price-affected securities.

An individual is not guilty of insider dealing by virtue of a **disclosure** of information if he shows that:

- He did not, at the time, expect any person, because of the disclosure, to deal in securities either through a regulated market or via a professional intermediary
- Although he had such an expectation at the time, he did not expect the dealing to result in a profit attributable to the fact that the information was price sensitive in relation to the securities

5.5 Special defences

5.5.1 Market makers

A market maker is a person who holds himself out at all normal times in compliance with the rules of a RIE as willing to acquire or dispose of securities and is required to do so under those rules. An individual is not guilty of insider dealing by virtue of dealing in securities or encouraging another to deal if he can show that he acted in **good faith** in the course of market making.

5.5.2 Market information

An individual is not guilty of an offence under the Act if he can show that the information which he had as an insider was **market information** (information concerning transactions in securities that either have been or are about to be undertaken) and that it was reasonable for an individual in his position to have acted in that manner when in possession of inside information. Consideration will be taken as to the content of the information, the circumstances of receiving the information and the capacity in which the recipient acts, to determine whether it is reasonable.

This defence will also cover the **facilitation of takeover bids**.

5.5.3 Price stabilisation

An individual is not guilty of an offence under the Act by virtue of dealing in securities or encouraging another person to deal if he can show that he acted in conformity with the **price stabilisation rules**.

5.6 Enforcement by the FSA

objective **6.3.9 Explain** the FSA's powers to prosecute under insider dealing.

The FSA has powers under S401 and S402 FSMA 2000 to prosecute a range of criminal offences, including **insider dealing**, in England, Wales and Northern Ireland.

Under s168 FSMA 2000, inspectors from the FSA have the power to require persons who they believe may have information to:

- Produce any relevant documents
- Attend before them
- Give all assistance possible

In addition to prosecuting for insider dealing, the FSA may revoke the authorisation of an authorised firm where individuals have been allowed to insider deal. They could also remove a person's approval.

Amendments made in 2009 to the Serious Organised Crime and Police Act 2005 give the FSA additional statutory powers, including the **power to grant 'immunity notices'**, when investigating criminal cases such as insider dealing.

While the Department for Business, Innovation and Skills has the power to prosecute, since 2001 the **FSA** will now normally prosecute insider dealing cases. Accordingly, the London Stock Exchange (as the person who often initiates an investigation) will pass information directly to the FSA.

5.7 Penalties

Insider dealing is a **criminal offence** and the penalties available depend on the method of prosecution.

- **Magistrates' Court** – maximum of six months' imprisonment and a £5,000 fine
- **Crown Court** – maximum of seven years' imprisonment and an unlimited fine

There are no automatic civil sanctions contained in CJA 1993. In addition, no contract is automatically void or unenforceable by reason only that it is the result of insider dealing.

6 MARKET ABUSE

objective **6.3.10 Understand** the nature of behaviours defined as market abuse (MAR 1.3, 4, 5, 6, 7, 8 & 9).

6.1 Overview

Market abuse is a **civil offence** under **S118 FSMA 2000,** which provides an alternative civil regime for enforcing the criminal prohibitions on insider dealing and misleading statements/practices.

The UK market abuse rules conform with the **EU Market Abuse Directive**.

The **territorial scope** of market abuse is very wide. It covers everyone, not just authorised firms and approved persons. Firms or persons outside the UK are also covered by the offence.

As market abuse is a **civil offence**, the FSA must prove, on the balance of probabilities, that a person:

- Engaged in market abuse, or
- By taking or refraining from action, required or encouraged another person to engage in market abuse

As shown in the following diagram, there are seven types of behaviour that can amount to market abuse.

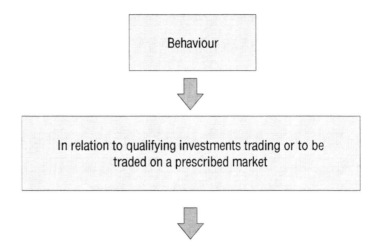

6.2 Requiring and encouraging

Section 123(1)(b) FSMA 2000 allows the FSA to impose penalties on a person who, by taking or refraining from taking any action, has required or encouraged another person or persons to engage in behaviour, which if engaged in by A, would amount to market abuse.

The following are **examples** of behaviour that might fall within the scope of section 123(1)(b).

- A director of a company, while in possession of inside information, instructs an employee of that company to deal in qualifying investments or related investments in respect of which the information is inside information. (This could amount to **requiring**.)

- A person recommends or advises a friend to engage in behaviour which, if he himself engaged in it, would amount to market abuse. (This could be **encouraging** market abuse.)

6.3 The regular market user test

A regular user is a **hypothetical reasonable person** who regularly deals on that market in investments of the kind in question. The **regular market user test** then determines in light of the circumstances whether an offence has been committed.

Since the implementation of the Market Abuse Directive, the regular market user is only used to determine whether market abuse has occurred in relation to the behaviours 'Misuse of Information', 'Misleading Behaviour' and 'Distortion'.

Therefore, the regular market user decides:

- Whether information that is not generally available would be relevant when deciding which transactions in qualifying investments or related investments should be undertaken, and

- Whether behaviour is below the expected standard, or creates a false or misleading impression or distorts the market

6.4 Qualifying investments and prescribed markets

Behaviour will only constitute market abuse if it occurs **in the UK or in relation to qualifying investments traded on a prescribed market**. The term 'behaviour' is specifically mentioned as the offence of market abuse can cover both action and inaction.

A **prescribed market** means any UK RIE, and any regulated market. **Qualifying investment** thus means any investment traded on a UK RIE or a regulated market. **Regulated markets** comprise the main EEA exchanges.

The definition of prescribed market and qualifying investment are amended slightly with reference to the offences of '**Misuse of Information**', '**Misleading Behaviour**' and '**Distortion**'. Here, a prescribed market means any UK RIE. Qualifying investment thus means any investment traded on a UK RIE. Therefore, these offences are only relevant to the UK markets.

In addition, the rules confirm that a prescribed market accessible electronically in the UK would be treated as operating in the UK.

As behaviour must be **in relation to** qualifying investments, the regime is not limited to on-market dealings. A transaction in an OTC (Over The Counter) derivative contract on a traded security or commodity would be covered by the regime. In addition, abusive trades on foreign exchanges could constitute market abuse if the underlying instrument also trades on a prescribed market. This makes the regime much wider than the criminal law offences.

6.5 The definition of market abuse

Market abuse is behaviour, whether by one person alone or by two or more persons jointly or in concert, which occurs in relation to:

- Qualifying investments admitted to trading on a prescribed market, or

- Qualifying investments in respect of which a request for admission to trading on a prescribed market has been made, or

- Related investments of a qualifying investment (strictly, this is only relevant to the offences of 'Insider Dealing' and 'Improper Disclosure' – see below)

and falls within one or more of the offences below.

6.6 The seven types of market abuse offence

The seven types of behaviour that can constitute market abuse are as follows:

1. **Insider Dealing**. This is where an insider deals, or attempts to deal, in a qualifying investment or related investment on the basis of **inside information**.

2. **Improper Disclosure**. This is where an insider discloses **inside information** to another person otherwise than in the proper course of the exercise of his employment, profession or duties.

3. **Misuse of Information**. This fills gaps in '1' or '2' above and is where the behaviour is

    –   Based on information which is not generally available to those using the market but which, if available to a regular user of the market, would be regarded by him as relevant when deciding the terms on which transactions in qualifying investments should be effected, and

    –   Likely to be regarded by a regular user of the market as a failure on the part of the person concerned to observe the standard of behaviour reasonably expected of a person in his position.

4. **Manipulating Transactions**. This consists of effecting transactions or orders to trade (otherwise than for legitimate reasons and in conformity with accepted market practices) which

    –   Give, or are likely to give a false or misleading impression as to the supply, demand or price of one or more qualifying investments, or

    –   Secure the price of one or more such investments at an abnormal or artificial level.

5. **Manipulating Devices**. This consists of effecting transactions or orders to trade which employ fictitious devices or any other form of deception.

6. **Dissemination**. This consists of the dissemination of information by any means which gives, or is likely to give, a false or misleading impression as to a qualifying investment by a person who knew or could reasonably be expected to have known that the information was false or misleading.

7. . **Misleading Behaviour** and **Distortion**. This fills any gaps in '4', '5' and '6' above and is where the behaviour

    –   Is likely to give a regular user of the market a false or misleading impression as to the supply of, demand for, or price or value of, qualifying investments, or

    –   Would be regarded by a regular user of the market as behaviour that would distort the market in such an investment and is likely to be regarded by a regular user of the market as a failure on the part of the person concerned to observe the standard of behaviour reasonably expected of a person in his position.

6.7 Intention

The market abuse regime is **effects based** rather than 'intent based'. Thus, whether the perpetrator intended to abuse the market is largely irrelevant – the key question is whether the action **did** abuse the market.

6.8 Code of Market Conduct

While the law is set out in FSMA, the FSA also has a duty to draft a **Code of Market Conduct**.

The main provisions of the Code of Market Conduct are that it sets out:

*   Descriptions of behaviour that, in the opinion of the FSA, do or do not amount to market abuse. Descriptions of behaviour which do not amount to market abuse are called '**safe harbours**'

- Descriptions of behaviour that are or are not **accepted market practices** in relation to one or more identified markets

- Factors that, in the opinion of the FSA, are to be taken into account in determining whether or not behaviour amounts to market abuse

The Code does not exhaustively describe all types of behaviour that may or may not amount to market abuse.

6.9 Enforcement and penalties

g objective 6.3.11 **Explain** the enforcement powers of the FSA relating to market abuse (MAR 1.1.4, 5 & 6).

The FSA may impose one or more of the following **penalties** on those found to have committed market abuse.

- An unlimited **fine**

- Issue a **public statement**

- Apply to the court to seek an **injunction** or **restitution order**

- Where an authorised/approved person is guilty of market abuse, they will also be guilty of a breach of the FSA's Principles and they could, in addition to the above penalties, have disciplinary proceedings brought against them, which may result in withdrawal of authorisation/approval.

The case of Paul Davidson ('The Plumber') has led to change in perceptions about how market abuse may be treated. The current position is that a **civil standard of proof** (on the balance of probabilities) of the appropriate degree can still be used by the FSA in market abuse cases. However, even when the punishment (in accordance with S123 FSMA 2000) is treated as **civil** for domestic law purposes, market abuse is a **criminal** charge (with a standard of proof 'beyond reasonable doubt') for the purposes of the European Convention on Human Rights, and someone committing it is subject to possible criminal prosecution.

In addition to being able to impose penalties for market abuse, the FSA is given criminal prosecution powers to enforce insider dealing and S397. The FSA has indicated that it will not pursue both the civil and criminal regime. In terms of the enforcement process for market abuse, this is the same as FSA's disciplinary process.

6.10 Safe harbours

If a person is within one of the **safe harbours** set out in the **Code of Market Conduct** they are not committing market abuse. These are indicated by the letter **C** in the Handbook.

Generally, there are no rules in the Takeover Code that permit or require a person to behave in a way which amounts to market abuse.

However, the following rules provide a **safe harbour** meaning that behaviour conforming with that rule does not amount to market abuse.

6.10.1 FSA rules

Behaviour caused by the proper operation of a Chinese wall or behaviour that relates to the timing, dissemination or content to a disclosure under the Listing Rules will not amount to market abuse.

6.10.2 Takeover Code

Behaviour conforming with any of the rules of the Takeover Code about the timing, dissemination or content of a disclosure does not, of itself, amount to market abuse. This is subject to the behaviour being expressly required or permitted by a rule and provided it conforms to the General Principles of the Takeover Code.

6.10.3 Buy-back programmes and stabilisation

Behaviour which conforms with the **Buy-Back and Stabilisation Regulation** (in the Market Conduct Sourcebook of the FSA's Handbook) will **not** amount to market abuse.

However, buy-back programmes which do not follow the Buy-Back and Stabilisation Regulation are not automatically seen as market abuse, but do not have an automatic safe harbour.

6.11 Due diligence defence

Under Section 123 FSMA 2000, the FSA may not impose a financial penalty in relation to market abuse where it is satisfied that the person believed, on reasonable grounds, that his behaviour did not amount to market abuse or he took all reasonable precautions and exercised all **due diligence** to avoid engaging in market abuse.

6.12 Notification of suspicious transactions by firms

The FSA's Supervision manual (**SUP**) stipulates that an authorised **firm** which:

- Arranges or executes a transaction with or for a client in a qualifying investment admitted to trading on a prescribed market, and

- Has reasonable grounds to suspect that the transaction might constitute market abuse

must **notify the FSA** without delay.

7 CUSTOMER COMPLAINTS AND COMPENSATION

6.4.1 **Explain** the FSA rules relating to handling of complaints (DISP 1.3).

7.1 General points

Firms carrying on regulated activities may receive **complaints** from their clients about the way the firm has provided financial services or in respect of failure to provide a financial service. This could include allegations of financial loss whether or not such losses have actually yet occurred: for example, in the case of a mis-sold pension contract, future losses may be involved. Under the FSA's rules, a firm must have **written procedures** to ensure complaints from eligible complainants are properly handled.

A **complaint** is defined as 'any **oral or written** expression of dissatisfaction, whether justified or not, from, or on behalf of, a person about the provision of, or failure to provide, a financial service, which alleges that the complainant has suffered (or may suffer) financial loss, material distress or material inconvenience'.

Firms are permitted to **outsource complaints handling**, or to arrange a 'one-stop shop' for handling complaints with other firms.

7.2 Eligible complainants

The rules on how firms must handle complaints apply to **eligible complainants**. An eligible complainant is a person eligible to have a complaint considered under the Financial Ombudsman Service.

Eligible complaints is someone who is

- A consumer

- An enterprise with fewer than 10 employees and turnover or annual balance sheet not exceeding €2 million (called a 'micro-enterprise')

- A charity with annual income of less than £1 million, or

- A trust with net asset value of less than £1 million

The rules do not apply to **authorised professional firms** (such as firms of accountants or solicitors) in respect of their **non-mainstream regulated activities**.

For **MiFID business**, the **complaints handling and record rules** apply to

- Complaints from **retail clients**, but not those who are not retail clients

- Activities carried on from a **branch** of a UK firm in another EEA state, but not to activities carried on from a branch of an EEA firm in the UK

- If a firm takes responsibility for activities **outsourced** to a third party processor, the firm is responsible for dealing with complaints about those activities

7.3 Consumer awareness rule

To aid **consumer awareness** of the complaints protection offered, firms must:

- Publish a **summary** of their internal processes for dealing with complaints promptly and fairly.
- Refer eligible customers in writing to this summary at, or immediately after, the point of sale.
- Provide the summary on request, or when acknowledging a complaint.

7.4 Complaints handling

Firms, and UK firms' branches in the EEA, must establish procedures for the reasonable handling of complaints which

- Are effective and transparent.

- Allow complaints to be made by any reasonable means (which might include email messages, or telephone calls, for example).

- Recognise complaints as requiring resolution.

In respect of non-MiFID business, firms must ensure that they identify any **recurring or systemic problems** revealed by complaints. For MiFID business, the requirement is that firms must use complaints information to detect and minimise risk of '**compliance failures**'.

There is an expectation that firms should maintain standards of ethics and professional integrity in their handling of complaints:

- Having regard to FSA **Principle 6** (*Customers' Interests*), which requires that firms **treat customers fairly**, firms should consider acting on their own initiative in respect of customers who may have been disadvantaged but have not complained.

- This is an example of how, in line with its emphasis on 'principles-based regulation', the FSA expects firms to adopt an **ethical stance** and to consider themselves how to apply the Principles for Businesses.

7.5 Complaints resolution

Learning objective 6.4.4 **Explain** the procedure and time limits for the resolution of complaints (DISP 1.4, 1.5 & 1.6).

For all complaints received, the firm must:

- Investigate the complaint **competently, diligently and impartially**
- Assess **fairly, consistently and promptly**:
  - whether the complaint should be upheld
  - what remedial action and/or redress may be appropriate
  - whether another respondent may be responsible for the matter (in which case, by the **complaints forwarding rule**, the complaint may be **forwarded** to that other firm, promptly and with notification of the reasons to the client)
- Offer any redress or remedial action
- Explain the firm's assessment of the complaint to the client, its decision, including any offer of redress or remedial action made – in a fair, clear and not misleading way

Factors relevant to assessing a complaint

- All the available evidence and circumstances
- Similarities with other complaints
- Guidance from the FSA, FOS or other regulators

The firm should aim to resolve complaints as early as possible, minimising the number of unresolved complaints referred to the FOS – with whom the firm must cooperate fully, complying promptly with any settlements or awards.

7.6 Complaints resolved the next day

Complaints **time limit, forwarding and reporting rules** do not apply to complaints which are **resolved by the next business day** after the complaint is made.

7.7 Time limit rules

On receiving a complaint, the firm must

- Send to the complainant a prompt written acknowledgement providing 'early reassurance' that it has received the complaint and is dealing with it, and
- Ensure the complainant in kept informed of progress on the complaint's resolution thereafter.

By the end of **eight weeks** after receiving a complaint which remains unresolved, the firm must send:

- A final response, or
- A holding response, which explains why a final response cannot be made and gives the expected time it will be provided, informs the complainant of his right to complain directly to the FOS if he is not satisfied with the delay, and encloses a copy of the FOS explanatory leaflet

The FSA expects that, within eight weeks of their receipt, almost all complaints will have been substantively addressed.

7.8 Firms with a two-stage complaints procedure

Some firms operate a **two-stage complaints procedure** that provides for a complainant who is not satisfied with the firm's initial response to refer the matter back to the firm or to its head office.

These firms are subject to the time limits set out above, but the rules recognise that some complainants may never respond to the initial reply or may take a long time to do so. Therefore, where the firm sends a response to the complainant offering redress or explaining why they do not propose to give redress and setting out how the complainant can pursue the claim further within the firm or apply to the FOS, it is permissible for the firm to regard the matter as closed if the firm does not get a reply within eight weeks.

If the complainant does reply indicating that they remain dissatisfied, then the general time limits will resume. However, the firm can discount any time in excess of a week taken by the complainant to reply.

7.9 Time barring

Complaints received outside the FOS **time limits** (see below) may be rejected without considering their merits in a final response, but this response should state that the FOS may waive this requirement in exceptional circumstances.

7.10 Complaints record rule

objective   **6.4.8 Explain** the rules relating to record keeping and reporting (DISP 1.9, 1.10).

Records of complaints and of the measures taken for their resolution must be retained for:

- **Five years**, for MiFID business
- **Three years**, for other complaints

after the date the complaint was received

7.11 Complaints reporting

Firms must provide a complete **report to the FSA** on complaints received **twice a year**. There is a standard format for the report, which must show, for the reporting period:

- Complaints broken down into categories and generic product types

- Numbers of complaints closed by the firm: within four weeks of receipt; within four to eight weeks; and more than eight weeks from receipt

- Numbers of complaints: upheld; known to have been referred to and accepted by the FOS; outstanding at the beginning of reporting period; outstanding at the end of the reporting period

- Total amount of redress paid in respect of complaints

8 THE FINANCIAL OMBUDSMAN SERVICE

8.1 Function of the Ombudsman

Learning objective 6.4.2 **Explain** the role of the Financial Ombudsman Service (DISP Introduction and DISP 2).

A **complainant** must first go to the authorised firm against which the complaint is being made. If the authorised firm does not resolve the complaint to his satisfaction, the complainant may refer it to the **Financial Ombudsman Service (FOS)**.

The FOS offers an informal method of independent adjudication of disputes between a firm and its customer, which is relatively cheap compared with the alternative of taking action through the Courts.

8.2 Powers of the FOS

Learning objective 6.4.3 **Distinguish** compulsory from voluntary jurisdiction (DISP Introduction).

The FOS is a body set up by statute and, while its Board is appointed by the FSA, it is **independent** from the FSA and authorised firms. The FOS is, however, accountable to the FSA and is required to make an annual report to the FSA on its activities.

The FOS can consider a complaint against an authorised firm for an act or omission in carrying out any of the firm's regulated activities together with any ancillary activities that firm does. This is known as the **Compulsory Jurisdiction** of the FOS.

In addition to the Compulsory Jurisdiction, the FOS can consider a complaint under its '**Voluntary Jurisdiction**'. Firms or businesses can choose to submit to the voluntary jurisdiction of the FOS by entering into a contract with the FOS. This is available, for example, to unauthorised firms, and can cover activities such as credit and debit card transactions and ancillary activities carried on by that voluntary participant where they are not regulated activities.

A further **Consumer Credit Jurisdiction** applies under the Consumer Credit Act 2006, which gives to the FOS powers to resolve certain disputes regarding loans against holders of licences issued by the Office of Fair Trading under the Consumer Credit Act 1974.

8.3 Eligible complainants

Only **eligible complainants** who have been customers of authorised firms or of firms which have voluntarily agreed to abide by the FOS rules may use the FOS. The scope of what is meant by 'eligible complainants' is explained in section 1 of this chapter.

Where an eligible complainant refers a matter to the Ombudsman, a firm has no definitive right to block the matter being referred, but may dispute the eligibility of the complaint or the complainant. In such circumstances, the Ombudsman will seek representations from the parties. The Ombudsman may investigate the merits of the case and may also convene a hearing if necessary.

8.4 FOS time limits

The following **time limits** apply to taking a complaint to the FOS.

- When **six months** have passed since the firm sent the consumer a final response (which has to mention the six-month time limit)

- When more than **six years** have passed **since the event** complained about, **or**
- More than **three years** since the person became aware of or could reasonably be expected to have become **aware** of the problem

After these time limits have expired, the firm complained about can choose to object to the Ombudsman looking at the complaint on the grounds that it is 'time-barred'.

8.5 Outcome of FOS findings

objective 6.4.6 **Explain** the rules relating to determination by the Ombudsman (DISP 3).

Where a complaint is determined in favour of the complainant, the Ombudsman's determination may include one or more of the following.

- A **money award** against the respondent
- An **interest award** against the respondent
- A **costs award** against the respondent
- A **direction** to the respondent

The Ombudsman may give a **direction** to the firm to take just and appropriate steps to remedy the position including to pay a money award of up to a maximum of **£100,000** plus reasonable costs (although awards of costs are not common). This figure will normally represent the financial loss the eligible complainant has suffered but can also cover any pain and suffering, damage to their reputation and any distress or inconvenience caused. If the Ombudsman considers that a sum greater than £100,000 would be fair, he can recommend that the firm pays the balance, although he cannot force the firm to pay this excess.

An **interest award** may provide for interest from a specified date to be added to the money award.

Once the Ombudsman has given a decision, the complainant may decide whether to accept or reject that decision.

- If the complainant **accepts** the Ombudsman's decision, **the authorised firm is bound** by it
- . If the complainant **rejects** the decision, they can pursue the matter further through the **Courts**

9   COMPENSATION

9.1 Purpose of FSCS

objective 6.4.7 **Explain** the purpose of the Financial Services Compensation Scheme (FSCS) (COMP 1.1.7).

The **Financial Services Compensation Scheme (FSCS)** is set up under FSMA 2000. The FSCS is designed to compensate **eligible claimants** where a relevant firm is unable or likely to be unable to meet claims against it. Generally speaking, therefore, the scheme will only apply where the firm is declared **insolvent or bankrupt**. The FSCS is seen as part of the 'toolkit' the FSA will use to meet its statutory objectives.

The compensation scheme is independent, but accountable, to the FSA and HM Treasury for its operations and works in partnership with the FSA in delivering the FSA's objectives, particularly that of consumer protection. The FSCS is funded by **levies on authorised firms**.

9.2 Entitlement to compensation

Learning objective **6.4.8 Explain** the circumstances under which the FSCS will pay compensation (COMP 1.3.3, 3.2.1(1) & (2), 4.2.1 & 2 (1) to (6)).

To be entitled to compensation from the scheme, a person must:

1.   Be an **eligible claimant**. This covers most individuals (including, following August 2009 rule changes, directors of the failed entity and their close relatives, in respect of **deposits**) and small businesses. Broadly, an eligible claimant is defined as a claimant who is **not**:

   –   A large company or large partnership/mutual association. What is meant by a large company and partnership will depend on rules established under the UK Companies Acts, which are amended from time to time

   –   An authorised firm, unless they are a sole trader/small business and the claim arises out of a regulated activity of which they have no experience, i.e. do not have permission to carry out

   –   An overseas financial services institution, supranational body, government and local authority

2.   Have a '**protected claim**'. This means certain types of claims in respect of deposits and investment business. Protected investment business means **designated investment business**, the activities of the manager/trustee of an authorised unit trust and the activities of the authorised corporate director/depository of an ICVC. These activities must be carried on either from an establishment in the UK or in an EEA State by a UK firm which is passporting their services there.

3.   Be claiming against a '**relevant person**' who is **in default**. A relevant person means:

   –   An authorised firm, except an EEA firm passporting into the UK (customers who lose money as a result of default by an EEA firm must normally seek compensation from the firm's Home State system, unless the firm has **top-up cover** provided by the FSCS in addition to, or in the absence of, compensation provided by the Home State).

   –   An appointed representative of the above

4.   Make the claim within the relevant **time limits** (normally six years from when the claim arose)

The scheme will normally award financial compensation in cash. The FSCS may require the eligible claimant to assign any legal rights to them in order to receive compensation as they see fit.

Consumer awareness of the FSCS will be promoted by a new rule which came into force on 1 January 2010, requiring firms to **provide information** on the existence of the **FSCS** and level of **protection** it offers to depositors, as well as proactively informing customers of any **additional trading names** under which the firm operates.

9.3 Compensation limits

Learning objective **6.4.9 Identify** the limits on the compensation payable by the FSCS (COMP 10.2.1, 2 & 3).

Maximum compensation levels for failures of firms occurring since **1 January 2010** are shown in the Table below. The limits are per person and per claim, and not per account or contract held.

	Limits from 1 January 2010
Protected investments and home finance	£50,000 (i.e. 100% of the first £50,000)
Protected deposits	£50,000 or €50,000, whichever is greater (i.e. 100% of the first £50,000 or €50,000)
Long-term insurance policies (for both UK and EEA risks)	90% of the claim
General insurance	100% for compulsory insurance; in other cases, 90% of the claim

The FSA has extended, until 30 December 2010, its interim rules which allow separate compensation cover for customers with deposits in two **merging building societies**. The same extension has been made for customers whose deposits are transferred from a failed firm to another deposit taker where they already have an account.

From 31 December 2010, the **Deposit Guarantee Schemes Directive (DGSD)** will require payout of compensation within twenty days. The FSA is aligning its rules with that requirement but expects that payout will be faster, with a target of seven days.

The DGSD proposes a fully harmonised compensation limit set at €100,000 per authorised entity from **31 December 2010**.

CHAPTER ROUNDUP

- Those carrying out a controlled function need to meet a 'fit and proper' test to be approved persons. This test covers honesty, integrity and reputation; competence and capability; and financial soundness.

- Controlled functions include exerting significant influence on the firm, and dealing with customers or their property.

- A firm is responsible for ensuring that there is appropriate training for employees and that employees remain competent.

- Minimum periods are set down for retaining records (five years for MiFID business) and there are requirements on reporting executions of trades and on periodic reporting.

- Money laundering has three typical stages: placement, layering, integration. Those in the financial services industry must keep alert to possible offences relating to the proceeds of any crime.

- Joint Money Laundering Steering Group 2007 guidance requires firms to assess risks when implementing money laundering precautions. The 'Know Your Customer' principle implies that firms should, where appropriate, take steps to find out about the customer's circumstances and business.

- It is a criminal offence to assist laundering the proceeds of crime, to fail to report it satisfactorily or, in the regulated sector, to tip off someone who is involved in laundering the proceeds of crime.

- The Money Laundering Regulations 2007 apply to all authorised firms and individuals. Each firm must have a Nominated Officer, who will decide whether to report suspicions to the Serious Organised Crime Agency.

- Fund raising, use and possession, funding arrangements and money laundering are offences under the Terrorism Act 2000. There is a duty to report suspected terrorism to the police.

- The Counter-Terrorism Act 2008 allows the Treasury, subject to certain conditions, to make directions to financial services firms to address financial crime risks.

- To act on information not freely available to the market is to commit the criminal offence of insider dealing.

- Various types of behaviour, including insider dealing and manipulation of transactions, can constitute market abuse.

- Firms must have transparent and effective complaints procedures, and must make customers aware of them. Firms must investigate complaints competently, diligently and impartially.

- Time limits apply to complaints processing, and the firm must report data on complaints to the FSA twice-yearly.

- If the firm does not resolve a customer's complaint to the customer's satisfaction, the Financial Ombudsman Service is available to adjudicate the dispute.

- The FOS has a Compulsory Jurisdiction (covering authorised firms' regulated activities) and a Voluntary Jurisdiction (for unregulated activities where a firm opts for it).

- The FOS can order a firm to pay up to £100,000 plus costs, in respect of a complaint.

- The Financial Services Compensation Scheme – set up under FSMA 2000 – will pay out within the claim limits to eligible depositors and investors if a firm becomes insolvent.

TEST YOUR KNOWLEDGE

1.   What are the important considerations a person must show to the FSA in order to become approved?

2.   For how long must a firm keep records to demonstrate compliance with the training and competence rules for MiFID business?

3.   What are the three typical stages of money laundering?

4.   Explain what is meant by the 'Nominated Officer' in money laundering prevention provisions.

5.   What is the definition of an insider under criminal law?

6.   What is the maximum penalty for the civil offence of market abuse?

7.   Within what time period does the FSA expect almost all complaints to have been substantively addressed?

8.   What is the maximum award the FOS may make?

TEST YOUR KNOWLEDGE: ANSWERS

1.   Honesty, integrity and reputation; competence and capability; financial soundness.

     (See Section 1.1)

2.   At least five years.

     (See Section 2.4)

3.   Placement, layering and integration.

     (See Section 4.2)

4.   The Nominated Officer is someone who has been nominated by their employer to receive reports of suspected money laundering. This will normally be the Money Laundering Reporting Officer (MLRO) or his deputy.

     (See Section 4.7.3)

5.   Under CJA 1993, an insider is an individual who knowingly has inside information and knows it is from an inside source.

     (See Section 5.2)

6.   An unlimited fine. Other sanctions also include a public statement, an injunction or restitution order.

     (See Section 6.9)

7.   Eight weeks.

     (See Section 7.7)

8.   £100,000 plus costs.

     (See Section 8.5)

7

The Regulatory Advice Framework

INTRODUCTION

The FSA Principles for Businesses are central to the 'principles-based' approach to regulation. Recall that protection of consumers is one of the FSA's statutory objectives. The FSA has made detailed rules in the 'Conduct of Business Sourcebook' (COBS) which are aimed largely at providing such protection.

The COBS rules cover a wide range of operational areas, and have been substantially revised in 2007 following the implementation of the Markets in Financial Instruments Directive (MiFID). This underlines the fact that regulation is increasingly being determined at the European level.

Regulations on client assets segregate those assets to protect clients in the event of failure of the firm.

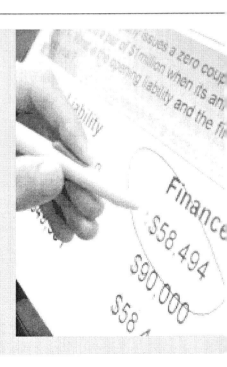

CHAPTER LEARNING OBJECTIVES

7   The regulatory advice framework

Demonstrate the ability to apply the regulatory advice framework in practice for the consumer

7.1   Accepting customers for business

7.1.1 **Explain** the purpose of client classification

7.1.2 **Distinguish** between a retail client, a professional client and an eligible counterparty (COBS 3.4, 3.5, 3.6)

7.1.3 **Apply** the rules relating to treating a client as an elective professional client (3.5.3)

7.1.4 **Apply** the rules relating to treating a client as an elective eligible client (COBS 3.6.4)

7.1.5 **Apply** the rules relating to providing clients with a higher level of protection (COBS 3.7)

7.1.6 **Explain** the rules relating to client agreements (COBS 8.1)

7.2   Financial promotions and other communications with customers

7.2.1 **Explain** the purpose and scope of the financial promotions rules and the exceptions to them (COBS 4.1)

7.2.2 **Explain** the fair, clear and not misleading rule (COBS 4.2)

7.2.3 **Explain** the rules relating to communications with retail clients (COBS 4.5)

7.2.4 **Explain** the rules relating to past, simulated past and future performance (COBS 4.6)

7.2.5 **Explain** the rules relating to direct offer promotions (COBS 4.7)

7.2.6 **Explain** the rules relating to cold calls and other promotions that are not in writing (COBS 4.8)

7.2.7 **Explain** the rules relating to systems and controls in relation to approving and communicating financial promotions (COBS 4.10)

7.2.8 **Explain** the record keeping requirements relating to financial promotions (COBS 4.11)

7.2.9 **Explain** the rules relating to distance marketing communications (COBS 5.1)

7.2.10 **Explain** the rules relating to providing information about the firm and compensation information (COBS 6.1)

7.3   Identifying client needs, information about the firm and investment research

7.3.1 **Explain** the rules relating to assessing suitability (COBS 9.2)

7.3.2 **Explaining** the rules relating to assessing appropriateness (COBS 10.2)

7.3.3 **Explain** the rules relating to warning a client (COBS 10.3)

BPP LEARNING MEDIA

7.3.4 **Identify** circumstances when assessing appropriateness is not required (COBS 10.4, 10.5 & 10.6)

7.3.5 **Identify** circumstances where own authority or expertise is limited and the need to refer to specialists

7.3.6 **Explain** the rules relating to investment research produced by a firm and disseminated to clients (COBS 12.2)

7.3.7 **Explain** the rules relating to the publication and dissemination of non-independent research (COBS 12.3)

7.3.8 **Explain** the disclosure requirements relating to the production and dissemination of research recommendations (COBS 12.4)

7.4 Product disclosure – packaged products

7.4.1 **Explain** the obligations relating to preparing product information (COBS 13.1)

7.4.2 **Explain** the rules relating to the form and content of a key features document (COBS 13.2 and 13.3)

7.4.3 **Explain** the rules relating to cancellation rights (COBS 15)

7.5 Client assets and client money rules

7.5.1 **Explain** the concept of fiduciary duty

7.5.2 **Explain** the application and purpose of the rules relating to custody of client assets held in connection with MiFID business (CASS 6.1)

7.5.3 **Explain** the rules relating to the protection of clients' assets and having adequate organisation arrangements (CASS 6.2)

7.5.4 **Explain** the rules relating to depositing assets with third parties (CASS 6.3)

7.5.5 **Explain** the purpose of the rules relating to the use of clients' assets (CASS 6.4)

7.5.6 **Explain** the rules relating to records, accounts and reconciliations of clients' assets (CASS 6.5)

7.5.7 **Explain** the application and general purpose of the client money rules (CASS 7.2)

7.5.8 **Explain** the rules relating to the segregation of client money (CASS 7.4)

7.5.9 **Explain** the rules relating to records, accounts and reconciliations of client money (CASS 7.6)

7.6 Dealing and managing

7.6.1 **Explain** the rules relating to best execution (COBS 11.2)

7.6.2 **Explain** the rules relating to client order handling (COBS 11.3)

7.6.3 **Explain** the rules relating to the use of dealing commission (COBS 11.6)

7.6.4 **Explain** the rules on personal account dealing (COBS 11.7)

1 ACCEPTING CUSTOMERS FOR BUSINESS

Learning objective   7.1.1 **Explain** the purpose of client classification.

1.1 Conduct of Business Sourcebook (COBS)

Classifying clients into different types allows different regulatory rules to be applied to each type of client, who may therefore be afforded different degrees of protection under the regulatory system. The main corpus of rules affected by the categorisation of any particular client is that found in the **Conduct of Business Sourcebook (COBS)** in the FSA Handbook.

The Conduct of Business rules have been revised extensively, and shortened, with the implementation of the Markets in Financial Instruments Directive (MiFID), with effect from November 2007. The new Sourcebook has sometimes been referred to as 'NEWCOB', but is now referred to by the abbreviation '**COBS**'. (The version which COBS replaced had the abbreviation 'COB'.) Before looking at how clients are categorised, we explain the activities to which COBS applies.

1.2 General application rule

The **general application rule** is that **COBS** applies to an authorised **firm** in respect of the following activities when carried out from one of its (or its **appointed representative's**) **UK** establishments.

- Accepting deposits
- Designated investment business
- Long-term life insurance business

Many rules (except the financial promotion rules) only apply when the firm is doing **designated investment business** with customers.

The term '**designated investment business**' has a narrower meaning than the concept of '**regulated activities**' by excluding activities relating to Lloyd's business, deposits, funeral plans, mortgages, pure protection policies and general insurance contracts. Following the implementation of MiFID, operating a **multilateral trading facility (MTF)** is designated investment business.

There are **modifications** to the general application rule. Only some of the COBS rules apply to **eligible counterparty business** which is MiFID or equivalent third country (that is, **non-EEA**) business. The term 'eligible counterparty' is explained later in this chapter. The following COBS rules **do not** apply to such business.

- Conduct of business obligations, except 'Agent as client' and 'Reliance on others' rules
- Communicating with clients (including financial promotions rules)
- Rules on information about the firm and its services
- Client agreements
- Appropriateness rules (for non-advised sales)
- Best execution, client order handling and use of dealing commission
- Information about designated investments
- Reporting information to clients

1.3 Further general provisions

The **territorial scope** of COBS is modified to ensure compatibility with European law: this is called the '**EEA territorial scope rule**'. One of the effects of the EEA territorial scope rule is to override the application of COBS to the overseas establishments of EEA firms in a number of cases, including circumstances covered by MiFID, the Distance Marketing Directive or the Electronic Commerce Directive. In some circumstances, the rules on financial promotions and other communications will apply to communications made by UK firms to persons located outside the United Kingdom and will not apply to communications made to persons inside the United Kingdom by EEA firms.

For a UK **MiFID investment firm**, COBS rules within the scope of MiFID generally apply to its MiFID business carried on from a **UK branch or establishment**. COBS also applies to EEA MiFID investment firms carrying out business from a UK establishment. However, certain provisions (on investment research, non-independent research and on personal transactions) apply on a **'Home State' basis**: those rules will apply to all establishments in the EEA for the UK firm, and will not apply to a non-UK EEA firm.

COBS provisions on **client limit orders** do not apply to transactions between the operator of a MTF and its members, for MiFID or equivalent third country business. Members or participants in a **regulated market** do not have to apply client limit orders rules to each other, again for MiFID or equivalent third country business. However, in both cases, these rules must be applied if the members are executing orders on behalf of **clients**.

1.4 Communications by electronic media

Where a rule requires a notice to be delivered in writing, a firm may comply using **electronic media**. The COBS rules often specify that communication must be in a **durable medium**.

Durable medium means:

- Paper, or

- Any instrument (e.g. an email message) which enables the recipient to store information addressed personally to him in a way accessible for future reference for a period of time adequate for the purposes of the information and which allows the unchanged reproduction of the information stored. This will include the recipient's computer hard drive or other storage devices on which the electronic mail is stored, but not internet websites unless they fulfil the criteria in this definition.

Some communications are allowed to be delivered either in a durable medium or via a website, where the **website conditions** are satisfied.

The **website conditions** are specified as follows:

- The provision of the information in that medium must be appropriate to the context in which the business between the firm and the client is, or is to be, carried on (i.e. there is evidence that the client has regular access to the internet, such as the provision by the client of an e-mail address).

- The client must specifically consent to the provision of that information in that form.

- The client must be notified electronically of the address of the website, and the place on the website where the information may be accessed.

- The information must be up-to-date.

- The information must be accessible continuously by means of that website for such period of time as the client may reasonably need to inspect it.

1.5 Levels of protection for clients

Within any cost-effective regulatory system, protection provided ought to be **proportionate** to the need for protection. This is because there is not only a cost element to protection but also an inverse relationship with freedom. It is desirable that those who do not require high protection are given more freedom to trade without the restrictions that the rules inevitably bring.

The **size** and **financial awareness** of **clients** will determine the level of protection. As the size/knowledge increases, protection will decrease. A system of categorising clients can help determine that the level of protection is appropriate to the client.

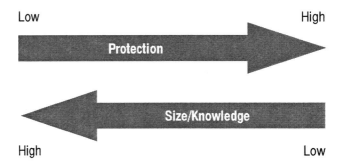

While this would ideally be a continuous process, gradually moving from full protection to no protection, in practical terms this is an impossibility.

1.6 Client categories

7.1.2 Distinguish between a retail client, a professional client and an eligible counterparty (COBS 3.4, 3.5, 3.6).

7.1.3 Apply the rules relating to treating a client as an elective professional client (3.5.3).

7.1.4 Apply the rules relating to treating a client as an elective eligible client (COBS 3.6.4).

7.1.5 Apply the rules relating to providing clients with a higher level of protection (COBS 3.7).

1.6.1 Overview

The terms used to classify clients has changed following the implementation of **MiFID** and the introduction of the new COBS.

Firms (unless they are providing only the special level of **basic advice** on a **stakeholder product**) are obliged to classify all clients who are undertaking **designated investment business,** before doing such business.

MiFID creates three client categories:

- **Eligible counterparties** – who are either **per se** or **elective** eligible counterparties
- **Professional clients** – who are either **per se** or **elective** professional clients
- **Retail clients**

As well as setting up criteria to classify clients into these categories, MiFID provides for clients to **change** their initial classification, on request.

A **customer** is a client who is not an eligible counterparty. The scheme of categorisation is summarised in the following diagram.

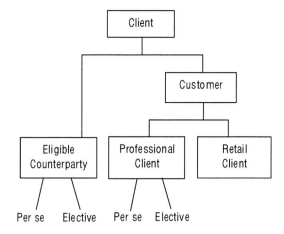

1.6.2 Clients

A **client** is a person to whom an authorised **firm** provides a service in the course of carrying on a **regulated activity** or, in the case of MiFID or equivalent third country business, a person to whom a firm provides an **ancillary service**.

1.6.3 Retail clients

Retail clients are defined as those clients who are not professional clients or eligible counterparties.

1.6.4 Professional clients

Some undertakings are automatically recognised as **professional clients**. Accordingly, these entities may be referred to as *per se* professional clients. (An **undertaking** is a company, partnership or unincorporated association.)

Clients who are *per se* **professional clients** are as follows.

- Entities that **require authorisation or regulation** to operate in the financial markets, including: credit institutions, investment firms, other financial institutions, insurance companies, collective investment schemes and pension funds and their management companies, commodity and commodity derivatives dealers, 'local' derivatives dealing firms, and other institutional investors

- In relation to **MiFID** or equivalent third country business, a **large undertaking** – meaning one that meets two of the following size requirements:

  - €20,000,000 Balance sheet total
  - €40,000,000 Net turnover
  - €2,000,000   Own funds

- In relation to business that is not **MiFID** or equivalent third country business, a **large undertaking** meeting **either** of the following requirements:

  - Called up share capital of at least £5,000,000 or equivalent, or

  - Two of the three following size tests:

    - €12,500,000 balance sheet total
    - €25,000,000 net turnover
    - 250 average number of employees in the year

- Central banks, international institutions, and national and regional government bodies

- Institutional investors whose main activity is to invest in financial instruments

A firm may treat a retail client as an **elective professional client** if the following tests are met.

- **Qualitative test.** The firm assesses adequately the client's **expertise**, **experience** and **knowledge** and thereby gains reasonable assurance that, for the transactions or services envisaged, the client is capable of making his own investment decisions and understanding the risks involved.

- **Quantitative test.** In the case of **MiFID** or equivalent third country business, at least **two** of the following three criteria must apply.

  - The client has carried out at least ten 'significant' transactions per quarter on the relevant market, over the last four quarters

  - The client's portfolio, including cash deposits, exceeds €500,000

  - The client has knowledge of the transactions envisaged from at least one year's professional work in the financial sector

Additionally, for professional client status to apply:

- The client must agree in writing to be treated as a professional client

- The firm must give written warning of the protections and compensation rights which may be lost

- The client must state in writing, separately from the contract, that it is aware of the consequences of losing protections

It is the responsibility of the professional client to keep the firm informed about changes (e.g. in portfolio size or company size) which could affect their categorisation.

COBS states that an elective professional client should not be presumed to have market knowledge and experience comparable to a *per se* professional client.

1.6.5 Eligible counterparties

In relation to MiFID or equivalent third country business, a client can only be an eligible counterparty in relation to eligible counterparty business.

The following, and their non-EEA equivalents, are *per se* **eligible counterparties** (i.e. they are automatically recognised as eligible counterparties).

- Investment firms
- Credit institutions
- Insurance companies
- UCITS collective investment schemes, and their management companies
- Pension funds, and their management companies
- Other financial institutions authorised or regulated under the law of the EU or an EEA state
- Certain own-account commodity derivatives dealers and 'local' derivatives firms
- National governments
- Central banks
- Supranational organisations

A firm may treat an undertaking as an **elective eligible counterparty** if the client:

- Is a *per se* professional client (unless it is such by virtue of being an institutional investor), or

- Is an elective professional client and requests the categorisation, but only in respect of the transactions and services for which it counts as a professional client, and

- In the case of MiFID or equivalent third country business, provides 'express confirmation' of their agreement (which may be for a specific transaction or may be general) to be treated as an eligible counterparty

If the prospective counterparty is established in another EEA state, for MiFID business the firm should defer to the status determined by the law of that other state.

1.7 Agent as client

One area that has proved complicated in the past is where a firm is dealing with an **agent**. For example, suppose that a solicitor is acting for his client and approaches a firm to sell bonds on his client's behalf. Clearly, it is important that the firm establish whether it owes duties to the solicitor or to the solicitor's client.

The agent is the client of the firm, unless an agreement in writing treats the other person as the client.

The relevant COBS rule applies to designated investment business and ancillary services. The rule states that the firm may treat the agent as its client if the agent is another authorised firm or an overseas financial services institution **or** if the agent is another person, provided that the arrangement is not to avoid duties which the firm would otherwise owe to the agent's clients.

An agreement may however be made, in writing, to treat the other person (in the above example, the solicitor's client) as the firm's client.

1.8 Providing a higher level of protection to clients

Firms must allow **professional clients** and **eligible counterparties** to re-categorise in order to get more protection. Such clients are themselves responsible for asking for higher protection if they deem themselves to be **unable** to assess properly or manage the risks involved.

Either on its own initiative or following a client request or written agreement:

- A *per se* **eligible counterparty** may be re-categorised as a **professional client** or **retail client**
- A *per se* **professional client** may be re-categorised as a **retail client**

The **higher level of protection** may be provided through re-categorisation:

- On a general basis
- · Trade by trade
- In respect of specified rules
- In respect of particular services, transactions, transaction types or product types

The client should (of course) be notified of a re-categorisation.

Firms must have written internal policies and procedures to categorise clients.

1.9 Client agreements

⌐ objective   **7.1.6 Apply** the rules relating to client agreements (COBS 8.1).

If a firm carries on **designated investment business**, other than advising on investments, for a **new retail client,** the firm must enter into a **basic agreement** with the client. Although little guidance is given in the rules as to the contents, the agreement will set out the essential rights and obligations of the firm, and must be in writing – on paper or other durable medium. For a **professional client**, there is no requirement for an agreement, although most firms will wish there to be one.

In good time, normally **before** the client is bound by any agreement relating to designated investment business or ancillary services, the firm must provide to the retail client – either in a durable medium or on a website, if the website conditions are satisfied:

- The terms of the agreement

- Information about **the firm and its services** (see below), including information on communications, conflicts of interest and authorised status

The agreement and information may be provided **immediately after** the client is bound by the agreement if the agreement was concluded using a means of distance communication (e.g. telephone).

Relevant material changes to the information provided must be notified to the client in **good time**.

A **record** of the client agreement should be kept for five years, or for the duration of the relationship with the client if longer. For pension transfers or opt-outs, or FSAVCs, the record should be kept indefinitely.

2 FINANCIAL PROMOTIONS AND COMMUNICATIONS

Learning objective | 7.2.1 **Explain** the purpose and scope of the financial promotions rules and the exceptions to them (COBS 4.1).

2.1 Introduction

A **financial promotion** is an **invitation** or **inducement** to **engage** in investment activity. The term therefore describes most forms and methods of marketing financial services. It covers traditional advertising, most website content, telephone sales campaigns and face-to-face meetings. The term is extended to cover **marketing communications** by MiFID.

The purpose of regulation in this area is to create a regime where the quality of financial promotions is scrutinised by an authorised firm who must then comply with lengthy rules to ensure that their promotions are **clear**, **fair and not misleading** (Principle 7) and that customers are treated **fairly** (Principle 6).

2.2 Application of the financial promotions rules

The **financial promotions rules** within COBS apply to a firm:

- Communicating with a **client** in relation to **designated investment business**

- **Communicating** or **approving** a **financial promotion** (with some exceptions in respect of: credit promotions, home purchase plans, home reversion schemes, non-investment insurance contracts and unregulated collective investment schemes)

Firms must also apply the rules to promotions issued by their **appointed representatives**.

2.3 Territorial scope

For financial promotions, the **general application rule** applies. This indicates that the rules apply to a firm in respect of designated investment business carried out from an establishment maintained by the firm or its appointed representative in the UK. Additionally, in general the rules apply to firms carrying on business with a client in the UK from an establishment overseas.

The financial promotions rules also apply to:

- Promotions communicated to a person in the UK

- Cold (unsolicited) calling to someone outside the UK, if the call is from within the UK or is in respect of UK business

2.4 Fair, clear and not misleading

g objective **.7.2.2 Explain** the fair, clear and not misleading rules (COBS 4.2).

A firm must ensure that a communication or financial promotion is **fair, clear and not misleading**, and is **appropriate** and **proportionate** considering the means of communication and the information to be conveyed.

This rule applies to **communications** in relation to designated investment business other than a third party prospectus.

It applies to **financial promotions** approved by the firm, and to financial promotions communicated by the firm which are not non-retail, or excluded and are not a third party prospectus.

The **fair, clear and not misleading rule** is specifically interpreted in COBS as it applies to financial promotions in some aspects, as follows.

- If a product or service places a client's capital at risk, this should be made clear

- Any yield figure quoted should give a balanced impression of both short-term and long-term prospects for the investment

- Sufficient information must be provided to explain any complex charging arrangements, taking into account recipients' needs

- The regulator (FSA) should be named, and any non-regulated aspects made clear

- A fair, clear and not misleading impression should be given of the producer for any packaged product (a term explained later) or stakeholder products not produced by the firm

The British Bankers' Association / Building Societies Association **Code of Conduct for the Advertising of Interest Bearing Accounts** is also relevant in the case of financial promotions relating to deposits.

2.5 Identifying promotions as such

A firm must ensure that a **financial promotion** addressed to a **client** is clearly **identifiable as such**.

- This rule does not apply to a third party prospectus in respect of **MiFID** (or equivalent third country) business.

- There are also some exceptions in respect of **non-MiFID** business, including prospectus advertisements, image advertising, non-retail communications, deposits and pure protection long-term care insurance (LTCI) products.

2.6 Exceptions

As mentioned earlier, the **financial promotions rules** in COBS do **not apply** to promotions of qualifying credit, home purchase plans, home reversion schemes, non-investment insurance contracts, and certain unregulated collective investment schemes whose promotions firms may not communicate or approve.

Except in regard to disclosure of compensation arrangements, the COBS rules on communications (including financial promotions) do **not** apply when a firm communicates with an **eligible counterparty**.

The financial promotions rules also do **not** apply to incoming communications in relation to **MiFID business** of an investment firm **from another EEA state** that are, in its home state, regulated under MiFID.

2.7 Excluded communications

A firm may rely on one or more of the following aspects which make a communication into an **excluded communication** for the purposes of the rules.

- A financial promotion that would benefit from an exemption in the Financial Promotion Order (see below) if it were communicated by an unauthorised person, or which originates outside the UK and has no effect in the UK

- A financial promotion from outside the UK that would be exempt under articles 30, 31, 32 or 33 of the Financial Promotion Order (Overseas communicators) if the office from which the financial promotion is communicated were a separate unauthorised person

- A financial promotion that is subject to, or exempted from, the Takeover Code or to the requirements relating to takeovers or related operations in another EEA state

- A personal quotation or illustration form

- A **'one-off' financial promotion** that is not a cold call. The following conditions indicate that the promotion is a 'one-off', but they need not necessarily be present for a promotion to be considered as 'one-off'.

  (i)   The financial promotion is communicated only to one recipient or only to one group of recipients in the expectation that they would engage in any investment activity jointly

  (ii) The identity of the product or service to which the financial promotion relates has been determined having regard to the particular circumstances of the recipient

  (iii) The financial promotion is not part of an organised marketing campaign

2.8 Financial Promotions Order

Section 21 FSMA 2000 makes it criminal for someone to undertake a financial promotion, i.e. invite or induce another to engage in investment activity, unless they are either

- An **authorised firm** (i.e. **issuing the financial promotion**), or
- The content of the communication is **approved** by an authorised firm

Contravention of section 21 is punishable by up to **two** years in jail and an **unlimited** fine.

There are a number of exemptions from s21 set out in the **Financial Promotions Order**. The effect of being an **exemption** is that the promotion would **not** need to be issued or approved by an authorised firm. It would therefore not have to comply with the detailed financial promotion rules.

The main examples are as follows. (Other exemptions cover certain one-off and purely factual promotions.)

Exemption	Comments
1. Investment professional	A communication to an authorised or exempt person.
2. Deposits and insurance	Very limited application of COBS.

Exemption	Comments
3. Certified high net worth individuals*	Anyone may promote **unlisted securities** to persons who hold certificates of high net worth (normally signed by their accountant or employer, however, these can now be self-certified by an individual) and who have agreed to be classified as such. Requirements for a certificate are that a person must have a net income of £100,000 or more, or net assets (excluding principal property) of £250,000 or more. Note that, if applicable, the financial promotion should not invite or induce the recipient to engage in business with the firm that signed the certificate of high net worth.
4. Associations of high net worth individuals	Anyone can promote non-derivative products to associations of high net worth investors.
5. Sophisticated investors	Anyone can promote products to a person who holds a certificate indicating that they are knowledgeable in a particular stock (normally signed by an authorised firm, however, individuals can now self-certify themselves as sophisticated in relation to unlisted securities) and who have signed a statement agreeing to be such. Note that the financial promotion should not invite or induce the recipient to engage in business with the authorised firm that signed the certificate.
6. Takeover Code	Promotions subject to the Takeover Code.

2.9 Prospectus advertisements

Where a **prospectus** is issued on an offer or an admission of transferable securities to trading, there are rules governing advertisements relating to it.

The **advertisement**:

- Must state that a prospectus has been or will be published, and indicate where it can be obtained
- Must be clearly recognisable as an advertisement
- Must not contain inaccurate or misleading information
- Must be consistent with information in the prospectus

A written advertisement should contain a **bold and prominent statement** indicating that it is not a prospectus but an advertisement and that investors should not subscribe for transferable securities mentioned except on the basis of information in the prospectus.

All information issued – oral or written, even if not for advertising purposes – must be consistent with the prospectus.

2.10 Communicating with retail clients

objective **7.2.3 Explain** the rules relating to communications with retail clients (COBS 4.5).

2.10.1 General rule

The general rule on **communicating with retail clients** in relation to **designated investment business** states that firms must ensure that the information:

- Includes the **name of the firm** (which may be the **trading name** or **shortened name**, provided the firm is identifiable)
- Is accurate and does not emphasise potential benefits of investment without also giving a **fair and prominent indication of relevant risks**

- Is **sufficient** for and presented so as to be **likely to be understood** by the **average member** of the group to whom it is directed or by whom it is likely to be received

- Does **not disguise, diminish** or **obscure** important **items, statements** or **warnings**

In deciding whether and how to communicate to a target audience, the firm should **consider**: the nature of the product/business, risks, the client's commitment, the average recipient's information needs and the role of the information in the sales process.

The firm should consider whether omission of a relevant fact will result in information being **insufficient, unclear, unfair** or **misleading**.

2.10.2 Comparative information

Information comparing business / investments / persons must

- Present **comparisons** in a meaningful, fair and balanced way

- In relation to MiFID or equivalent third country business, specify **information sources**, key facts and assumptions

2.10.3 Tax treatment

If **tax treatment** is referred to, it should be stated prominently that the tax treatment depends on the individual circumstances of the client and may be subject to change in future. (One of a couple of exceptions to this rule is that it does not apply to deposits other than cash ISAs or CTFs.)

2.10.4 Consistency

The firm should ensure that information in a financial promotion is **consistent** with other information provided to the retail client. (**Deposits** are an exception to this rule.)

2.11 Past, simulated past and future information

Learning objective 7.2.4 **Explain** the rules relating to past, simulated past and future performance (COBS 4.6).

2.11.1 Introduction

Rules on **performance information** apply to information disseminated to retail clients, and to financial promotions. In the case of non-MiFID business, the rules do not apply to deposits generally nor to pure protection long-term care insurance (LTCI) contracts.

2.11.2 Past performance information

Past performance information must:

- **Not** be the most prominent feature of the communication

- Include appropriate information covering at least the **five preceding years**, or the whole period the investment/service has been offered/provided or the whole period the financial index has been established, if less than five years

- Be based on and must show complete **12-month periods**

- State the **reference period** and **source of the information**

- Contain a **prominent warning** that the figures refer to the past and that past performance is not a reliable indicator of future results

- If denominated in a foreign **currency**, state the currency clearly, with a warning that the return may increase or decrease as a result of currency fluctuations

- If based on gross performance, disclose the effect of **commissions**, fees or other charges

The above provisions are to be interpreted in a way that is '**appropriate and proportionate**' to the communication. For example, in a periodic statement issued for investments managed, past performance may be the most prominent feature, in spite of the first bullet point immediately above.

For a **packaged product** (except a unitised with-profits life policy or a stakeholder pension scheme), information should be given on:

- An **offer to bid** basis (which should be stated) for an actual return or comparison with other investments, or

- An **offer to offer**, **bid to bid** or **offer to bid** basis (which should be stated) if there is a comparison with an index or with movements in the price of units, or

- A **single pricing** basis with allowance for charges

2.11.3 Simulated past performance information

Simulated past performance information must

- Relate to an investment or a financial index

- Be based on actual past performance of investments/indices which are the same as, or underlie, the investment concerned

- Contain a **prominent warning** that figures refer to simulated past performance and that past performance is not a reliable indicator of future performance

2.11.4 Future performance information

Future performance information must:

- **Not** be based on nor refer to simulated past performance
- Be based on **reasonable assumptions** supported by **objective data**
- If based on gross performance, disclose the effect of **commissions**, fees or other charges
- Contain a **prominent warning** that such forecasts are not a reliable indicator of future performance
- Only be provided if **objective data** can be obtained

2.12 Financial promotions containing offers or invitations

ɔ objective   **7.2.5 Explain** the rules relating to direct offer promotions (COBS 4.7).

A **direct offer financial promotion** is a form of financial promotion which enables investors to purchase investments directly 'off the page' without receiving further information.

A direct offer financial promotion to retail clients must contain whatever **disclosures** are relevant to that offer or invitation (as outlined earlier, such as information about the firm and its services, and costs and charges) and, for non-MiFID business, additional appropriate information about the relevant business and investments so that the client is reasonably able to understand their nature and risks, and consequently to take investment decisions on an informed basis. This information may be contained in a separate document to which the client must refer in responding to the offer or invitation. Alternatively, information disclosures may be omitted if the firm can demonstrate that the client referred to the required information before making or accepting the offer.

A firm may wish to include in a direct offer financial promotion a summary of **tax** consequences, and a statement that the recipient should seek a **personal recommendation** if he has any doubt about the suitability of the investments or services.

2.13 Unwritten promotions and cold calling

Learning objective

7.2.6 Explain the rules relating to cold calls and other promotions that are not in writing (COBS 4.8).

An **unwritten financial promotion** outside the firm's premises may only be initiated if the person communicating it

- Does so at an appropriate time of day
- Identifies himself and his firm, and makes his purpose clear
- Clarifies if the client wants to continue or terminate the communication, and terminates it on request at any time
- If an appointment is arranged, gives a contact point to a client

Firms may only make **cold (unsolicited) calls** if

- The recipient has an established client relationship with the firm, such that the recipient envisages receiving them, or
- The call is about a generally marketed packaged product (not based on a high volatility fund), or
- The call relates to controlled activities by an authorised person or exempt person, involving only readily realisable securities (not warrants)

Note that the rules on unwritten promotions and cold calling apply only to **retail clients**.

2.14 Financial promotions for the business of overseas persons

An 'overseas person' here means a firm carrying on regulated activities who does not do so within the UK.

Any financial promotion for the business of such an **overseas person** must

- Make clear which firm has approved or communicated it
- Explain that rules for protection of retail clients do not apply
- Explain the extent and level of any available compensation scheme (or state that no scheme applies)
- Not be issued if the firm has any reason to doubt that the overseas person will deal with UK retail clients in an honest and reliable way

2.15 Approving financial promotions

Learning objective

7.2.7 Explain the rules relating to systems and controls in relation to approving and communicating financial promotions (COBS 4.10).

The rules in **SYSC** require that a firm which communicates with a client regarding designated investment business, or communicates or approves a financial promotion, puts in place **systems and controls** or **policies and procedures** in order to comply with the COBS rules.

Section 21(1) FSMA 2000 prohibits an unauthorised person from communicating a financial promotion, unless either an exemption applies or the financial promotion is approved by an authorised firm.

Approval of a financial promotion by an **authorised firm** enables it to be communicated by an **unauthorised firm**.

A firm **approving** a financial promotion must confirm that it **complies** with the **financial promotion rules**. The firm must withdraw its approval, and notify anyone it knows to be relying on its approval, if it becomes aware that it no longer complies with the financial promotion rules.

A promotion made during a personal visit, telephone conversation or other interactive dialogue cannot be approved.

Approval given by the firm may be '**limited**', e.g. limited to communication to **professional clients** or **eligible counterparties**.

In communicating a financial promotion, a firm is permitted to **rely on another firm's confirmation of compliance** with the financial promotions rules. The firm must take reasonable care to ensure that the promotion is only communicated to types of recipients for whom it was intended.

2.16 Record keeping requirements relating to financial promotions

objective | **7.2.8 Explain** the record keeping requirements relating to financial promotions (COBS 4.11).

A firm must make an adequate record of any financial promotion it communicates or approves. The record must be retained for:

- indefinitely for a pension transfer, opt-out or FSAVC

- Six years for a life policy, occupational pension scheme, SSAS, personal pension scheme or stakeholder scheme

- Five years for MiFID or equivalent third country business

- Three years for other cases

2.17 Distance marketing communications

objective | **7.2.9 Explain** the rules relating to distance marketing communications (COBS 5.1).

2.17.1 Overview

The EU **Distance Marketing Directive (DMD)** covers the distance marketing of financial services and has been enacted in the UK via the **Financial Services (Distance Marketing) Regulations 2004**.

COBS Chapter 5 on *Distance communications* includes provisions conforming to the DMD. COBS clarifies how the **Distance Marketing Directive (DMD)** and the Regulations should be interpreted by authorised firms. It requires that certain product disclosures are given to **consumers** who conclude contracts at a distance.

The FSA has taken the view that responsibility for the DMD requirements applies to the Home State except in the case of a branch, in which case responsibility rests with the EEA State in which the branch is located. This means that the relevant COBS rules will apply to branches in the UK, including branches of foreign (EEA or non-EEA) firms.

2.17.2 Disclosure requirements

The DMD introduced requirements to provide consumers with certain **detailed information** before a contract is concluded, including information about:

- The identity of the supplier (including geographical address)
- Product details (including price and fees), and
- Particulars of the contract (including rights of cancellation)

During **voice telephony** communications, only specified abbreviated distance marketing information needs to be provided. However, the standard distance marketing information must still be provided on a durable medium in good time before the customer is bound by any distance contract or offer.

2.17.3 Consumer

The DMD provides protections for any individual who is a **consumer**, meaning a natural person (i.e. an individual) who concludes a **distance contract** outside of their trade, business or profession.

The Directive covers individuals acting, for example:

- As personal representatives, including executors, unless they are acting in a professional capacity, e.g. a solicitor acting as executor, or
- In personal or other family circumstances for example, as trustee of a family trust

but excludes individuals acting, for example:

- As trustee of a trust, such as a housing or NHS trust, or
- As member of the governing body of a club or other unincorporated association, such as a trade body or a student union, or
- As a pension trustee

2.17.4 Distance contract

A **distance contract** is one which is concluded under an '**organised distance sales or service-provision scheme**' directly or through an intermediary with exclusive use of one or more **means of distance communication**.

Concluding a contract by **means of distance communication** includes by post, telephone, fax or the internet.

The following factors help determine whether a contract is concluded under an '**organised distance sales or service-provision scheme**'.

- There must have been no '**simultaneous physical presence**' of the firm and the **consumer** throughout the offer, negotiation and conclusion of the contract. So, for example, contracts offered, negotiated and concluded over the internet, through a telemarketing operation or by post will normally be **distance contracts**. A **consumer** may visit the local office of the firm in the course of the offer, negotiation or conclusion of the contract with that firm. Wherever, in the literal sense, there has been 'simultaneous physical presence' of the firm and the **consumer** at the time of such a visit, any ensuing contract will **not** be a **distance contract**.

- Services provided on a strictly occasional basis and outside a commercial structure dedicated to the conclusion of **distance contracts** are not governed by the DMD.

- A one-off transaction effected exclusively by distance means to meet an emergency will not be a **distance contract**.

- If a firm normally operates face-to-face and has no facilities in place enabling a **consumer** to deal with it customarily by distance means, the DMD will not apply.

2.17.5 Initial service agreement and successive operations

A firm's contract with a customer may take the form of an **initial service agreement** followed by a **series of separate operations** over time. Where this is the case, the DMD disclosure and cancellation requirements apply in relation to the initial service agreement only and not to the successive or separate operations.

However, if new elements are added to the **initial service agreement**, the addition of those new elements is treated as a new contract, to which the DMD disclosure and cancellation requirements apply. For example, the opening of a bank account would be a initial service agreement, the deposit or withdrawal of funds from that account would be a successive or series of separate operations, but adding a debit card to the account constitutes a new element to which the DMD disclosure and cancellation requirements apply.

Other examples of **initial service agreements** and **successive operations** are as follows.

- Opening a brokerage account for the purposes of trading securities, and transactions under that account

- Establishing a facility to enable a customer to subscribe to an ISA for the present and future tax years, and successive subscriptions under that agreement

- Subscribing to an investment trust savings scheme, and successive purchases or sales of shares under that scheme

- Concluding a life policy, pension contract or stakeholder pension scheme that includes a pre-selected option providing for future increases or decreases in regular premiums or payments, and subsequent index-linked changes to those premiums or increases or decreases to pension contributions following fluctuations in salary

The DMD disclosure requirements will not apply to **successive operations** of the same nature over time, e.g. the subscription of units into the same Collective Investment Scheme provided there has been an operation of the same nature within the past year. If there has been a break of longer than a year, the next operation will be treated as the first in a new series of operations and the DMD disclosure requirements will apply.

2.17.6 Use of intermediaries

The mere fact that an intermediary (acting for the firm or for the **consumer**) is involved does not make the sale of a financial product or service a **distance contract**.

2.17.7 Distance contracts for intermediation services

In a small number of cases, intermediaries will themselves fall within the scope of DMD, e.g. where the intermediary agrees to provide continuing advisory, broking or portfolio management services for a **consumer**.

However, the DMD is only relevant if:

- There is a contract between the intermediary and the consumer in respect of the intermediary's mediation services, and

- The contract is a distance contract, and

- The contract is concluded other than merely as a stage in the provision of another service by the intermediary or another person

2.18 Information about the firm

Learning objective 7.2.10 **Explain** the rules relating to providing information about the firm and compensation information (COBS 6.1).

Information about a firm and its services which must be provided to a **retail client** comprises the following general information.

- The firm's **name and address** (permanent place of business), and **contact details** which allow effective communication

- For MiFID and equivalent third country business, the **languages** the firm uses for documents and other communication

- **Methods of communication with clients** which are used by the firm, including those for sending and receiving orders where relevant

- Statement that the firm is **authorised**, and the name of the authorising **competent authority** (e.g. the Financial Services Authority) – with the authority's contact address, in the case of MiFID business

- If the firm is acting through an **appointed representative or tied agent**, a statement of this fact specifying the EEA State in which the representative/agent is registered

- The nature, frequency and timing of **performance reports** provided by the firm (in accordance with rules on reporting to clients)

- For a MiFID or common platform firm or a third country (non-EEA) investment firm, the firm's **conflicts of interest policy** (or a summary of it)

- For other firms, details of **how the firm will ensure fair treatment** of clients when material interests or conflicts of interest arise

2.19 Information about compensation

For MiFID business, the firm must tell the client about the applicable **investor compensation scheme** (generally, **FSCS**), giving information in a durable medium or via a web site meeting the web site conditions and in the language of the EEA State:

- On the amount and scope of cover offered
- At the client's request, on conditions and formalities involved in claiming compensation

3 IDENTIFYING CLIENT NEEDS

3.1 Assessing suitability

Learning objective 7.3.1 **Explain** the rules relating to assessing suitability (COBS 9.2).

Suitability rules apply when a firm makes a **personal recommendation** in relation to a **designated investment** (but not if the firm makes use of the rules on basic scripted advice for stakeholder products).

The firm has obligations regarding the assessment of **suitability**: the firm must take reasonable steps to ensure that, in respect of designated investments, a personal recommendation or a decision to trade is **suitable for its client**.

To meet this obligation, the firm must **obtain necessary information** regarding the client's:

- **Knowledge and experience** in the relevant investment field (including: types of investment or service with which the client is familiar; transactions experience; level of education and profession or former profession; understanding of risks)

- **Investment objectives** (including: length of time he wishes to hold the investment; risk preferences; risk profile; purposes of the investment)

- **Financial situation** (including: extent and source of regular income; assets including liquid assets; investments and real property; regular financial commitments) (Is he able to bear any investment risks, consistent with his investment objectives?)

The firm is entitled to **rely** on **information provided by the client**, unless it is aware that the information is out of date, inaccurate or incomplete.

A **transaction** may be **unsuitable** for a client because of

- The risks of the designated investments involved
- The type of transaction
- The characteristics of the order
- The frequency of trading
- It resulting in an unsuitable portfolio (in the case of **managing investments**)

For non-MiFID business, these rules apply to business with **retail clients**. When making personal recommendations or managing investments for **professional clients**, in the course of MiFID or equivalent third country business, a firm is entitled to assume that the client has the necessary experience and knowledge, in relation to products and services for which the professional client is so classified.

3.2 Suitability report

3.2.1 Requirement

A firm must provide a **suitability report** to a retail client if the firm makes a personal recommendation and the client:

- Buys or sells shares/units in a regulated collective investment scheme

- Buys or sells shares through an investment trust savings scheme or investment trust ISA or PEP

- Buys, sells, surrenders, cancels rights in or suspends contributions to a personal or stakeholder pension scheme

- Elects to make income withdrawals from a short-term annuity

- Enters into a pension transfer or pension opt-out

A suitability report is required for all personal recommendations in relation to **life policies**.

A suitability report is **not** required:

- If the firm acts as investment manager and recommends a regulated collective investment scheme

- If the client is habitually resident outside the EEA and is not in the UK when acknowledging consent to the proposal form

- For small life policies (not >£50 p.a.) recommended by friendly societies

- For recommendations to increase regular premiums on an existing contract

- For recommendations to invest further single contributions to an existing packaged product

3.2.2 Timing

The suitability report must generally be provided to the client **as soon as possible after the transaction is effected**. For personal or stakeholder pension schemes requiring notification of cancellation rights, the report must be provided no later than 14 days after the contract is concluded.

3.2.3 Contents

The suitability report must, at least

- Specify the client's **demands and needs**

- Explain the firm's **recommendation** that the transaction is suitable, having regard to information provided by the client

- Explain any possible **disadvantages** of the transaction to the client

The firm should give details appropriate to the **complexity** of the transaction.

For **income withdrawals** from a **short-term annuity**, the explanation of possible disadvantages should include **risk factors** involved in income withdrawals or purchase of a short-term annuity.

3.3 Appropriateness

Learning objectives

7.3.2 Explain the rules relating to assessing appropriateness (COBS 10.2).

7.3.3 Explain the rules relating to warning a client (COBS 10.3).

7.3.4 Identify circumstances when assessing appropriateness is not required (COBS 10.4, 10.5, 10.6).

The **appropriateness** rules we outline here apply to a firm providing **investment services** in the course of **MiFID** or equivalent third country business, **other than** making a personal recommendation and managing investments. (Note that, as we have seen, the **suitability** rules apply where there is a personal recommendation.) One firm may rely on another MiFID firm's assessment of appropriateness, in line with the general rule on reliance on other investment firms.

The rules apply to arranging or dealing in **derivatives** or **warrants** for a **retail client**, when in response to a **direct offer financial promotion**.

To **assess appropriateness**, the firm must ask the client to provide information on his knowledge and experience in the relevant investment field, to enable the assessment to be made.

The firm will then:

- Determine whether the client has the necessary **experience and knowledge** to understand the **risks** involved in the product/service (including the following aspects: nature and extent of service with which client is familiar; complexity; risks involved; extent of client's transactions in designated investments; level of client's education and profession or former profession)

- Be entitled to assume that a **professional client** has such experience and knowledge, for products/services for which it is classified as 'professional'

Unless it knows the information from the client to be out-of-date, inaccurate or incomplete, the firm may rely on it. Where reasonable, a firm may infer knowledge from experience.

The firm may seek to increase the client's level of understanding by providing appropriate information to the client.

If the firm is satisfied about the client's experience and knowledge, there is **no duty to communicate** this to the client. If, in doing so, it is making a personal recommendation, it must comply with the **suitability** rules. But if the firm concludes that the product or service is **not appropriate** to the client, it must **warn** the client. The warning may be in a standardised format.

If the client provides insufficient information, the firm must **warn** the client that such a decision will not allow the firm to determine whether the service or product is appropriate for him. Again, the warning may be in a standardised format.

If a client who has received a warning asks the firm to go ahead with the transaction, it is for the firm to consider whether to do so 'having regard to the circumstances'.

A firm **need not assess appropriateness**:

- For an execution-only service in listed shares provided on the initiative of the client, if the client is warned that there will be no suitability assessment and the firm meets conflict of interest requirements

- If it is receiving or transmitting an order in relation to which it has assessed suitability

- If it is able to rely on a recommendation made by an investment firm

- On each occasion, in new dealings with a client engaged in a course of dealings

3.4 Referring to specialists

objective | 7.3.5 **Identify** circumstances where own authority or expertise is limited and the need to refer to specialists.

Very few financial advisers have extensive or sufficient knowledge in all areas of financial planning.

If dealings with a client involve actions that are beyond the authority of the adviser, either as a result of the firm's rules or the regulator's requirements and rules, then the adviser should seek authority from an appropriate person.

The adviser should be able to refer to other specialists within the firm, and should be willing to do so if necessary. Advisers may also need to refer to specialists outside their business in certain areas of advice and should explain to the client when it would be necessary.

4 INVESTMENT RESEARCH

4.1 Investment research and conflicts of interest

objective | 7.3.6 **Explain** the rules relating to investment research produced by a firm and disseminated to clients (COBS 12.2).

There have been concerns that analysts have been encouraged to write favourable research on companies in order to attract lucrative investment banking work. There have also been concerns about firm's employees recommending particular securities while privately trading contrary to the recommendation.

COBS rules on investment research apply to MiFID business carried on by a MiFID investment firm. Rules on disclosure of research recommendations apply to all firms.

There are rules covering investment research which is intended or likely to be disseminated to clients or to the public.

Firms must ensure that its measures for **managing conflicts of interest** cover the **financial analysts** who produce its investment research, and any other relevant staff.

The firm's arrangements must ensure that:

- The financial analysts and other staff involved do not undertake personal transactions or trade on behalf of other persons, including the firm (unless they are acting as a market maker in good faith), in financial instruments to which unpublished investment research relates, until the **recipients** of the research have had a **reasonable opportunity** to act on it

- In other circumstances, personal transactions by financial analysts and other staff in financial instruments related to investment research they are producing which is **contrary to current recommendations** must only occur in **exceptional circumstances** and with **prior approval** of the firm's legal or compliance function

- The firm and its staff must not **accept inducements** from those with a material interest in the subject matter of investment research, and they must not **promise issuers favourable research coverage**

- Issuers and persons other than financial analysts must not be allowed to **review pre-publication drafts** of investment research for any purpose **other than to verify compliance** with the firm's legal obligations, if the draft includes a recommendation or a target price

There is an exemption from the rules in this section (7.3.2) where a firm distributes investment research **produced by a third party** which is not in the firm's group, provided that the firm does not alter the recommendations and does not present the research as produced by the firm. The firm is required to verify that the independent producer of the research has equivalent arrangements in place to avoid conflicts of interest.

4.2 Non-independent research

Learning objective   7.3.7 **Explain** the rules relating to the publication and dissemination of non-independent research (COBS 12.3).

Investment research is research which Is described as investment research or in similar terms, or is otherwise presented as an objective or independent explanation of the matters contained in the recommendation. Research not meeting this requirement falls within the definition of **non-independent research**.

Non-independent research must:

- Be clearly identified as a **marketing communication**

- Contain a clear and prominent statement that it does not follow the requirements of independent research and is not subject to prohibitions on dealing ahead of dissemination of research

Financial promotions rules apply to non-independent research as if it were a marketing communication.

Firms must take **reasonable care** to ensure that research recommendations are fairly presented, and to disclose its interests or indicate conflicts of interest.

Situations where conflicts can arise include:

- Employees trading in financial instruments which they know the firm has or intends to publish non-independent research about, before clients have had a reasonable opportunity to act on the research (other than where the firm is acting as a market maker in good faith, or in the execution of an unsolicited client order

- Non-independent research intended first for internal use and for later publication to clients

4.3 Research recommendations

7.3.8 Explain the disclosure requirements relating to the production and dissemination of research recommendations (COBS 12.4).

The **identity** (name, job title, name of firm, competent authority) of the person responsible for the research should be disclosed clearly and prominently.

The research should meet certain **general standards** for example to ensure that facts are distinguished from interpretations or opinions. Projections should be labelled as such. Reliable sources should be used, and any doubts about reliability clearly indicated. The substance of the recommendations should be possible to be substantiated by the FSA on request.

Additionally, the firm must take reasonable care to ensure **fair presentation**, broadly covering the following aspects.

- Indication of material sources, including the issuer (if appropriate)
- Disclosure of whether the recommendation was disclosed to the issuer and then amended
- Summary of valuation basis or methodology
- Explanation of the meaning of any recommendation (e.g. 'buy', 'sell', 'hold')
- Risk warning if appropriate
- Planned frequency of updates
- Date of release of research, and date and time of prices mentioned
- Details of change over any previous recommendation in the last year

Firms must make **disclosures** in research recommendations broadly covering the following areas.

- All **relationships and circumstances** (including those of affiliated companies) that may reasonably be expected to impair the objectivity of the recommendation (especially, financial interests in any relevant investment, and a conflict of interest regarding the issuer)

- Whether employees involved have **remuneration** tied to investment banking transactions

- **Shareholdings** held by the firm (or an affiliated company) of over 5% of the share capital of the issuer

- **Shareholdings** held by the issuer of over 5% of the share capital of the firm (or an affiliated company)

- Other **significant financial interests**

- Statements about the **role of the firm** as market maker, lead manager of previous offers of the issuer in the last year, provider of investment banking services

- Statements about **arrangements** to prevent and avoid conflicts of interest, prices and dates at which employees involved acquired shares

- **Data** on the proportions of the firm's **recommendations** in different categories (e. g. 'buy', 'sell', 'hold'), on a quarterly basis, with the proportions of relevant investments issued by issuers who were investment banking clients of the firm during the last year

- Identification of a **third party** who produced the research, if applicable, describing also any alteration of third party recommendations and ensuring that any summary of third party research is fair, clear and not misleading

For shorter recommendations, firms can make reference to many of the relevant disclosures, e.g. by providing a website link.

5 PRODUCT DISCLOSURE AND CANCELLATION RIGHTS

Learning objective   7.4.1 **Explain** the obligations relating to preparing product information (COBS 13.1).

5.1 Advising on packaged products

5.1.1 Packaged products

The term '**packaged products**' relates to products that can be bought 'off-the-shelf', with the terms and conditions and price identical for all potential investors. These are typically products sold through an intermediary, for example an Independent Financial Adviser (IFA).

A **packaged product** is defined as one of the following:

- A unit in a regulated collective investment scheme
- A life policy
- An interest in an investment trust savings scheme
- A personal pension scheme
- A stakeholder pension scheme

whether or not (in the case of the first three types listed above) it is held within an ISA or a Child Trust Fund (CTF) and whether or not the packaged product is also a stakeholder product.

Exam tip

> Use the word **CLIPS** to remember the types of packaged product.
>   **C**ollective Investment Schemes (regulated)
>   **L**ife policies
>   **I**nvestment trust savings schemes
>   **P**ersonal pensions
>   **S**takeholder pensions

There are disclosure rules, described below, which apply when a firm makes a **personal recommendation** to a **retail client** to buy a **packaged product**. These rules do not apply when special rules on (scripted) **basic advice** for stakeholder products are being followed.

These rules apply to a UK firm's business carried out in another EEA State for a retail client in the UK, subject to certain exclusions. They also apply to business carried out in the UK for a client in another EEA state.

5.1.2 Selling products from the firm's scope

The firm's disclosures should indicate whether it expects its **scope** to be:

- The whole of the market or market sector
- Limited to several product providers
- Limited to a single product provider

What is meant by the **scope** and **range** of a firm's advice?

- The **scope** relates to the product providers whose products it sells
- The **range** relates to which products from those providers it sells

> The **client's best interests rule** (in COBS) states:
> 'Firms must act honestly, fairly and professionally in accordance with the **best interests of the client**.'

In accordance with the **client's best interests rule** and the **fair, clear and not misleading rule**, a firm must ensure that:

- Its representatives consider, based on adequate knowledge, products across its scope

- Products outside the scope are not recommended

- All representatives advising on packaged products and making recommendations can recommend and sell each product in the relevant range. (If a representative is not competent to advise on a product or category, a client to whom a recommendation ought to be made should be referred to a representative who is competent.)

- The scope disclosed to the client is not narrowed without appropriate new disclosure to the client

- The scope is not extended in a way that alters remuneration arrangements unless it provides new disclosures on inducements, charges and costs (e. g. by providing a further '**menu**')

A firm may use sufficient '**panels' of product providers** to cover the whole of the market, and if so should review these regularly.

5.2 Disclosure requirements

A firm must prepare a **key features document** for each packaged product, cash deposit ISA and cash deposit CTF it produces, in good time before that document has to be provided.

The firm does **not** have to prepare the document if **another firm** has agreed to prepare it. There are some further **exceptions**, including certain collective investment schemes for which a simplified prospectus is produced instead of a key features document, and stakeholder and personal pension schemes if the information appears prominently in another document.

A **single document** may be used as the key features document for **different schemes**, if the schemes are offered through a '**funds supermarket**' and the document clearly describes the difference between the schemes.

5.2.1 Product information standards

A **key features document** must:

- Be produced / presented to **at least** the quality / standard of **sales and marketing material** used to promote the product

- Display the **firm's brand** as prominently as any other

- Include the **keyfacts logo** prominently at the top

- Include the following **statement**, in a prominent position:

  'The Financial Services Authority is the independent financial services regulator. It requires us, [provider name], to give you this important information to help you to decide whether our [product name] is right for you. You should read this document carefully so that you understand what you are buying, and then keep it safe for future reference.'

- Not include anything that might reasonably cause a retail client to be **mistaken** about the **identity** of the firm that produced, or will produce, the product

5.2.2 Contents of key features document

7.4.2 Explain the rules relating to the form and content of a key features document (COBS 13.2 and 13.3).

Required headings in a **key features document** are as follows. (The **order** shown below must be followed.)

- *Title:* '**key features of the [name of product]**'

- *Heading:* '**Its aims**' – followed by a brief description of the product's aims

- *Heading:* '**Your commitment**' or '**Your investment**' – followed by information on what a retail client is committing to or investing in and any consequences of failing to maintain the commitment or investment

- *Heading:* '**Risks**' – followed by information on the material risks associated with the product, including a description of the factors that may have an adverse effect on performance or are material to the decision to invest

- *Heading:* '**Questions and answers**' – (in the form of questions and answers) about the principal terms of the product, what it will do for a retail client and any other information necessary to enable a retail client to make an informed decision

The **key features document** must:

- Include **enough information** about the nature and complexity of the product, any minimum standards / limitations, material benefits / risks of buying or investing for a retail client to be able to make an **informed decision** about whether to proceed

- Explain arrangements for handling **complaints**

- Explain the **compensation** available from the FSCS if the firm cannot meet its liabilities

- Explain whether there are **cancellation / withdrawal rights**, their duration and conditions, including amounts payable if the right is exercised, consequences of not exercising, and practical instructions for exercising the right, including the address to which any notice must be sent

- For **child trust funds (CTFs)**, explain that stakeholder, cash deposit and share CTFs are available, and which type the firm is offering

- For personal pension schemes, explain clearly and prominently that **stakeholder pension schemes** are available and might meet the client's needs as well as the scheme on offer

5.3 Additional information requirements

Note the requirements to provide **general information** to clients about **designated investments**, which were explained earlier in this chapter. As we noted there, a **key features document** may meet those requirements.

5.4 Cancellation and withdrawal rights

objective **7.4.3 Explain** the rules relating to cancellation rights (COBS 15).

5.4.1 Introduction

Cancellation and withdrawal rights are of relevance to firms that enter into a cancellable contract, which means most providers of retail financial products, including distance contracts, based on deposits or designated investments.

5.4.2 Cancellation periods

Minimum **cancellation periods** where a consumer has a right to cancel are summarised below (and are subject to certain exemptions in special situations which are beyond the syllabus). (Note that a **wrapper** means an ISA or CTF. Personal pension contracts, including SIPPs, and pension contracts based on regulated collective investment schemes, fall within the definition of a **pension wrapper**.)

Life and pensions contracts: 30 calendar days

- Life policies, including pension annuities, pension policies or within a wrapper (For a life policy effected when opening or transferring a wrapper, the 30-day right applies to the entire arrangement.)
- Contracts to join a personal or stakeholder pension scheme
- Pension contracts
- Pension transfers
- Initial income withdrawals from an existing personal or stakeholder pension scheme

Cash deposit ISAs: 14 calendar days

Non-life/pensions contracts (advised but not at a distance): 14 calendar days – these rights arise only following a personal recommendation

- Non-distance contracts to buy units in a regulated collective investment scheme (including within a wrapper or pension wrapper) (For units bought when opening or transferring a wrapper or pension wrapper, the 14-day right applies to the entire arrangement.)
- Opening or transferring an ISA or CTF
- Enterprise Investment Schemes

Non-life/pensions contracts (at a distance): 14 calendar days

- Accepting deposits
- Designated investment business

If one transaction attracts more than one right to cancel, the longest period applies.

The **cancellation period begins**

- **Either:** From the day the contract is concluded (but, for life policies, when the consumer is informed that the contract has been concluded),
- **Or:** From the day when the consumer receives the contract terms and conditions, if later

5.4.3 Disclosure of rights to cancel or withdraw

Where the consumer would not already have received similar information under another rule, the firm must **disclose** – in a durable medium and in good time or, if that is not possible, immediately after the consumer is bound – the right to cancel or withdraw, its duration and conditions, information on any further amount payable, consequences of not exercising the right, practical instructions for exercising it, and the address to which notification of cancellation or withdrawal should be sent.

5.4.4 Exercising a right to cancel

A consumer's notification of exercise of a right to cancel is deemed to have observed the deadline if it is **dispatched**, in a durable medium, before the deadline expires.

The consumer need **not** give any **reason** for exercising the right to cancel.

6 CLIENT ASSETS AND CLIENT MONEY RULES

Learning objectives

7.5.1 Explain the concept of fiduciary duty.

7.5.2 Explain the application and purpose of the rules relating to custody of client assets held in connection with MiFID business (CASS 6.1).

6.1 Introduction

The rules in this section link to Principle 10 of the *Principles for Businesses*. The rules aim to restrict the commingling of client's and firm's assets and minimise the risk of client's investments being used by the firm without the client's agreement or contrary to the client's wishes, or being treated as the firm's assets in the event of its **insolvency**.

The firm has a **fiduciary duty** (a duty of care) to look after client assets and money. The focus therefore is on two main issues, namely custody of investments, and client money.

The client assets rules have a broader coverage than the rules contained in COBS, the Conduct of Business Sourcebook, in that they afford protection not only to retail and professional clients, but also to **eligible counterparties**.

Under MiFID, client assets are regulated by the **home state**. Therefore, for example, if a French firm is **passporting** into the UK, it will adhere to French client assets rules.

The implementation of MiFID has resulted in more onerous requirements on firms in respect of custody of client assets and client money.

- Except in the case of credit institutions, firms may not use client funds for their own account in any circumstances.

- Sub-custodians and depositaries must be selected in accordance with specified rules.

- There are rules specifying that client funds be held with particular types of bank and (if the client does not object) certain money market funds meeting specified criteria.

- One of the most significant impacts of MiFID implementation on the existing client money regime is that MiFID firms will no longer be able to allow professional clients to 'opt-out' of the client money rules, for MiFID business.

The **Client Assets (CASS)** section of the *FSA Handbook* includes custody rules for **custody** and **client money** which apply to a firm which holds financial instruments belonging to a client.

6.2 Holding client assets

objectives **7.5.3 Explain** the rules relating to the protection of clients' assets and having adequate organisation arrangements (CASS 6.2).

7.5.4 Explain the rules relating to depositing assets with third parties (CASS 6.3).

7.5.5 Explain the purpose of the rules relating to the use of clients' assets (CASS 6.4).

Firms sometimes hold investments on behalf of clients in physical form, e.g. bearer bonds, or may be responsible for the assets but not physically holding them as they are held elsewhere, e.g. with another custodian or via CREST.

Firms which hold financial instruments belonging to clients must make arrangements to **safeguard clients' ownership rights**, especially in the event of the firm's insolvency. Firms are not permitted to use financial instruments which are held for clients **for their own account** unless they have the express consent of the client.

The firm must have **adequate organisational arrangements** to minimise risk of loss or diminution of clients' financial instruments or of rights over them resulting from misuse, fraud, poor administration, inadequate record-keeping or other negligence.

As far as practicable, the firm must effect registration or recording of legal title to financial instruments, normally in the name of

- The client, or
- A nominee company

For nominee companies controlled by the firm, the firm has the same level of responsibility to the client regarding custody of the assets.

In the case of **overseas financial instruments**, where it is in the client's best interests, the instruments may be held by

- Any other party, in which case the client must be notified in writing

- The firm, subject to written consent (if a retail client) or notification of the client (for professional clients)

6.3 Requirement to protect client money

objectives **7.5.7 Explain** the application and general purpose of the client money rules (CASS 7.2).

7.5.8 Explain the rules relating to the segregation of client money (CASS 7.4).

A firm must make adequate arrangements to safeguard clients' rights over **client money** the firm holds, and to prevent the use of client money for the firm's own account.

As with financial instruments, the firm must have **adequate organisational arrangements** to minimise risk of loss or diminution of clients' money or of rights over such money resulting from misuse, fraud, poor administration, inadequate record-keeping or other negligence.

If a firm leaves some of its own money in a client money account, this will be referred to as a '**pollution of trust**' and, if the firm fails, the liquidator will be able to seize all the money held in the client account for the general creditors of the firm.

6.4 Client accounts

Client money must be deposited with

- A central bank
- An EEA credit institution
- A bank authorised in a third country, or
- A qualifying money market fund

6.5 Financial instruments: reconciliations with external records

Learning objective **7.5.6 Explain** the rules relating to records, accounts and reconciliations of clients' assets (CASS 6.5).

The firm should ensure that any **third party** holding clients' **financial instruments** provides regular statements.

To ensure accuracy of its records, the firm must carry out regular reconciliations between its own records and those of such third parties

- As regularly as is necessary, and
- As soon as possible after the date to which the reconciliation relates

The person, who may be an employee of the firm, carrying out the reconciliation should, whenever possible, be someone who is independent of the process of producing and maintaining the records. (This type of control is called **segregation of duties**.)

If a firm has not complied with the reconciliation requirements 'in any material respect', then it must inform the FSA without delay.

6.6 Financial instruments: reconciliation discrepancies

Any **discrepancies** revealed in the reconciliations – including items recorded in a suspense or error account – must be corrected promptly.

Any unreconciled shortfall must be made good, if there are reasonable grounds for concluding that the firm is responsible. If the firm concludes that someone else is responsible, steps should be taken to resolve the position with that other person.

If a firm has not made good an unreconciled shortfall 'in any material respect', then it must inform the FSA without delay.

6.7 Client money: reconciliations with external records

Learning objective **7.5.9 Explain** the rules relating to records, accounts and reconciliations of client money (CASS 7.6).

Broadly, if a firm holds money that belongs to someone else, then that money is client money.

As with financial instruments, to ensure accuracy of its records, the firm must carry out regular reconciliations between its own client money records and those of third parties, such as a bank, holding **client money**

- As regularly as is necessary, and
- As soon as possible after the date to which the reconciliation relates

In determining the **frequency** of reconciliations, the firm should **consider relevant risks**, such as the nature, volume and complexity of the business, and where the client money is held.

The FSA recommends that reconciliations should compare and identify discrepancies between

- The balance of each **client bank account** as recorded by the firm, *and* the balance shown on the bank's statement, and

- The balance as shown in the firm's records, currency by currency, on each **client transaction account** – for **contingent liability investments**, which includes certain derivatives, spot forex trades, spread bets and contracts for difference (CFDs) – *and* the balance shown in the third party's records.

Any **approved collateral** held must be included in the reconciliation.

6.8 Client money: reconciliation discrepancies

The **reason** for any **discrepancy** must be identified, unless it arises solely from timing differences between a third party's accounting systems and those of the firm.

Any **shortfall** must be paid into (or any **excess** withdrawn from) the client bank account by the close of business on the day the reconciliation is performed.

If a firm cannot resolve a difference between its internal records and those of a third party holding client money, the firm must pay its own money into a relevant account to make up any difference, until the matter is resolved.

As with financial instruments held, If a firm has not complied with the reconciliation requirements in respect of client money 'in any material respect', then it must inform the FSA without delay.

6.9 Statutory trust

Section 139(1) FSMA 2000 provides for creation of a fiduciary relationship (a **statutory trust**) between the firm and its client, under which client money is in the legal ownership of the firm but remains in the beneficial ownership of the client.

In the event of failure of the firm, costs relating to the distribution of client money may have to be borne by the trust.

6.10 Exemptions from CASS rules

There are some circumstances in which the client money rules do not apply.

6.10.1 Credit institutions

The client money rules do not apply to **Banking Consolidation Directive (BCD) credit institutions** in respect of deposits. Institutions whose business is to receive deposits from the public are credit institutions.

6.10.2 Coins held for intrinsic value

Client money rules do not apply to **coins** held on behalf of a client, if the firm and client have agreed that the money is to be held by the firm for the **intrinsic value** of the **metal** in the coin.

6.10.3 DVP transactions

Money arising through **delivery versus payment (DVP) transactions** through a commercial settlement system need not be treated as client money, if it is intended that:

- Money from the client, in respect of a client's purchase, will be due to the firm within one business day, on fulfilment of a delivery obligation, or

- Money is due to the client, in respect of a client's sale, within one business day following the client's fulfilment of a delivery obligation

DVP is a form of securities trading in which payment and transfer of the subject security occur simultaneously.

6.11 Discharge of fiduciary duty

Money **ceases to be client money** if it is paid

- To the client or his authorised representative

- Into a bank account of the client

- To the firm itself, when it is due and payable to the firm, or is an excess in the client bank account

- To a third party, on the client's instruction, unless it is transferred to a third party to effect a transaction – for example, a payment to an intermediate broker as initial or variation margin on behalf of a client who has a position in derivatives. In these circumstances, the firm remains responsible for that client's equity balance held at the intermediate broker until the contract is terminated and all of that client's positions at that broker closed

7 DEALING AND MANAGING

7.1 Application of rules

COBS rules on **dealing and managing** (except for the rules on personal account dealing – see below) apply to **MiFID business** carried out by a **MiFID investment firm**, and to equivalent third country business.

The provisions on **personal account dealing** apply to designated investment business carried on from a UK establishment. They also apply to passported activities carried on by a UK MiFID investment firm from a branch in another EEA state, but not to the UK branch of an EEA MiFID investment firm in relation to its MiFID business.

7.2 Best execution

Learning objective   **7.6.1 Explain** the rules relating to best execution (COBS 11.2).

The basic COBS rule of **best execution** is as follows.

A firm must take all reasonable steps to obtain, when executing orders, the best possible result for its clients taking into account the execution factors.

When a firm is **dealing on own account with clients**, this is considered to be execution of client orders, and is therefore subject to the best execution rule.

If a firm provides a best quote to a client, it is acceptable for the quote to be executed after the client accepts it, provided the quote is not manifestly out of date.

The obligation to obtain best execution needs to be interpreted according to the particular type of financial instrument involved, but the rule applies to **all types of financial instrument**.

The **best execution criteria** are that the firm must take into account **characteristics of**:

- The client, including categorisation as retail or professional
- The client order
- The financial instruments
- The execution venues

The '**best possible result**' must be determined in terms of **total consideration** – taking into account any costs, including the firm's own commissions in the case of competing execution venues, and not just quoted prices. (However, the firm is not expected to compare the result with that of clients of other firms.) Commissions structure must not discriminate between execution venues.

7.3 Order execution policy

7.3.1 Policy requirements

The firm must establish and implement an **order execution policy**, and it must monitor its effectiveness regularly.

The policy must include, for each class of financial instruments, information on different execution venues used by the firm, and the factors affecting choice of execution venue.

The firm should choose venues that enable it to obtain on a consistent basis the best possible result for execution of client orders. For each client order, the firm should apply its execution policy with a view to achieving the best possible result for the client.

If orders may be executed outside a regulated market or multilateral trading facility, this must be disclosed, and clients must give prior express consent.

A firm must be able to demonstrate to clients, on request, that it has followed its execution policy.

7.3.2 Client consent and clients' specific instructions

The firm must provide a **retail client** with details on its execution policy before providing the service, covering the relative importance the firm assigns to execution factors, a list of execution venues on which the firm relies, and a clear and prominent warning that **specific instructions** by the client could prevent the firm from following its execution policy steps fully.

If the client gives **specific instructions**, the firm has met its best execution obligation if it obtains the best result in following those instructions. The firm should not induce a client to gives such instructions, if they could prevent best execution from being obtained. However, the firm may invite the client to choose between execution venues.

The firm must obtain the **prior consent** of clients to its execution policy, and the policy must be **reviewed annually** and whenever there is a material change in the firm's ability to achieve the best possible result consistently from execution venues.

7.3.3 Portfolio management and order reception and transmission services

Firms who act as **portfolio managers** must comply with the **clients' best interests rule** when placing orders with other entities. Firms who provide a service of **receiving and transmitting orders** must do the same when transmitting orders to other entities for execution. Such firms must:

- Take all reasonable steps to obtain the best possible result for clients

- Establish and maintain a policy to enable it to do so, and monitor its effectiveness

- Provide appropriate information to clients on the policy

- Review the policy annually or whenever there is a material change affecting the firm's ability to continue to obtain the best possible result for clients

7.4 Client order handling

Learning objective **7.6.2 Explain** the rules relating to client order handling (COBS 11.3).

The general rule on **client order handling** is that firms must implement procedures and arrangements which provide for the prompt, fair and expeditious execution of client orders, relative to other orders or the trading interests of the firm.

These procedures and arrangements must allow for the execution of otherwise comparable orders in accordance with the time of their reception by the firm.

When carrying out **client orders**, firms must:

- Ensure that orders are promptly and accurately recorded and allocated

- Carry out otherwise comparable orders sequentially and promptly, unless this is impracticable or not in clients' interests

- Inform a retail client about any material difficulty in carrying out orders promptly, on becoming aware of it

Where it is not practicable to treat orders sequentially e.g. because they are received by different media, they should not be treated as 'otherwise comparable'.

Firms must not allow the **misuse of information** relating to pending client orders. Any use of such information to deal on own account should be considered a misuse of the information.

When overseeing or arranging **settlement**, a firm must take reasonable steps to ensure that instruments or funds due are delivered to the client account promptly and correctly.

7.5 Use of dealing commission

Learning objective **7.6.3 Explain** the rules relating to the use of dealing commission (COBS 11.6).

The practice of using dealing commission (previously called **soft commission**) dates back many years. The practice developed from brokers effectively **rebating** part of the commission paid by large fund management clients, to be used to cover the costs of services such as equity research. The effect was to reduce the 'real' commission paid for the execution of the trade. It is therefore necessary to control these arrangements to ensure that customers who ultimately pay the commissions, namely the fund managers' clients are protected from abuse.

The rules on the use of dealing commission aim to ensure that an investment manager's arrangements, in relation to dealing commissions spent on acquiring services in addition to execution, are transparent and demonstrate accountability to customers so that customers are treated fairly.

The rules therefore ensure firms comply with Principle 1 (Integrity), Principle 6 (Customers' Interests) and Principle 8 (Conflicts of Interest).

The rules on the use of dealing commission apply to investment managers when executing customer orders through a broker or another person in shares or other investments which relate to shares, e.g. warrants, hybrids (ADRs and options) and rights to, or interests in, investments.

When the investment manager passes on the broker's or other person's charges (whether commission or otherwise) to its customers and in return arranges to receive goods or services **the rules require the investment manager to be satisfied that the goods or services:**

- Relate to the execution of trades, or
- Comprise the provision of research

This is subject to a clause that the goods or services will reasonably assist the investment manager in the provision of services to its customers and do not impair compliance with the duty of the investment manager to act in the best interests of its customers.

In relation to goods or services relating to the execution of trades, the FSA have confirmed that post-trade analytics, e.g. performance measurement, is not going to be an acceptable use of dealing commission. Where the goods or services relate to research, the investment manager will have to be satisfied that the research:

- Is capable of **adding value** to the investment or trading decisions by providing **new insights** that inform the investment manager when making such decisions about its customers' portfolios

- In whatever form its output takes, represents **original thought**, in the critical and careful consideration and assessment of new and existing facts, and does not merely repeat or repackage what has been presented before

- Has **intellectual rigour** and does not merely state what is commonplace or self-evident, and

- Involves analysis or manipulation of data to reach **meaningful conclusions**

Examples of goods or services that relate to the execution of trades or the provision of research that are **not** going to be **acceptable** to the FSA include the following.

- Services relating to the valuation or performance measurement of portfolios

- Computer hardware

- Dedicated telephone lines

- Seminar fees

- Subscriptions for publications

- Travel, accommodation or entertainment costs

- Office administration computer software, such as word processing or accounting programmes

- Membership fees to professional associations

- Purchase or rental of standard office equipment or ancillary facilities

- Employees' salaries

- Direct money payments

- Publicly available information

- Custody services relating to designated investments belonging to, or managed for, customers other than those services that are incidental to the execution of trades

Investment managers must make **adequate prior disclosure** to customers about receipt of goods and services that relate to the execution of trades or the provision of research. This should form part of the summary form disclosure under the rule on inducements. **Periodic disclosures** made on an annual basis are recommended.

7.6 Inducements

A firm must **not** pay or accept any fee or commission, or provide or receive any non-monetary benefit, in relation to designated investment business, other than:

■ Fees, commissions and non-monetary benefits paid or provided to or by the client or a person on their behalf

■ Fees, commissions and non-monetary benefits paid or provided to or by a third party or a person acting on their behalf, if the firm's duty to act in the best interests of the client is not impaired, and (for MiFID and equivalent business, and where there is a personal recommendation of a packaged product, but not for 'basic advice') clear, comprehensive, accurate, understandable disclosure (except of 'reasonable non-monetary benefits', listed later) is made to the client before the service is provided (Thus, the rule on inducements does not apply to discloseable commissions.)

This rule supplements Principles 1 and 6 of the *Principles for Businesses*. It deals with the delicate area of inducements and seeks to ensure that firms do not conduct business under arrangements that may give rise to conflicts of interest.

In relation to the sale of **packaged products**, the following are broadly deemed to be **reasonable non-monetary benefits**.

■ Gifts, hospitality and promotional prizes of reasonable value, given by product provider to the firm
■ Assistance in promotion of a firm's packaged products
■ Generic product literature which enhances client service, with costs borne by the recipient firm
■ 'Freepost' envelopes supplied by a product provider
■ Product specific literature
■ Content for publication in another firm's magazine, if costs are paid at market rate
■ Reasonable costs of business conferences attended costs by a product provider
■ 'Freephone' links
■ Quotations and projections, and advice on completion of forms
■ Access to data and data processing, related to the product provider's business
■ Access to third party dealing and quotation systems, related to the product provider's business
■ Appropriate informational software
■ Cash or other assistance to develop computer facilities and software, if cost savings are generated
■ Information about sources of mortgage finance
■ Generic technical information
■ Training facilities
■ Reasonable travel and accommodation expenses, e.g. to meetings or training

If a product provider makes benefits available to one firm but not another, this is more likely to impair compliance with the **client's best interests rule**. Most firms deliver against the inducements requirements by drafting detailed '**gifts policies**' (although the rule does **not** explicitly require firms to have a gifts policy). These contain internal rules regarding disclosure, limits and clearance procedures for gifts.

7.7 Personal account dealing

Learning objective | 7.6.4 **Explain** the rules on personal account dealing (COBS 11.7).

Personal account dealing relates to trades undertaken by the staff of a regulated business for themselves. Such trades can create **conflicts of interest** between staff and customers.

A firm conducting **designated investment business** must establish, implement and maintain adequate **arrangements** aimed at preventing employees who are involved in activities where a conflict of interest could occur, or who has access to inside information, from:

- Entering into a transaction which is prohibited under the **Market Abuse Directive**, or which involves misuse or improper disclosure of confidential information, or conflicts with an obligation of the firm to a customer under the regulatory system

- Except in the course of his job, advising or procuring anyone else to enter into such a transaction

- Except in the course of his job, disclosing any information or opinion to another person if the person disclosing it should know that, as a result, the other person would be likely to enter into such a transaction or advise or procure another to enter into such a transaction

The **firm's arrangements** under these provisions must be designed to ensure that:

- All relevant persons (staff involved) are aware of the personal dealing restrictions

- The firm is informed promptly of any personal transaction

- A service provider to whom activities are outsourced maintain a record of personal transactions and provides it to the firm promptly on request

- A record is kept of personal transactions notified to the firm or identified by it, including any related authorisation or prohibition

The rule on personal account dealing is **disapplied** for personal transactions:

- Under a discretionary portfolio management service where there has been no prior communication between the portfolio manager and the person for whom the transaction is executed

- In UCITS collective undertakings (e.g. OEICs and unit trusts) where the person is not involved in its management

- In life policies

- For successive personal transactions where there were prior instructions in force, nor to the termination of the instruction provided that no financial instruments are sold at the same time

7.8 Churning and switching

Churning and switching are similar wrongs. They involve the cynical **overtrading** of customer accounts for the purpose of generating commission. This would clearly contravene the **client's best interests rule**.

The difference between the two lies in the **different products** in which the transactions are undertaken.

- **Churning** relates to investments generally
- **Switching** describes overtrading within and between packaged products

Churning or switching will often be difficult to isolate, unless blatant. Much would depend upon the market conditions prevailing at the time of dealing.

The **COBS rules** on churning and switching state that:

- A series of transactions that are each suitable when viewed in isolation may be unsuitable if the recommendations or the decisions to trade are made with a frequency that is not in the best interests of the client

- A firm should have regard to the client's agreed investment strategy in determining the frequency of transactions. This would include, for example, the need to switch within or between packaged products

CHAPTER ROUNDUP

- The Conduct of Business Sourcebook (COBS) generally applies to authorised firms engaged in designated investment business carried out from their (or their appointed representatives') UK establishments. Some COB rules do not apply to eligible counterparty business.

- 'Designated investment business' is business involving regulated activities, except mortgages, deposits, pure protection policies, general insurance, Lloyd's business and funeral plans.

- The level of protection given to clients by the regulatory system depends on their classification, with retail clients being protected the most. Professional clients and eligible counterparties may both be either *per se* or elective. Both professional clients and eligible counterparties can re-categorise to get more protection.

- Firms doing designated investment business, except advising, must set out a basic client agreement. Firms must provide to clients appropriate information about the firm and its services, designated investments and their risks, execution venues and costs. Firms managing investments must establish a performance benchmark and must provide information about valuations and management objectives.

- It is generally acceptable for a firm to rely on information provided by others if the other firm is competent and not connected with the firm placing the reliance.

- A financial promotion inviting someone to engage in investment activity must be issued by or approved by an authorised firm. Communications must be fair, clear and not misleading. Prospectus advertisements must clearly indicate that they are not a prospectus. Communications with retail clients must balance information about benefits of investments with information about risks.

- Unwritten financial promotions rules cover cold calling, which must be limited to an 'appropriate time of day'.

- Rules on assessing suitability of a recommendation apply when a firm makes a personal recommendation in relation to a designated investment.

- For certain packaged products, a suitability report is required, specifying the client's demands and needs and explaining the firm's recommendation.

- There are obligations to assess 'appropriateness' – based on information about the client's experience and knowledge – for MiFID business other than making a personal recommendation and managing investments.

- Key Features Documents, which must be produced to at least the same quality as marketing material, disclose product information for packaged products.

- Retail clients must be given the opportunity to change their mind (cancel) after agreeing to the purchase of a packaged product.

- Inducements must not be given if they conflict with acting in the best interests of clients, and there are controls on the use of dealing commission.

- The client asset rules are contained within the Client Assets (CASS) section of the FSA Handbook.

- Firms must make adequate arrangements to safeguard clients' money, and to prevent the use of client money for the firm's own account.

- A firm must in general take all reasonable steps to obtain, when executing orders, the best possible result for its clients. This is the requirement of best execution. There must be arrangements for prompt, fair and expeditious client order handling, and a fair order allocation policy. Unexecuted client limit orders must normally be made public, to facilitate early execution.

BPP
LEARNING MEDIA

- Firms must establish arrangements designed to prevent employees entering into personal transactions which are prohibited forms of market abuse. Staff must be made aware of the personal dealing restrictions.

- Churning (investments generally) and switching (packaged products) forms of unsuitable overtrading of customer accounts in order to generate commission.

TEST YOUR KNOWLEDGE

Check your knowledge of the Chapter here, without referring back to the text.

1. Name the three main categories of client.

2. Name three types of per se eligible counterparty.

3. A firm's communications and financial promotions must be '....................... , ... and not .... '. *Fill in the blanks.*

4. What information will the firm need to obtain from the client to enable it to assess the appropriateness of a product or service to the client?

5. List the different types of packaged product.

6. What different types of 'scope' may apply to a firm selling packaged products?

7. What is the effect of a statutory trust created under s139(1) FSMA 2000?

8. What does the rule on best execution require?

TEST YOUR KNOWLEDGE: ANSWERS

1. Eligible counterparties, professional clients and retail clients.

    (See Section 1.6.1)

2. Investment firms, national governments and central banks are all examples.

    (See Section 1.6.5)

3. Fair, clear and not misleading.

    (See Section 2.4)

4. The firm will need to ask the client for information about his knowledge and experience in the relevant investment field, so that it can assess whether the client understands the risks involved

    (See Section 3.3)

5. Use the mnemonic CLIPS: Collective Investment Schemes (regulated); Life policies; Investment trust savings schemes; Personal pensions; Stakeholder pensions.

    (See Section 5.1.1)

6. A firm's scope may be:

    - The whole of the market or market sector
    - Limited to several product providers
    - Limited to a single product provider

    (See Section 5.1.2)

7. Section 139(1) FSMA 2000 provides for creation of a fiduciary relationship (a statutory trust) between the firm and its client, under which client money is in the legal ownership of the firm but remains in the beneficial ownership of the client.

    (See Section 6.9)

8. The best execution rule requires a firm to take all reasonable steps to obtain, when executing orders, the best possible result for its clients, taking into account the execution factors.

    (See Section 7.2)

8

Principles and Outcomes Based Regulation

INTRODUCTION

The FSA Principles for Businesses are central to the 'principles-based' approach to regulation. Recall that protection of consumers is one of the FSA's statutory objectives.

For approved persons carrying out controlled functions, there are Statements of Principles by which they must abide. The Code of Practice for Approved Persons provides some guidance on whether or not an approved person's conduct does comply with the Statements of Principle.

CHAPTER CONTENTS

BPP LEARNING MEDIA

8 The FSA's use of principles and outcomes based regulation

Demonstrate an understanding of the FSA's use of principles and outcomes based regulation to promote ethical and fair outcomes

8.1.1 Explain the application and purpose of the FSA's Principles for Businesses (PRIN 1.1.1 & 2)

8.1.2 Explain the consequences of breaching the FSA's Principles for Businesses (PRIN 1.1.7 to 9 and DEPP 6.2.14 & 15)

8.1.3 Identify the FSA's Principles for Businesses (PRIN 2.1.1 and PRIN 4)

8.1.3 Explain the importance of corporate culture and leadership

8.1.4 Explain the application and purpose of the Statements of Principle and Code of Practice for approved persons (APER)

1 PRINCIPLES FOR BUSINESSES

Learning objective | **8.1.1 Explain** the application and purpose of the FSA's Principles for Businesses (PRIN 1.1.1 & 2).

1.1 Application of the Principles for Businesses

The **High Level Standards** known as the **Principles for Businesses** apply in whole or in part to every **authorised firm** carrying out a regulated activity. Approved persons are subject to a separate set of principles, known as **Statements of Principle** – see later in this Chapter.

While the *Principles for Businesses* apply to regulated activities generally, with respect to the activities of accepting deposits, general insurance and long-term pure protection policies (i.e. that have no surrender value and are payable upon death), they apply only in a 'prudential context'. This means the FSA will only proceed where the contravention is a serious or persistent violation of a principle that has an impact on confidence in the financial system, the fitness and propriety of the firm or the adequacy of the firm's financial resources.

As we have seen, the implementation of **MiFID** – the EU **Markets in Financial Instruments Directive** – (with effect from **1 November 2007**) has had a significant impact on various aspects of FSA rules. The application of the Principles is modified for firms conducting MiFID business (including investment services and activities, and ancillary services, where relevant), and for EEA firms with the right (often referred to as a '**passport**') to do business in the UK.

1.2 The Principles

Learning objective | **8.1.3 Identify** the FSA's Principles for Businesses (PRIN 2.1.1 and PRIN 4).

The **eleven** *Principles for Businesses* are as follows.

Principles for Businesses	
1.	**Integrity**
	A firm must conduct its business with integrity.
2.	**Skill, care and diligence**
	A firm must conduct its business with due skill, care and diligence.
3.	**Management and control**
	A firm must take reasonable care to organise and control its affairs responsibly and effectively, with adequate risk management systems.
4.	**Financial prudence**
	A firm must maintain adequate financial resources.
5.	**Market conduct**
	A firm must observe proper standards of market conduct.
6.	**Customers' interests**
	A firm must pay due regard to the interests of its customers and treat them fairly.
7.	**Communications with clients**
	A firm must pay due regard to the information needs of its clients and communicate information to them in a way that is clear, fair and not misleading.
8.	**Conflicts of interest**
	A firm must manage conflicts of interest fairly, both between itself and its customers and between a customer and another client.
9.	**Customers: relationships of trust**
	A firm must take reasonable care to ensure the suitability of its advice and discretionary decisions for any customer who is entitled to rely upon its judgement.
10.	**Clients' assets**
	A firm must arrange adequate protection for clients' assets when it is responsible for those assets.
11.	**Relations with regulators**
	A firm must deal with its regulators in an open and co-operative way and must disclose to the FSA appropriately anything relating to the firm of which the FSA would reasonably expect notice.

1.3 Scope of the Principles

Some of the principles (such as Principle 10) refer to **clients**, while others (such as Principle 9) refer to **customers**. This difference affects the scope of the relevant principles.

- 'Client' includes everyone from the smallest retail customer through to the largest investment firm. It therefore includes, under the terminology of MiFID, eligible counterparties, professional customers and retail customers.

- 'Customer' is a more restricted term that includes professional and retail clients but excludes 'eligible counterparties'. 'Customers' are thus clients who are not **eligible counterparties**. Principles 6, 8 and 9, and parts of Principle 7, apply only to **customers**.

In line with MiFID, a firm will not be subject to a Principle to the extent that it is contrary to the EU Single Market Directives. Principles 1, 2, 6 and 9 may be disapplied for this reason, in the case of:

- Eligible counterparty business

- Transactions on a regulated market (e.g. the London Stock Exchange), and member transactions under a **multilateral trading facility** – a system that enables parties (e.g. retail investors or other investment firms) to buy and sell financial instruments

Note that Principle 3 would not be considered breached if the firm failed to prevent **unforeseeable** risks.

1.4 Breaches of the Principles

8.1.2 Explain the consequences of breaching the principles (PRIN 1.1.7, 8 & 9 and DEPP 6.2.14 & 15).

The consequence of breaching a Principle makes the firm liable to **enforcement or disciplinary sanctions**. The FSA may bring these sanctions where it can show that the firm has been at fault in some way. The definition of 'fault' will depend upon when Principle has been breached.

S150 FSMA 2000 creates a right of action in damages for a '**private person**' who suffers loss as a result of a contravention of certain **rules** by an authorised firm. However, a 'private person' may not sue a firm under S150 FSMA 2000 for the breach of a **Principle**.

1.5 Treating customers fairly (TCF)

In addition to meeting its regulatory objectives, the FSA aims to maintain efficient, orderly and clean markets and help retail customers achieve a fair deal. Since 2000, the FSA has been examining what a fair deal for retail customers actually means. This has led to much discussion of the concept of **TCF** – 'treating customers fairly'.

The FSA does not define **treating customers fairly (TCF)** in a way that applies in all circumstances. By adopting a '**Principles-based approach**' to TCF through Principle 6, the FSA puts the onus on firms to determine what is fair in each particular set of circumstances. Firms therefore need to make their own assessment of what TCF means for them, taking into account the nature of their business.

The emphasis of the Authority's philosophy is not so much on the principles themselves. It is on the actual consequences of what firms do. Increasingly, the term used for the FSA's current approach (in 2009 and beyond) is **outcomes-focused regulation**.

TCF is now treated as a part of the **FSA's core supervisory work**. Firms – meaning senior management, including the Board – are expected to be able to demonstrate to themselves and to the FSA that they deliver **fair outcomes to their customers**.

The FSA wants firms to focus on delivering the following six TCF consumer outcomes.

- Consumers can be confident that they are dealing with firms where the fair treatment of customers is central to the corporate culture.

- Products and services marketed and sold in the retail market are designed to meet the needs of identified consumer groups and are targeted accordingly.

- Consumers are provided with clear information and are kept appropriately informed before, during and after the point of sale.

- Where consumers receive advice, the advice is suitable and takes account of their circumstances.

- Consumers are provided with products that perform as firms have led them to expect, and the associated service is both of an acceptable standard and also as they have been led to expect.

- Consumers do not face unreasonable post-sale barriers imposed by firms to change product, switch provider, submit a claim or make a complaint.

2 CORPORATE CULTURE AND LEADERSHIP

objective '8.1.4 Explain** the application and purpose of the Statements of Principle and Code of Practice for approved persons (APER).

2.1 Societal and corporate values

The concept of **societal values** is of values that are generally agreed by reasonable people and that are widely accepted. At a **corporate** level, reference to values or the **corporate culture** suggests that particular ways of acting can become prevalent throughout a firm, whether by design or not. A 'culture' of pursuing short-term profit or revenue even if customers are misled ('having the wool pulled over their eyes') may pervade through a firm, either at the instigation of an aggressive if short-sighted and unethical senior management team, or as the unintended consequence of mis-judged target-setting incentive structures for employees.

2.2 Corporate culture

Firms have to follow the **law and regulation**s, or else they will be subject to fines and their officers might face similar charges. **Ethics** in organisations relates to **social responsibility** and **business practices.**

People who work for organisations bring their own **values** into work with them. Organisations encompass a variety of ethical frameworks.

- **Personal ethics** deriving from a person's upbringing, religious or non-religious beliefs, political opinions, personality and so on.

- **Professional ethics**, for example the CFA's Code of Ethics.

- **Corporate culture** (e.g. 'Customer first'). Culture, in denoting what is normal behaviour, also denotes what is the right behaviour in many cases.

- **Organisation systems**. Ethics might be contained in a formal code, reinforced by the overall statement of values. A problem might be that good ethics does not always save money, and there is a real cost to ethical decisions. Equally, there can be substantial risk, and costs, if poor ethics results in loss of reputation for the firm.

2.3 Leadership

As the FSA states (in CP10/12), promoting **standards of ethical behaviour** improves outcomes for consumers and their perception of the financial services industry. Consumer perception stems from consumers' view of the behaviour and culture established by senior management in large firms as much as in that of a sole trader.

It is recognised that, beyond mere compliance with rules, organisations and firms must – through their **leaders** – foster a corporate culture that is congruent with the purpose of regulatory rules and principles, if regulation is to be effective.

For example, this is recognised in respect of financial crime. One of the suggested guiding principles for a firm's anti-money laundering and anti-terrorist financing policy statement is:

'An unequivocal statement of the culture and values to be adopted and promulgated throughout the firm towards the prevention of financial crime.'

Senior management must use their **leadership** positions to move the culture of their firm in the desired direction. A programme to imprint a corporate culture on the firm should be backed up by:

- Communication of the principles to all levels of the organisation, and possibly external stakeholder groups

- Leaders (senior management, and team leaders) setting an example

- Appropriate training of staff

3 APPROVED PERSONS: STATEMENTS OF PRINCIPLE AND CODE OF PRACTICE

Learning objective   **8.1.5 Explain** the application and the purpose of the Statements of Principle and Code of Practice for Approved Persons (APER).

3.1 Approved persons

Section 59 FSMA 2000 states that a person (an individual) cannot carry out certain **controlled functions** unless that individual has been approved by the FSA. This requirement gives rise to the term '**approved person**', and the FSA's Supervision Manual (SUP) covers the approval process. We looked at the approval process, and at what are controlled functions, earlier in this Study Text.

3.2 Statements of Principle for Approved Persons

FSA **Statements of Principle** apply generally to all **approved persons** (i.e. to relevant employees of FSA firms) when they are performing a **controlled function**. The scope of 'controlled' functions is covered later in this Study Book.

The Statements of Principle will not apply where it would be contrary to the UK's obligations under EU Single Market Directives. Under **MiFID** rules, the requirement to employ personnel with the necessary knowledge, skills and expertise is reserved to the firm's **Home State**. As a result, the FSA does not have a role in assessing individuals' competence and capability in performing a controlled function in relation to an **incoming EEA firm** providing MiFID investment services.

There are **seven Statements of Principle**.

- The first four Principles apply to all approved persons (which includes those doing a **significant influence function** as well as those not doing a significant influence function).

- As noted in the following Table, the final three Principles only apply to approved persons performing a significant influence function.

Statements of Principle for Approved Persons	
1 Integrity	
2 Skill, care and diligence	Apply to all approved persons
3 Proper standard of market conduct	
4 Deal with the regulator in an open way	
5 Proper organisation of business	Apply only to those doing a significant influence function
6 Skill, care and diligence in management	
7 Comply with regulatory requirements	

3.3 The Code of Practice for Approved Persons

FSMA 2000 requires the FSA to issue a code of practice to help approved persons to determine whether or not their conduct complies with the Statements of Principle. The FSA has complied with this obligation by issuing the **Code of Practice for Approved Persons**. This sets out descriptions of conduct which, in the FSA's opinion, does not comply with any of the statements, and factors which will be taken into account in determining whether or not an approved person's conduct does comply with the Statements of Principle. These descriptions have the status of **evidential provisions**.

The Code is not conclusive – it is only evidential towards indicating that a Statement of Principle has been breached. Account will be taken of the context in which the course of conduct was undertaken. In determining whether there has been a breach of Principles 5 to 7, account will be taken of the nature and complexity of the business, the role and responsibilities of the approved person, and the knowledge that the approved person had (or should have had) of the regulatory concerns arising in the business under their control. The examples in the Code that would breach a principle are not exhaustive.

The Code may be amended from time to time and the current published version at the time of the approved person's conduct will be the Code that the FSA will look to in determining whether or not there has been a breach. The FSA will examine all the circumstances of a particular matter and will only determine that there has been a breach where the individual is '**personally culpable**', i.e. deliberate conduct or conduct below the reasonable standard expected of that person in the circumstances.

We now look at the **seven Statements of Principle** in detail, taking into account the treatment of each by the **Code of Practice for Approved Persons**.

3.4 The Statements of Principle in detail

Statement of Principle 1

An approved person must act with integrity in carrying out his controlled functions.

The Code of Practice provides examples of behaviour that would not comply with this Statement of Principle. These include an approved person:

- **Deliberately misleading clients**, his firm or the FSA, or

- Deliberately failing to inform a customer, his firm, or the FSA, that their understanding of a material issue is incorrect.

Statement of Principle 2

An approved person must act with due skill, care and diligence in carrying out his controlled function.

Examples of non-compliant behaviour under Statement of Principle 2 include failing to inform a **customer**, or his firm, of material information or failing to control client assets.

The coverage of Statement of Principle 2 is similar to Principle 1. The difference is that Principle 1 states that each act needs to be **deliberate**. Principle 2 may be breached by acts which, while not deliberate wrongdoing, are **negligent**.

Statement of Principle 3

An approved person must observe proper standards of market conduct in carrying out his controlled function.

Examples of non-compliant behaviour under Statement of Principle 3 include:

- A breach of market codes and exchange rules

- A breach of the *Code of Market Conduct*

The FSA expects all approved persons to meet proper standards, whether they are participating in organised markets such as exchanges, or trading in less formal over-the-counter markets.

Statement of Principle 4

An approved person must deal with the FSA and with other regulators in an open and co-operative way and must disclose appropriately any information of which the FSA would reasonably expect notice.

This Statement of Principle concerns the requirement to co-operate, not only with the FSA, but also with other bodies such as an overseas regulator or an exchange.

Approved persons do not have a duty to report concerns directly to the FSA unless they are responsible for such reports. The obligation on most approved persons is to report concerns of '**material significance**' in accordance with the firm's **internal procedures**. If no such procedures exist, the report should be made direct to the FSA.

It would also be a breach of this Statement of Principle if an approved person did not attend an interview or meeting with the FSA, answer questions or produce documents when requested to do so and within the time limit specified.

Statement of Principle 5

An approved person performing a significant influence function must take reasonable steps to ensure that the business of the firm for which he is responsible in his controlled function is organised so that it can be controlled effectively.

As stated above, Principles 5 to 7 relate only to those approved persons performing a significant influence function. This principle requires those performing a significant influence function to **delegate** responsibilities responsibly and effectively. Paramount to this is a requirement that they should delegate only where it is to a suitable person. In addition, they must provide those persons with proper reporting lines, authorisation levels and job descriptions. Clearly, all of these factors (and in particular the suitability requirement) should be regularly reviewed.

Principle 5 will be particularly relevant to the person whose responsibility it is to ensure appropriate apportionment of responsibilities under the Senior Management Arrangements, Systems and Controls (SYSC) section of the FSA Handbook.

Statement of Principle 6

An approved person performing a significant influence function must exercise due skill, care and diligence in managing the business of the firm for which he is responsible in his controlled function.

This principle requires those performing a significant influence function to inform themselves about the affairs of the business for which they are responsible. They should not permit transactions or an expansion of the business unless they fully **understand the risks** involved. They must also take care when monitoring highly profitable or unusual transactions and in those or other cases, must never accept implausible or unsatisfactory explanations from subordinates.

This principle links to Principle 5 as it makes it clear that **delegation is not an abdication** of responsibility. Therefore, where delegation has been made, a person must still monitor and control that part of the business and, therefore, should require progress reports and question those reports where appropriate.

Statement of Principle 7

An approved person performing a significant influence function must take reasonable steps to ensure that the business of the firm for which he is responsible in his controlled function complies with the relevant requirements and standards of the regulatory system.

This has a clear link to Principle 3 of the *Principles for Businesses – Management and Control.* Those exerting a significant influence on the firm must take reasonable steps to ensure that the requirements set out therein are implemented within their firm. They should also review the improvement of such systems and controls, especially where there has been a breach of the regulatory requirements. Principle 7 will be particularly relevant to the person whose responsibility it is to ensure appropriate apportionment of responsibilities under the Senior Management Arrangements, Systems and Controls section of the FSA Handbook.

CHAPTER ROUNDUP

- The High Level Standards known as the Principles for Businesses apply in whole or in part to every authorised firm carrying out a regulated activity. Approved persons are subject to a separate set of principles, known as Statements of Principle.

- Breaching a Principle makes the firm liable to enforcement or disciplinary sanctions. Additionally, S150 FSMA 2000 creates a right of action in damages for a 'private person' who suffers loss as a result of a contravention of certain rules by an authorised firm. However, a 'private person' may not sue a firm under S150 FSMA 2000 for the breach of a Principle.

- Although the FSA stresses the Principles for Businesses over and above compliance with detailed rules, the emphasis of the Authority's philosophy is on the actual consequences of what firms do. Increasingly, the term used for the FSA's regulatory approach has been outcomes-focused regulation.

- Ethical conduct by all team members should be a major concern for management. Inside the organisation, a compliance-based approach highlights conformity with the law. An integrity based approach suggests a wider remit, incorporating ethics in the organisation's values and corporate culture, which is promoted through leadership.

- FSA Statements of Principle apply generally to all approved persons (i.e. relevant employees of FSA firms) when they are performing a controlled function. The Code of Practice for Approved Persons sets out types of conduct breaching the Statements of Principle.

TEST YOUR KNOWLEDGE

Check your knowledge of the Chapter here, without referring back to the text.

1. List six of the FSA Principles for Businesses.

2. 'Section 150 FSMA 2000 creates a right of action in damages for a private person who suffers loss from contravention of a rule or principle by an authorised firm.' Is this statement *True* or *False*?

3. State three methods by which senior management might seek to ensure adoption of a corporate culture throughout a firm.

4. Which Statements of Principle apply to all approved persons?

5. State the first Statement of Principle for Approved Persons.

6. Give two examples of behaviour that would breach Statement of Principle 1.

TEST YOUR KNOWLEDGE: ANSWERS

1. You could have listed any six of the following: Integrity, Skill, Care & Diligence, Management and Control, Financial Prudence, Market Conduct, Customers' Interests, Communications with Clients, Conflicts of Interest, Customers: Relationships of Trust, Clients' Assets, Relations with Regulators.

   (See Section 1.2)

2. False. A private person may sue a firm under s150 for the breach of a rule, but not of a Principle.

   (See Section 1.4)

3. Through communication, setting an example, and appropriate training.

   (See Section 2.3)

4. The first four Statements of Principle apply to all approved persons. These are: Integrity; Skill, care and diligence; Proper standards of market conduct; Deal with the regulator in an open way.

   (See Section 3.2)

5. An approved person must act with integrity in carrying out his controlled functions.

   (See Section 3.4)

6. The following are examples.

   - Deliberately misleading clients, his firm or the FSA, or
   - Deliberately failing to inform a customer, his firm, or the FSA, that their understanding of a material issue is incorrect

   (See Section 3.4)

9

Ethical Behaviour and Professional Standards

INTRODUCTION

Ethical conduct is a matter of continuing debate. There have been many examples of misbehaviour at all levels of large organisations in recent years, including for example the frauds associated with Enron. All professional bodies are alarmed by these events and what they say about ethical standards in everyday life.

What do individuals, firms and the financial sector stand to lose if there are slips in professional standards, even if those slips are put right? Probably the most significant thing at stake is the reputation of the individuals and firms involved, which can have implications for the reputation of the whole sector. In business as in other areas of life, reputation must typically be built up by small steps over a long time, but it can be lost in a moment.

CHAPTER CONTENTS

9 Code of Ethics and Professional Standards

Demonstrate an ability to apply the Code of Ethics and professional standards to business behaviours of individuals

9.1.1 Identify the elements of the CFA Code of Ethics

9.1.2 Explain the professional principles and values on which the Code is based

9.1.3 Apply the Code to a range of ethical dilemmas

10 Ethical and compliance driven behaviour

10.1.1 Identify typical behavioural indicators

10.1.2 Critically evaluate the outcomes which may result from behaving ethically – for the industry, individual advisers and consumers

10.1.3 Critically evaluate the outcomes which may result from limiting behaviour to compliance with the rules – for the industry, firm, individual advisers and consumers

1 CFA CODE OF ETHICS

Learning objectives

9.1.1 Identify the elements of the CFA Code of Ethics.
9.1.2 Explain the professional principles and values on which the Code is based.
9.1.3 Apply the Code to a range of ethical dilemmas.

1.1 Overview

The **CFA Institute** has set out a **Code of Ethics** and **Standards of Professional Conduct** for CFA members and candidates,

The Institute states: 'High ethical standards are critical to maintaining the public's trust in financial markets and in the investment profession'.

Institute members (including holders of the Chartered Financial Analyst® [CFA®] designation) and CFA candidates must abide by the Code and Standards and are encouraged to notify their employer of this responsibility.

- Violations may result in disciplinary sanctions by CFA Institute.

- Sanctions can include revocation of membership, revocation of candidacy in the CFA Program, and revocation of the right to use the CFA designation.

The **Standards of Practice Handbook** (Tenth edition, 2010) explains the Standards of Professional Conduct in greater detail, with accompanying case studies, and is available on the CFA Institute web site **www.cfainstitute.org**.

1.2 The Code

Members of CFA Institute (including CFA charterholders) and **Candidates** for the CFA designation must:

- Act with integrity, competence, diligence, respect, and in an ethical manner with the public, clients, prospective clients, employers, employees, colleagues in the investment profession, and other participants in the global capital markets

- Place the integrity of the investment profession and the interests of clients above their own personal interests

- Use reasonable care and exercise independent professional judgment when conducting investment analysis, making investment recommendations, taking investment actions, and engaging in other professional activities

- Practice and encourage others to practice in a professional and ethical manner that will reflect credit on themselves and the profession

- Promote the integrity of and uphold the rules governing capital markets

- Maintain and improve their professional competence and strive to maintain and improve the competence of other investment professionals

1.3 Standards Of Professional Conduct

The CFA Standards of Professional Conduct are as follows.

I. Professionalism

A. Knowledge of the Law. Members and Candidates must understand and comply with all applicable laws, rules, and regulations (including the CFA Institute Code of Ethics and Standards of Professional Conduct) of any government, regulatory organization, licensing agency, or professional association governing their professional activities. In the event of conflict, Members and Candidates must comply with the more strict law, rule, or regulation. Members and Candidates must not knowingly participate or assist in and must dissociate from any violation of such laws, rules, or regulations.

B. Independence and Objectivity. Members and Candidates must use reasonable care and judgment to achieve and maintain independence and objectivity in their professional activities. Members and Candidates must not offer, solicit, or accept any gift, benefit, compensation, or consideration that reasonably could be expected to compromise their own or another's independence and objectivity.

C. Misrepresentation. Members and Candidates must not knowingly make any misrepresentations relating to investment analysis, recommendations, actions, or other professional activities.

D. Misconduct. Members and Candidates must not engage in any professional conduct involving dishonesty, fraud, or deceit or commit any act that reflects adversely on their professional reputation, integrity, or competence.

II. Integrity of capital markets

A. Material Non-public Information. Members and Candidates who possess material non-public information that could affect the value of an investment must not act or cause others to act on the information.

B. Market Manipulation. Members and Candidates must not engage in practices that distort prices or artificially inflate trading volume with the intent to mislead market participants.

III. Duties to clients

A. Loyalty, Prudence, and Care. Members and Candidates have a duty of loyalty to their clients and must act with reasonable care and exercise prudent judgment. Members and Candidates must act for the benefit of their clients and place their clients' interests before their employer's or their own interests.

B. F air Dealing. Members and Candidates must deal fairly and objectively with all clients when providing investment analysis, making investment recommendations, taking investment action, or engaging in other professional activities.

C. Suitability.

1. When Members and Candidates are in an advisory relationship with a client, they must:

a. Make a reasonable inquiry into a client's or prospective client's investment experience, risk and return objectives, and financial constraints prior to making any investment recommendation or taking investment action and must reassess and update this information regularly.

b. Determine that an investment is suitable to the client's financial situation and consistent with the client's written objectives, mandates, and constraints before making an investment recommendation or taking investment action.

c. Judge the suitability of investments in the context of the client's total portfolio.

2. When Members and Candidates are responsible for managing a portfolio to a specific mandate, strategy, or style, they must make only investment recommendations or take only investment actions that are consistent with the stated objectives and constraints of the portfolio.

D. Performance Presentation. When communicating investment performance information, Members and Candidates must make reasonable efforts to ensure that it is fair, accurate, and complete.

E. Preservation of Confidentiality. Members and Candidates must keep information about current, former, and prospective clients confidential unless:

1. The information concerns illegal activities on the part of the client or prospective client,

2. Disclosure is required by law, or

3. The client or prospective client permits disclosure of the information.

IV. Duties to employers

A. Loyalty. In matters related to their employment, Members and Candidates must act for the benefit of their employer and not deprive their employer of the advantage of their skills and abilities, divulge confidential information, or otherwise cause harm to their employer.

B. Additional Compensation Arrangements. Members and Candidates must not accept gifts, benefits, compensation, or consideration that competes with or might reasonably be expected to create a conflict of interest with their employer's interest unless they obtain written consent from all parties involved.

C. Responsibilities of Supervisors. Members and Candidates must make reasonable efforts to detect and prevent violations of applicable laws, rules, regulations, and the Code and Standards by anyone subject to their supervision or authority.

V. Investment analysis, recommendations, and actions

A. Diligence and Reasonable Basis. Members and Candidates must:

1. Exercise diligence, independence, and thoroughness in analyzing investments, making investment recommendations, and taking investment actions.

2. Have a reasonable and adequate basis, supported by appropriate research and investigation, for any investment analysis, recommendation, or action.

B. Communication with Clients and Prospective Clients.

Members and Candidates must:

1. Disclose to clients and prospective clients the basic format and general principles of the investment processes they use to analyze investments, select securities, and construct portfolios and must promptly disclose any changes that might materially affect those processes.

2. Use reasonable judgment in identifying which factors are important to their investment analyses, recommendations, or actions and include those factors in communications with clients and prospective clients.

3. Distinguish between fact and opinion in the presentation of investment analysis and recommendations.

C. Record Retention. Members and Candidates must develop and maintain appropriate records to support their investment analyses, recommendations, actions, and other investment-related communications with clients and prospective clients.

VI. Conflicts of interest

A. Disclosure of Conflicts. Members and Candidates must make full and fair disclosure of all matters that could reasonably be expected to impair their independence and objectivity or interfere with respective duties to their clients, prospective clients, and employer. Members and Candidates must ensure that such disclosures are prominent, are delivered in plain language, and communicate the relevant information effectively.

B. Priority of Transactions. Investment transactions for clients and employers must have priority over investment transactions in which a Member or Candidate is the beneficial owner.

C. Referral Fees. Members and Candidates must disclose to their employer, clients, and prospective clients, as appropriate, any compensation, consideration, or benefit received from or paid to others for the recommendation of products or services.

VII. Responsibilities as a CFA Institute Member or Candidate

A. Conduct as Members and Candidates in the CFA Program. Members and Candidates must not engage in any conduct that compromises the reputation or integrity of CFA Institute or the CFA designation or the integrity, validity, or security of the CFA examinations.

B. Reference to CFA Institute, the CFA Designation, and the CFA Program. When referring to CFA Institute, CFA Institute membership, the CFA designation, or candidacy in the CFA Program, Members and Candidates must not misrepresent or exaggerate the meaning or implications of membership in CFA Institute, holding the CFA designation, or candidacy in the CFA program.

2   ETHICAL BEHAVIOUR AND PROFESSIONAL INTEGRITY

objectives   **10.1.1 Identify** typical behavioural indicators.

10.1.2 Critically evaluate the outcomes which may result from behaving ethically – for the industry, individual advisers and consumers.

10.1.3 Critically evaluate the outcomes which may result from limiting behaviour to compliance with the rules – for the industry, firm, individual advisers and consumers.

2.1 Values – personal, corporate, societal

Beyond merely developing rules, human groups and individuals have formulated **values** which, if followed by all, result in a better outcome than if individuals acted only out of their own **self-interest**.

For example, a commonly espoused **personal value** is that of **concern for others**, or acting towards others in the way that you would wish them to act towards you. Some have associated the rules, principles and values they have personally sought to live by with **religion**, while others have seen the rules, principles and values as having a **rational** basis.

The concept of **societal values** is of values that are generally agreed by reasonable people and that are widely accepted. At a corporate level, reference to values or the corporate culture suggests that particular ways of acting can become prevalent throughout a firm, whether by design or not. A 'culture' of pursuing short-term profit or revenue even if customers are misled ('having the wool pulled over their eyes') may pervade through a firm, either at the instigation of an aggressive if short-sighted and unethical senior management team, or as the unintended consequence of mis-judged target-setting incentive structures for employees.

2.2 Societal values and business

Social attitudes, such as a belief in the merits of education, progress through science and technology, and fair competition, are significant for the management of a business organisation. Other beliefs have either gained strength or been eroded in recent years.

- There is a growing belief in preserving and improving the **quality of life** by reducing working hours, reversing the spread of pollution, developing leisure activities and so on. Pressures on organisations to consider the environment are particularly strong because most environmental damage is irreversible and some is fatal to humans and wildlife.

- Many pressure groups have been organised in recent years to protect social minorities and under-privileged groups. Legislation has been passed in an attempt to prevent racial discrimination and discrimination against women and disabled people.

- Issues relating to the environmental consequences of corporate activities are currently debated, and respect for the environment has come to be regarded as an unquestionable good.

- There remains a debate about whether consumers should be protected by a comprehensive set of rules with the objective of making sure that they do not enter into bad deals or transactions, or whether the rule of *caveat emptor* ('let the buyer beware') should guide all transactions.

2.3 Sources of rules and principles

The rules or principles that regulate behaviour of individuals and businesses derive from:

- The **law**
- The requirements of **rules and regulations**
- **Regulatory guidance** that is not mandatory
- **Professional standards** and **codes of conduct**
- **Ethics** and ethical **values**

2.4 Ethics: moral principles to guide behaviour

Whereas the political environment in which an organisation operates consists of laws, regulations and government agencies, the social environment consists of the customs, attitudes, beliefs and education of society as a whole, or of different groups in society; and the ethical environment consists of a set (or sets) of well-established rules of personal and organisational behaviour.

2.5 The ethical environment

The ethical environment refers to justice, respect for the law and a moral code. The conduct of an organisation, its management and employees will be measured against ethical standards by the customers, suppliers and other members of the public with whom they deal.

An example of unethical behaviour is to **present misleading information** to a customer which wrongly claimed that they would be likely to be better off transferring from a work-based pension scheme to a personal pension, when this is not the case. Such pension transfers led to the widespread pensions mis-selling scandal in recent years.

More recently, excessively zealous selling of 'sub-prime' and 'undocumented' or 'self-certified' mortgages to those who lacked the resources to meet future payments has been seen by many as a root cause of the financial crisis on 2007-2009, particularly in the US housing market. However, views vary about which behaviours are unethical in such a situation, and attributing 'blame' for such a crisis is complex.

- Were consumers to blame for over-committing themselves?

- Were mortgage brokers to blame for selling mortgages to those who were likely to default?

- Were lenders to blame for making the funds available, while knowing that the mortgages could be 're-packaged' and sold on to investors in securitised form?

Because of differences about where to draw the line between ethical and unethical behaviour, there is much to be said for formulating clearly stated **principles** and **codes** that will apply to particular professional groups or to particular regulated activities.

2.6 Self-interest in the organisational context

The **free market model** of society is based on the idea that individuals act to maximise their own utility. They seek to do this by making decisions to enter into transactions based on the utility gained compared with the opportunity cost on the transaction: the opportunity cost is typically the utility to be gained from spending the same amount of money on the next best alternative. The basic economic model assumes that the economic actor makes decisions out of **self-interest**, as well as being in possession of full **information**.

By and large, we can expect that people will act to better their own interests. But how is this best achieved?

The *Harvard Business Review* reported that the US retailer, Sears Roebuck was deluged with complaints that customers of its car service centre were being charged for unnecessary work: apparently this was because mechanics had been given targets of the number of car spare parts they should sell. The mechanics were seeking to advance their own self-interest in trying to meet the targets set by the organisation.

When targets are set, the key consideration may be to enhance revenues, in the interests of shareholders of the firm. Sales targets for the sale of financial products might, for example, encourage advisers, acting out of self-interest, to advise unnecessary **switching** of client's investments in order to generate commission.

- As well as attracting regulatory sanctions, excessive switching of customers' investments by a firm may, as soon as it becomes known to customers or the media, damage the **firm's reputation**. A poorer reputation could hit sales significantly, thus hurting the business and shareholders' profits that the targets were originally seeking to enhance.

- The adviser responsible for unnecessary switching of customer investments is also liable to damage **his or her own reputation** as a professional. Through the practice of excessive switching having been discovered, the adviser has in fact damaged the self-interest he or she was seeking to promote.

Such examples illustrate how the interaction of self-interest with motivation and with a firm's rules can be complex. Self-interest can be a powerful motivator, encouraging employees to do a better job, but the wrong incentives can lead to sub-optimal outcomes arising.

2.7 Role of the agent

Agency, as we have seen, is a contractual relationship where one party hires or engages another party to act on his behalf in transactions with a third party. There are many examples of agency within the world of financial services. Clients and their financial adviser or their stockbroker are two obvious relationships, with solicitors and estate agents being other agency situations in the world of commerce.

A person who enlists the services of another is the principal and the person so engaged is the agent.

The **duties of an agent** are usually set out in an agreement between principal and agent. However, where there is no agreement or where the agreement does not expressly cover all matters, there are certain duties implied by law which apply – a duty to:

- **Obey instructions** – if the agent exceeds his authority, he may be personally liable to the third party

- **Exercise skill and care**

- **Act in person** – the duties must not be delegated to someone else

- Account and to **keep accounts**

- **Act in good faith** – conflicts of interest must be disclosed to the principal, with everything the agent does being for the principal's benefit

2.8 Rights

The idea that individuals have natural **inherent rights** that should not be abused is a further, long-established influence on Western ethical thinking and one that has led to the development of law to protect certain 'human rights'.

2.9 Reasons for unethical behaviour

Unethical behaviour can arise for a number of different reasons. The FSA's **Discussion Paper 18** *An ethical framework for financial services* (2002) suggested some of them, as outlined below.

- The pressure of short-term gain could be seen to encourage undesirable behaviour. Staff bonus payments may often seem to be geared to pure bottom line success. How risks and tensions can be identified is a constant issue – e.g. truth versus loyalty, one person versus the many? In all of this, it is usual for the values and actions of senior management to influence employee levels.

- Some individuals behave unethically because they think it is worth the risk. This may be related to a short-termist agenda, or may simply be personally selfish. People weigh up the pros and cons and take a chance. It is a deliberate risk/reward trade off. Others may believe they are behaving ethically but come to operate by a different yardstick to that used by others. They might do something which is deemed unethical, but which seems acceptable from their own perspective.

- Others (and some of these groups are not mutually exclusive) may be unaware of the values embedded in existing regulatory standards. So, they comply (or don't comply!) blindly with the 'letter of the law', rather than thinking about the wider effects their behaviour might have.

2.10 Ethical principles

2.10.1 Overview

Much of the practical difficulty with ethics lies in the absence of an **agreed basis** for decision-making. Effective **legal systems** are certain in their effects upon the individual. While the complexity of such matters as tax law can make it difficult to determine just what the law says in any given case, it is still possible to determine the issue in court. Once the law is decided, it is definite and there is little scope for argument.

The **certainty of legal rules** does not have a counterpart in ethical theory. Different ideas apply in different cultures.

Ethics and morality are about right and wrong behaviour. Western thinking about ethics tends to be based on ideas about **duty** and **consequences**. Unfortunately, such thinking often fails to indicate a single clear course of action. Ethical thinking is also influenced by the concepts of **virtue** and **rights**.

2.10.2 Ethics based on consequences

This approach judges actions by reference to their outcomes or consequences.

Utilitarianism, propounded by Jeremy Bentham, is the best known version of this approach and can be summed up as choosing the action that is likely to result in the **greatest good for the greatest number of people**.

This approach has been refined by other moral philosophers who distinguish this 'act utilitarianism' with an alternative 'rule utilitarianism' which involves choosing and living by the **rules** that are most likely to result in the greatest good for the greatest number of people.

2.10.3 Ethics based on duty

We use **duty** as a label for the ethical approach technically called **deontology** (which means much the same thing as 'duty' in Greek). This set of ideas is associated with the German thinker Immanuel Kant and is based upon the idea that behaviour should be governed by **absolute moral rules** that apply in all circumstances.

2.10.4 Ethics based on virtue and personal qualities

Virtue ethics continues to exert a subtle influence. The idea is that if people cultivate certain **values / principles** or **virtues / qualities**, their **behaviour** is likely to be inherently ethical. Today it is suggested that managers should attempt to incorporate such **personal qualities** as firmness, fairness, objectivity, charity, forethought, loyalty and so on into their daily behaviour and decision-making.

2.11 Two approaches to business ethics

Lynne Paine (*Harvard Business Review*, March-April 1994) suggests that ethical decisions are becoming more important as penalties, in the US at least, for companies which break the law become tougher. Paine suggests that there are two approaches to the management of ethics in organisations.

- Compliance-based (or 'rules-based')
- Integrity-based

2.11.1 Compliance-based approach

A rules-based compliance approach is primarily designed to ensure that the company **acts within the letter of laws and regulations**, and that violations are prevented, detected and punished. Some organisations, faced with the legal consequences of unethical behaviour take legal precautions such as those below.

- Compliance procedures to detect misconduct
- Audits of contracts
- Systems for employees to report criminal misconduct without fear of retribution
- Disciplinary procedures to deal with transgressions

2.11.2 Integrity-based programmes

An integrity-based approach combines a concern for the law with an **emphasis on managerial responsibility** for ethical behaviour. Integrity strategies strive to define companies' guiding values, aspirations and patterns of thought and conduct. When integrated into the day-to-day operations of an organisation, such strategies can help prevent damaging ethical lapses, while tapping into powerful human impulses for moral thought and action.

The integrity-based approach, as compared with a rules-centred or compliance-based approach, echoes the **FSA's principles-based approach** to financial regulation. The principles-based approach requires firms to act with integrity and to treat customers fairly, for example. Unlike rules, such principles require senior management to apply higher-level professional values in how they run their business.

A compliance-based approach suggests that bureaucratic control is necessary; an integrity-based or principles-based approach relies on cultural control.

Basing our professional work on integrity, instead of asking 'Show me where it says we can't...', we ask 'How can we improve our standards and conduct our business with integrity?'.

2.12 Professional integrity

2.12.1 The principle of integrity

Financial services is an important industry, affecting the lives of most people. The industry needs not simply to provide the necessary expertise, but to do so with integrity.

The FSA's first Principle for Businesses is **Integrity**:

'A firm must conduct its business with integrity.'

The first Statement of Principle for Approved Persons is also **Integrity**:

'An approved person must act with integrity in carrying out his controlled functions.'

What do we mean by professional integrity? Among the attributes that contribute to integrity are:

- **Honesty** – which will mean that the person will not deliberately mislead another

- **Reliability** – meaning that the person can be relied upon to maintain appropriate levels of competence and skill in practice

- **Impartiality** – this means treating different people fairly, where the people involved could be customers, or employees

- **Openness** – which implies transparency, where appropriate and where justifed confidentiality is not breached

2.12.2 Examples of behaviour lacking integrity

The **Code of Practice for Approved Persons (APER)** includes examples of behaviour that would breach the Statement of Principle.

The integrity principle will be contravened, in the view of the regulator, and indeed on any commonsense interpretation of the principle, if the approved person **deliberately misleads**, or **attempts to mislead**, by act or omission, a client, his firm, its auditors or actuaries, or the FSA.

The following examples of behaviour of this type are provided in APER:

- Falsifying documents

- Misleading a client about the risks of an investment

- Misleading a client about the charges or surrender penalties of investment products

- Misleading a client about the likely performance of investment products by providing inappropriate projections of future investment returns

- Misleading a client by informing him that products require only a single payment when that is not the case

- Mismarking the value of investments or trading positions

- Procuring the unjustified alteration of prices on illiquid or off-exchange contracts, or both

- Misleading others within the firm about the credit worthiness of a borrower

- Providing false or inaccurate documentation or information, including details of training, qualifications, past employment record or experience

- Providing false or inaccurate information to the firm (or to the firm's auditors or an actuary appointed by the firm

- Providing false or inaccurate information to the FSA

- Destroying, or causing the destruction of, documents (including false documentation), or tapes or their contents, relevant to misleading (or attempting to mislead) a client, his firm, or the FSA

- Failing to disclose dealings where disclosure is required by the firm's personal account dealing rules

- Misleading others in the firm about the nature of risks being accepted

- Deliberately recommending an investment to a customer, or carrying out a discretionary transaction for a customer where the approved person knows that he is unable to justify its suitability for that customer

- Deliberately failing to inform, without reasonable cause a customer, the firm or its auditors or actuary, or the FSA, of the fact that their understanding of a material issue is incorrect, despite being aware of their misunderstanding, including failing to disclose false documents

- Deliberately preparing inaccurate or inappropriate records or returns, including performance reports for customers and training records

- Deliberately misusing the assets or confidential information of a client or of his firm

- Deliberately designing transactions so as to disguise breaches of requirements and standards of the regulatory system

- Deliberately failing to disclose the existence of a conflict of interest

- *[Draft 2010 addition to APER]* Deliberately not paying due regard to the interests of a customer

- *[Draft 2010 addition to APER]* Deliberate acts, omissions or business practices that could be reasonably expected to cause consumer detriment

2.12.3 Behaviour reflecting professional integrity

The following types of behaviour reflect professional integrity.

- **Commitment and capacity to work to accepted professional values and principles, beyond professional norms**. Firstly, employees and prospective employees should receive training about professional values, either through professional or company training programmes. Individuals' capacity to abide by these values can be tested through employee selection (e.g. at interview). Employees' technical and professional training needs to be sufficient to enable the employee to understand how the application of professional values affects consumers, the firm and its stakeholders, and the industry.

- **Relating professional values to personally held beliefs**. Ideally, the professional standards required in an employee's workplace should be congruent with his or her personally held beliefs and ethical standards. If this is not the case, tensions may result. An adviser who values regulatory compliance highly may find it difficult to work in a firm where a 'blind eye' may be turned to some rule breaches. If the professional finds themselves in a difficult ethical situation they cannot easily resolve alone, or if they are aware of failings in the organisation that are not within their immediate control, they should consider and take further action, which may include discussion with a superior, with their professional body or possibly with the regulator. If the situation remains unresolved, the individual will need to consider the position further, ultimately resigning if appropriate.

- **Giving a coherent account of beliefs and actions**. When holding discussions with a client, the ethical beliefs of an adviser with professional integrity are likely to show through. Where contraventions of ethical standards are at issue, the ability of employees to give a coherent account of actions is key to resolving this issue. A professional adviser should be disciplined in note-taking and in recording their actions, so that an accurate account of events can be assembled if necessary.

- **Strength of purpose and ability to act on values**. The qualities of a positive attitude and an assertive personality can be cultivated to promote a strong sense of purpose. The firm can help to promote an environment in which strength of purpose will thrive if it is clear about its objectives, which may be expressed in a mission statement.

2.12.4 Professional integrity and ethics in financial services

Professional integrity and ethical issues within financial services can be demonstrated in various ways.

- **The workings of financial markets**. There are various wrongs that can occur. Trading on inside information is an offence and corrodes confidence in markets. If investors believe that price movements may be caused by such practices, then they perceive that the market is rigged against them, and they may suffer financial losses as a result. Research analysis firms are showing lack of integrity if they or their employees deal ahead of publication of research, which could take an unfair advantage of price movements caused by publication of research. There are various other conduct of business rules which we cover elsewhere in this Study Text and which have a bearing on professional integrity, such as rules on personal account dealing by employees and rules on inducements.

- **The operation of institutions**. Organisations need to make arrangements that ensure as far as possible that employees, and the firm, will operate with integrity. These arrangements can take various forms, and should include training in matters of ethics. Conflicts of interest should be avoided, wherever possible, before they become a problem. This can sometimes be achieved by

'Chinese walls' which are organisational or physical barriers separating departments or employees where exchange of information between them could be unethical.

- **Personal conduct of finance professionals and representatives**. Professional employees, and appointed representatives who may be acting as **agents**, should act with integrity, and there should be transparency: they should be *seen* to act with integrity, to encourage **consumer** confidence. As individuals, they must play their part in complying with conduct of business rules of the regulator, and also rules set out by the firm.

2.13 Responsibilities to stakeholders

Managers have a duty (in most enterprises) to aim for profit. At the same time, modern ethical standards impose a duty to guard, preserve and enhance the value of the enterprise for the good of all touched by it, including the general public. The various groups with an interest of some kind in the business and its activities are termed **stakeholders** in the business and include shareholders, employees, customers and suppliers. Large organisations tend to be more often held to account over this duty than small ones.

In the area of **products and production**, managers have responsibility to ensure that the public and their own employees are protected from danger. Attempts to increase profitability by cutting costs may lead to dangerous working conditions or to inadequate safety standards in products. In the United States, **product liability litigation** is so common that this legal threat may be a more effective deterrent than general ethical standards.

Business ethics are also relevant to competitive behaviour. This is because a market can only be free if competition is, in some basic respects, fair. There is a distinction to be drawn between competing aggressively and competing unethically.

In **Discussion Paper 18** *An ethical framework for financial services* (2002), the FSA commented on how the highest ethical standards can generate significant benefits for all stakeholders, for example with the following potential benefits.

- **Market confidence.** High ethical standards offer the potential of differentiating the UK financial services sector as being renowned for good ethical practice. A good ethical track record for the sector could help it (and its regulator) to absorb some 'shocks'.

- **Consumer protection.** Improved ethical standards might include a better relationship between firms and consumers which would be reflected in, for example, improved financial promotions.

- **Financial crime.** High ethical standards could change the perception that it is easy to launder money in the UK, and reduce the scope for our firms and markets to be targeted by criminals in the first place. This can be done by developing individual responsibility and a sense of involvement by all staff.

- **Public awareness and confidence.** Higher business and individual standards of behaviour promote the integrity and the general probity of all working in financial services, enhancing public perceptions and trust in the firms and individuals concerned.

CHAPTER ROUNDUP

- The CFA Code of Ethics covers placing the integrity of the profession and the interests of clients above your own interests; acting with integrity, competence, and respect; and improving and maintaining your professional competence.

- The CFA Standards of Professional Conduct cover: professionalism, integrity of the capital markets, duties to clients, duties to employers, investment analysis and recommendations, and conflicts of interest

- Ethics is about rules, principles and standards to be observed, by people, by firms, and in society generally.

- The conduct of an organisation, its management and employees will be measured against ethical standards by the customers, suppliers and other members of the public with whom they deal. Perceptions of its conduct will determine the reputation of the organisation, which can take time to build up, while it can be reduced quickly.

- There are rules-based and compliance-based approaches to business ethics. Professional integrity encompasses such attributes as honesty, reliability, impartiality and openness.

- Ethical conduct by all team members should be a major concern for management. Inside the organisation, a compliance based approach highlights conformity with the law. An integrity based approach suggests a wider remit, incorporating ethics in the organisation's values and culture. Organisations sometimes issue codes of conduct to employees. Many employees are bound by professional codes of conduct.

BPP LEARNING MEDIA

TEST YOUR KNOWLEDGE

Check your knowledge of the chapter here, without referring back to the text.

1.   Theodore is a Chartered Financial Analyst and works for a City of London firm. His role is as an investment analyst, and he is based in a developing country. The country where he works is modernising rapidly but does not yet have laws prohibiting insider dealing. Theodore becomes aware of a takeover of a local firm which he expects to take place at a substantial premium, making a purchase of shares in the local firm potentially very attractive.

     Comment on whether Theodore has relevant obligations under the CFA Standards of Professional Conduct.

2.   Scott Hambling is a CFA member and private client adviser who has been intensifying his marketing efforts recently in order to increase his client base. Scott presents a seminar at a golf club, to which selected club members have been invited. He discusses the recent performance of the stock market and explains that he has developed a method to predict future movements in stock market indices through identifying patterns in historical data. This method, he tells his audience, shows that there is certain to be an uplift in the main UK indices over the next six months.

     Comment on what Scott has told his audience with regard to the CFA Standards of Professional Conduct.

3.   Gabriel is a Candidate in the CFA programme. He has spent eight weeks as an intern, without pay, at Renfrew Burton Advisers. In the course of the internship, Gabriel played a major role in drafting a compliance manual for the firm, as part of its efforts to prepare for the Retail Distribution Review. Towards the end of his internship, Gabriel accepts a paid position with Forward Point plc, another company which is seeking to prepare for implementation of the RDR. Gabriel makes copies of his work at Renfrew Burton, before his internship has ended, for use in his new role.

     Comment on Gabriel's actions with regard to the CFA Standards of Professional Conduct.

4.   How do Principle for Businesses 1 and Statement of Principle 1 relate to professional standards?

5.   How could high ethical standards in financial services firms help in the fight to stop financial crime?

TEST YOUR KNOWLEDGE: ANSWERS

1. In the event of any conflict, Members and Candidates must comply with requirements and standards that are more strict than those of the country in which he is based. Theodore has received material non-public information and must abide by Standard II(A). He must not act nor cause others to act on the information.

    (See Section 1.3)

2. Scott has contravened Standard III(B), *F air dealing*, which states that Members and Candidates must deal fairly and objectively with all clients when providing investment analysis, making investment recommendations, taking investment action, or engaging in other professional activities. The future course of stock market indices is uncertain and cannot be known with certainty.

    (See Section 1.3)

3. Although Gabriel's internship is unpaid, he has used resources of the firm in drafting the manual and he would be considered an employee because of the work experience and knowledge he is able to gain through the internship. By copying the material, Gabriel is in violation of his duties to an employer under Standard IV(A).

    (See Section 1.3)

4. The FSA's first Principle for Businesses is Integrity: 'A firm must conduct its business with integrity.'

    The first Statement of Principle for Approved Persons is also Integrity: 'An approved person must act with integrity in carrying out his controlled functions.'

    (See Section 2.12.1)

5. High ethical standards could change the perception that it is easy to launder money in the UK, and reduce the scope for our firms and markets to be targeted by criminals in the first place. This can be done by developing individual responsibility and a sense of involvement by all staff.

    (See Section 2.13)

10

Client Objectives and Investment Advice

INTRODUCTION

The investment adviser needs to identify a client's objectives and make recommendations or construct portfolios to meet these objectives. The adviser must operate within the confines of the risk tolerance of the client whilst facing the general economic financial circumstances.

Investment management may be conducted at an institutional level for companies or at an individual level. There are different approaches and philosophies behind managing money, ranging from hands-on active approaches, to more passive approaches.

When dealing with retail clients, or consumers who are not yet clients, the adviser needs to adapt his or her communication to suit the capabilities of the individual involved. In practice, there is a wide range of investment solutions to suit different circumstances.

CHAPTER CONTENTS

CHAPTER LEARNING OBJECTIVES

11 Retail clients

Demonstrate an understanding of how the retail customer is served by the financial services industry

11.1.1 Explain the obligations of a firm towards consumers and their perceptions of financial services

11.1.2 Explain the main needs of consumers and how they are prioritised

11.1.3 Identify suitable investment solutions to suit different needs of consumers

12 Client objectives and the investment advice process

Demonstrate an ability to apply the investment advice process

12.1 The client's financial objectives

12.1.1 Explain the importance of establishing and quantifying a client's objectives
12.1.2 Explain the need to prioritise objectives to accommodate a client's affordability

12.2 The client's current circumstances

12.2.1 Explain the importance of the fact finding process in establishing a client's current financial circumstances

12.2.2 Identify the factors shaping a client's circumstances

12.3 The client's attitude to risk

12.3.1 Analyse the main types of investment risk as they affect investors
12.3.2 Explain the role of diversification in mitigating risk
12.3.3 Analyse the impact of timescale on a client's attitude to risk
12.3.4 Explain the key methods of determining a client's attitude to risk

12.4 Advice and recommendations

12.4.1 Explain why asset allocation always comes before investment or product selection

12.4.2 Explain the key roles of past performance, charges and the financial stability of the provider as criteria within the fund selection process

12.4.3 Explain the importance of stability, independence and standing of trustees, fund custodians and auditors in the fund selection process

12.4.4 Identify benchmarks and other performance measures

12.4.5 Explain the importance of reviews within the financial planning process

1 SERVING RETAIL CUSTOMERS

1.1 Overview

Authorised **firms** have an obligation to abide by the FSA Principles for Businesses and detailed rules, as set out in the FSA Handbook, in their dealings with consumers. Over-arching principles include the requirement to treat customers fairly, while detailed rules cover many areas, including disclosures to be made to customers.

Beyond these requirements, firms will clearly serve themselves best if they work hard to maintain and enhance the **reputation** of the firm and of the financial services industry among consumers.

The **Retail Distribution Review (RDR)**, which we describe later below, is an initiative which seeks to set up arrangement that will enhance **consumers' confidence** in using financial services.

1.2 Consumers' ethical perceptions

In DP 18 *An Ethical Framework for Financial Services* (2002), the FSA recognised that consumers are increasingly understanding an ethical stance.

- Professional conduct and ethical behaviour could **strengthen the level of confidence** enjoyed by the industry.

- On the other hand, if consumers have **diminishing trust** in the sector and in individual firms, they will hesitate to use the products and services available.

Furthermore, there is increasing pressure from consumers and Government to 'put something back'. An example of this is the growing interest in policies to combat **social exclusion**, particularly from a financial standpoint.

Higher business and individual standards of behaviour promoting the integrity and the general probity of all working in financial services will, the FSA believes, enhance public perceptions and trust in the firms and individuals concerned.

1.3 Customer trust and confidentiality

The consumer must have every reason to **trust** a financial adviser. Trust is gained through respect, and an adviser will be able to project the attitudes needed by professional presentation at all times, and through the way the adviser deals with customers.

Acting as a professional means that it should be clear in the way business is conducted that all relevant regulations are being adhered to. Regulations exist to **protect the consumer**, and a client will be reassured if there is no suggestion that regulatory rules might be breached.

If the adviser is trusted, the client will be more open about his or her circumstances, and a more satisfactory basis for giving financial advice will be created. The adviser must always treat personal information with the utmost **confidentiality**.

Regarding confidentiality, all professional people need to be aware of the provisions of the **Proceeds of Crime Act 2002**. This Act requires a professional to disclose to the relevant authorities any information regarding possible crimes having been committed. These provisions mean that, by law, there are some circumstances – for example, if an adviser became aware of tax evasion having been committed – in which the professional requirement of confidentiality is overridden by the statutory requirement to breach that confidentiality by informing the authorities.

1.4 The adviser's fiduciary duty

The regulatory system codifies many obligations and many of the expectations that apply to professional investment advisers. Even if the various obligations had not been codified through written regulations and regulator's principles, the adviser may still owe a fiduciary duty to his or her client.

A decision in the Federal Court of Australia – *Australian Securities and Investment Commission v Citigroup Global Markets (2007)* – is likely to be persuasive in UK courts. In that decision, the court held that the parties' rights and liabilities could be excluded or modified by the terms of the contract between the parties (although **unfair terms regulations** discussed below would affect exclusions in consumer contracts). Citigroup's letter of engagement with a company it was advising had excluded any fiduciary relationship, and that exclusion was found to be effective by the court. The court stressed that, where there were **no explicit contractual exclusion or alteration**, a court would be likely to find that **a financial adviser has a fiduciary duty** towards its client.

An **adviser's fiduciary responsibility** implies that the adviser ought not to take advantage of a client's trust in him or her. The adviser (or firm) agrees to act in the sole interests of the client, to the exclusion of his or her own interests.

- The adviser's fiduciary duty implies that the adviser should act so as to avoid an influence being exerted by any conflict of interest the adviser may have.

- In fulfilling his or her fiduciary duty, the adviser must always act in the client's best interests. This is codified in the FSA's **client's best interests rule**.

- The adviser must make a full and fair disclosure of material facts, particularly where there may be a conflict of interest.

The adviser's fiduciary duty runs through all of his or her work and his or her relationships with clients. The adviser must do more than merely stick to the letter of the regulations. Under its **principles-based regulation** approach, the FSA expects the industry to pay due attention to the **higher level Principles for Businesses** it has formulated, rather than only to slavishly tick checklists of detailed regulations and codes.

1.5 Fair treatment of customers

The FSA aims to maintain efficient, orderly and clean markets and to help retail customers achieve a fair deal. Since 2000, the FSA has examined what a fair deal for retail customers actually means and this has led to much discussion of the concept of **TCF** – 'treating customers fairly'.

The FSA does not define **treating customers fairly (TCF)** in a way that applies in all circumstances. **Principle for Businesses 6** states that a firm must pay due regard to its customers and treat them fairly. By adopting a 'principles-based approach' to TCF through Principle 6, the FSA puts the onus on firms to determine what is fair in each particular set of circumstances. Firms therefore need to make their own assessment of what TCF means for them, taking into account the nature of their business.

The emphasis of the Authority's philosophy is not so much on the principles themselves. It is on the actual consequences of what firms do. Increasingly, the term used for the FSA's current approach has been **outcomes-focused regulation**.

TCF is now treated as a part of the **FSA's core supervisory work**. Firms – meaning senior management, including the Board – are expected to be able to demonstrate to themselves and to the FSA that they deliver **fair outcomes to their customers**.

With regard to TCF, the FSA specifically expects firms to focus on delivering the following six **consumer outcomes**.

- **Corporate culture**: consumers can be confident that they are dealing with firms where the fair treatment of customers is central to the corporate culture.

- **Marketing**: products and services marketed and sold in the retail market are designed to meet the needs of identified consumer groups and are targeted accordingly.

- **Clear information**: consumers are provided with clear information and are kept appropriately informed before, during and after the point of sale.

- **Suitability of advice**: where consumers receive advice, the advice is suitable and takes account of their circumstances.

- **Fair product expectations**: consumers are provided with products that perform as firms have led them to expect, and the associated service is both of an acceptable standard and also as they have been led to expect.

- **Absence of post-sale barriers**: consumers do not face unreasonable post-sale barriers imposed by firms to change product, switch provider, submit a claim or make a complaint.

1.6 Requirements for fair agreements

In communications relating to designated investment business, a firm must not seek to **exclude or restrict any duty or liability** it may have under the **regulatory system**. If the client is a retail client, any other exclusion or restriction of duties or liabilities must meet the 'clients' best interests rule' test.

The general law, in particular the **Unfair Terms in Consumer Contracts Regulations 1999**, also limits a firm's scope for excluding or restricting duties or liabilities to a consumer. As a qualifying body, the FSA has an agreement with the Office of Fair Trading – the lead enforcer of these Regulations – that the Authority will apply the Regulations to financial services contracts issued by regulated firms and appointed representatives for carrying out regulated activities.

- As well as its principles and rules which require firms to treat their customers fairly, the FSA has powers under the Regulations to challenge firms that use unfair terms in their standard consumer contracts.

- The Authority may consider the fairness of consumer contracts, make recommendations to firms, and apply for injunctions against them to prevent the use of such terms.

- The FSA also has a statutory duty to consider all complaints made to it about unfair contract terms.

The FSA has made clear that it considers fairness in consumer contracts to be an important visible factor in firms treating their customers fairly.

1.7 The Retail Distribution Review (RDR)

The **Retail Distribution Review (RDR)** is a key component of the FSA's overall retail market strategy, complementing the Authority's initiatives on Treating Customers Fairly (TCF) and financial capability.

The RDR aims to enable more consumers to have sufficient confidence in the market to want to use its products and services more often. To achieve this objective, the financial services industry needs more clearly to act in the best interests of its customers and to treat them fairly.

The FSA's **Discussion Paper 07/1** (DP07/1) considered the efficiency of the retail financial services distribution marketplace and proposals to improve it, to the benefit of all participants, particularly consumers. The Discussion Paper set out a possible view of the future of retail distribution based on the work of industry practitioners, consumer representatives and other market stakeholders. In April 2008, the Authority produced an Interim Report on the future for the retail distribution of savings and investments.

Many respondents to DP07/1 called for a simpler framework, and for a clearer distinction between advice and sales. The Interim Report therefore sets out a much simplified landscape consisting of the following three components.

- **Advice**. There would be only one type of adviser and a step change in the standards required by advisers, building on the existing requirement that a firm must act honestly, fairly and professionally in line with the best interests of its clients. So all advisers would be independent, both in terms of status and in their practices. Advisers would recommend products from across the whole market and operating remuneration would be determined without product provider input.

- **Sales**. The FSA's starting point for sales is services that are strictly non-advised. These services are intended to encourage higher levels of savings and protection so that the needs of more consumers are met.

- **Money Guidance**. This is an information and guidance initiative and is not a regulated activity. Alongside the FSA's other work on **financial capability**, money guidance has the potential to stimulate more consumers to seek out regulated advice and sales services. Thus, this demand-side initiative may be highly relevant to the future for retail distribution. The Moneymadeclear Money Guidance service is being rolled out by the CFEB across the UK from Spring 2010.

Under the FSA's 2009 proposals (**Consultation Paper 09/18** *Distribution of retail investments: delivering the RDR*), all firms that give investment advice must set their own charges, in agreement with their clients, and will have to meet new standards regarding how they determine and operate these charges. The proposals bring to an end the current, commission-based system of adviser remuneration: the FSA proposes to ban product providers from offering amounts of commission to secure sales from adviser firms and, in turn, to ban adviser firms from recommending products that automatically pay commission. Consumers will still be able to have their adviser charges deducted from their investments if they wish, but these charges will no longer be determined by the product providers they are recommended.

The RDR proposals, due to take effect from the **end of 2012**, impact on all regulated firms involved in producing or distributing retail investment products and services, including banks, building societies, insurers, wealth managers and financial advisers.

2 GIVING INVESTMENT ADVICE

2.1 The financial planning process

The **financial planning** process can be summarised as comprising the following six stages.

1   **Obtaining relevant information** – sometimes termed fact finding
2   **Establishing and agreeing** the client's financial objectives
3   **Processing and analysing the data** obtained
4   **Formulating recommendations** in a comprehensive plan with objectives
5   **Implementing the recommendations** as agreed with the client
6   **Reviewing and regularly updating** the plan

It is helpful to consider **client objectives** below (stage **2** in the process) before we go on to discuss the **fact-find** (stage **1** in the process).

2.2 Client objectives

2.2.1 Overview

Broadly speaking, the requirements of clients fall into one of two categories:

- To **maximise returns**, e.g. positive net worth individuals looking for a portfolio to match their risk/return preferences

- To **match liabilities**, e.g. pension funds, where the aim is to match assets and liabilities or minimise any mismatch

2.2.2 Return maximisation

Given the choice, most investors would elect to have a high performance fund with minimal risk. However, this is not achievable and some trade-off between the two will have to take place. Understanding the **risk/reward trade-off** is crucial to understanding the overall objectives of a return maximising fund and then to establishing the policy of a fund.

Lower risk aversion or greater risk tolerance will tend to result in greater allowable portfolio risk, along with greater potential gains (and potential losses)

The primary concern in this type of fund is, therefore, to fully understand the client's risk tolerance, whether the clients are private or institutional clients.

2.2.3 Liability matching

The only way to guarantee the matching of any liability is through investment in government bonds where the income and capital inflows exactly match those liabilities.

If the return from bonds is insufficient to achieve this required return, then we must use other assets. The result of the use of other assets is that we may achieve the higher return required. However, the risk associated with the use of these other assets means that the liabilities may not be exactly met – there may be a mismatch.

Again, a key requirement here will be to establish the client's attitude to risk, though here we have more specific financial objectives to meet, i.e. a future liability to satisfy.

2.2.4 Mixed requirements

For most institutional clients, the primary requirement will be quite clear-cut – collective investments are generally return-maximising funds whereas pension funds are liability-driven.

For many private clients, however, the requirements may be more mixed. A wealthy private client may have certain liabilities to meet such as paying for children's/grandchildren's school and college fees, repaying loans/mortgages or providing financial protection for relatives/dependents, but may wish that any 'spare' resources be managed to maximise returns.

There are a number of stages that need to be undertaken when considering client objectives.

2.3 Quantifying and prioritising clients' objectives

12.1.1 Explain the importance of establishing and quantifying a client's objectives.

The first stage is to determine all of the objectives that the client is looking to meet and to prioritise and quantify those objectives, especially quantifying any liability targets since they will invariably be the top priorities.

From a priority viewpoint, this will clearly be specific to and determined by the client.

From a quantification viewpoint, the fund liabilities may include such factors as school/college fees, loans, dependent pensions, and a primary consideration here will be whether those liabilities are nominal or real.

- A **nominal liability** is one that is fixed in monetary terms irrespective of future inflation. An example of a nominal liability would be a bank loan or mortgage where the monetary sum borrowed must be paid off at the end of the term and does not alter with inflation over that time.

- In contrast, a **real liability** is one which changes in monetary terms as we experience inflation. For example, in order to maintain a standard of living a pension needs to pay out the same amount each year in real terms, ie a rising monetary amount to cover the impacts of inflation, and this sum needs to be paid for the remaining life from the retirement – an indeterminate term.

Whatever the liability, assessment will involve a **present value analysis** of the anticipated future liabilities that the fund is aiming to meet. For example, to pay a pension of £20,000 pa for a period of 20 years when real returns (asset returns in excess of inflation) are 3% will require a fund value at retirement of almost £300,000 and so we would be looking to achieve this fund value at the retirement date.

2.4 Affordability of client's objectives

objective

12.1.2 Explain the need to prioritise objectives to accommodate a client's affordability.

Based on the quantification, the fund manager will be able to determine any lump sum or annual contributions that needs to be paid into the fund in order to establish the required pool and at this stage the issue of affordability needs to be considered. **Affordability** is the primary issue since if a client cannot afford a proposal then it is not suitable.

If the current assets and/or disposable income of the client are more than sufficient to meet the liability needs then the surplus funds are available for (return-maximising) savings. If, on the other hand, there is a deficit or shortfall then the client's targets and, potentially, priorities will need to be reconsidered.

2.5 The fact find process

objectives

12.2.1 Explain the importance of the fact finding process in establishing the client's current financial circumstances.

12.2.2 Analyse the factors shaping the clients' circumstances.

Key to the assessment of the affordability, therefore, is the client's current personal and financial circumstances which may be determined through the fact find.

The fact find will seek to establish both personal and financial information. **Personal information** detailed in the fact find would, for a retail client, include family names and addresses, dates of birth, marital status, employment status, tax status. **Financial information** would include current income and expenditure levels, levels of savings and investments, the scale of any financial liabilities (usually mortgages, loans and credit cards), the existence of any life assurance policies and pensions etc.

The client will have much of this information easily to hand, however certain information may need to be obtained from third parties. For example, the current performance and value of any pension schemes or life policies such as endowments will probably need to be obtained from the relevant pension fund manager or life assurance fund manager. The overall financial plan will need to take account of any payments that are committed to such funds, any receipts that may be expected from them and whether it is worth considering changing providers.

Other areas that may be considered at this stage are current mortgage terms and the terms of other loans as it may again be appropriate to refinance at better rates.

In order to obtain this information from a third party, the fund manager will require a **letter of authority** from the client that authorises the release of the information. Such enquiries typically take several weeks to get resolved and may cause a substantial delay in finalising the fund investment plan.

The objective information regarding the client's personal and financial situation may be referred to as **hard facts**. One final aim of the fact find will be to seek to understand the more subjective information that may be relevant, such as client aspirations, risk tolerances and any other subjective factors such as their attitude towards issues such as socially responsible investment. This subjective information may be referred to as **soft facts**.

Understanding such soft facts requires face-to-face meeting with the client to discuss and consider the issues alongside them. Establishing a client's risk tolerance, for example, is far from straight forward as standard risk measures are far from familiar to most retail clients and approaches are covered below.

2.6 Risks affecting clients

12.3.1 Analyse the main types of investment risk as they affect investors.

12.3.2 Identify the role of diversification in mitigating risk.

12.3.3 Analyse the impact of timescales on a client's attitude to risk.

12.3.4 Explain the key methods of determining a client's attitude to risk.

2.6.1 Overview

The main risks that a **client** faces and that they need to understand are as follows.

- **Capital risk** – the potential variability in investment values

- **Inflation risk** – the potential variability in inflation rates, which will impact significantly on return requirements for funds looking to finance real liabilities

- **Interest rate risk** – the risk of changes in bank base rates and the knock-on effect that this may have on asset returns

- **Shortfall risk** – the risk of a fund failing to meet any specified liabilities. This can be reduced by minimising targets, increasing sums invested or extending investment terms.

2.6.2 Diversification

One of the key benefits of employing a fund manager is that the investor's funds are being pooled with those of other investors. This pooling allows the investor's money to be spread over a range of assets.

Consider an **investment** in shares (equities). Two sorts of risk can be distinguished:

- The general **market risk** of investing in shares or bonds
- The **specific risk** of any individual investment

For example, if an investor were to put all their money into the shares of a company, there would firstly be the risk that the market in all shares would fall, causing the value of the investment to fall, and secondly the risk that the specific company itself may suffer from a specific incident causing the share price to fall.

If an investor is able to buy more investments, he will be taking on board specific risks of different companies. Eventually, there will be a situation where, because of specific risks, some of the investments will fall but others will rise. Overall, through this process of **diversification**, investors are able to rid themselves of the specific risk of a stock. It is, however, impossible to remove the market risk.

Having established the general principle of diversification, we can see that there are the following different types of diversification:

- **Diversification by asset class.** This is achieved by holding a combination of different kinds of asset within a portfolio, possibly spread across: cash, fixed interest securities, equity investments, property-based investments, and other assets.

- **Diversification within asset classes.** An investor can diversify a portfolio by holding a variety of investments within the particular asset types that he holds. This may be achieved by holding various fixed interest securities, by holding equities in a number of different companies, by spreading investments across different industry sectors and geographical markets, and by holding a number of different properties or property-based investments.

- **Diversification by manager.** Diversifying risk across different funds with different managers reduces the risks from a manager performing poorly. This is one of the attractions of '**manager of manager**' and '**fund of fund**' structures.

The **principle of diversification** should be clearly explained to the client as it will have a significant impact on the potential asset allocations. As part of the fact find, the fund manager will probably illustrate various possible asset allocations and discuss in detail the potential returns and risks of each.

2.6.3 Timescales

A client's attitude to risk may be influenced by **investment timescales**.

If, for example, we are managing a pension fund, our attitude to risk will be highly dependent on timescales. If the fund is a young scheme with 30 or 40 years to client retirement then it can afford to take a reasonably aggressive attitude to capital risk and invest in what may be regarded as the riskier assets. By taking a high risk, we may experience some poor years but we are also likely to experience some very good years. The effect is that risk averages out over time, giving rise to a good overall long-term return, thus minimising shortfall risk.

If, on the other hand, the scheme is very mature and retirement is imminent, then there is insufficient time for this averaging effect to take place. As a result, any poor performance this year may have a significantly adverse effect on the fund, ie a high capital risk in this circumstance increases the shortfall risk.

The fund managers approach will, therefore, be very much affected by investment timescales.

2.6.4 Client's risk tolerance

There are two approaches that a fund manager will utilise in order to get an understanding of the clients risk tolerance, specifically the fact find soft facts discussion and undertaking a review of any current investments. Since a full appreciation of risk is essential to how the fund is managed, the fund manager will investigate both.

The process will probably start with a review of the client's current investments and risks, which will clearly illustrate the client's historical attitude to risk. As we noted above, however, risk tolerance changes over time, so this historical information, whilst a very useful insight, is not of itself sufficient for a full understanding of the client's risk tolerance.

To augment this, the fund manager will also undertake the fact find soft facts review. The standard fact find approach is to ask the client to select a mix of, say, equities and bonds, to give an idea of the normal mix (and hence risk) that the client wishes to face. We noted above that as part of the fact find process the fund manager will illustrate various possible asset allocations and discuss in detail the potential returns and risks of each. Such targeted discussions should enable the manager to get an understanding of the clients general risk tolerance. The fund manager will also be looking to establish limits for each asset class, maximum and minimum holdings of the different assets available, representing investment risk limits.

2.6.5 Investment risks and rewards

We have already mentioned the trade-off between risk and potential reward. This is fundamental to an understanding of investment management.

- **Low risk** investments offer low returns, but low probability of loss
- **High risk** investments offer the possibility of high returns, and a high probability of loss

The following table gives a broad indication of where various investments can be placed in a 'spectrum' of overall investment risk.

Negligible risk	NS&I deposit products Gilts (income) Gilts (redemption)
Low risk	Bank deposits Building society deposits Cash ISAs Annuities
Low / medium risk	Gilts (pre-redemption capital) With-profits funds
Medium risk	Unit-linked managed funds Unit trusts and OEICs/ICVCs (UK funds) Investment trusts (UK) Residential and commercial property
Medium / high risk	Unit-linked overseas funds Unit trusts and OEICs/ICVCs (overseas funds) UK single equities Commodities
High risk	Venture Capital Trusts Unlisted shares Warrants Futures and Options when used to speculate Enterprise Investment Scheme Enterprise Zone Property

Before offering any investment advice, it is vital to ensure that the risk and returns match the customer's criteria.

2.7 The investment management process

The objectives and constraints of the fund or portfolio lead the fund or portfolio manager to consider a variety of strategies or possible asset allocations, and within these to select specific stocks that meet the fund objectives. The fund manager will be judged by his performance with regard to the objectives of the fund and, in the highly competitive world of fund management, an under-performing manager will not be given many second chances.

The approach to fund management

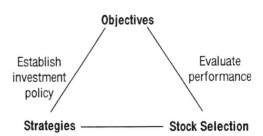

Once the objectives and constraints of the particular fund have been established, the next stage is to develop the investment policy/strategies that will be used in order to achieve these objectives. All these considerations will be detailed as recommended investment policy/strategy options.

These recommendations must then be submitted to the client for approval. In simple situations there may be one obvious approach for the manager to adopt, in more complex situations, several alternatives may be presented to the client forming the basis of a discussion leading to the finally agreed investment policy/strategy statement.

2.8 Asset allocation

The resultant investment policy/strategy statement forms the basis of the management approach. This strategy will detail the long term **strategic asset allocation** options selected to achieve the client's objectives. Asset allocations should not, however, be set in stone. Different asset categories perform better in different economic situations and the fund manager must be ready to respond to such circumstances.

Along with the long term strategic **asset allocation**, the strategy may also detail **market timing/tactical asset allocation** options that may be adopted by the fund in those differing circumstances. The strategy details asset allocations and limits but will not detail **stock or product recommendations**.

Finally, the investment strategy will probably detail any performance **benchmarks** against which the fund performance is to be assessed.

2.9 Investment and product selection

2.9.1 Introduction

When the overall strategy and policy of the fund have been determined, the final stage is to select the stock that will make up the portfolio.

The precise approach adopted depends on the investment management style adopted, i.e. **active** or **passive**.

2.9.2 Active versus passive management

There are two styles that the investment manager can adopt. On the one hand, an active investment manager is one who intervenes with the portfolio on a regular basis, attempting to use individual expertise in order to enhance the overall return of the fund. Passive investment management, on the other hand, establishes a strategy which, once established, should guarantee the appropriate level of return for the fund. These are, perhaps, two extreme versions of investment management. There are alternatives that represent hybrids between the two extremes.

2.9.3 Active management

As mentioned above, active investment management means the fund manager constantly takes decisions and appraises the value of investments within the portfolio. Whilst, to many, this may seem the only thing a fund manager could do, it has to be appreciated that in practice there are costs involved with all transactions, and hence limits on the number of active interventions taking place are likely to be to the advantage of the fund holder.

Moreover, from a more theoretical point of view, there are a number of theories (such as efficient market hypothesis) that indicate that the market itself is efficient and therefore the prices currently quoted in the market contain within them all available information. If this is so, then the only reason that a price will move is because of information which is not already known to the market and, as such, fund managers buying and selling (switching between stocks) will only make money if they are 'lucky' and switch to the right stock at the right time.

Active fund managers do not believe that the securities markets are continuously efficient. Instead, they believe that securities can be mis-valued and that at times **winners** can be found. They also attempt to correctly **time** their purchase or sale on the basis of specific stock information, market information, economic factors, etc.

Active fund managers may obtain research from external sources such as investment banks. In this instance analysts are referred to as 'sell-side' analysts. Alternatively they may establish an in-house research department, made up of 'buy-side' analysts. The benefit of generating unbiased internal research needs to be weighed against the costs of setting up the department.

2.9.4 Passive management

Passive management involves the establishing of a strategy with the intention of achieving the overall objectives of the fund. Once established, this strategy should not require active intervention, but should be self-maintaining. The simplest strategy is to 'buy and hold'. However, perhaps the most common form of passive management is indexation.

2.9.5 Indexation

With **indexation**, the fund manager selects an appropriate index quoted in the market place. Having established the index, the fund manager builds a portfolio which mimics the index, the belief being that this portfolio will then perform in line with the index numbers. Such funds are known as **index** or **tracker** funds.

Overall, the likelihood is that the fund will underperform the index for a number of reasons. Firstly, there is the initial cost of creating the portfolio. Secondly, and perhaps more importantly, all index funds tend to be based on a sampling approach and consequently exhibit a degree of **tracking error**.

It should be noted that indexation itself is not a totally passive form of investment management since the constitution of each index will, over time, change and the portfolio will also be required to change. Tracker funds will, however, incur lower transaction costs as a result of the lower levels of turnover, an advantage over actively managed funds.

2.9.6 Hybrids

Increasingly, fund managers are being requested to outperform indexes, rather than merely track them, and this inevitably requires a less passive, more interventionist approach, potentially with an **indexed core fund** and a **peripheral** or **satellite fund** (which is more actively managed and potentially involves the use of derivatives in order to establish larger trading positions than the fund itself can obtain). The regulator of collective investment schemes such as unit trusts, the FSA, has established a number of important rules limiting the extent to which a fund can invest in futures and options.

Alternatively, the fund manager may combine both active and passive fund management methods by **tilting** the fund. Tilting involves holding all (or a representative sample) of the constituents of an index (like a passive tracker fund), but with larger proportions in areas that the manager favours. This asset allocation decision constitutes the active management component.

2.10 Review

The final stage of the process is to evaluate whether the fund is achieving its objectives through a consideration of its performance. Fund performance should be **reviewed** no less than once a year, certainly more regularly for short term funds, and will look to achieve a number of objectives.

BPP
LEARNING MEDIA

- **Client circumstances** – we should firstly look to determine whether any client circumstances have altered as this may result in an alteration of the client's objectives. Any significant changes may require a modification to the investment strategy.

- **Performance review** – we need to monitor the performance of the fund against the selected benchmark to ensure that it is achieving its objectives.

- **Portfolio rebalancing** – following on from the performance review we should consider whether there is any need to update the agreed asset allocations. Care needs to be taken here in respect of the tax liabilities that may arise from the effects of any rebalancing.

The fund management process cannot, however, be thought of as a step-by-step process that finishes at this stage, rather it is an ongoing process. This review will establish the strategy for the next period and the process will continue.

Throughout this process there are, however, a number of considerations that must be kept in mind in carrying out this fund management process. These include the following.

- Should the fund management be conducted on an active or a passive basis?
- Should fund management be conducted top-down or bottom-up?
- Should the fund manager be conducting a value or growth style of management?

2.11 Benchmarks

2.11.1 Overview

An investor who has been paying someone to actively manage their portfolio will wish to monitor how well the fund manager is doing his job. Such information can then be used to:

- Alter or update the portfolio investment constraints in order to achieve a particular objective

- Communicate investment objectives to the fund manager to ensure that the fund is managed efficiently

- Identify strengths and weaknesses of particular fund managers

When measuring a fund's performance, it is important to establish whether the fund performance was relatively good or bad (i.e. a performance measure is required).

There are three main forms of comparable analysis of a fund's performance.

- Comparison to relevant stock/index, e.g. a published market index

- Comparison to similar funds, i.e. performance of other fund managers with similar objectives and constraints. PPM consultants maintain extensive databases on statistical performance, e.g. CAPS Ltd and WM Company, Micropal. These companies measure:

  - Short and long-term investment return
  - Asset distribution of funds
  - Review specific client fund performance against peer groups and/or market indices
  - Fund performance relative to benchmarks and market medians

- Comparison with a customised benchmark for funds that have a unique objective or constraint, e.g. ethical funds that cannot invest in arms/tobacco (although the standardised FTSE4Good indices meeting ethical criteria are available)

2.11.2 Using indices

Movements of an **index** over a period of time can be used by analysts to give an indication of general trends, and also indicate whether the market appears overpriced or underpriced relative to previous years. To be useful in this context, however, the index must be comparable over the period being considered, and great efforts must be made to ensure that any index is both **relevant** and **comparable**. If an index is to be used as a performance yardstick against which the performance of a fund is to be assessed, it must provide a reasonable comparison.

This is particularly important when a client will want to compare the performance of the fund in which they are investing. There are several private client performance indices available, the best known being the WM Performance Indices, in addition to FTSE Indices.

The WM Performance Indices include a series of benchmarks based upon **income**, **growth** as well as a **balanced fund** index.

An investor will need to understand how the index deals with the payment of income by a security (dividends for shares and interest for bonds). The normally quoted **FTSE Indices** do **not** include dividend income in their evaluation. In contrast, bond indices, such as the **Citigroup World Government Bond Indices**, most frequently **do** include the value of coupon payments and hence represent **total return indices**.

2.11.3 Benchmark indices

Indices may be used for a variety of reasons. Historically, their purpose was to give an indication of the mood of the market. More frequently now, they are used as a benchmark for performance assessment.

To be appropriate for benchmarking purposes, an index must be indicative of the performance that could realistically have been achieved.

The characteristics that are required to render an index suitable as a benchmark are therefore that it is:

- Specified and unambiguous

- Appropriate to the nature of the fund (e.g. a UK blue chip fund may utilise the FTSE 100 Index)

- Appropriate to the currency of the fund

- Investable, i.e. composed of investments that could conceivably be held in the fund

- Measurable, i.e. the return can be calculated on a frequent basis as required

- Representative of achievable performance, i.e. it has an arithmetic weighted composition (remember that the return of a portfolio is an arithmetic weighted average of the individual stock returns)

- Measures the relevant component of performance, i.e. total return indices for total return performance and capital value indices for capital growth

2.12 Recommending funds

Learning objectives   **12.4.2 Explain** the key roles of past performance, charges and the financial stability of the provider as criteria within the fund selection process.

12.4.3 Explain the importance of stability, independence and standing of trustees, fund custodians and auditors in the fund selection process.

2.12.1 Introduction

Where the fund is too small to be efficiently managed or the clients objectives are too specialised to be handled in-house, the fund management will need to be outsourced. The decision to outsource will be determined when the overall strategy and policy are developed, towards the end of the initial fund management process.

The range of funds that a manager can use may be restricted if the manager is 'tied', however if they are independent then they will have the whole market to choose from. Irrespective of the range available to them there are certain factors to consider, including the following.

2.12.2 Past performance

Though appropriate warnings must be given regarding relying on past performance, consistency of past performance is accepted as an indication of the manager's skill.

2.12.3 Charges

The best fund manager in the world will not be worth using if his charges eat up all of the fund's returns so it is essential that these are considered. Fund charges tend to come in one of two forms

- Entry and exit charges – charges made when funds are invested or when funds are withdrawn

- Annual charges – generally charged as a percentage of the value of funds under management, though they may include a performance related element

The higher the overall fee burden, the greater the fund performance needs to be in order to outperform its peer group.

2.12.4 Financial stability of the provider

For many funds this is of little relevance, however it is key to 'with profits' funds run by life assurance companies whose performance accumulates over many years. 'With profits' funds aim to smooth the fund returns across the years through the application of bonuses. In very good years part of the fund return will be retained rather than being allocated as an annual bonus. In poorer years these retained funds can be called on to continue to provide the annual bonus. For this process to function requires a good degree of financial stability within the provider.

2.12.5 Stability, independence and standing of trustee, fund custodians and auditors

Financial regulation came into being as a result of certain financial scandals and despite these regulations scandals still arise, though they are now much rarer in the UK. In many respects, fund management is an industry ripe for fraud. One individual, the fund manager, has control of potentially quite substantial funds owned by others, the investors. As a result, there needs to be controls and checks in place to ensure that neither the fund manager nor anyone else involved in the process is either tempted or able to abuse their position.

Typically, within a fund where a trustee is involved:

- The fund manager controls how and where the assets are invested but never personally has access to them

- Any trades are transacted by a broker

- The funds are held in the name of the trustee who is charged with the task of ensuring that the fund manager operates in accordance with his remit

- Periodically, the fund accounts are checked by the fund auditor

Any action taken by any one of these parties is immediately transparent to the others, so this segregation of duties should ensure the safety and security of the investor's funds (except in the case of collusion between all of the parties involved).

The trustee and auditor are the primary controlling influences in this system, hence their independence from the fund manager and each other as well as their reputation and standing in those roles are of great importance to the investor.

3 INSTITUTIONAL INVESTMENT MANAGEMENT

Learning objectives

12.5.1 Explain the features and objectives of the following funds in the UK: pension funds (defined benefit and defined contribution), life assurance funds and general insurance funds.

12.5.2 Distinguish among the typical asset allocations for the above funds.

12.5.3 Explain the return objectives of the major fund types.

12.5.4 Classify funds by their income/capital growth requirements.

12.5.8 Identify the other types of legal requirements that affect person, insufficient funds and private clients.

3.1 Introduction

Over the last 50 years, the power of the institutional investor has grown dramatically in line with the decline in individual investors.

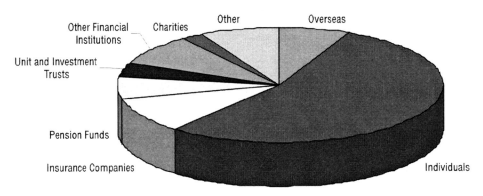

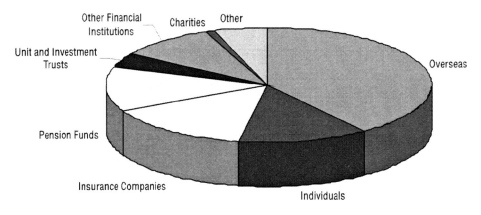

BPP
LEARNING MEDIA

3.2 Types of fund

Each type of institutional fund has its own particular risk/reward profile stemming from:

- Its initial objectives, return maximising/liability matching
- The value and time horizons of the liabilities it has to meet (if any)
- The assets it can invest in
- The liquidity they require within the fund
- The risk they can tolerate in the fund
- Its tax status
- Legislation governing its powers

3.3 IMA classifications

The **Investment Management Association (IMA)** publishes sector definitions to classify unit trusts and OEICs. The table below shows the groupings of funds in the IMA classifications.

The groups correspond to different investment objectives.

- Some **income funds** principally target **immediate income**, while others aim to achieve **growing income**.
- **Growth funds** which mainly target **capital growth or total return** are distinguished from those that are designed for **capital protection**.
- **Specialist funds** form a further category.

UK fund classifications

Income funds			Growth funds	Specialist funds
Immediate income	**Growing income**	**Capital protection**	**Capital growth/total return**	
UK Gilts UK Index Linked Gilts Sterling Corporate Bond Sterling High Yield Sterling Strategic Bond Global Bonds UK Equity & Bond Income	UK Equity Income UK Equity Income & Growth	Money Market Protected /Guaranteed Funds	UK All Companies UK Smaller Companies Japan Japanese Smaller Companies Asia Pacific including Japan Asia Pacific excluding Japan North America North American Smaller Companies Europe including UK Europe excluding UK European Smaller Companies Cautious Managed Balanced Managed Active Managed Global Growth Global Emerging Markets UK Zeros	Absolute Return Property Specialist Technology & Telecomms Personal Pensions

3.4 Pension funds

3.4.1 Assets and liabilities

A pension fund is an example of a liability matching fund or a return maximising fund. It represents a pool of money to be invested now, to achieve either:

- A specific return based on the employee's salary and number of years' service with the company – a **defined benefit/final salary scheme**, or

- A general increase in value of the contributions paid on behalf of the employee – a **defined contribution/money purchase scheme**

Occupational pension schemes, where the scheme is set up by the employer for the benefit of the employees, tend to be defined benefit schemes, though defined contribution schemes are becoming increasingly popular.

Personal pension schemes, set up by an individual who is, perhaps, self-employed or is not a member of an occupational scheme, are defined contribution pensions.

Generally speaking, pension funds have fairly **long-term horizons** and, therefore, are prepared to take on board a higher degree of risk, since any shortfall in the fund can be made up in future investment performance. This **investment policy** depends on the **maturity** of the fund. If the fund beneficiaries are close to retirement, then it would be more appropriate to select relatively short-term safe investments. However, in general the above comment is applicable.

Pension funds also have to keep control over the real rate of return that they earn since their liabilities, the potential pension payments calculated by the fund actuaries, will be expanding in line with inflation. As a consequence, pension funds tend to invest in slightly more speculative assets often referred to as **real assets**, such as **equities** and **property**, since these offer a degree of protection against the impact of inflation.

In addition, they tend to keep only a small proportion of the fund in fixed interest instruments. In particular, they will tend to be substantial holders of index-linked stocks, partly because these guarantee real returns over a period of time, but also because the bonds themselves tend to have fairly high durations and are therefore sensitive to movement in real interest rates.

Equally, the pension fund will need to keep some assets in a liquid form and government bond markets represent a highly liquid market place in which to invest money gaining a moderate but **risk-free** return.

3.4.2 Tax status

Generally, within certain limits, **contributions** paid to pension funds are **tax free**, i.e. no income tax burden is suffered by individuals on contributions paid on their behalf, and tax relief can be claimed on contributions that they pay themselves.

In addition, pension funds approved by HMRC are **gross funds**, i.e. they pay no UK tax on either fund income or capital gains.

However, pension funds are not able to reclaim the 10% income tax that is assumed to have been paid on UK dividends received. In addition, there may be withholding tax on overseas investments that may not be recoverable.

The only occurrence of tax in relation to pension funds occurs (in the form of **income tax) on receipt of pensions in retirement**.

3.5 Life assurance companies

3.5.1 Assets and liabilities

Life assurance is a form of insurance against an eventuality that is **assured** (hence the name) to arise, i.e. that people will die. As such, it is another form of liability matching fund. Life assurance policies take a number of forms.

■ **Term assurance policies** – where an individual's life is insured for a specific period or term (usually ten years or more) in a similar way to normal car or household insurance.

■ **Whole of life policies** – where a capital sum will be paid upon the death of the policyholder, whenever that may be.

■ **Endowment policies** – which combine life insurance and savings. These policies are generally associated with mortgages where the savings element is designed to pay off the capital borrowed at the end of the term of the policy, and the life insurance will repay the mortgage should the policyholder die before the end of that term.

In common with pension funds, life assurance companies tend to have reasonably **long-term** liabilities and, as such, are able to take on board a higher degree of risk. Once again, this tends to involve a high proportion of their assets being invested into equities and property with only a smaller proportion being invested into the fixed interest markets.

As a long-term fund, life assurance companies are able to take reasonably higher degrees of risk and again may be tempted towards the higher duration stocks in the bond markets.

Within the industry there are a variety of policies available ranging from with profits policies, which share in the profits of the fund but attract higher premiums, to without profits policies, where the premiums are lower but the profits go to the insurance company.

3.5.2 Tax status

There is **no tax relief on the payment of life assurance premiums** on new policies (although there is on certain older policies).

All fund income and capital gains are taxable, which will result in the investment manager selecting investment vehicles that are more tax efficient.

Proceeds paid from life policies are taxable unless the policy is a **qualifying** policy, in which case the proceeds are **tax free**.

3.5.3 Legislation

In terms of regulation, there is a considerably stronger regime imposed upon the insurance industry than that currently operating in the pensions market. The key regulator is the FSA which, under FSMA 2000, is given a range of interventionist powers.

Both life assurance funds and general insurance funds are closely monitored to ensure that the solvency of the company is in no way called into question. Overall, this tends to make both of them more risk adverse than pension funds, but there is a marked difference between life assurance companies and general insurance companies in the risk/reward profile they adopt.

The basic measure of solvency is that the assets of the fund must exceed the liabilities of the fund, both derived using prudent measures. Where there are concerns about the solvency of a fund, then they may intervene in order to guarantee the policyholders' rights.

The FSA operates a compensation scheme for UK investment, banking and insurance firms who become insolvent and unable to meet their obligations. Claims under the scheme are subject to limits set out in the FSA Handbook.

3.6 General insurance companies

3.6.1 Assets and liabilities

General insurance companies clearly aim to be able to match their liabilities. They have a much shorter liability profile than life funds. In essence, insurance is like taking a bet. The insured person pays the company the premium.

The insurance company makes money if they are able to take in this premium and earn investment income on it that exceeds the amounts of any claims arising on the policy.

Since claims are likely to arise in the immediate future, for example in the next year, then they are unable to take substantial risks, forcing them to invest a greater proportion of their fund into **short-term** 'risk-free' government securities. Whilst the returns may not be as high, the fund simply cannot take any risk.

Both life assurance funds and general insurance funds are closely monitored by the FSA to ensure that the solvency of the company is in no way called into question. Overall, this tends to make both of them more risk adverse than pension funds but there is a marked difference between life assurance companies and general insurance companies in the risk/reward profile they adopt.

3.6.2 Tax status

General insurance business profits are subject to normal corporation tax rates.

3.6.3 Legislation

General insurance business is governed by the same rules and regulations as life insurance business discussed above.

3.7 Constraints on funds

Learning objective | **12.5.5 Explain** the effect of each of the following on a fund's asset allocation: time horizons; liability structure and liquidity requirements.

3.7.1 Introduction

Given the client's objectives, the key to understanding the investment strategy is to appreciate the various constraints that operate on the fund itself.

3.7.2 Time horizons

The **time horizon** for the attainment of the return, or the matching of the liabilities, will clearly influence the types of investments that will be worthwhile for the fund.

A fund whose purpose is to meet some liabilities in, say, two years' time, may find that the investment vehicle is low coupon gilts. This will especially be the case if the client is a high rate taxpayer as he will be able to benefit from a tax-free capital gain on these gilts at redemption.

For a fund that has liabilities to meet in 20 years' time, such investments would be inappropriate.

The time horizon will also influence the level of risk that can be taken in order to achieve the objectives. A fund with a long-term time horizon can probably stand a higher risk, as any poor returns in one year will be cancelled by high returns in subsequent years before the fund expires. Clearly, this sort of risk cannot be taken in a very short-term fund which may only span a couple of years and, therefore, may not have counterbalancing good and bad years.

3.7.3 Liabilities

As mentioned above, certain funds have liabilities that they are obliged to meet and the investment manager's objective must take these into consideration. For example, pension funds and life assurance companies will have statistical projections of their liabilities into the future and the fund must attempt to achieve these.

A further consideration is the exposure to currency risk. A pension fund may have all its liabilities denominated in sterling. If the fund were to invest heavily in overseas assets this would expose it to an additional risk, other than the risk inherent in the assets themselves. However, if the pension fund has liabilities in, say, dollars, then buying US investments matches their currency exposure and, therefore, minimises risk as well as taking on board an acceptable investment.

3.7.4 Liquidity needs

Within any fund, there must be the ability to respond to changing circumstances and, consequently, there needs to be a degree of liquidity. Government fixed interest instruments can guarantee a tranche of the investment portfolio which will give easy access to cash should the fund need it. In general, exchange traded investments (equities and bonds) tend to be highly liquid whilst investments that are not exchange traded, such as property, have low liquidity.

3.7.5 Risk aversion and risk tolerances

We commented above on the risk/reward trade-off, which impacts on the ways in which the fund's requirements can be achieved.

3.8 Asset allocation

Asset allocation is the allocation of the funds available between the various instruments or financial markets.

All fund managers require a knowledge of asset allocation according to more fundamental principles. This is perhaps the most subjective area of fund management, and one where there will never be a single correct answer. Given the same fund and client, it is unlikely that any two fund managers would produce exactly the same asset allocation and make exactly the same investment decisions. However, it would be reasonable to assume that any allocations would have a broadly similar effect. The justification for this last statement is that the fund or portfolio manager has a legal and professional duty to **base the asset allocation on the client's wishes** with particular regard to the criteria discussed above when identifying the client's objectives, specifically the following.

- Matching liabilities
- Meeting any ethical considerations
- Remaining within risk tolerances
- Maximising fund performance

Asset allocation must, therefore, be the first step in the investment management process.

There are three basic rules the fund manager should bear in mind when trying to satisfy the client's investment objectives.

- The fund manager should take every step to diversify risk, a process requiring an understanding of the different risk factors affecting all the investments in which he may be investing as well as the impact of foreign exchange.

- The fund manager should be aware that the best way to match the client's liabilities if they are fixed in money terms is by investing in bonds, since this will generate cash flows from interest and redemption proceeds which will allow the liabilities to be met as they arise.

- Asset allocation is effectively a compromise between matching investments to client liabilities and investing assets in more attractive markets in order to maximise fund performance.

The optimal asset allocation should be based on the objectives and constraints of the fund and the fund manager's estimate of the risks and returns offered by the various securities.

The idea is that the objectives and constraints of a fund direct the investment manager towards certain asset classes and away from others, leading towards the asset allocation decision. For example, if real liabilities are to be met, these must be matched by real assets (equities/property/index-linked bonds), or if high liquidity is needed, then property is inappropriate.

As an illustration of this, we consider in the table below the various constraints for common liability matching funds and a potential resultant asset allocation.

Constraint	Young pension fund	Mature pension fund	Life assurance fund	General insurance fund
Time	Long-term	Short-term	Long-term	Short-term
Liability	Real	Real	Nominal	Nominal
Liquidity	Very low	High	Low	Very high
Risk tolerance	High	Low	Medium/High	Very low
Tax status	Gross fund, no tax on income or gains*	Gross fund, no tax on income or gains*	Tax on income and gains	Tax on income and gains
Asset allocation				
Equities	60% - 80%	20% - 30%	55% - 65%	0%
Property	5% - 10%	0% (illiquid)	0% - 5%	0%
Bonds	15% - 25%	55% - 65%	15% - 30%	100%
Cash	0% - 5%	15% - 25%	5% - 15%	

* Pension funds are not able to recover the 10% tax credit on dividend distributions.

3.9 Tax status

Learning objectives

12.5.6 Explain the taxation of the various types of funds in the UK.

12.5.7 Explain the effect that tax legislation may have on the stock selection and asset allocation of a fund.

Taxation is a consideration for all investment managers. The investment portfolio and the strategy adopted must be consistent with the fund's tax position. In some cases, such as pension funds, the fund does not suffer taxation. For these **gross funds**, the manager should, normally, avoid those stocks which involve the deduction of tax at source. For, even though it may be possible to reclaim any tax suffered, the fund will have incurred the opportunity cost of the lost interest on the tax deducted.

3.10 Other preferences and legal constraints

Obviously, when constructing a portfolio for any investor, the manager should consider the legal constraints that may exist. The regulatory framework adopted in the market needs to be adhered to. For collective investment schemes in the UK, there are certain investments into which the fund may not invest, such as derivatives.

Equally, a **trust deed** may exist which binds the investment manager to invest in certain securities and, consequently, the manager must abide by this trust document. Where there is no trust deed, the **Trustee Act 2000** provides guidance on the appropriate mix of investments. This places a duty of care on the trustees to exercise reasonable care in investments.

4 ADVISING INDIVIDUALS

objectives

13.1.1 Communicate clearly, assessing and adapting to the differing capabilities of clients.

13.1.2 Evaluate the factors shaping a clients' needs and circumstances.

13.1.3 Identify suitable investment solutions to suit different types of circumstances.

4.1 Client questionnaire

Information collected about the client should be **recorded carefully and meticulously**. The standard method of doing this is the use of a **questionnaire** designed to ensure that all relevant information is sought.

Comprehensive information gathering can serve the function of helping to generate business for the adviser but it is also important from the compliance point of view. It ensures that a proper record is kept, that information was sought from a client, that it was either given or refused and, combined with documents recording recommendations made to a client, can confirm that the advice given to the client was sound and suitable.

4.2 Client's attitudes

The following questions concern attitudes of the client.

- What is the client's attitude to existing savings/investment/protection?

- Are existing arrangements **sufficient**?

- Are they **suitable**?

- Have they been **reviewed recently**?

- Is the level of **investment risk acceptable** to a client?

- Is the client prepared to accept **more or less risk**?

- Are there any **constraints** on investment, e.g. ethical investments?

- Does the client consider that the **existing investments meet current needs**?

- **Do you consider that they meet current and existing needs**? (Remember that with long-term contracts such as life policies, surrender is not precluded but it must be recommended only when such a course is obviously suitable. This is likely to happen in very few cases, except perhaps with term assurance, where better terms may be obtained if premium rates have fallen.)

4.3 Client's objectives

The **client's objectives** and **expected liabilities** should be considered under headings such as the following.

- Is the client expecting to buy **property** or move house or incur expenses for school fees or change jobs or buy a car or face major repairs?

- What is the client's **timespan** for investments, i.e. short-term or long-term or both?

- How **accessible** must the client's funds be?

- What is the client's **current and future tax position**?

- Are the client's needs for **income or growth** or both?

- Does the client want any **personal involvement** in the direction of investment?

- Does the client have **ethical views or preferences** which could influence their investment choices?

4.4 Present client circumstances

The analysis of a client's current circumstances begins with an analysis of the financial figures for the client's current circumstances. For a typical retail client, this would show a list of the client's **assets and liabilities**, and reveal whether there is a surplus or a deficit. It will also include an **income and expenditure** account to reveal whether there is **surplus** income or a **shortfall**: this is effectively a **budget**.

- If there is a **surplus**, it will enable the client to put into effect at least some of any recommendations which involve an additional outlay.

- If there is a **shortfall**, this reveals the need for the client to take action not to increase liabilities and perhaps to reduce existing liabilities.

Current income needs should be measured and this will enable you to check whether or not the **protection** against death and disability is adequate to meet those needs.

4.5 Future client circumstances

The adviser must also analyse the client's possible **changing circumstances** and **lifestyle**.

- What are the consequences, for example, of moving to another house or a prospective job change or children approaching fee paying school age? There may be additional housing or education costs, for example.

- If the client is employed and is planning to become self-employed, are any arrangements in hand for replacing company group life and disability cover with personal life and disability cover?

- Are arrangements in hand to ensure that finance is available to enable the move to take place?

4.6 Analysing client needs

In order to formulate a **recommendation** for a client, an adviser must always **identify** and **analyse** the **client's needs**.

By now, you have all the information necessary regarding the client and you can quantify a client's protection needs against the existing provision and compare future income needs against expectations.

You can also assess the client's current and future **tax position** and evaluate the tax efficiency of existing investments.

After all this has been done, the chances are that **most clients will not be able to achieve all of their objectives**. This will mean prioritising their objectives according to their resources.

An adviser must take into account all the **regulatory compliance requirements** that apply before dealing with the client (such as giving to the client a **business card**, a **services and costs disclosure document or SCDD**, and **terms of business letter**) through the process to the stage where recommendations are given, when the reasons for those recommendations are required.

4.7 Discretionary and non-discretionary portfolio management

If the client is to own a portfolio, we should be clear about the nature of the advice being given.

- With **discretionary portfolio management**, the investment manager makes and implements decisions to buy and sell investments in the portfolio without asking the client each time.

- The **non-discretionary portfolio manager** provides advice to the client to assist the client in making their own investment decisions.

4.8 Execution-only customers

Execution-only customers are those who are not given any advice by the firm when they make investment decisions. The only responsibility of the firm to such customers is one of 'best execution': to implement the customer's investment decisions at the best price available.

4.9 Client needs and circumstances

It is possible to characterise individual investors by their situation, which may cover:

- Source of wealth
- Amount of wealth
- Stage of the life cycle

4.10 Wealth and investment exposure

When considering investment, the **wealth** of the investor is clearly an important consideration. If there is free capital to invest, then clearly it is sensible for the individual to take steps to make the best use of that capital.

It is possible, although not generally advisable, for someone with little wealth to gain exposure to investment markets, for example by **borrowing money to invest**, or by using investments such as derivatives or spread betting to gain a greater exposure than the individual's free resources. When investing in **risky assets** such as **equities**, a good principle is the often-stated one that **someone should only invest what they can afford to lose**. Someone who borrows to invest without having other capital to back it up if things go wrong, has the problem that they may end up with liabilities in excess of their assets.

An investor who uses instruments such as derivatives to increase their exposure should maintain other accessible resources (for example, cash on deposit) that can be used to meet losses that may arise. Clearly, it is also important that they understand the risks they are undertaking.

Major investments, including housing, should be appropriately **safeguarded**. For investments, the soundness of institutions holding funds, and any compensation arrangements where applicable, should be considered. Good title to housing should be ensured, and appropriate insurance taken out against risks such as fire.

4.11 Source of wealth

The way in which people received their wealth may affect their characteristics as investors. Investors may have acquired their wealth **actively** or **passively**.

Passive wealth

- People who have acquired their wealth passively, for example, through inheritance, or those who have acquired savings gradually from their salaries.

- These people are frequently less experienced with risk and do not believe that they could rebuild their wealth were they to lose it.

- They have a greater need for security and a lower tolerance for risk.

Active wealth

- People who have earned their own wealth, often by risking their own capital in the process.
- These types of people are assumed to be more confident and familiar with risk.
- They have a higher tolerance for risk.
- They dislike losing control over anything, including their investments.

4.12 Amount of wealth

The amount or **measure** of someone's wealth will affect his views on risk, since it will affect a person's sense of financial health. However, this sense of financial health is highly subjective. This makes it difficult to use this approach as a means of categorising investors.

Generally, if people perceive their wealth to be small, they are less inclined to take risks with their portfolios.

A portfolio that is only just sufficient to cover lifestyle needs could be viewed as small. A portfolio that is well in excess of that needed for the person's lifestyle could be considered large.

4.13 Taxation

4.13.1 Tax planning points

In giving financial advice in other aspects, there are of course tax considerations to be borne in mind:

- Is the client a non-taxpayer, savings income starting rate (10%), basic rate (20%), higher rate (40%) or top rate (50%) taxpayer? (Keep aware of current rates.)

- Are all personal allowances for income tax purposes being used?

- What is the likely capital gains tax position, and is there a way for the client to make use of annual CGT exemptions, or any brought forward capital losses that can be set against capital gains?

- What is the tax position of financial products being considered? Are proceeds exempt from tax? Are there planning steps that can ensure that tax effects are mitigated?

- At the **end of a tax year**, key issues are whether an individual wishes to top up **pension plans** or **ISAs,** for which there are limits on contributions within a tax year.

4.13.2 Tax planning in context

It is important to consider tax planning in the light of all the client's circumstances and needs, and in the context of all of their plans and wishes.

Any **tax advantages** should not be sought at all costs, without considering other aspects. For example, there will be no benefit to a client if a particular financial product carries a tax advantage which is cancelled out by the effect of higher charges on that particular product, or by exposure to **investment risks** that the client would not otherwise wish to be exposed to.

4.14 Factors shaping individual circumstances

There are various **life stages**, and people have differing financial needs. Every case is different, and there may be many variations in individual circumstances that cannot easily be fitted into easily formulated categories.

As an individual gets older, different priorities and needs take effect. Each person will clearly be different and therefore it is difficult to generalise to any degree. However, analysing by reference to where someone is in their life cycle will give some insight into investor characteristics.

Typically, but not always, **risk tolerance** declines as someone passes through his life cycle. Younger people have a long time horizon and a lower net worth. They may be more willing and able to take risk as a result.

As a person gets older, his net worth may increase and long-term spending goals will start to appear. The investor is still investing for the long term, but risk tolerance has declined, reflecting a fear of capital losses. These will be harder to recover over the shorter time available.

Later in a person's life, when they have paid off all their liabilities (e.g. mortgage), they will find that their personal net worth increases more quickly. The person who is close to retirement age has the prospect that earnings will no longer be able to counterbalance falls in the portfolio value. As a result, risk tolerance will fall even more.

4.15 Life cycle, age and commitments

The **age** of an investor, the stage of **life cycle** that he is at, and his **commitments**, all affect the investor's **risk profile**.

Adventurous risk-taking may be unwise for someone with heavy financial **commitments**, for example to children and other dependants. Another aspect of an investor's commitments is that of how much time he has available: if he works full-time and has a family, there may be little time left for him to manage his own investments even if he has an interest and knowledge to do so, and his commitments may mean that he is more likely to wish to seek professional financial advice.

4.16 An individual's risk profile

The financial adviser must recognise that each client has their own views, aspirations and attitudes. **Attitudes to risk** vary widely, and accordingly investment choices vary widely too. Some individuals will be reluctant to take on any significant risk of loss of their capital while others are prepared to 'gamble' with their savings.

People are likely to take notice of the growth potential of an investment while some could be less willing to appreciate the risk involved. The adviser needs to take especial care to make such a client aware of risks.

Attitudes to risk vary according to the different objectives of the investor. An investor may have a core holding of deposits that he wishes to keep as an emergency fund, while he may be prepared to take greater risks with other funds he holds. If a client has a specific target for a particular investment – for example, to pay for children's education, or to pay for a vacation – then he may choose lower risk investments for the funds intended to reach that target than for other his other investments.

One way of classifying investors is to look at an investor's views on risk and the way that investor makes decisions. This will give a classification system based on how **cautious**, **methodical**, **spontaneous** or **individualistic** the investor is.

	Decision making is rational/based on thought	Decision making is emotional/based on feeling
High risk aversion	Methodical	Cautious
Low risk aversion	Individualist	Spontaneous

Source: Bronson, Scanlan, Squires

The following is a general guide to typical characteristics.

Cautious investors

- Highly loss averse
- Need for security
- Want low-risk investments with safe capital
- Do not like making decisions but do not listen to others
- Tend not to use advisers
- Portfolios are low risk and with low turnover

Methodical investors

- Analytical and factual
- Make decisions slowly
- Little emotional attachment to investments and decisions
- Tend to be conservative in investment approach

Spontaneous investors

- High portfolio turnover
- Do not trust the advice of others
- Some are successful investors, but most do less well, particularly because of high transaction costs due to high turnover
- Make decisions quickly and are fearful of missing out on opportunities

Individualist investors

- Self-confident
- Prepared to do analysis and will expect to achieve their long-term goals

4.17 Customer understanding

It is a basic regulatory requirement that a firm should not recommend a transaction or act as an investment manager for a customer unless it has taken reasonable steps to help the customer **understand the nature of the risks** involved.

In the case of **warrants** and **derivatives**, the firm should provide to the customer any appropriate **warrants and derivatives risk warnings**.

If recommending to a retail customer transactions in investments that are not readily realisable, the adviser should explain the difficulties in establishing a market price.

Following the recording of recommendations in a **report**, the adviser can check whether the client has read and understood the contents of the report, and can be asked whether he has any **questions** to ask about it.

4.18 Affordability and accessibility

The **affordability** of any investments and protection policies to be recommended for the client must be considered. The client's prospective disposable income should be ascertained in order to assess the affordability of regular contributions to policies and investment plans. Existing assets and policies, such as life assurance contracts and other savings need to be taken into account in quantifying the sizes of investments needed to meet client needs.

4.19 Client reviews

The adviser is concerned with identifying and satisfying client needs. This is not just a 'one-off' process. Clients will have a continuing need for financial advice. Their circumstances will change, and there may need to be a review of whether products initially recommended continue to be suitable.

Regular **reviews** of client circumstances will enable the adviser to make best use of future business opportunities with that client. For the client, there are the benefits of the advice arising from the review.

4.20 Review dates

Many financial advisers conduct client reviews **annually**. This may fit well with the client's needs, if pay or bonuses are reviewed annually for example, or to fit in with the accounting cycle of a business. A review at the time of a client's birthday is another possibility: some life assurance risks are assessed in annual steps linked to the birth date.

Client reviews should not be restricted to **pre-determined review dates**. Clients' circumstances may change in unpredictable ways. An individual may be made redundant, or may start a new job. There could be a change in family health circumstances, or a new baby may be expected. These are examples of changes that could have a significant impact on financial planning, and so the client should be encouraged to seek advice and appropriate review of their circumstances, when such events occur.

Events in the financial world may produce an opportunity for the adviser to contact the client to review their effect on his or her circumstances.

- For example, **new tax rules** may be announced, or investment conditions may change, for example if there are significant movements in share prices.

- A **new tax year** can present possible **tax planning** opportunities, for example relating to ISA investments and pension contributions.

It may be most appropriate for an adviser to agree with the client that there will be an annual review date, but with the proviso that either client or adviser may make contact if an additional review is appropriate.

5 CLIENT INTERACTION

| objective | **Demonstrate** an understanding of the range of skills required when advising clients: communicate clearly, assessing and adapting to the differing capabilities of clients.

5.1 The financial adviser

The adviser must work within the scope of the activities for which their firm is **authorised** or for which they are individually **approved**. The adviser needs to be aware of the extent of their own **professional competence** and not attempt to work outside this, or beyond the **job description** laid out by their firm.

5.2 Communication techniques

Good **communication skills** are important for the financial adviser and wealth manager. Much of the information the adviser acquires is likely to be by interviewing – asking questions of – the client.

You should appreciate the difference between objective **factual information** and evaluative statements which express opinions or feelings. The latter type of statement may be expressed in terms of someone's hopes, wants or plans.

Examples of factual information

- Disregarding dividends, the Clearfield Unit Trust has grown in value by more than the FTSE 100 benchmark index over the three-year period to 31 December 2007.

- Brenda has fallen into two months' arrears on her mortgage payments.

Examples of non-factual statements

- Graham thinks that he should invest more of his portfolio in foreign stocks, in order to diversify risk.

- Matilda was disappointed by the service provided by her previous financial adviser.

Closed questions ask for a **specific** piece of **information**, for example a National Insurance number or a figure for the value of a property. Examples could be:

- Could you please tell me your address?
- Do you have any ISAs?

The answer to a closed question is typically a single word, or a short phrase, or 'Yes' or 'No'. The client may tire of having too much of this form of questioning quickly, and the questioner will not find out much about the client's views or feelings in the process.

Open questions give the client more opportunity to **express his views** or **feelings** in a **longer response**. Examples of open questions are:

- How do you feel about taking risks with your investments?
- What do you think are the most immediate financial needs to be addressed?

5.3 'Know your customer'

You will be well aware of the need to possess a lot of **information** about your client before you can give them advice. This need is reflected in one of the basic requirements of the regulatory regime: to '**know your customer**' **(KYC)**. This is one of the basic requirements of the regulatory regime as well as being part of the **fiduciary duty** of the adviser.

This includes obtaining sufficient information about a customer's personal and financial situation, before giving advice or (if applicable) before constructing a portfolio for the customer. The process of obtaining this information is not only essential in ensuring that you give suitable advice on a current issue. It can also reveal further areas where you might help your clients in the future.

A further aspect of knowing one's customer is know the **customer's capabilities**, so that one can **adapt** one's communication to suit the customer. Such adaptation should cover the extent of use of technical terminology and the extent of quantitative analysis presented to the customer. The adaptation should cover both **spoken and written communication**.

Earlier, we mentioned initiatives such as **Money Guidance**, which targets consumers generally, many of whom may have had limited if any contact with financial services firms. Firms themselves can help to widen their customer base and be more inclusive through initiatives to write **printed and website content** in plain English, and to train advisers in communicating with a range of consumers.

In **presentations** to clients, the adviser who is an effective communicator will be checking for indications that the client understands what is being said as the presentation develops, so that the adviser can explain a point again if necessary, perhaps simplifying aspects of the explanation. Checks on understanding can be made by asking open questions. Just to ask 'Do you follow what I am saying?' will not be sufficient: the less assertive client may say 'Yes' even if they do not fully understand.

5.4 Written reports to clients

Providing a **written report** to clients is an important part of the process of giving financial advice.

The **parts of a financial planning report** to a client are typically as follows.

- A statement of the client's objectives

- A summary of the client's income and assets and other relevant circumstances or problems

- Recommendations, including any proposals for immediate action as well as longer-term suggestions for the client to consider in the future

- Appendices, including any data that is best presented separately, if appropriate

Product quotations, illustrations and brochures should be presented in an orderly way, possibly with an index listing the various items being sent to the client.

The **language** in the report should be phrased as concisely as possible and, again, with explanations to suit the capabilities of the particular client while also meeting all regulatory requirements. Jargon should be avoided except where necessary to explain points being made.

When a client has agreed a set of recommendations, there will be a considerable amount of work involved in arranging investments, along with any pension arrangements and protection policies also being taken out.

5.5 Formulating a plan

The prime objective of the **comprehensive plan** is to make **recommendations** regarding the action needed to meet the client's stated and agreed objectives.

As well as **regulatory considerations,** the plan must **take account of economic conditions** which could affect the client, such as the possibility of redundancy, the prospects for a self-employed person's business and the effect of inflation.

The plan should take account of a client's **current financial position**. Is there a surplus of assets over liabilities? If so, is the surplus in a form where it can be better used?

If liabilities exceed assets then can **liabilities be rearranged**? For example, if part of the reason is an expensive loan, can the loan be repaid (provided any repayment charges are acceptable) and replaced by a more effective loan such as borrowing on the security of a with profits policy where interest rates tend to be below average?

How liquid are the client's assets? How much of the client's assets is in a form which can be turned into cash quickly, if necessary?

The client's current **tax position** is of prime importance.

The client's protection requirements will be affected not only by current needs but by **changing economic conditions**.

Full account must be taken of the **client's attitude and understanding of risk** when it comes to arranging investments. Widows with small capital sum and whose only income is the state pension should not be advised to invest in futures and options! Equally, high net worth individuals with substantial excess of income over expenditure could spread their investments in a way which provides a balanced mix of caution, medium risk and high risk.

5.6 Ethical preferences

In taking account of any **ethical preferences** affecting investment choice that a client may have, the adviser needs to bear in mind the differences between funds. As we have seen, there are many **'ethical' funds**, but these cover a range of criteria, for example between 'dark green' funds that use **negative criteria** to exclude companies to other 'lighter green' funds that use **positive criteria** to include companies that pursue positive policies on the environment or social factors. The adviser should ensure that funds chosen match the expressed concerns of the client.

CHAPTER ROUNDUP

- Given consumers' experience and perception of financial services, firms will do well to treat customers fairly, as the regulator requires, and to ensure that ethical practices prevail in their business.

- The financial planning process involves six stages: 1: Obtaining relevant information – fact finding. 2: Establishing and agreeing the client's financial objectives. 3: Processing and analysing the data obtained. 4: Formulating recommendations in a comprehensive plan with objectives. 5: Implementing the recommendations as agreed with the client. 6: Reviewing and regularly updating the plan.

- Clients' objectives may need to be prioritised and quantified, resulting in a present value analysis of anticipated future liabilities. Affordability should be assessed.

- Information on the client's current personal and financial circumstances is collected through the fact find process.

- Higher risk investments are needed to produce the potential of high returns, but also bring the chance of loss. Specific risks of investments can be diversified away, but general market risk will remain. A client's attitude to risk may be influenced by investment timescales.

- Investment management is the management of an investment portfolio on behalf of a private client or an institution.

- The objective of the fund/investors will either be to match future liabilities or to maximise returns within given risk parameters.

- There are two main types of pension scheme: defined benefits schemes, which pay a proportion of final salary at retirement; and defined contribution schemes, which pay a pension based on the amount of contributions and investment performance up to retirement.

- Life assurance and general insurance companies also invest the premiums they receive to generate returns.

- Discretionary, advisory and execution-only are different service levels offered to clients.

- The investment management process involves asset allocation, market timing and stock selection, asset allocation being the primary step since it is based on the client's objectives and fixed constraints.

- Investment managers may follow an active process of trying to outperform the market, or a passive approach of merely aiming to track the market.

- Differences in individuals' circumstances may include variability in sources of wealth (whether passively or actively acquired), amount of wealth and the current life cycle stage of the individual. The level of an individual's tolerance to risk needs to be considered by an adviser.

- Advisers should aim to employ good communication skills. The desirability of avoiding social exclusion underlines the idea that communications with consumers be adapted suit the capabilities of the consumer to which the communication is directed.

TEST YOUR KNOWLEDGE

Check your knowledge of the chapter here, without referring back to the text.

1. What does it mean to say that the adviser owes a fiduciary duty to the client?

2. Outline the six stages of the financial planning process.

3. What different types of diversification might an investor or adviser consider?

4. List the activities in the investment management process.

5. What term is used to describe the risk that index tracking funds will not follow the index?

6. What are the two different types of pension schemes?

7. Name three different types of life assurance product.

8. Distinguish discretionary and non-discretionary portfolio management, and execution only business.

9. In the context of communicating verbally with a client, give examples of closed questions and open questions.

TEST YOUR KNOWLEDGE: ANSWERS

1. An **adviser's fiduciary responsibility** implies that the adviser ought not to take advantage of a client's trust in him or her. The adviser (or firm) agrees to act in the sole interests of the client, to the exclusion of his or her own interests.

    (See Section 1.4)

2. Stages of the financial planning process

    1   Obtaining relevant information – fact finding
    2   Establishing and agreeing the client's financial objectives
    3   Processing and analysing the data collected
    4   Formulating recommendations in a comprehensive plan
    5   Implementing the agreed recommendations
    6   Reviewing and regularly updating the plan

    (See Section 2.1)

3. Diversification may be:

    - By asset class
    - Within asset classes
    - Across different fund managers

    (See Section 2.6.2)

4. Asset allocation, market timing and stock selection.

    (See Section 2.8)

5. Tracking error.

    (See Section 2.9.5)

6. Defined contribution and defined benefit schemes.

    (See Section 3.4.1)

7. Term assurance policies, whole of life policies and endowment policies.

    (See Section 3.5.1)

8. With discretionary portfolio management, the investment manager makes and implements decisions to buy and sell investments in the portfolio without asking the client each time. The non-discretionary portfolio manager provides advice to the client to assist the client in making their own investment decisions.

    Execution-only customers are those who are not given any advice by the firm when they make investment decisions. The only responsibility of the firm to such customers is to implement the customer's investment decisions at the best price available ('best execution').

    (See Section 4.7-4.8)

9. **Closed questions**:

    - Could you please tell me your address?
    - Do you have any ISAs?

Open questions:

- How do you feel about taking risks with your investments?
- What do you think are the most immediate financial needs to be addressed?

(See Section 5.2)

.

The UK Tax System

INTRODUCTION

Companies are liable to pay corporation tax on their profits. The amount varies dependent on the size of a company's profits. Individuals are liable to pay income tax on any salary, interest and dividends earned. Gains made from assets are also potentially liable to capital gains tax if they rise above the annual exceptions.

CHAPTER CONTENTS

CHAPTER LEARNING OBJECTIVES

14   The UK Tax System

Demonstrate an understanding of the UK tax system as relevant to the needs and circumstances of individuals and trusts

14.1.1 **Explain** the principles of income tax applicable to earnings, savings and investment income in the UK

14.1.2 **Explain** in relation to income tax the system of allowances, reliefs and priorities for taxing income

14.1.3 **Explain** the taxation of the income of trusts and beneficiaries

14.1.4 **Explain** the system of national insurance contributions

14.1.5 **Explain** the principles of capital gains tax in the UK

14.1.6 **Explain** the principles of inheritance tax

14.1.7 **Explain** the implications of residence and domicile in relation to liability to income, capital gains and inheritance tax

14.1.8 **Explain** the system of UK tax compliance including self assessment, Pay As You Earn (PAYE), tax returns, tax payments, tax evasion and avoidance issues

14.1.9 **Explain** the principles of stamp duty land tax (SDLT) as applied to property transactions – buying/selling and leasing

14.1.10 **Explain** the principles of stamp duty reserve tax (SDRT)

14.1.11 **Explain** how companies are taxed in the UK

14.1.12 **Explain** in outline the principles of Value Added Tax (VAT)

17   Application of personal tax planning to investment advice

Demonstrate an ability to apply the knowledge of personal taxation to the provision of investment advice

17.1.1 **To carry out computations** on the most common elements of income tax

1   INCOME TAX FOR INDIVIDUALS

1.1 Introduction

Learning objectives   **14.1.1 Explain** the principles of income tax applicable to earnings, savings and investment income in the UK.

14.1.2 Explain in relation to income tax the system of allowances, reliefs and priorities for taxing income.

14.1.7 Explain the implications of residence and domicile in relation to liability to income, capital gains and inheritance tax.

17.1.1 To carry out computations on the most common elements of income tax.

1.1.1 Who pays income tax?

Income tax is payable by all individuals and trusts (see later) **resident in the UK on their worldwide income**. Non-residents are only liable to income tax if they have a source of income derived in the UK (see later).

1.1.2 Tax years

Income tax is calculated by reference to the tax year. It runs from 6 April one year to 5 April the next year. The 2009/10 tax year is the year ending 5 April 2010.

1.2 Taxable income

1.2.1 What is taxable income?

Taxable income is virtually any income that an individual receives from whatever source.

1.2.2 Tax-free income

Some income is specifically **tax free** (free of both income tax and capital gains tax (CGT)), such as the income and/or gains from:

- **National Savings & Investments Certificates**
- **National Savings & Investments Certificate Children's Bonus bonds**
- **Individual Savings Accounts (ISAs)**
- **Child Trust Funds (CTFs)**
- **Qualifying Life Assurance Policies** in the hands of the original owner
- Save As You Earn (SAYE) schemes (interest and gains)
- Premium bond prizes
- Gambling wins, such as from the lottery
- Compensation payments of up to £30,000 when employment ends
- **Life assurance bond withdrawals** of up to 5% pa (cumulative) of the original premium, withdrawals above this level are taxable.

The items in **bold** are covered in further detail later in this Text.

1.3 Income tax liability

1.3.1 Tax rates

Different tax rates apply to different types of income so it is important to determine what income an individual has received.

The main types of income you will see in the exam are:

- Income from employment or self employment ('earnings'), and
- Savings income, including interest (eg bank interest and interest from securities – see later) and dividends.
- Investment income, including property income.

If a taxpayer receives income from a number of different sources it is taxed in the following order:

(1) Earnings and property income ('non-savings' income)
(2) Interest
(3) Dividends

1.3.2 Calculating tax

Before applying the appropriate tax rate(s), an individual can deduct the **personal allowance** from his income to arrive at his taxable income. In 2010/11, the personal allowance is £6,475. It is deducted from non-savings income first, then from savings income and lastly from dividend income (see later).

1.3.3 Income tax rates for non-savings income

There are three different rates of income tax that apply to non-savings income:

Tax rates for earnings	2010/11
20% – Basic rate	The basic rate is charged on the **first £37,400** of taxable income
40% –Higher rate	The higher rate is charged on any taxable income above **£37,400**.
50% – Additional rate	The additional rate is charged on taxable income above **£150,000**

Employment earnings are received after income tax has been deducted by the employer under the Pay As You Earn system (see later).

Self employment earnings and property income are only taxed at the end of the tax year under the self assessment system (see later).

Example

Mr Anderson is an employed electrician. In the tax year 2010/11, his total earnings were £65,000 (PAYE £15,930). Calculate Mr Anderson's tax due for the year.

Solution

	£
Total earnings	65,000
Less: personal allowance	(6,475)
Taxable income	58,525
Tax on first £37,400 @ 20%	7,480
Tax on next £21,125 @ 40%	8,450
Total tax liability	15,930
Less: tax deducted at source via PAYE	(15,930)
Tax due	Nil

1.3.4 Income tax rates for interest income

There is a starting rate of 10% for the **first £2,440 of interest** income. This **only applies** where **savings income falls below the starting rate limit**.

Remember that non-savings income is taxed first. So, in most cases, an individual's non-savings income will exceed the starting rate limit and the savings income starting rate will not be available on savings income. In this case, the individual's savings income will be charged to tax at 20% up to the basic rate limit of £37,400, 40% up to the higher rate limit of £150,000 and 50% thereafter.

Example

Sandra is a self employed hairdresser. In the tax year 2010/11 she has earnings of £50,000 and interest of £8,000. Calculate Sandra's tax due for the year.

Solution

	Earnings £	Interest £
Total earnings	50,000	
Interest £8,000 × 100/80*		10,000
Less: personal allowance	(6,475)	
Taxable income	43,525	10,000
Tax on first £37,400 @ 20%	7,480	
Tax on next £6,125 @ 40%	2,450	
Tax on £10,000 @ 40%	4,000	
Total tax liability	13,930	
Less: tax deducted at source Interest: £10,000 × 20%	(2,000)	
Total tax due	11,930	

*£8,000 is the net amount received, representing 80% of the gross amount, due to the 20% tax that is automatically deducted. Therefore the gross amount is £10,000.

1.3.5 Income tax rates for dividend income

UK dividends are treated as if received net of a deemed (or 'notional')10% tax credit so are grossed up by 100/90.

Dividends falling in the basic rate tax band are taxed at 10%. As they come with a 10% deemed tax credit, no further tax is payable on dividends for basic rate taxpayers. Dividends falling into the higher rate tax band are taxed at 32.5% and at 42.5% for additional rate taxpayers.

The 10% tax credit on dividends is deductible from the tax liability. However, since it is not a real tax credit, it cannot be repaid to the taxpayer.

Example

In the tax year 2010/11 Nikki receives earnings from employment of £50,000, interest of £8,000 and dividends of £27,000. Calculate Nikki's tax due for the year.

Solution

	Earnings £	Interest £	Dividends £
Total earnings	50,000		
Interest £8,000 × 100/80		10,000	
Dividends £27,000 × 100/90			30,000
Less: personal allowance	(6,475)		
Taxable income	43,525	10,000	30,000
Tax on first £37,400 @ 20%	7,480		
Tax on next £6,125 @ 40%	2,450		
Tax on £10,000 @40%	4,000		
Tax on £30,000 @ 32.5%	9,750		
Total tax liability	23,680		

Less: tax deducted at source	
On dividends: £30,000 × 10%	(3,000)
On interest: £10,000 × 20%	(2,000)
Total tax due	18,680

1.4 Allowances and reliefs

1.4.1 Introduction

There are various allowances and reliefs available through the UK tax system. These either reduce the amount of income that is taxable or reduce the tax liability. It is essential to distinguish between the different types.

1.4.2 Allowances

Personal allowance

Every individual (including a child) is allowed to deduct the **personal allowance of £6,475** in the tax year 2010/11 from his net income before arriving at his taxable income.

It is deducted from **non-savings income first, then from savings income and lastly from dividend income**.

If an individual's net income for 2010/11 exceeds £100,000, the personal allowance is reduced by £1 for every £2 excess income. So, an individual with net income of £112,950 in 2010/11 receives no personal allowance in 2010/11.

People aged over 65 have a higher age-rated personal allowance.

Blind person's allowance

An individual who is formally registered as blind is entitled to an additional allowance of £1,890 in 2010/11.

1.4.3 Interest payments

Certain loan interest payments can be deducted from total income. An individual who pays interest in a tax year is entitled to relief in that year if the loan is for one of the following purposes, subject to certain conditions:

- Loan to buy plant or machinery for partnership use (interest allowed for three years)
- Loan to buy plant or machinery for employment use (interest allowed for three years)
- Loan to buy interest in unquoted employee-controlled company
- Loan to invest in a partnership
- Loan to invest in a co-operative

Tax relief is given by deducting the interest from total income for the tax year in which the interest is paid. It is deducted from non-savings income first, then from savings income and lastly from dividend income.

1.4.4 Relief for gifts to charity

Payroll giving

Under the **payroll giving scheme**, employees can authorise their employer to deduct charitable donations from their gross salary before calculating tax via the Pay As You Earn system (see later), giving the employee automatic tax relief at his or her marginal (ie highest) rate of tax.

Gifts of shares and securities

If an individual makes a gift of certain shares and securities to a charity, he can deduct the market value of the shares or securities at the date of the charitable gift, again giving the employee automatic tax relief at his marginal rate of tax.

The shares must be listed on a recognised stock exchange in the UK or overseas. A gift of AIM shares can qualify.

Gift Aid

The tax calculation may be affected by cash donations to charity made under the Gift Aid scheme.

All cash donations are treated as being paid net, ie after deduction of income tax at the basic rate (20%). So, a net donation of £800 is worth £1,000 (£800 × 100/80) as the charity can claim £200 (20% × £1,000) from Her Majesty's Revenue & Customs (HMRC).

If the donor is a higher or additional rate taxpayer, their basic rate band is increased by an amount equal to the gross amount of the gift (£1,000 in our example). This means that an additional £1,000 of income is taxed at the basic rate instead of the higher or additional tax rate providing additional relief.

1.4.5 Pension contributions

Contributions to occupational pension schemes

Within certain limits (see later), an individual's contributions to his employer's pension scheme can be deducted from his earnings from that employment. This provides tax relief at the individual's highest rate.

Personal pension contributions

Within the same limits as mentioned above, an individual's contributions to a personal pension scheme may affect his tax rate if he is a higher or additional rate taxpayer. Relief is given in broadly the same way as for cash gift aid donations (see later).

1.4.6 Tax reductions

Tax reductions do not affect income, they reduce the amount of tax calculated on income.

The tax reductions, which are both covered in more detail later in this Text, are:

(a)   Investments in **venture capital trusts (VCTs)** and
(b)   Investments under the **enterprise investment scheme**.

Investments in the above companies may qualify for a tax reduction of up to the lower of:

(a)   A percentage of the amount subscribed for qualifying investments, and
(b)   The individual's tax liability.

For investments in VCTs, the percentage is 30% for 2010/11. For investments under the EIS, the percentage is 20%. Further details are given later in this Text.

A tax reduction can only reduce an individual's tax liability to zero. It cannot create a repayment.

If an individual is entitled to both tax reductions, the VCT reducer is deducted first.

1.5 Overseas aspects of income tax

1.5.1 Residence

A taxpayer's residence and domicile have important consequences for determining the UK tax treatment of his income.

Generally, a **UK resident is liable to UK income tax on his worldwide (ie UK and overseas) income as it arises (arising basis)**.

A **non-UK resident is liable to UK income tax only on income arising in the UK**.

1.5.2 Domicile

An individual who is UK resident but not UK domiciled may claim to be taxed on overseas income on the remittance basis (unless it applies automatically in certain circumstances).

This means that he is only liable to UK income tax on overseas income only to the extent that it is brought in (remitted) to the UK.

1.5.3 Remittance basis

Where the remittance basis applies, the income is taxed in the same way as earnings, ie at 20% in the basic rate band, 40% in the higher rate band and 50% for additional rate taxpayers, even if it is dividends.

If an individual:

- **Claims the remittance basis for the tax year,** and
- **Is aged 18 or over in the tax year, and**
- **Has been UK resident for at least seven of the nine tax years preceding that tax year,**

then he must pay an **additional £30,000 remittance basis charge in order to be able to use the remittance basis**.

2 NATIONAL INSURANCE CONTRIBUTIONS

2.1 Introduction

2.1.1 Who pays National Insurance Contributions (NICs)?

National insurance contributions are payable by employees and their employers and also by self employed individuals.

2.1.2 Scope of NICs

The main classes of NICs are:

- **Class 1**. This is divided into:
    - **Primary**, paid by employees
    - **Secondary**, paid by employers
- **Class 2**. Paid by the self-employed
- **Class 4**. Paid by the self-employed

2.2 Class 1 for employed persons

2.2.1 Class 1 NICs

Both employees and employers pay NICs related to the employee's earnings.

Employees pay main primary contributions of 11% of earnings between the earnings threshold of £5,715 and the upper earnings limit of £43,875 or the equivalent monthly or weekly limit. They also pay additional primary contributions of 1% on earnings above the upper earnings limit.

Employers pay secondary contributions of 12.8% on earnings above the earnings threshold of £5,715 or the equivalent monthly or weekly limit. There is no upper limit.

Example

Brian works for Red plc. He is paid £4,000 per month. What are Brian's primary contributions and the secondary contributions paid by Red plc for 2010/11?

Solution

Earnings threshold £5,715
Upper earnings limit £43,875
Annual salary £4,000 × 12 = £48,000

	£
Brian	
Primary contributions	
£(43,875 − 5,715) = £38,160 × 11% (main)	4,198
£(48,000 − 43,875) = £4,125 × 1% (additional)	41
Total primary contributions	4,239
Red plc	
Secondary contributions	
£(48,000 − 5,715) = £42,285 × 12.8%	5,412

2.3 Class 2 and Class 4 NICs for self-employed persons

2.3.1 Introduction

The self employed pay two Classes of NICs: Class 2 and Class 4.

2.3.2 Class 2 NICs

Class 2 contributions are payable at a flat rate. **The Class 2 rate for 2010/11 is £2.40 a week.** Contributions are usually paid by direct debit.

2.3.3 Class 4 NICs

Additionally, **the self employed pay Class 4 NICs,** based on the level of their taxable business profits.

Main rate Class 4 NICs are calculated by applying a fixed percentage (8% for 2010/11) to the individual's profits between the lower limit (£5,715) and the upper limit (£43,875). Additional rate contributions are 1% on profits above that limit.

Example

Dennis's self employment profits are £46,000. How much are his Class 4 NICs?

Solution

	£
Upper limit	43,875
Less lower limit	(5,715)
	38,160
Main rate Class 4 NICs 8% × £38,160	3,053
Additional rate Class 4 NICs £(46,000 − 43,875) = £2,125 × 1%	21
	3,074

Class 4 NICs are paid at the same time as the associated income tax liability (see later).

3 CAPITAL GAINS TAX

3.1 Introduction

14.1.5 Explain the principles of capital gains tax in the UK.

14.1.7 Explain the implications of residence and domicile in relation to liability to capital gains tax.

17.1.1 To carry out computations on the most common elements of CGT.

3.1.1 Who pays capital gains tax?

Capital gains tax (CGT) is payable by **chargeable persons** on the **chargeable disposal** of a **chargeable asset**. A chargeable person is one who is **resident or ordinarily resident** in the UK.

3.1.2 Chargeable persons

Chargeable persons include:

- Individuals
- Companies (see later)
- Trusts (see later).

3.1.3 Chargeable assets

Virtually all assets are chargeable assets, wherever in the world they are situated, except for certain exempt assets.

The **key exempt assets** to be aware of are the following:

- Private cars

- National Savings & Investments certificates and premium bonds

- Investments held in ISAs

- Foreign currency for private use, eg used for holidays or homes abroad

- An individual's **principal private residence**, ie his main home.

- **Gilts** (treasury stock).

- **Qualifying corporate bonds (QCBs)**, ie non-convertible debt instruments (debentures) issued by companies and denominated in sterling.

- Enterprise Investment Scheme investments held for three years

Chargeable assets include such items as foreign currency, shares and other investments.

If an asset is an exempt asset any gain is not chargeable and any loss is not allowable.

3.1.4 Chargeable disposals

A **chargeable disposal** occurs when an asset is sold (in whole or in part), is given away or is received as a result of a liquidation of a company. When an individual dies, the assets disposed of as a result, through inheritance, etc, are not subject to CGT. Unfortunately, this does not mean tax is avoided – the government just charges inheritance tax instead!

The disposal can occur either in the UK or overseas, but is only treated as subject to CGT when made by a UK resident.

Disposals to spouses or civil partners are tax neutral for CGT purposes (ie there is no gain and no loss).

3.2 Overseas aspects of CGT

3.2.1 General principles

Individuals are liable to CGT on the disposal of assets situated anywhere in the world if for any part of the tax year in which the disposal occurs they are resident in the UK.

Non-UK residents are not chargeable to UK CGT unless they are carrying on a trade or profession in the UK.

3.2.2 Domicile

If a person is UK resident but is not UK domiciled, they may be able to use the remittance basis of taxation usually by making a claim. If the remittance basis applies, the individual's gains on the disposal of assets located overseas (see below) are only chargeable to CGT when the gains are remitted to the UK.

If a non-UK domiciled individual over the age of 18 makes a claim to use the remittance basis (ie it does not apply automatically) and he has been UK resident for seven out of the previous nine tax years, he must pay an additional tax charge of £30,000.

3.3 Calculation of Capital Gains and Losses

3.3.1 The basic computation

The calculation of a capital gain on the disposal of an asset in a tax year can be illustrated as follows:

	£
Disposal value (say)	10,000
less: assumed allowable deductions	(3,000)
Capital gain	7,000

If allowable deductions exceed the disposal value, a capital loss will arise.

The disposal value will typically be the **sale proceeds**. The allowable deductions will be the purchase price and other relevant costs of acquisition and disposal such as stamp duty land tax paid on purchase (see later), legal fees and estate agency commission.

3.3.2 The annual exempt amount

An individual pays capital gains tax (CGT) on his net chargeable gains (his gains minus his losses) for a tax year, less unrelieved losses brought forward from previous years and the annual exempt amount.

There is an **annual exempt amount** for each tax year. In 2010/11 it is £10,100.

It is the last deduction to be made in the calculation of taxable gain.

Trustees (see below) are only entitled to half of the individual's annual exempt amount, ie £5,050 for 2010/11.

3.3.3 Capital losses

Allowable losses of the same year

Capital losses in a tax year are deducted from capital gains arising in the same tax year to come to a net overall position for the year. Only then is the annual exempt amount deducted.

Any loss which cannot be set off is carried forward to set against future gains. Losses must be used as soon as possible (but see below).

Allowable losses brought forward

Allowable losses brought forward are only set off to reduce current year gains less current year allowable losses to the annual exempt amount. No set-off is made if net chargeable gains for the current year do not exceed the annual exempt amount.

Example

George has gains for 2010/11 of £11,000 and allowable losses of £6,000. What is his net CGT position for 2010/11?

Solution

As the losses are current year losses they must be fully relieved against the £11,000 of gains to produce net gains of £5,000 despite the fact that net gains are below the annual exempt amount.

Example

Bob has gains of £14,000 for 2010/11 and allowable losses brought forward of £6,000. What is his net CGT position for 2010/11?

Solution

Bob restricts his loss relief to £3,900 so as to leave net gains of £(14,000 − 3,900) = £10,100, which will be exactly covered by his annual exempt amount for 2010/11. The remaining £2,100 of losses will be carried forward to 2011/12.

Example

Tom has gains of £10,000 for 2010/11 and losses brought forward of £4,000. What is his net CGT position for 2010/11?

Solution

He will leapfrog 2010/11 and carry forward all of his losses to 2011/12. His gains of £10,000 are covered by his annual exemption for 2010/11.

3.3.4 Tax rate

A flat rate of 18% applies to capital gains in excess of the annual exempt amount for basic rate taxpayers. Higher rate taxpayers are subject to a flat rate of 28% for that tax year.

3.3.5 Entrepreneurs' relief

Entrepreneurs relief is available to reduce the tax rate on the first £2m of chargeable gains (£1m in 2009/10) from 18% to 10%.

The relief applies to gains arising on the disposal of:

- The whole or part of a trading business
- Assets used in a business that has ceased
- Shares in a trading company where the individual held 5% or more of the voting shares
- Assets used in a partnership
- Certain disposals by trustees.

The actual mechanics applied to achieve this 10% rate is to reduce the eligible gains by a factor of 4/9 leaving 5/9ths chargeable and applying the 18% rate to this reduced figure (5/9 × 18% = 10%).

Example

In the 2010/11 tax year, Mr Barnes makes capital gains of £20,200, which are not eligible for entrepreneurs' relief, and capital losses of £1,000. What amount of CGT should he pay?

Solution

	£
Capital gains	20,200
Capital losses	(1,000)
Net capital gains	19,200
Annual exempt amount	(10,100)
Amount chargeable to CGT	9,100

Since the gain does not attract entrepreneur's relief, CGT will be due on the £9,100 at a rate of 18%, ie £1,638.

4 INHERITANCE TAX AND TRUSTS

14.1.6 Explain the principles of inheritance tax.

14.1.7 Explain the implications of residence and domicile in relation to liability to inheritance tax.

14.1.3 Explain the taxation of the income of trusts and beneficiaries.

17.1.1 To carry out computations on the most common elements of IHT including the impact of lifetime transfers and transfers at death

4.1 Introduction to inheritance tax

IHT is a tax on gifts, or **'transfers of value'**, made by **chargeable persons**. This generally involves a transaction as a result of which wealth is transferred by one person to another, either directly or via a trust.

IHT is primarily a tax on **wealth left on death**. It also applies to **gifts within seven years of death** and to certain **lifetime transfers of wealth to trusts**.

4.2 Basic principles

For income tax and CGT we asked the basic question: how much money has the taxpayer made?

For IHT, we generally need to ask: how much has he given away?

We tax the amount which the taxpayer has transferred (the 'transfer of value') – the amount by which he is worse off.

4.3 Scope of IHT

IHT applies to:

- **Lifetime gifts to trusts (see below)**
- **Gifts on death (usually in someone's will), and**
- **Lifetime gifts if the person making the gift (the 'donor') dies within seven years of making that gift.**

All UK domiciled individuals are liable to inheritance tax (IHT) on their worldwide assets. For individuals who are not domiciled in the UK, only transfers of UK assets are liable to IHT. UK assets are broadly assets located in the UK.

4.4 Lifetime gifts

A **potentially exempt transfer (PET)** is a **lifetime gift made by an individual to another individual**.

A PET is exempt from IHT when made, and will remain so if the donor survives for at least seven years from making the gift. If he dies within seven years of making the gift, it will become chargeable to IHT.

Any other lifetime transfer by an individual (eg gift to a trust) not covered by an exemption (see below) is a **chargeable lifetime transfer (CLT)**.

4.5 Exemptions

4.5.1 Introduction

Various exemptions are available to eliminate or reduce the chargeable amount of a lifetime transfer or property passing on an individual's death.

- Some exemptions apply *only* to lifetime transfers
- Other exemptions apply to both lifetime gifts and property passing on death, including those for gifts between spouses and civil partners

4.5.2 Exemptions applying to lifetime transfers only (including PETs)

Small gifts exemption

Outright gifts to individuals totalling £250 or less per donee in any one tax year are exempt. If gifts are more than £250 the whole amount is chargeable. A donor can give up to £250 each year to each of as many donees as he wishes. The small gifts exemption cannot apply to gifts into **trusts**.

Annual exemption

The first £3,000 of value transferred in a tax year is exempt from IHT. The annual exemption is used only after all other exemptions (such as for transfers to spouses/civil partners – see below). If several gifts are made in a year, the £3,000 exemption is applied to earlier gifts before later gifts. The annual exemption is used up by PETs as well as CLTs, even though the PETs might never become chargeable.

Any **unused portion of the annual exemption** is **carried forward for one year** only. Only use it in the following year after that year's annual exemption has been used.

Normal expenditure out of income

IHT is a tax on **transfers of capital**, not on **gifts of income.** So the gift is exempt if it is:

(a)   Made as part of the donor's normal expenditure
(b)   Out of income, and
(c)   Leaves the transferor with sufficient income to maintain his usual standard of living

This exemption mainly covers such gifts as paying grandchildren's school fees.

Wedding gifts

Wedding gifts (and gifts made on the occasion of a same sex civil partnership ceremony) are exempt up to:

(a)   £5,000, if from a parent of a party to the marriage or civil partnership
(b)   £2,500, if from a grandparent of one of the parties to the marriage or civil partnership
(c)   £1,000, if from any other person.

The limits apply to gifts from any one donor per marriage or civil partnership.

4.5.3 Exemptions applying to both lifetime transfers and transfers on death

Gifts to charity

Gifts to UK charities are exempt from IHT.

Gifts between spouses/civil partners are exempt if the donee is domiciled in the UK. The exemption covers lifetime gifts between them and property passing on death.

If the donor is UK domiciled but the donee is not UK domiciled, the exemption is limited to £55,000 in total. Any lifetime gift over £55,000 will be a PET.

If neither spouse/civil partner is domiciled in the UK there is no limit on the exemption.

A claim can also be made to transfer any unused nil rate band (see later) from one spouse/civil partner to the surviving spouse/civil partner.

4.6 Lifetime IHT

After all available exemptions have been applied, the first £325,000 of a CLT is taxed at 0% (the **nil rate band**), and is therefore effectively tax free.

To stop people from avoiding IHT by, for example, giving away £1,625,000 in five lots of £325,000, the IHT rules look back seven years every time a transfer is made to decide how much of the nil rate band is available to set against the current transfer.

Any excess over the available nil rate band is taxable at 20%.

Example

Eric makes a gift of £336,000 to a trust on 10 July 2010. He has not used his annual exemption in 2010/11 nor in 2009/10. The trustees agree to pay the tax due.

Eric made a gift of £100,000 in June 2008.

Calculate the lifetime tax payable by the trustees.

Solution

	£	£
Gift		336,000
Less AE 2010/11 & 2009/10 b/f		(6,000)
CLT		330,000
Nil rate band	325,000	
Less: gifts in previous 7 yrs	(100,000)	
Less: available nil rate band		(225,000)
		105,000
IHT @ 20%		21,000

The amount of this gift that uses up the nil rate band in the future would be £330,000.

If the taxpayer pays the IHT on the gift, his wealth has reduced by both the amount of the gift and the tax. The gift is therefore a net gift and must be grossed up to find the gross value of the transfer. **We do this by working out the tax as follows:**

Chargeable amount (ie not covered by nil rate band) $\times \dfrac{20\,(\text{rate of tax})}{80\,(100\,\text{minus the rate of tax})}$

Example

If Eric, in the above example, paid the tax on the gift of £336,000 on 10 July 2010 what would be the tax due?

Solution

	£	£
Gift		336,000
Less AE 2010/11 & 2009/10 b/f		(6,000)
CLT		330,000
Nil rate band	325,000	
Less: gifts in previous 7 yrs	(100,000)	
Less: available nil rate band		(225,000)
		105,000
IHT @ 20/80		26,250

The gross gift that uses up the nil rate band in the future is: £330,000 + £26,250 = £356,250.

4.7 Death tax on lifetime transfers

Although PETs are exempt from IHT when they are made, if the donor dies within seven years of making the gift it will become chargeable to IHT.

In addition, if a donor dies within seven years of making a CLT, additional IHT may become due on the gross gift amount. In this case, any lifetime tax already paid can be deducted.

Gross gifts in the seven years before the original gift use up the nil rate band. On death, therefore, you need to look back for up to 14 years to work out how much nil rate band is left.

The rate of IHT on death is 40%. However, the longer the transferor survives after making the gift, the lower the rate applied. This is because a **taper relief** applies to lower the amount of death tax payable as follows:

Years between transfer and death	% reduction in death tax	Effective IHT rate
3 years or less	0	40%
More than 3 but less than 4	20	32%
More than 4 but less than 5	40	24%
More than 5 but less than 6	60	16%
More than 6 but less than 7	80	8%

IHT on a lifetime transfer on death is payable by the **transferee**.

Example

If Eric, in the above example (gross gift of £356,250), dies on 10 August 2010, how much additional IHT would be due?

Solution

	£	£
Gross gift		356,250
Nil rate band	325,000	
Less: gifts in 7 yrs before the gift	(100,000)	
Less: available nil rate band		(225,000)
		105,000
IHT @ 40% (no taper relief as dies within 3 years)		42,000
Less: lifetime tax		(26,250)
IHT due		15,750

Example

If Eric, above, dies instead on 10 August 2014, how much additional IHT would be due?

Solution

	£	£
Gross gift		356,250
Nil rate band	325,000	
Less: gifts in 7 yrs before the gift	(100,000)	
Less: available nil rate band		(225,000)
		105,000
IHT @ 24% (taper relief at 40% as dies 4 – 5 years after making gift)		25,200
Less: lifetime tax		(26,250)
IHT due		Nil

Note that there is no repayment of lifetime tax paid.

4.8 Introduction to Trusts

4.8.1 Terminology

A trust is an arrangement under which a person, the 'settlor', transfers property to another person, the 'trustee' or trustees, who is required to deal with the trust property on behalf of certain specified persons, the 'beneficiaries'.

4.8.2 Types of trusts

A trust may be either:

- An **interest in possession (IIP) trust**, where the beneficiaries are automatically entitled to receive all of the income of the trust as it arises, or

- A **discretionary trust**, where the trustees can determine which beneficiaries to make payments to and how much they will receive.

Although both trusts are treated the same for IHT purposes, it is essential to recognise the type of trust the income tax treatment is very different for each.

You are likely only to have to deal with the taxation of savings and investment income of a trust.

4.8.3 Income tax for IIP trusts

IIP trustees' tax position

- Interest income is taxed at **20%**
- **Dividends** are taxed at **10%**.

Interest is usually received net of a 20% tax credit by the trust (as it is by an individual). Dividends are received with a 10% notional tax credit. As both of these tax credits satisfy the trustees' liability for these types of income, no further tax is due from the trustees.

IIP beneficiary's tax position

The IIP beneficiary (sometimes called the 'life tenant') is entitled to receive the trust income once the trustees have paid the tax due.

The beneficiary will receive a statement of income from the trust showing the amounts they are entitled to receive along with the associated tax credit (ie the tax paid by the trustees). They will then include these amounts in their own tax calculation.

The income paid to the beneficiary retains its nature so if it is interest income in the trustees' hands it will be taxed as interest income on the beneficiary and so on.

Example

An interest in possession trust receives net bank interest of £1,600 and dividends of £900 net in 2010/11. There is one life tenant who is a higher rate taxpayer. What is the trust's and the beneficiary's tax position?

Solution

Trustees' income tax position	£	£
Interest £1,600 × 100/80	2,000	
Dividends £900 × 100/90		1,000
Total income	2,000	1,000
Tax @ 20%/ 10%	400	100
Less: tax credits		
On interest	(400)	
On dividends £1,000 × 10%		(100)
Tax due	Nil	Nil
The trust can distribute the after tax income:	1,600	900

Beneficiary's income tax position	£	£
Interest £1,600 × 100/80	2,000	
Dividends £900 × 100/90		1,000
Total income	2,000	1,000
Tax @ 40%/ 32.5%	800	325
Less: tax paid by trustees	(400)	(100)
Tax due from beneficiary	400	225

4.8.4 Income tax for discretionary trusts

Discretionary trustees' tax position

Discretionary trusts have a standard, or basic rate, band of £1,000. The first £1,000 of income is taxed at the basic rates, ie at 10% (dividends), 20% (interest income). As for individuals, the basic rate band is applied first to non savings income, then savings income and finally dividends. Many smaller trusts will have no further tax to pay.

Any remaining income is taxed at the rates that apply to additional rate taxpaying individuals:

- Interest income is taxed at **50%** (the 'trust rate')
- **Dividends** are taxed at **42.5%** (the 'trust dividend rate').

Discretionary beneficiary's tax position

Beneficiaries of discretionary trusts are only taxed if they receive income payments from the trust.

Any payments of income to beneficiaries are made net of tax at 50% and are taxed on them at the rates that apply to earnings income. The trustees will again provide a statement of income to the beneficiaries showing the relevant figures.

If the trustees have not paid sufficient tax to cover this tax credit, they must make an additional payment. Beneficiaries who are basic or higher rate taxpayers may obtain repayments. Additional rate taxpaying beneficiaries will have no further tax liability.

Example

A discretionary trust receives net bank interest of £1,600 and dividends of £900 net in 2010/11. The trustees make a payment of £500 to one of the beneficiaries who is a higher rate taxpayer. What is the trust's and the beneficiary's tax position?

Solution

Trustees' income tax position	£	£
Interest £1,600 × 100/80	2,000	
Dividends £900 × 100/90	____	1,000
Total income	2,000	1,000
£1,000 @ 20% (interest income in the basic rate band)	200	
£1,000 @ 50% (interest income at the trust rate)	500	
£1,000 @ 42.5% (dividend income at the trust dividend rate)	425	
	1,125	
Less: tax credits		
On dividends £1,000 × 10%	(100)	
On interest	(400)	
Tax due	625	

Beneficiary's income tax position	£	£
Payment £500 × 100/50	1,000	
Tax @ 40%	400	
Less: tax paid by trustees	(500)	
Tax rebate due to beneficiary	100	

5 UK Tax Compliance

objective **14.1.8 Explain** the system of UK tax compliance including self assessment, Pay As You Earn (PAYE), tax returns, tax payments, tax evasion and avoidance issues.

5.1 Introduction

In earlier sections we have explored the principles of income tax, capital gains tax and national insurance.

In this chapter we see how individuals and trusts must 'self assess' their tax liability. We also look at the Pay As You Earn system for individuals in employment and also consider the difference between tax avoidance and tax evasion.

In the remaining sections we will consider the remaining taxes within the syllabus: stamp taxes, corporation tax and VAT.

5.2 Self assessment

5.2.1 General principles

The self assessment system relies upon the taxpayer completing and filing a tax return and paying the tax due on time.

Many taxpayers have very simple affairs: an individual receiving a salary under deduction of tax through Pay as You Earn (PAYE) or an IIP trustee receiving only interest. These individuals and trustees will not normally have to complete a tax return. Self-employed taxpayers and trustees with more complicated affairs will have to complete a self assessment tax return.

5.2.2 Tax returns

Individuals who are chargeable to income tax or CGT for any tax year and who have not received a notice to file a return must notify HMRC that they are chargeable within six months from the end of the year, ie by 5 October 2011 for 2010/11. HMRC will then send them a multi-page tax return to complete.

The latest filing date for a self assessment tax return for a tax year (Year 1) is:

- **31 October in the next tax year (Year 2), for a non-electronic return (ie a paper return).**
- **31 January in Year 2, for an electronic return (ie sent to HMRC via the internet).**

If the taxpayer is filing a **paper return, he may make the tax calculation on his return or ask HMRC to do so on his behalf**.

If the taxpayer wishes HMRC to make the calculation for Year 1, a paper return must be filed on or before 31 October in Year 2.

If the taxpayer is filing an **electronic return, the calculation of tax liability is made automatically when the return is made online**.

There are penalties for late returns.

5.2.3 Payment of tax

The self-assessment system may result in the taxpayer making three payments of income tax and Class 4 NICs.

Date	Payment
31 January in the tax year	1st payment on account
31 July after the tax year	2nd payment on account
31 January after the tax year	Final payment to settle the remaining liability

Payments on account are usually required where the income tax and Class 4 NICs due in the previous year exceeded the amount of income tax deducted at source; this excess is known as **'the relevant amount'**. Income tax deducted at source includes tax suffered (eg 20% on interest income), PAYE deductions and tax credits on dividends.

The payments on account are each equal to 50% of the relevant amount for the previous year.

Payments on account of CGT are never required.

Payments on account are not required if the relevant amount falls below a de minimis limit of £1,000. Also, payments on account are not required from taxpayers who paid 80% or more of their tax liability for the previous year through PAYE or other deduction at source arrangements.

The balance of any income tax and Class 4 NICs together with all CGT due for a year, is normally payable on or before the 31 January following the year.

5.2.4 Late payment of tax

If tax is paid late, interest is chargeable from the due date until the day before the actual date of payment.

If the tax is still unpaid at 30 days, six months and twelve months there are **penalties** of 5% of the unpaid tax at these dates.

5.3 Pay As You Earn (PAYE)

5.3.1 General principles

PAYE is the method by which **income tax and national insurance contributions are deducted from the earnings of employees**.

5.3.2 Payment of PAYE

Employers are **required to pay PAYE and NIC deductions** made on paydays falling between 5th of a calendar month and the 6th of the next calendar month to HMRC **within 14 days of the end of the tax month**. For example, PAYE deducted on 26 September 2010 payday must be paid by 19 October 2010.

If **payments are made electronically** the payment **date is extended by three days,** ie to 22 October 2010 in this example.

PAYE end of year reporting

After the end of each tax year, the employer must provide each employee with a **form P60.** This shows total taxable earnings for the year, tax deducted, tax code, NI number and the employer's name and address. The P60 must be provided by **31 May** following the tax year so that the employee can complete his self assessment tax return on time.

5.4 Tax avoidance and evasion

Tax avoidance is a valid way for a taxpayer to use existing tax rules to his advantage so that he does not pay more than is legally due.

Tax evasion, on the other hand, is illegal and includes, for example, a taxpayer not reporting all of his income on his tax return to reduce his tax liability.

These concepts are discussed further later in this text.

6 STAMP TAXES

14.1.9 Explain the principles of stamp duty land tax (SDLT) as applied to property transactions - buying /selling and leasing.

14.1.10 Explain the principles of stamp duty reserve tax (SDRT).

6.1 Stamp Duty Land Tax (SDLT)

6.1.1 Basic principles

Stamp duty land tax (SDLT) applies to land transactions. A land transaction is a transfer of land or an interest in, or right over, land.

SDLT is generally payable as a percentage of the consideration paid for the land. It is payable by the purchaser.

6.1.2 SDLT rates

The amount of the charge to SDLT depends on whether the land is residential or non-residential and whether or not it is in a designated disadvantaged area. The following rates apply:

Rate (%)	All land in the UK		Land in disadvantaged areas	
	Residential	**Non-residential**	**Residential**	**Non-residential**
Zero	£0 – £125,000[1][2]	£0 – £150,000[3]	£0 – £125,000[1][2]	£0 – £150,000[3]
1	£125,001[1][2] – £250,000	£150,001 – £250,000	£125,001[1][2] – £250,000	£150,001 – £250,000
3	£250,001 – £500,000	£250,001 – £500,000	£250,001 – £500,000	£250,001 – £500,000
4	Over £500,000	Over £500,000	Over £500,000	Over £500,000

Notes　(1)　A higher threshold of £250,000 applies to purchases by first time buyer completed between 25.3.10 and 24.3.12.

(2)　A higher threshold of £150,000 applies to transactions in residential land in disadvantaged areas.

(3)　For non-residential property, where the transaction involves a grant of a lease, the zero rate band is not available if annual rent exceeds £1,000.

6.1.3 New leases - SDLT on lease rentals

Rate (%)	Net present value (NPV) of rent	
	Residential	**Non-residential**
Zero	£0 – £125,000*	£0 - £150,000
1%	Over £125,000*	Over £150,000

SDLT on the net present value (NPV) of the rent is payable in addition to SDLT on any lease premium.

The rate applies to the amount of NPV in the slice, not to the whole value.

6.2 Stamp Duty Reserve Tax (SDRT)

6.2.1 Basic principles

Stamp Duty Reserve Tax (SDRT) is a tax on electronic (ie paperless) share transactions. It is also payable on electronic purchases of units in unit trusts or shares in open-ended investment companies (see later).

6.2.2 SDRT rates

SDRT is payable by the purchaser at a flat rate of 0.5% based on the amount paid for the shares.

For example, if an individual buys shares for £1,000, they must pay SDRT of £5.

7 CORPORATION TAX

Learning objective	**14.1.11 Explain** how companies are taxed in the UK.

7.1 Who pays corporation tax?

Companies must pay corporation tax on their **total income and gains** for each **accounting period.**

An **accounting period** is the period for which corporation tax is charged and cannot exceed 12 months.

An accounting period is based on the company's **period of account**, which is the period for which it prepares its financial accounts. Usually this will be 12 months in length but it may be longer or shorter than this. If it is longer, the period of account must be split into two accounting periods. The first accounting period is always twelve months in length.

7.2 Taxable profits

7.2.1 General principles

Corporation tax is self-assessed by the company and is calculated as a percentage of the taxable profits of the company.

The taxable profits are based on the profit before tax figure in the company's annual financial accounts. There is quite a bit of scope for a company to manipulate this profit, for example by using particular depreciation rates (see below) for assets. For this reason, tax legislation requires that a number of adjustments be made to this profit figure.

7.2.2 Trading profit

Disallowed expenses

Certain expenses that are deducted from profits in the financial accounts cannot be deducted for tax purposes. Examples include **client or supplier entertainment expenditure** and provisions for **uncertain debts** (although **bad debts** are allowed).

Capital allowances and depreciation

Depreciation charged by a company in its financial accounts is not allowable expenditure for tax purposes, since the company determines the depreciation rates. However, the company can deduct **capital allowances** instead. This is essentially tax terminology for tax depreciation, but calculated by reference to special rules in the tax legislation.

7.2.3 Interest

Companies receive interest gross, ie without deduction of 20% tax at source. As interest is investment income and not trading income, it **must be deducted from the profit before tax** shown in the accounts when calculating taxable profits. It is then added to the rest of the company's income and gains to arrive at total profits.

Interest paid by a company, for example on debentures (see later), **is deductible for tax purposes** and does not usually have to be adjusted for.

7.2.4 Dividends

Dividends received by a company from another company are tax free and do not form part of the company's taxable profits.

Although dividend income is exempt from corporation tax, the gross dividend (ie the dividend received plus the 10% notional tax credit) is added to the company's total profits to arrive at the augmented profits, which determine the rate of corporation tax that it must pay (see below).

However, it is only the total profits are actually taxed.

7.2.5 Capital gains

Capital gains made by a company on the disposal of its fixed assets are chargeable to corporation tax and not to capital gains tax. Only individuals pay capital gains tax.

A company's chargeable gains are calculated in a similar way as an individual's gains are calculated, but with an additional deduction to strip out the effect of inflation on the value of the asset.

Illustration: Computation of taxable profits

	£	£
Profit before tax from the financial accounts		300,000
Add back: expenditure not allowable for tax purposes		
Entertainment expenses	30,000	
Provisions for doubtful debts	3,000	
Depreciation	10,000	
		43,000
Less: income included but exempt/ not taxable as trading profits		
– Dividends from UK companies		(9,000)
– Interest receivable		(10,000)
Less:		
– Capital allowances		(12,000)
Trading profits		312,000
Add: income included but not taxable as trading profits		
– Interest		10,000
Total profits		322,000
Add: gross dividends		10,000
Augmented profits		332,000

7.3 Corporation tax rates

The rates of corporation tax are fixed for financial years

A financial year runs from 1 April to the following 31 March and is identified by the calendar year in which it begins.

For example, the year from 1 April 2010 to 31 March 2011 is the Financial year 2010 (FY 2010). This should not be confused with a tax year, which (as we saw earlier) runs from 6 April to the following 5 April.

Current UK Corporation Tax Rates
The **main rate** is 28%.
The **small profits rate** is 21%.

The **main rate** of corporation tax of 28% is payable by companies with 'augmented' profits (ie total profits plus gross dividends) of **£1,500,000 or more** in their chargeable accounting period.

The **small profits rate** of 21% is payable by companies with profits of **less than £300,000** in their chargeable accounting period.

Companies whose profits lie between £300,000 and £1,500,000 pay a rate that effectively lies between 21% and 28%. This is achieved by the form of marginal relief, where profits between £300,000 and £1,500,000 are taxable at **29.75%.** So, the full 28% is only paid once profits reach £1,500,000.Remember, these rates are applied to the company's **total profits**.

7.4 Corporation tax losses

If a company suffers a trading loss, it can set this off against any other income and gains in the year (say from investments).

If it is still showing a loss for the year then clearly there will be no tax charge for that year. In this case the company can make a claim to carry these losses back against the profits of the prior year (but usually just the prior year) in order to obtain tax relief and thus generate a tax repayment.

If the company does not make a claim to carry the losses back, it can carry them forward indefinitely and offset them against future profits **from the same trade**.

8   VALUE ADDED TAX (VAT)

Learning objective   **14.1.12 Explain** in outline the principles of value Added Tax (VAT).

8.1 The scope of VAT

VAT is a tax on turnover, not on profits.

The basic principle is that VAT should be borne by the final consumer. VAT-registered traders may deduct the tax which they suffer on supplies to them (input tax) from the tax which they charge to their customers (output tax) at the time this is paid to HMRC.

So, at each stage of the manufacturing or service process, the net VAT paid is on the value added at that stage.

The burden is borne by the final consumer.

8.2 Rates of VAT

VAT is charged on taxable supplies. A taxable supply is a supply of goods or services other than an exempt supply.

A taxable supply can either be standard rated or zero rated. The standard rate is 17.5%.

Certain supplies, which fall within the classification of standard rate supplies, are charged at a reduced rate of 5%. An example is the supply of domestic fuel.

Zero-rated supplies are taxable at 0%. An example is the supply of books. A taxable supplier whose outputs are zero-rated but whose inputs are standard-rated will obtain repayments of the VAT paid on purchases.

An exempt supply is not chargeable to VAT. An example is the supply of financial services or insurance. **A person making exempt supplies is unable to recover VAT on inputs**. The exempt supplier thus has to shoulder the burden of VAT. Of course, he may increase his prices to pass on the charge, but he cannot issue a VAT invoice which would enable a taxable customer to obtain a credit for VAT, since no VAT is chargeable on his supplies.

8.3 VAT registration and deregistration

8.3.1 Registration

A trader becomes liable to register for VAT if:

- The value of **taxable supplies in any 12 month period exceeds £70,000** (the historical test) or
- If there are reasonable grounds for believing that the value of the **taxable supplies will exceed £70,000 in the next 30 days** (the future test).

A trader may also register **voluntarily**, for example to give the impression of a substantial business.

8.3.2 Deregistration

A trader may deregister voluntarily if he expects the value of his taxable supplies in the following one year period will not exceed £68,000.

Alternatively, a trader who no longer makes taxable supplies may be **compulsorily deregistered**.

8.4 Calculating VAT

If a trader's output VAT exceeds his input VAT at the end of a VAT period (usually a period of three months), he must **pay over the excess** to HMRC.

If his input VAT exceeds his output VAT he will receive a **repayment**.

Note that **not all input VAT is deductible**, for example VAT on motor cars and on business entertaining.

CHAPTER ROUNDUP

- The tax year runs from 6 April to 5 April the following year.

- Income tax is payable on earnings, savings and investments. These are taxed at different rates.

- A number of reliefs and allowances are available to either reduce income (eg the personal allowance) or the tax liability (eg investments in the EIS).

- UK resident and domiciled individuals are taxed on their worldwide income. Non-UK domiciled individuals may be taxed on their foreign income on the remittance basis. Non-UK residents are only taxable in the UK on their UK income.

- Employees and their employers pay Class 1 NICs.

- Self employed individuals pay Class 2 (fixed amount) and Class 4 (based on their taxable business income).

- Capital gains tax is payable by individuals and trustees on the disposal of chargeable assets (ie assets that are not exempt, such as cars).

- Non-UK domiciled individuals may be taxable on their overseas gains on the remittance basis.

- Inheritance tax is payable on lifetime gifts to trusts (CLTs). It is also due if an individual dies within seven years of making any gift (ie to a trust (CLT) or to an individual (PET)).

- UK domiciled individuals are liable to IHT on their worldwide assets. Non-UK domiciled individuals are only liable on transfers of their UK assets.

- IIP trusts are taxed at the basic tax rates.

- Discretionary trusts have a basic rate band but the rest of their income is taxed at the special trust rates.

- Individuals and trusts may need to complete a self assessment tax return and make three payments of tax (two payments on account and a balancing payment).

- PAYE is the system used for deducting income tax and Class 1 NIC from employees' earnings.

- SDLT is payable on property purchases by the buyer at rates dependent on the transaction value.

- SDRT is payable at 0.5% on electronic share purchases.

- The main rate of tax for corporations is 28%. There is a lower rate for smaller companies of 21%.

- Companies calculate their tax liability based on their taxable profits in a chargeable accounting period.

- VAT is a tax on turnover borne by the final consumer.

- The standard rate of VAT is 17.5% although supplies may be zero rated or even exempt from VAT completely.

TEST YOUR KNOWLEDGE

1. When does a tax year start and end?

2. What rate of tax does a higher rate taxpayer pay on dividends?

3. What is the personal allowance for the tax year 2010/11?

4. What rate of Class 1 NICs must employers pay in respect of their employees' earnings?

5. How much is the CGT annual exempt amount for 2010/11?

6. How long must someone survive from the date of making a PET for it to be completely exempt?

7. What rate of tax is the 'trust rate' and the 'trust dividend rate'?

8. When is a self assessment tax return due if the taxpayer submits it via the Internet?

9. What is the rate of SDRT?

10. What rate of tax must a company with profits of £2 million pay?

11. What level of turnover must a business have before it is required to register for VAT?

TEST YOUR KNOWLEDGE: ANSWERS

1. A tax year starts on 6 April one year and ends on 5 April the following year.

    (See Section 1.1.2)

2. 32.5%.

    (See Section 1.4.5)

3. £6,475

    (See Section 1.5.2.1)

4. 12.8%

    (See Section 2.2.1)

5. £10,100

    (See Section 3.3.2)

6. 7 years

    (See Section 4.4)

7. Trust rate is 50% and the trust dividend rate is 42.5%

    (See Section 4.9.4.1)

8. 31 January after the end of the tax year

    (See Section 5.2.2)

9. 0.5%

    (See Section 6.2.2)

10. 28% (main rate)

    (See Section 7.3)

11. £70,000

    (See Section 8.3.1)

The Taxation of Investments

INTRODUCTION

All investment are taxable. We look at the tax impliocations of direct investment such as cash and cash equivalents, fixed interest securities, equities and property. We end this chapter with study of the taxation of indirect investment such as ISAs, GTFs, REITs, collective investment schemes, VCTs and EISs.

CHAPTER CONTENTS

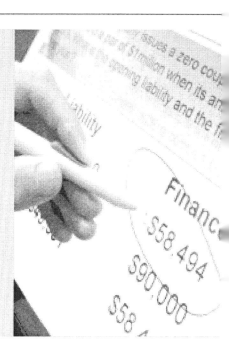

15 The taxation of investments

Demonstrate an ability to analyse the taxation of investments as relevant to the needs and circumstances of individuals and trusts

15.1.1 Analyse the taxation of direct investments including cash and cash equivalents, fixed interest securities, equities and property

15.1.2 Analyse the taxation of indirect investments including pension arrangements, individual savings accounts (ISAs) , child trust funds(CTFs), onshore and offshore collective investment schemes and investment companies, onshore and offshore life assurance policies, real estate investment trusts and Venture Capital Trusts (VCTs) and Enterprise Investment Schemes (EISs).

17 Application of personal tax planning to investment advice

Demonstrate an ability to apply the knowledge of personal taxation to the provision of investment advice

17.1.1 To carry out computations on the most common elements of income tax and NICs; CGT; IHT including the impact of lifetime transfers and transfers at death

1 DIRECT INVESTMENTS

1.1 Introduction

Learning objectives   **15.1.1 Analyse** the taxation of direct investments including cash and cash equivalents, fixed interest securities, equities and property.
17.1.1 To carry out computations on the most common elements of income tax and NICs; CGT; IHT including the impact of lifetime transfers and transfers at death

In this first section, we look at direct investments, which involve the investor spending their money, either personally or through a broker, on a particular investment, for example shares or property.

1.2 Cash and cash equivalents

1.2.1 General principles

Cash investments, or deposits, are used by individuals looking for secure, low risk, liquid investments.

1.2.2 Cash investments

The principle UK deposit takers are **banks and building societies**.

National Savings & Investments (NS&I) is a government agency that also takes cash deposits. Their investments are guaranteed by the government so are completely secure. They offer two different savings accounts, the Easy Access Savings Account and the Investment Account. They also offer Savings Certificates, Children's Bonus Bonds and Cash ISAs (see later).

Other cash investments include:

- Time deposits (or term accounts).
- Money market accounts which allow deposits for periods ranging from overnight to five years
- Foreign currency accounts.

1.2.3 Income from cash investments

The income receivable from cash investments is interest.

1.2.4 Tax treatment of cash investments

Income tax

We have already seen that UK resident individuals are taxable on bank and building society interest in the **tax year the interest is paid**.

The rates, which we saw earlier are:

- 10% starting rate (where there is non-savings income below £2,440 for 2010/11)
- 20% basic rate
- 40% higher rate
- 50% additional rate.

Bank and building society interest is generally paid **net of 20% income tax**.

The investor's tax position will be as follows:

- Non taxpayers can reclaim the full 20% tax deducted
- Starting rate taxpayers can reclaim a 10% refund
- Basic rate taxpayers have no further tax liability
- Higher rate taxpayers pay a further 20% through their self assessment tax return
- Additional rate taxpayers pay a further 30%, also via self assessment.

Interest on NS&I Easy Access Savings Accounts and Investment Accounts is paid gross. This means that no tax is deducted by NS&I so the taxpayer cannot claim the 20% tax credit. The tax liability will usually have to be paid through the self assessment system.

Interest from Savings Certificates and Children's Bonus Bonds is tax free (exempt).

Capital gains tax

Cash on a deposit investment does not grow in value, it simply produces income, so there is no charge to capital gains tax.

1.3 Fixed interest securities

1.3.1 What are fixed interest securities?

Fixed interest or 'fixed income' securities are securities that pay a pre-specified return, in the form of capital and income. Such securities are also generally called **bonds**.

Gilts, corporate bonds, loan stock, debentures and loan notes are names given to types of bonds.

Bonds are loans, with the investor as the lender. The holder of the bond – that is, the investor – will receive any interest payment (the coupon), and normally repayment of capital on maturity of the bond.

The issuers of bonds include:

- Government (gilts), and
- Companies (corporate bonds).

1.3.2 Features of fixed interest securities

Fixed interest securities generally have:

- A **fixed redemption value** which the issuer will repay to the bondholder on maturity

- A **fixed rate of interest** (the coupon) expressed as a percentage of face value, usually paid every six months

- A **pre-specified redemption date** (or maturity date).

For example, a holding of £10,000 Lloyds TSB 2.75% 2011 corporate bond will pay £137.50 interest every six months until 2011, when the holder will be repaid the £10,000.

1.3.3 Accrued income scheme

Interest payments are made to the holder who was registered seven business days before the interest payment date. If the stock is sold before this date it is sold with the interest (**cum interest**). The purchaser will receive the interest payment. However, the sale proceeds will include interest accrued to the date of sale.

Sales after this date are made without the interest (**ex interest**). In this case the next interest payment will be paid to the seller. This time, the sale proceeds will exclude interest accruing after the date of sale.

Under the **accrued income scheme**, where securities are transferred the accrued interest reflected in the value of securities is taxed separately as savings income. The seller is treated as entitled to the proportion of interest which has accrued since the last interest payment. The buyer is entitled to relief against the interest he receives. This relief is equal to the amount assessable on the seller.

Conversely, where the transfer is ex interest, the seller will receive the whole of the next interest payment. He will be entitled to relief for the amount of interest assessed on the purchaser. The purchaser is treated as entitled to the proportion of the interest accrued between the sale and the next payment date and it is taxed as savings income.

The **accrued income scheme does not apply where the seller's holdings of gilts and corporate bonds did not exceed £5,000**

- In the tax year in which the next interest due date falls, and
- The previous tax year.

Example

Nigel bought £10,000 5% Loan Stock a few years ago. Interest is payable on 30 June and 31 December each year. Nigel sells the loan stock to Evie on 30 November 2010 cum interest.

What are the amounts assessable for Nigel and Evie in respect of the loan stock for 2010/11?

Solution

Nigel	£
Interest paid 30.6.10	
£10,000 × 5% × 6/12	250
Accrued interest deemed received 31.12.10	
£10,000 × 5% × 5/12	208
Total assessable	458

Evie	£
Interest paid 31.12.10	
£10,000 × 5% × 6/12	250
Less relief for accrued interest	
£10,000 × 5% × 5/12	(208)
Total assessable (ie 1 month's interest)	42

1.3.4 Tax treatment of fixed interest securities

Income tax

Interest received from fixed interest securities is taxed at the same rates as other (eg bank) interest.

Interest from government stocks (gilts) is paid gross unless:

- The investor elects to have 20% tax deducted from it, or
- The gilt was purchased before 6 April 1998 and the investor has not elected for gross payments

Interest on corporate bonds (debentures) is generally paid **net of 20% income tax**.

The investor's tax position is as shown above for other interest.

Capital gains tax

Individuals pay no CGT on disposals of their holdings of:

- **Gilts**
- **Qualifying corporate bonds** (most company loan stock and debentures).

Gains on such disposals are exempt and losses are not allowable (ie cannot be set off against other gains).

1.4 Equities

1.4.1 What are equities?

The term **'equities'** refers to the ordinary shares of companies. The ordinary shareholders of a company are its owners.

Many smaller **'Limited'** companies are private companies, which may be owner managed and cannot offer their shares to the general public. The use of the term 'limited' indicates that the shareholder have limited liability: if the company fails, shareholders can lose their entire investment in the company but the company's creditors cannot pursue the shareholders for any further money.

To offer shares for sale to the public, a company must be a **'plc'** (public limited company), which can either:

- Seek a full **listing** on the **main market of the London Stock Exchange (LSE),** or

- Join the less closely regulated **Alternative Investment Market (AIM),** that is also operated by the LSE, or

- Join **Plus Markets**, the UK's **independent public market**, dedicated to smaller companies.

Equities are **bought and sold** by private investors, by large institutions, such as life assurance companies and pension funds, and by foreign investors.

An investor buys ordinary shares for two main reasons:

- To receive dividends from the company's earnings stream (**income**)
- To gain from increases in the value of the share (**capital gain**).

1.4.2 Buying and selling shares

Direct holdings of ordinary shares are appropriate for investors who obtain advice on an ongoing basis or who wishes to spend the time researching his own investments.

Equities are usually bought and sold through a stockbroker.

1.4.3 Tax treatment of shares

Income tax

Shareholders receive **dividends**, which, as we saw earlier, are **paid with a 10% tax credit**. The tax credit is $1/9 \times$ the dividend received. Remember, this tax credit is not real tax so cannot be repaid to the taxpayer, although it can **reduce the taxpayer's liability**.

The position for a dividend received of £90 for different types of taxpayer can be summarised as follows:

	Non-taxpayer £	Basic rate taxpayer (10%) £	Higher rate taxpayer (32.5%) £	Additional rate taxpayer (42.5% £
Net dividend	90.00	90.00	90.00	90.00
Tax credit (net × 1/9)	10.00	10.00	10.00	10.00
Gross dividend (net × 100/90)	100.00	100.00	100.00	100.00
Additional tax due	Nil	Nil	22.50	32.50
Net income	90.00	90.00	67.50	57.50

Note that the **effective rate of tax on the net dividend** for a higher rate taxpayer is ($22.5/90 \times 100$) 25%, and for an additional rate taxpayer is ($32.5/90 \times 100$) around 36%.

Capital gains tax

If the investor makes a capital gain on the disposal of shares it may be subject to capital gains tax at 18%, after deduction of the annual exempt amount (£10,100 for 2010/11).

The basic calculation is:

Profit = Proceeds (less expenses of sale) *less* costs of investing in the shares.

Expenses of sale include broker's commission.

The main costs of originally investing in shares that can be deducted are:

- Purchase cost
- Broker's commission
- Stamp duty reserve tax (SDRT) (0.5% on electronic purchases of UK equities).

If the investor holds at least 5% of the shares in a company that he also works for and has owned the shares for at least one year, he is entitled to **entrepreneurs' relief**. This reduces the effective tax rate to 10% (see earlier).

1.5 Property

1.5.1 Property markets

There is a high level of **owner-occupation of residential property** in the UK, ie many people own their own home.

Individuals can also invest in property in the following ways:

- **'Buy-to-let' ownership of residential property**, ie purchasing residential property specifically to rent out to individuals.

- **Commercial property** (eg retail, offices and industrial units), although insurance companies and pension funds are more likely to invest in this.

1.5.2 Tax treatment of residential property

Income tax

Profits from renting out property are taxed in the same way as earnings, ie they are taxed as **non-savings income at 20%, 40% or 50%**.

Mortgage interest on the let property is a deductible expense when calculating the letting profit.

Other costs are also deductible such as:

- Maintenance costs

- 10% (× the rental income) 'wear and tear' allowance or, alternatively, the cost of replacing (but not the original purchase price of) furniture, fixtures and fittings

- Estate agent's commission

- Management expenses.

Improvement expenditure (eg adding an extension to the property) is not deductible.

If the landlord is **non-UK resident**, the tenant or letting agent must deduct basic rate tax from the property income before paying the rent to the non-resident landlord. The landlord may apply to HMRC to be allowed to receive gross payments of rent if he completes a self assessment tax return and keeps his tax affairs up to date.

Capital gains tax

If the property being let has ever been the investor's **principal private residence (PPR)**, ie his main home that he has lived in at any time, the gain on the sale of the property may be fully or partly exempt from capital gains tax, depending on how long he has owned the property and how long he actually lived in it before renting it out.

If the property has never been the investor's PPR, the gain will be taxable in full.

Expenses of sale that can be deducted include legal fees.

The main **costs of originally investing in property** that can be deducted when calculating the gain:

- Purchase cost
- Legal fees

- **Stamp duty land tax (SDLT)** (percentage based on original value of the property).

The property will not usually qualify for entrepreneurs' relief.

2 INDIRECT INVESTMENTS

2.1 Introduction

Learning objectives

15.1.2 Analyse the taxation of indirect investments including pension arrangements, individual savings accounts (ISAs) , child trust funds(CTFs), onshore and offshore collective investment schemes and investment companies, onshore and offshore life assurance policies, real estate investment trusts and Venture Capital Trusts (VCTs) and Enterprise Investment Schemes (EISs).

17.1.1 To carry out computations on the most common elements of income tax and NICs; CGT; IHT including the impact of lifetime transfers and transfers at death

We now turn to **indirect investments**, where the investor, instead of spending his money directly on an investment such as shares or property, invests in a **product** that in turn invests in those shares or property.

Indirect investment is a simple and effective way for the investor to invest without becoming involved in the problems and costs of buying and selling shares on his own account. It also allows him to diversify his risk.

2.2 Pension arrangements

2.2.1 What is a pension?

An individual is encouraged by the Government to make financial provision to cover his needs when he reaches a certain age. There are state pension arrangements which provide some financial support, but the Government would like an individual not to rely on state provision but to make his own pension provision.

Therefore tax relief is given for such pension provision. This includes relief for contributions to a pension and an exemption from tax on income and gains arising in a pension fund.

In order for the tax advantages described below to apply to a pension scheme, the scheme must be registered with HMRC.

2.2.2 Pension arrangements

An individual may make pension provision in a number of ways:

- **Personal pension schemes**, set up by an individual who is, perhaps, self-employed or is not a member of an occupational scheme, are **defined contribution** pensions. This means that the level of pension that the member can draw from such schemes will depend on the investment performance of the money invested.

- **Occupational pension schemes**, where the scheme is set up by the employer for the benefit of the employees, historically tended to be **defined benefit** (final salary) schemes, where the pension depends on the period for which the individual has been a member of the scheme and his salary at the time of retirement. Modern occupational schemes are more likely to be defined contribution schemes.

Pension funds invest the pension contributions of individuals who belong to the pension.

2.2.3 Tax treatment of pension funds

Income from investments within the pension is tax free, as is any growth in value when the pension fund disposes of the investments.

You can think of a pension as a **tax-free wrapper** around the investments within it.

2.2.4 Tax treatment of pension contributions

Tax relief for pension contributions

An individual can make tax relievable contributions to his pension arrangements up to the **higher of**:

- His **earnings** (employment and self employment income) in the tax year, and
- **£3,600**.

Contributions to personal pensions are paid net of basic rate tax, which gives immediate relief to all taxpayers. **Further tax relief is given if the individual is a higher or additional rate taxpayer. The relief is given by increasing the basic rate limit for the year by the gross amount of contributions for which he is entitled to relief.**

Example

Joe has earnings of £60,000 in 2010/11. He pays a personal pension contribution of £7,200 (net). He has no other taxable income. Show Joe's tax liability for the year.

Solution

	£
Total earnings	60,000
Less: personal allowance	(6,475)
Taxable income	53,525
Tax on first £37,400 @ 20%	7,480
Tax on next £9,000 @ 20% (£7,200 × 100/80)	1,800
Tax on next £7,125 @ 40%	2,850
Tax liability	12,130

Employers normally operate 'net pay' arrangements in respect of employees' contributions to their occupational schemes. **In this case, as we saw earlier, the employer will deduct gross pension contributions from the individual's earnings before operating PAYE.** The individual therefore obtains tax relief at his marginal rate of tax without having to make any claim.

Excess contributions

There is an overriding limit on the total pension that can be input into a pension scheme for each tax year. This is called the *annual allowance*.

The amount of the annual allowance for 2010/11 is £255,000.

If the amount put into the pension exceeds this annual allowance there is an income tax charge on the individual at the rate of 40%.

2.3 Changes to tax relief for pension contributions from 2011/12

From 6 April 2011, income tax relief on pension contributions will be restricted for individuals with income of £150,000.

Between 22 April 2009 and 5 April 2011, individuals cannot take advantage of pension tax relief by making large additional pension contributions before the new rules take effect because of anti-forestalling rules which restrict tax relief on such contributions.

2.3.1 Tax treatment of pension benefits

Pension benefits

No pension payment can be made before the member reaches normal minimum pension age (55), unless the member is incapacitated by ill health. **At this age the member may take:**

- **An income pension, and/ or**
- **A lump sum**

from the pension scheme.

Up to 25% of the pension fund can be taken as a tax free lump sum, subject to the lifetime allowance limit (see below). **The remainder must be used to provide a pension income.**

Pension income is taxable as non savings income.

Lifetime allowance

An individual is not allowed to build up an indefinitely large pension fund. **There is a maximum value for a pension fund (for money purchase arrangements) or for the value of benefits (for defined benefits arrangements). This is called the *lifetime allowance*.**

The amount of the lifetime allowance in 2010/11 is £1,800,000.

If the pension fund exceeds the lifetime allowance this will give rise to an income tax charge on the excess value of the fund.

The rate of the charge depends on the type of benefit that will be taken from the excess funds:

- **Lump sum**: charge at **55%** on the value of the lump sum.
- **Pension income**: charge at **25%** on the value of the vested funds.

2.4 Individual savings accounts (ISAs)

2.4.1 What is an ISA?

An ISA is a tax free savings account. There are two types of ISA account:

- **Cash**, including all the kinds of bank and building society accounts as well as NS&I products and similar, and
- **Stocks and shares**.

2.4.2 Who can invest in an ISA?

Individuals over 18, who are **resident and ordinarily resident in the UK, can invest in two ISA accounts each year,** one cash and one stocks and shares, so long as they keep within the investment limits (see below).

Trustees cannot invest in ISAs.

2.4.3 Main features of an ISA?

The main features of ISAs are as follows.

- There is an **annual subscription limit of £10,200**, of which no more than £5,100 can be in cash
- There is no statutory lock in period or minimum subscription
- There is **no lifetime limit**

Individuals under 18 but over 16 are allowed to subscribe up to £5,100 pa into a cash only ISA account.

Once the maximum amount has been subscribed for in any type of ISA for a year, it is not possible to make further investments even after a withdrawal is subsequently made.

2.4.4 Tax treatment of ISAs

All income (eg interest, dividends) and gains in respect of investments within an ISA are completely exempt from tax. You can think of an ISA as a **tax-free wrapper** around the investments within it.

A full or partial withdrawal may be made from an ISA at any time without loss of tax exemption.

Where an investor ceases to qualify by becoming **non-resident**, the benefits, including tax reliefs, of any ISAs held up to that time may be retained but **no further subscriptions** may be made (unless UK residence status is regained).

2.5 Child trust funds (CTFs)

2.5.1 What are CTFs?

CTF accounts are available for children born after 31 August 2002. The CTF is initially funded by a Government voucher (£250, or £500 for lower income families). A further sum is paid into the account by the Government on the child's 7th birthday, provided they remain eligible for the CTF.

It is also **possible for anyone, including friends and family, to contribute up to a total of £1,200 a year** to the account.

The CTF is held for the child until he reaches 18. There are different types of accounts including cash accounts, unit trusts and life products.

2.5.2 Tax treatment of CTFs

There is **no income tax or capital gains tax** payable on CTF account income or growth.

Usually income earned on contributions by a parent to an account held by their child (eg bank account) is taxed on the parent if that interest is more than £100 gross in the tax year. However, there is no tax if parental contributions are made to a CTF.

2.6 Collective investment schemes

2.6.1 What is a collective investment scheme?

A collective investment scheme is one in which investors **pool their money** into a single fund. Such schemes give an investor with fewer resources a means of investing in a range of stocks, shares, property, etc indirectly. As the fund contains a range of shares the risk is spread.

Instead of making direct purchases of stocks and shares on the market or through new issues, or buying land and buildings, the indirect investor entrusts his money to professional investment managers, who themselves place the total amount entrusted to them in direct investments.

2.6.2 Types of collective investment scheme?

Collective investment schemes include:

- **Unit trusts**
- **Investment trusts**
- **Open-Ended Investment Companies**.

2.6.3 Unit trusts

The unit trust is one of the **best known forms of managed fund investment**. The fund manager buys shares in a range of different companies and pools these in a fund. The investor (the unit holder) then buys 'units' in the fund.

The fund is **open-ended**, which means that the size of the fund and the number of units rises and falls as investors buy and sell units.

2.6.4 Investment trusts

Unlike unit trusts, **investment trusts are themselves companies**, listed on the LSE, in which the investor buys shares. The investment trust company invests in a broad range of assets, including shares, bonds and property. A holder of ordinary shares in the investment trust company has an indirect interest in the underlying portfolio.

An investment trust company is a **closed-ended** fund as opposed to a unit trust that is open-ended, which means that they have a fixed number of shares.

Investment trusts can do certain things that unit trusts and OEICs (see below) cannot, for example borrow money to invest ('gearing' or 'leverage').

2.6.5 Open-Ended Investment Companies (OEICs)

OEICs enable UK collective investment funds to be marketed around the European Union. Continental European investors are unused to either unit or investment trusts. They are much more familiar with **OEICs**.

In effect, these are a **hybrid** with many of the features of both unit and investment trusts.

2.6.6 Taxation of collective investment schemes

Taxation of the fund

If the **unit trust or OEIC is an equity fund it receives dividends** from its underlying investments net of a 10% tax credit and **has no further tax to pay**.

If the **unit trust or OEIC is a non-equity fund** it receives income from its underlying investments (eg interest or rental income) gross and has to pay **corporation tax at 20%** (equivalent to the basic rate of income tax).

This income is then passed on to investors at the distribution dates.

Investment trusts are taxed in the same way as other companies, ie dividends are exempt while other income is taxed at a rate up to 28% dependent on the total profits of the company.

With regard to **capital gains, unit trusts and OEICs are always exempt** from paying tax on their gains when they dispose of their investments. This allows the fund managers to trade in and out of shares without having to worry about the tax implications.

Investment trusts are also usually exempt from paying tax on their capital gains so long as the company receives HMRC approval.

Taxation of the investor

Income tax

The **taxation of unit trusts and OEICs is identical as far as the investor is concerned**.

If the fund is an **equity fund, income distributions to investors are dividends, which are taxed in the normal way** (see above).

Distributions from **non-equity funds (such as cash or bond funds) are treated as interest rather than dividends. They are subject to a 20% tax deduction at source** (see above) unless the funds are held within an ISA.

An investment trust shareholder will only ever receive dividends which are taxed as normal (see above).

Capital gains tax

Investors in a unit trust are liable for CGT on gains they make when they sell their units, or shares in the case of an OEIC or investment trust, regardless of whether the fund is investing in exempt assets such as gilts or not.

The chargeable gain is the difference between what the investor paid for the units or shares and what they sell them for.

2.6.7 Offshore funds

Offshore funds will be either classed as **distributor funds** (those which distribute at least 85% of their income) or a fund with non-distributor status ('**roll up' fund)** which accumulates income within the fund.

Neither type of offshore fund pays UK tax.

Income from offshore funds is usually received gross by the investor.

For distributor funds, income for the investor is treated as taxable income for UK residents and the profit encashment of the units (ie gain) is treated as a capital gain.

For a roll up fund, all income distributions and profits on encashment (ie gain) are treated as taxable income. As the charge is to income tax, there is no annual CGT exempt amount.

In most cases, the tax benefit is limited to a possible **deferral of tax payment** resulting from income being paid gross.

Non-UK residents pay no UK income tax or capital gains tax on income or gains arising from an offshore holding, although they may of course be subject to tax charges in their country of residence.

2.7 Life assurance policies

2.7.1 What is a life assurance policy?

Life assurance policies provide protection in the event of death. There are two types:

- Contracts for protection (insurance) purposes only, and
- Contracts with **both protection and investment elements**, which are the focus of this section.

2.7.2 Taxation of Life Assurance Policies

Overview

Unlike a pension fund, a **life assurance fund** is not a tax-free vehicle: it suffers corporation tax on its income and gains at a rate of 20%.

As the fund itself suffers tax, payouts from policies are often completely free of income tax and capital gains tax. This is the case if it is a qualifying policy.

A **qualifying policy is one where premiums have been paid for a minimum of one of the following**:

- Life of the life assured
- 10 years
- Three quarters of the term

If it is a **non-qualifying policy, there may be an income tax charge on encashment of the policy**. A non-qualifying policy is a **single premium bond** where a lump sum is invested in a life fund a small part of which buys cover in the event of death with the balance being invested. These are also known as **investment bonds** or **property bonds.**

Income tax

The encashment or partial encashment (withdrawal) of such a policy, is a **chargeable event** for **income tax** purposes. Depending on the circumstances, this event may produce an additional income tax charge in the year in which the event occurs.

A chargeable event may arise in certain circumstances where any withdrawal/encashment is **received by a higher rate or additional rate taxpayer**.

For such a bond, up to 5% of the original premium for each year of the bond's life (**including the year of the chargeable event**) may be withdrawn from the bond with no **immediate** tax implications until 100% is reached. For withdrawals above this 5% level the excess will be taxable.

Example: chargeable event gain & top slicing relief

If an investor purchases a single premium bond for £10,000 and after 3 years withdraws a sum less than or equal to £1,500 (3 years at £500 pa) then no chargeable event arises.

If this sum exceeds £1,500, the excess represents a chargeable event. So, if the investor withdraws £1,800 then £300 excess is potentially taxable.

This £300, however, is the total withdrawal for 3 years, representing £100 pa, the income has been 'sliced' or annualised. This £100 slice will be added as the 'top slice' of the investors income and if the investor is a higher or additional rate taxpayer then tax must be paid at either 20% (the difference between the higher and basic rate for savings income) which would be £20 here on each £100 slice (£60 in total on the three slices), or 30% (the difference between the additional and basic rate for savings income) which would be £90 in total).

On the final encashment of such bonds, any gains realised will be considered in a similar manner and will be subject to income tax in the hands of a higher rate taxpayer.

The gain will be 'sliced' as above to establish the annual gain, this annual gain will be added to the investors income to determine his tax status (basic/higher rate) with any higher rate part/region being taxed at 20%.

The total tax payable will be the tax on one slice × number of slices.

2.7.3 Offshore Life Assurance Policies

Overview

An offshore life assurance policy, often called an **offshore bond**, is broadly the same as a UK non-qualifying policy.

The advantage of an offshore bond is that the **underlying life funds suffer little or no tax (gross roll up)** compared with UK life funds which are taxed at 20%.

Taxation of offshore bonds

Withdrawals of up to 5% of the original investment may be taken for 20 years with no immediate tax liability. If the 5% allowance is not used in one year it can be carried forward to the next.

The **taxation of offshore policies on encashment is more stringent than for onshore products**. The chargeable gain on the bond is subject to basic, higher and additional rate tax.

When dividing to find the slice of gain, we use the **number of years since the beginning of the bond** not the years since the last chargeable event as with an onshore bond.

If the investor had been non-UK resident for part of the time he held the bond, then he receives **relief for the time that he was non-resident**. For example if he was non-UK resident for five of the ten years that he held the bond then the chargeable gain on encashment would be reduced by 50%.

If the investor is non-UK resident when the bond is encashed there are no UK tax consequences.

2.8 Real Estate Investment Trusts (REITs)

2.8.1 What are Real Estate Investment Trusts?

A REIT is a listed company (AIM does not count for this purpose) owning, managing and earning rental income from commercial or residential property.

The investor can use a REIT to spread his risk over a number of different properties.

2.8.2 Tax treatment of REIT investments

Income tax

REITs can elect for their property income (and gains) to be exempt from corporation tax and must withhold basic rate (20%) tax from distributions paid to shareholders (who cannot own more than 10% of a REIT's shares) out of these profits.

These distributions are taxed as property income on the investor, not as dividends.

Distributions by REITs out of other income (ie not property income or gains) are taxed as dividends in the normal way.

It is possible to hold REITs within **ISAs** and **CTFs.**

Capital gains tax

If the investor makes a capital gain on the disposal of REIT shares it may be **subject to capital gains tax** in the same way as shares in any other company (see above).

2.9 Enterprise Investment Schemes (EISs)

2.9.1 What is the Enterprise Investment Scheme?

The **Enterprise Investment Scheme (EIS)** is a scheme designed to promote enterprise and investment by helping high-risk, unlisted trading companies raise finance by the issue of ordinary shares to individual investors who are unconnected with that company.

Individuals can invest directly in the EIS company itself or via an EIS fund to diversify their exposure to risk.

2.9.2 Which shares qualify for the EIS?

Only shares in certain companies qualify for the EIS.

The company must be an **unquoted, trading company** that carries on a qualifying business activity for at least three years. Shares in AIM companies can qualify.

Non-qualifying business activities include:

- Banking,
- Dealing in commodities, and
- Property development.

The company's assets must not exceed £7 million immediately before and £8 million immediately after the share issue, and it must have **fewer than 50 full time equivalent employees** and must have **raised less than £2 million** in venture capital funds in the previous 12 months.

2.9.3 Tax treatment of EIS investments

Income tax

When an individual subscribes for eligible shares in a qualifying company, the **amount subscribed is a tax reduction** (see earlier), **saving income tax at 20%.**

The maximum total investment that can qualify for this income tax relief in a tax year is £500,000.

A 2010/11 investment will attract relief against the tax liability for that tax year. However, a taxpayer can claim to carry back his investment, up to the usual limit of £500,000, to the previous year.

The **relief may be withdrawn** if certain events, such as the sale of the shares, occur within three years.

Dividends from EIS shares are taxable under the normal rules.

Trustees cannot obtain any income tax relief.

Capital gains tax

Where EIS income tax relief is available there are also **capital gains tax reliefs** when the investor sells his EIS shares:

- Where an individual disposes of EIS shares after the three year period any **gain is exempt** from CGT. If the shares are disposed of within three years any gain is computed in the normal way.
- If the EIS shares are disposed of at a loss at any time, the **loss is allowable** but the acquisition cost of the shares is reduced by the amount of EIS relief attributable to the shares. The loss can be **set against capital gains**, as normal, and can **also be set against the investor's income**.

EIS CGT deferral relief allows the taxpayer to defer chargeable gains arising on the disposal of any asset if he invests in EIS shares in the period starting one year before and ending three years after the disposal of the asset. Note that this relief **does not depend on income tax relief being available and is also available to trustees**.

2.10 Venture Capital Trusts (VCTs)

2.10.1 What are Venture Capital Trusts?

Venture capital trusts (VCTs) are listed companies that invest in unquoted trading companies and meet certain conditions.

The investor can use a VCT to spread his risk over a number of higher-risk, unquoted EIS companies.

2.10.2 Tax treatment of VCT investments

Income tax

An individual investing in a VCT obtains the following **income tax benefits** on a **maximum qualifying investment of £200,000** in the tax year:

- A tax reduction of 30% of the amount invested. There is a withdrawal of relief if the shares are disposed of within five years or if the VCT ceases to qualify. Where both VCT and EIS relief are available in the same tax year, **deduct this VCT tax reduction first.**

- Dividends received are tax-free income

No relief is available for trustees.

Capital gains tax

Capital gains on the sale of shares in the VCT are exempt from CGT (and losses are not allowable).

In addition, capital gains which the VCT itself makes on its investments are exempt, so are not subject to corporation tax.

Note that there is no minimum holding period requirement for the benefits of tax-free dividends and CGT exemption.

CHAPTER ROUNDUP

- Bank and building society interest is usually paid net of 20% basic rate tax, while interest from NS&I accounts is paid gross (income from NS&I Certificates is exempt). Income tax is payable on interest income at 10%, 20%, 40 and 50%.

- There is no CGT on cash deposits.

- Interest from government stocks (gilts) is paid gross while interest on corporate bonds (debentures) is generally paid net of 20% income tax. The accrued income scheme applies when an investor buys or sells securities, so they are treated as receiving interest for the time they have owned the stock.

- Gilts and qualifying corporate bonds are exempt from CGT.

- Dividends from equities (ie shares) are paid with a 10% non-refundable tax credit. The gross dividend is taxed at either 10%, 32.5% or 42.5%.

- CGT is due on the disposal of shares at 18%, after deduction of the annual exempt amount.

- Property income (ie rent) is taxed as non-savings income at 20%, 40% or 50%.

- The gain on disposal of property is chargeable to CGT unless it has been the investor's main residence (PPR) at any point, in which case the gain may be fully or partly exempt.

- Income and gains within a pension fund are exempt from income tax and CGT.

- Individuals obtain tax relief when making contributions to their pension within the annual allowance. When an individual starts taking their pension they can take up to 25% of the fund (up to the lifetime allowance) as a tax free lump sum. The rest is taken as an income pension and is taxed at the non-savings rates.

- Individuals can invest up to £10,200 in cash (maximum £5,100) and shares a year in an Individual Savings Account. All income and gains are tax free.

- Up to £1,200 a year can be saved in a Child Trust Fund. Income and gains are tax free.

- Income from unit trusts and OEICs may be either interest or dividends and are taxed as such on the investor. Investment trusts are listed companies so distributions are always taxed as dividends.

- Capital gains tax is due on any growth in value when an investor disposes of their units or shares in any collective investment scheme.

- Payouts from qualifying life assurance policies are free of tax.

- Up to 5% of the original premium paid into a non-qualifying single premium life policy (bond) can be withdrawn tax free each year. Any excess is chargeable to income tax, but comes with a 20% tax credit.

- There may be further income tax (but not CGT) when a non-qualifying policy is encashed. Top slicing relief may apply for higher and additional rate taxpayers.

- Distributions from the tax exempt income of a REIT are taxed as property income on the investor, not as dividends. CGT will apply when the investor sells shares in a REIT.

- Income tax relief (a 20% tax reduction) is available for investments in EIS companies. Dividends from EIS companies are taxable as normal.

- There is no CGT if the investor sells the EIS shares after three years. EIS CGT deferral relief is available to defer the gain arising on any asset if the investor buys EIS shares within a four year period.

- Income tax relief (a 30% tax reduction) is available for investments in VCT companies. Dividends from VCTs are exempt from income tax. There is no CGT when the investor sells his VCT shares.

TEST YOUR KNOWLEDGE

1. What rate of tax is withheld from interest payments to individuals and trustees?

2. Is interest from gilts usually paid net or gross?

3. Is entrepreneurs' relief available on the disposal of shares and if so, in what circumstances?

4. What relief is available when an individual sells a property that they have lived in as their home?

5. David is a higher rate taxpayer. He pays £10,000 into his pension. By what amount will his basic rate band be extended?

6. What is the maximum amount that an individual can save in a cash ISA each year?

7. Name the three main types of collective investment scheme.

8. What is the maximum amount that can be withdrawn from a single premium bond each year?

9. Gerard, who is an additional rate taxpayer, receives a distribution of £2,500 from a REIT. What rate of tax must he pay on the income?

10. What is the income tax reduction available for individual investors in an EIS company?

11. Wayne sells his shareholding in Baronsmear VCT plc, making a gain of £10,000. How much CGT must he pay?

TEST YOUR KNOWLEDGE: ANSWERS

1.   20%.

    (See Section 1.2.4.1)

2.   Gross.

    (See Section 1.3.4.1)

3.   Yes. If the investor holds ≥5% and works for the company.

    (See Section 1.4.3.2)

4.   Principal private residence relief exempts all or part of the gain

    (See Section 1.5.2.2)

5.   £12,500 (£10,000 × 100/80)

    (See Section 2.2.4.1)

6.   £5,100

    (See Section 2.3.3)

7.   Unit trusts, investment trusts and OEICs

    (See Section 2.5.2)

8.   5% of the original premium

    (See Section 2.6.2.2)

9.   50% (taxed as property income not a dividend)

    (See Section 2.7.2.1)

10.   20%

    (See Section 2.8.3.1)

11.   Nil. No CGT on profit on sale of VCT shares.

    (See Section 2.9.2.2)

BPP
LEARNING MEDIA

13

Tax Planning

INTRODUCTION

Tax planning refers to the process of organising one's affairs so as to take best advantage of tax rules. With some of the more complex ways of taking advantage of tax rules HMRC will review to ensure their main aim is not the avoidance of tax.

CHAPTER CONTENTS

16 Tax planning

Demonstrate an ability to analyse the role and relevance of tax in the financial affairs of individuals and trusts

16.1.1 Explain the limitations of lifetime gifts and transfers at death in mitigating IHT

16.1.2 Analyse the key principles of income tax planning – spouse, civil partners, children, pension contributions, ISA allowances and other tax advantaged schemes (EIS and VCT's etc)

16.1.3 Analyse how the use of annual CGT exemptions, the realisation of losses, the timing of disposals, and sale and repurchase of similar assets can mitigate CGT

17 Application of personal tax planning to investment advice

Demonstrate an ability to apply the knowledge of personal taxation to the provision of investment advice

17.1.1 To carry out computations on the most common elements of income tax and NICs; CGT; IHT including the impact of lifetime transfers and transfers at death

17.1.2 To make elementary tax planning recommendations in the context of investments and pensions advice

1 INCOME TAX PLANNING

1.1 Introduction

Strategies for reducing the amount of income tax make use of the fact that not all income is subject to income tax and that all individuals are entitled to personal allowances. Investing in assets and products that produce exempt income, such as ISAs, is a simple and important way of reducing taxable income.

Learning objectives | **16.1.2 Analyse** the key principles of income tax planning – spouse, civil partners, children, pension contributions, ISA allowances and other tax advantaged schemes (EIS and VCTs etc).
17.1.1 To carry out computations on the most common elements of income tax and NICs; CGT; IHT including the impact of lifetime transfers and transfers at death.
17.1.2 To make elementary tax planning **recommendations** in the context of investments and pensions advice.

1.2 Spouses and civil partners

1.2.1 General principles

Spouses and civil partners are taxed as two separate people. Each spouse/civil partner is entitled to a personal allowance (or an age related personal allowance depending on his or her own age and income).

If one spouse's or civil partner's marginal rate of tax is higher than the other's marginal rate it would be tax efficient to **transfer the income-yielding asset (or part of it) to the individual with the lower rate to utilise their personal allowance and lower marginal tax rate.**

1.2.2 Joint property

When spouses/civil partners jointly own income-generating property, it is assumed that they are entitled to equal shares of the income.

If the spouses/civil partners are not actually entitled to equal shares in the income-generating property, they may make a joint declaration to HMRC specifying the proportion to which each is entitled. These proportions are used to tax each of them separately, in respect of income arising on or after the date of the declaration.

Example

Mr Buckle is a higher rate taxpayer who owns a rental property producing £20,000 of property income on which he pays tax at 40%, giving him a tax liability of £8,000. His spouse has no income.

What tax planning advice could you give Mr Buckle to reduce the couple's overall income tax liability?

Solution

If Mr Buckle transfers a small interest in the property, say 5%, to his wife, they will be treated, for income tax purposes, as jointly owning the property and will each be taxed on 50% of the income.

Mr Buckle's tax liability will be reduced to £4,000. His wife's liability is only £705 (£10,000 – £6,475 @ 20%), giving an overall tax saving of £3,295.

1.3 Children

A child is a separate taxable person for tax purposes so is entitled to a personal allowance in his own right.

There are rules to prevent the parent of a minor child (under the age of 18) from transferring income to the child to use his personal allowance and starting and basic rate tax bands. These rules **treat income received by the child that is directly transferred by the parent**, or is derived from capital transferred by the parent (eg by setting up a bank account in the child's name), **as income of the parent**, rather than the child's, for income tax purposes.

The child's income is not, however, treated as his parent's if it does not exceed £100 (gross) a year.

The rules only apply to gifts from parents, so a **tax saving is possible if other relatives (eg grandparents) make the gifts.**

It is also possible to use the child's personal allowance and starting and basic rate bands if the child is **employed in the parent's trade** because in this case there is no element of gift.

These rules do not apply to income from a **Child Trust Fund (CTF)** so a parent can make contributions to their child's CTF and the income will not be taxed on them (or on the child as the income is tax free – see earlier and below).

1.4 Tax efficient investments

There are a number of strategies involving tax efficient investments that may help to reduce the income tax liability. These include:

- **Investing in a pension.** All taxpayers receive immediate tax relief as contributions are paid **net of basic rate tax**. **Additional relief** is given to higher rate and additional rate taxpayers by increasing the basic rate limit for the year by the gross amount of contributions.

- **Employer contributions to a pension.** If an individual's **employer makes contributions** to his pension (within the annual allowance) there is no tax or NICs on the amount paid. It is therefore tax efficient for an individual to receive part of his earnings as a pension contribution rather than salary.

- **Open a cash and/ or share ISA account.** Income and gains are exempt within the ISA. Higher and additional rate taxpayers benefit from the fact that they have no further tax to pay on dividends in a stocks and shares ISA. Before making any other investments an individual should be encouraged to open an ISA account.

- **Open a Child Trust Fund account** for (most) under 18 year olds. Income and gains are exempt within the account. Even parents can make contributions to a CTF with no adverse tax consequences.

- **Invest in EIS company** shares to obtain a 20% **income tax reduction**. If the individual's tax rate was higher in the year before the investment, they should claim to deduct the tax reduction from the tax liability of the **previous year**. There are also CGT reliefs available for investments in EIS shares.

  EIS shares are **high risk investments** due to the size and nature of EIS qualifying companies. Only investors who are willing to accept this high level of risk, and possible losses on the eventual sale of the shares, should be advised to invest in EIS companies directly, although an EIS fund may be appropriate for a more risk-averse investor.

- **Invest in VCT company shares** to obtain a 30% **income tax reduction. Dividends received from VCTs are completely exempt** from income tax. **Less risky than EIS shares** as the investor is able to spread his risk across a number of higher-risk unquoted companies while investing in a listed company.

- **Invest in a single premium bond** (non-qualifying life assurance policy). Can make **regular withdrawals up to 5%** of the original premium each year, with no tax until the bond is encashed. Withdrawals come with **20% tax credit so no further liability** if investor is a basic rate taxpayer by that time. Particularly tax efficient for **investors nearing retirement age expecting a lower level of income**.

- **Invest in National Savings & Investments (NS&I) Certificates** and NS&I Children's Bonus Bonds. Income is tax free but paid irregularly.

2 CAPITAL GAINS TAX PLANNING

2.1 Introduction

Strategies for reducing the amount of capital gains tax make use of the fact that not all assets are subject to capital gains tax and that all individuals are entitled to an annual exempt amount as well as relief for their capital losses.

16.1.3 Analyse how the use of annual CGT exemptions, the realisation of losses, the timing of disposals, and sale and repurchase of similar assets can mitigate CGT.

17.1.1 To carry out computations on the most common elements of income tax and NICs; CGT; IHT including the impact of lifetime transfers and transfers at death

17.1.2 To make elementary tax planning **recommendations** in the context of investments and pensions advice.

2.2 CGT planning

As we have seen, each individual can make gains every year up to the level of the annual CGT exempt amount.

Only gains, net of losses for the year, in excess of the annual exempt amount are subject to CGT. Any unused annual exempt amount cannot be carried forward to future years.

Strategies to reduce the CGT liability include:

- **Transfer the ownership of assets to a spouse or civil partner.** The transfer will be tax neutral for CGT purposes and will allow the gifting spouse/ civil partner to use their annual exempt amount.

- **Phase asset disposals over more than one tax year**, if possible, to use more than one annual exempt amount. For example, make two separate disposals in March 2011 and April 2011, which uses two annual exempt amounts, ie those for the tax year 2010/11 and 2011/12.

- **Realise gains within the annual exempt amount**, so that there is no actual taxable gain, and repurchase a similar asset. This has the effect of increasing the base cost of the asset, reducing the risk of future gains exceeding future annual exempt amounts.

- **Dispose of EIS shares** (after three years of ownership) **or VCT shares** as any gain will be exempt. However, the investor should not sell an investment that he would prefer to keep just for the tax benefits. He should not let the 'tax tail' wag the dog!

- **Dispose of other exempt assets**, such as cars, treasury stock (gilts) or Qualifying Corporate Bonds (corporate stock).

- **Dispose of assets standing at a loss**. Remember capital losses must be set against gains of the same year. If there are any left, they can be carried forward and must be set against gains in future years, but only if those gains are not already covered by the annual exempt amount. **Losses arising on the disposal of EIS-type shares can be set against income as well as gains.**

3 INHERITANCE TAX PLANNING

3.1 Introduction

IHT arises as a result of the transfer of wealth in excess of the settlor's nil rate band. As we saw earlier, IHT is primarily a tax on wealth left on death and therefore most IHT planning focuses on reducing an individual's estate through lifetime gifts. It is, however, necessary to balance the desire to reduce the potential IHT liability through the gifting of assets versus the need to maintain sufficient assets to support the required standard of living.

Learning objectives

16.1.1 Explain the limitations of lifetime gifts and transfers at death in mitigating IHT.

17.1.1 To carry out computations on the most common elements of income tax and NICs; CGT; IHT including the impact of lifetime transfers and transfers at death

17.1.2 To make elementary tax planning **recommendations** in the context of investments and pensions advice.

3.2 Spouses and civil partners

3.2.1 General principles

Spouses and **civil partners** are taxed separately for IHT purposes. On the death of one spouse or civil partner, it is necessary to value his or her estate. That estate includes only the property (or share of property) actually belonging to the deceased. Each spouse or civil partner has their own **nil rate band**, exemptions and reliefs independently of the other spouse or civil partner.

Transfers between spouses or civil partners (whether or not living together) are **exempt**.

A simple planning point follows from this spouse exemption. Spouses/civil partners may avoid IHT, at least in the short term, if each makes a will leaving his property to the other.

3.2.2 Transferable nil rate band

When one spouse or civil partner dies, the unused portion of their nil rate band is transferred to the surviving spouse.

So, the second person's nil rate band on death will be their own remaining nil rate band plus the unused portion of the first person's (based on the nil rate band available on the second death).

Example

John dies on 1 June 2010 leaving £243,750 of assets to his children and the remainder of his assets to his wife, Tanya.

What is Tanya's estate's available nil rate band if she dies on 1 September 2015? Assume the nil rate band in 2015/16 is £400,000.

Solution

The assets John left to his children are within his nil rate band, consuming (£243,750/£325,000) ¾ of that band. The remaining unused ¼ of his nil rate band can be transferred to Tanya on her death.

The rest of the assets transferred to Tanya are exempt from IHT.

When Tanya dies her available nil rate band is:

	£
Tanya's own nil rate band	400,000
Unused portion of John's nil rate band (¼ × £400,000)	100,000
Tanya's available nil rate band on death	500,000

3.3 Gifts with reservation of benefit (GWR)

3.3.1 General principles

It is good IHT planning to make lifetime gifts rather than keep property and gift it on death as, if the donor survives seven years from the date of a lifetime gift, there is no further IHT to pay if it was a chargeable lifetime transfer or becomes completely exempt if the gift was a PET.

Many individuals would like to make lifetime gifts, but are unwilling to do so because they want to continue using the asset (for example, a house or a work of art). **One way around this would be for the individual to give the asset away and for the donee to allow the donor to continue to use the asset.**

This type of arrangement does not work because of the gift with reservation of benefit (GWR) rules.

3.3.2 What is a gift with reservation?

A GWR occurs when an individual gifts property and continues to enjoy the benefit of the asset, either rent free or at reduced cost, or the person getting the gift does so with conditions attached.

The following are the most common examples of a GWR:

- **Giving away a house but continuing to live in it rent-free** (or at a rent lower than a market rent)
- Giving away a holiday cottage but continuing to spend long holidays there without paying a market rent
- **Giving away a painting but the donor continuing to keep it hanging on his wall** without paying a market rent for its use
- Creating a trust from which the settlor can benefit

3.3.3 Tax treatment

Where a GWR is made, it is treated in the same way as any other gift at the time it is made, ie as either a PET or a CLT.

However **if the reservation still exists at the date of the donor's death, the asset is included in the donor's estate at its market value at the date of death** (probate value) and not its value at the date the gift was made.

If the donor has died within seven years of making the original GWR then, under basic principles, that gift will have death tax consequences (become chargeable if a PET, additional tax due if a CLT). **There will therefore be two IHT charges on the same asset. To avoid this double taxation HMRC will choose the higher total tax.**

Note that if the donor pays a full market rent for use of the property gifted, he will not be treated as having reserved a benefit and there will be no GWR implications.

Example

George gives his house to his son Owen on 1 April 2007 when it is worth £400,000. However, he continues to live in the house rent free. George dies on 2 January 2011. The house is then worth £460,000. George has made no previous transfers, other than to use his annual exemption each year. What are the IHT consequences of these events?

Solution

George makes a PET in April 2007 of £400,000. As he dies within seven years of the transfer (in January 2011), the PET becomes chargeable. However, he is also treated as still owning the house and this will be included in his death estate at the value at the date of death (£460,000).

This results in a double charge to IHT on the same property, so the 'double charges' rules ensure that only the IHT calculation that produces the higher tax applies. In this case, the charge on the house in the death estate will apply (higher value and no taper relief available for the death estate). The effect is the same as if George had never made the gift.

3.4 Other IHT planning

Other valid IHT planning steps include:

- **Make full use of all available exemptions** (eg annual, marriage, small gifts).

- **Use the normal expenditure out of income exemption**, for example to pay grandchildren's school fees.

- **Make lifetime gifts.** IHT will only be due on the asset gifted if the donor dies within seven years. The IHT charge will usually be based on a lower value (as the asset will often have increased by the date of death), and will take into account the lifetime annual and other exemptions as well as taper relief if the donor survives at least three years.

- **Make CLTs before making PETs in a tax year**. Annual exemptions are allocated chronologically during the tax year. CLTs are immediately chargeable to IHT so make these first, otherwise PETs will use up the annual exemption(s) if they are made earlier in the tax year. Remember, PETs only become chargeable if the donor dies within seven years of making PETs first will waste the annual exemption(s) if the donor survives for at least seven years.

- **Write life assurance benefits into trust** (ie make someone else – eg a family member – the beneficiary of the life policy) so that the policy proceeds are paid to another person and do not become part of the deceased's death estate.

- **Use life assurance policies (written into trust) to cover future IHT liabilities**, eg a seven year policy to cover the potential liability on a PET or additional liability on a CLT.

- **Leave assets to spouse/ civil partner.**

CHAPTER ROUNDUP

- Transfers between spouses/ civil partners are tax efficient from an income, capital gains and inheritance tax perspective.

- Successful income tax planning can involve simple steps such as ensuring both spouses/ civil partners are using their personal allowances and lower rate bands.

- Parents must beware of making gifts of assets or income to their children as this can lead to any income being taxed on them rather than the child, unless the income arises from a CTF or is less than £100 a year.

- Pensions are a very tax efficient way for individuals to make provision for retirement but they should be aware that they cannot use the pension fund until they reach retirement age.

- All investors should consider opening tax free Individual Savings Accounts (ISAs).

- Investors who are happy to take more risks with their investments could consider EIS and VCT shares, which provide a number of income and capital gains tax reliefs.

- Single premium bonds are useful investments for investors expecting their income to reduce by the date of encashment of the bond.

- Capital gains tax planning includes making use of the annual exempt amount (of both the investor and their spouse/ civil partner) and losses.

- Phasing asset disposals over more than one tax year allows for more than one annual exempt amount to be used.

- Investors should carefully consider whether they are happy to dispose of exempt assets to generate cash.

- Disposing of assets standing at a loss will allow offset of that loss against other gains in the same or later years.

- Transfers between spouses, both during lifetime and on death, are exempt for IHT purposes. The unused proportion of nil rate band on the death of one spouse/ civil partner can be transferred to the other on the second death.

- Lifetime gifts are effective for making use of available IHT lifetime exemptions.

- However, individuals must be careful when making lifetime gifts that they do not keep any benefit in respect of the asset gifted to avoid the application of the gift with reservation rules.

- The timing of CLTs and PETs is important to ensure tax efficient use of annual exemptions.

- Life assurance benefits should be written into trust to avoid unnecessary IHT charges.

TEST YOUR KNOWLEDGE

1. Mr and Mrs Smith own a holiday cottage jointly. The rental income during the year is £12,000. Mr Smith owns 15% of the property and Mrs Smith owns the remaining 85%. How much income is taxable on Mr Smith?

2. Celia Jones sets up a bank account for her daughter, Camilla, who is 12 years old. The interest received during the tax year was £240 (net). What is the income tax position in respect of the interest received on the account?

3. Which investment is higher risk: EIS shares or VCT shares?

4. Jeremy sold his shareholding in HighRisk Ltd, an EIS company, at a loss. Advise Jeremy what he can do with the loss.

5. Madeleine gifts the family home to her daughter, Cynthia, but continues to live in the property, rent free. Explain whether Madeleine has successfully reduced the value of her estate for IHT purposes.

6. Keith wishes to make a gift to his son, Sam, and a gift to a trust during 2010/11. Advise Keith which of the gifts he should make first and why.

TEST YOUR KNOWLEDGE: ANSWERS

1. Mr Smith is taxable on half of the income as the couple is treated as owning the property jointly. Mr Smith is therefore taxable on £6,000.

   (See Section 1.2.2)

2. The interest is treated as taxable on Celia because Camilla is her minor child and the interest is more than £100 gross. Celia is therefore taxable on £300 (£240 × 100/80).

   (See Section 1.3)

3. EIS shares are higher risk than VCT shares.

   (See Section 1.4)

4. Jeremy can set the capital loss against gains of the current year. If there is any remaining loss he can carry the loss forward.

   Alternatively, because this is a loss arising on the disposal of EIS shares, he can set the loss against his income rather than his gains which could save tax at a higher rate.

   (See Section 2.2)

5. Madeleine has made a gift with reservation of benefit as although she has made a PET of the house to her daughter, she continues to benefit from the asset so it is treated as still belonging to her. The gift is ineffective for IHT purposes.

   (See Section 3.3)

6. Keith should make the gift to the trust before the gift to Sam. This is because the gift to the trust is a CLT and is immediately chargeable to IHT, whereas the gift to Sam is a PET. If he were to make the PET first it would needlessly use up the annual exemption(s) and the tax due on the CLT, if any, would be higher.

   (See Section 3.4)

INDEX

Accessibility, 297

Active investment, 279

Administering investments, 113

Administration, 86

Administration of estates, 87

Administrative receiver, 87

Affordability, 275, 297

Age (of investor), 295

Agency, 80

Agent as client, 203

Aggregation, 5

All finanz, 11

Alternative Investment Market (AIM), 37, 48, 50

American Depository Receipts (ADRs), 61, 115

American Stock Exchange, 61

Ancillary services (MiFID), 26

Annual General Meeting (AGM), 56

Anti-Terrorism, Crime and Security Act 2001, 175

Appointed representative, 111

Appropriate examinations, 158

Appropriateness rules, 216

Approved person status, 155

Approved persons, 156, 244

ARROW II, 139

Artificial persons, 74

Asset allocation, 279, 289

Assistance (money laundering), 165

Attitudes to risk, 295

Audit committee, 55

Authorisation, 111

Authorisation (of firms), 136

Balance sheet test, 86

Bancassurers, 11

Bank of England, 10, 17, 99, 101

Bank of England Act 1998, 99

Banking system, 9

Bankruptcy, 83

Bankruptcy Restriction Order, 86

Banks, 7

Bare trust, 90

Barter economy, 2

Benchmark indices, 282

Benchmarks, 281

Borrowing, 4

Breach (of Principles), 242

Broker-dealers, 41

Budget, 19

Budgeting, 292

Building societies, 9

Building Societies Act 1986, 9

Business card, 293

Business sector, 3

Buy-back and stabilisation regulation, 184

Cancellation / withdrawal rights, 223

Cancelling permission, 143

Capacity to contract, 79

Capital markets, 6

Capital Requirements Directive (CRD), 27

Capital risk, 276

Cautious investor, 296

Censure (by FSA), 144

Central bank, 10

Central Securities Depository (CSD), 67

CFA Institute, 252

Chancellor of the Exchequer, 100

Chargeable lifetime transfer (CLT), 91

Charitable trusts, 91

Charities, 112

Chartered Financial Analyst, 252

Chattels, 82

Child trust funds (CTFs), 222

China, 14

Churning, 233

Circumstances (of individual), 295

City Code, 105

City Code on Takeovers and Mergers, 101

City of London, 11

Civil Partnership Act 2004, 88

Civil standard of proof (market abuse), 183

Client, 241

Client assets rules, 224

Client objectives, 273

Client order handling, 230

Clients' best interests rule, 221, 229, 271, 272

Close period, 51

Closed questions, 298

Code of conduct for the advertising of interest bearing accounts, 205

Code of Ethics (CFA), 252

Code of Market Conduct, 182